Birnbaum's

Walt Disney World®

STEPHEN BIRNBAUM
FOUNDING EDITOR

WENDY LEFKON
EDITOR

CYNTHIA AMBROSE
ART DIRECTOR

TRACY A. SMITH
ASSOCIATE EDITOR

DEANNA CARON
ASSISTANT EDITOR

ALEXANDRA MAYES BIRNBAUM
CONSULTING EDITOR

HYPERION AND HEARST BUSINESS PUBLISHING, INC.

CONTENTS

165 Disney-MGM Studios Theme Park

Here's the chance you've always wanted to be part of Hollywood in its Golden Years. Everything from the magic of animation to the excitement of daring stunts and special effects is here to enjoy. There's also an opportunity to be part of classic TV shows and to create sound effects. We've developed some strategies for seeing this tinseltown, guaranteeing the most fun and the least time standing around.

179 Everything Else in the World

Beyond the boundaries of the Magic Kingdom, Epcot Center, and the Disney-MGM Studios Theme Park are 27,000 acres full of the kinds of wonders for which WDW is famous.

State-of-the-art water parks, a nighttime entertainment complex, a nature preserve, and a shopping village are among the offerings.So if you want to ride down watery slides, dance the night away, shop at elegant boutiques, wander among exotic birds, or "go to school" behind the scenes, here's everything you need to find your way to the wonders of Walt Disney World.

201 Sports

Walt Disney World boasts more tennis courts and golf greens than most posh resorts, and there's lots of other acreage that's devoted to boats, bikes, horseback riding, swimming, and fishing. There also are programs to help improve your skills. Here's how to combine the broad spectrum of the athletic endeavors available with the rest of the fun at WDW to create a well-rounded holiday.

209 Good Meals, Great Times

Restaurants around the Walt Disney World property run the gamut from simple snack shops to bastions of haute cuisine. The choices are nearly endless, so we've organized all these eating places into alphabetical, area-by-area, and meal by meal directories that let you know which restaurants are where and what specialties they offer. We also tell you all about the various dinner shows, where to dine with the Disney characters, where to have Sunday brunch, and where to find the best ice cream.

For Steve, who merely made this all possible.

ISBN: 1-56282-803-7

Printed in the United States of America

Other 1994 Birnbaum Travel Guides

Bahamas, and Turks & Caicos	London
Berlin	Los Angeles
Bermuda	Mexico
Boston	Miami & Fort Lauderdale
Canada	Montreal & Quebec City
Cancun, Cozumel, and Isla Mujeres	New Orleans
Caribbean	New York
Chicago	Paris
Disneyland	Portugal
Eastern Europe	Rome
Europe	San Francisco
Europe for Business Travelers	Santa Fe & Taos
France	South America
Germany	Spain
Great Britain	United States
Hawaii	USA for Business Travelers
Ireland	Walt Disney World For Kids, By Kids
Italy	Washington, D.C.

A Word from the Editor

I will always remember my first days working with Steve Birnbaum on the preparation of this guidebook. It was very clear from the start what Steve expected of me. This guide was to be meticulously revised each year, leaving no attraction unexplored, no hotel unvisited, and no snack or meal untasted. When Steve became curious as to how the bus system ran at Walt Disney World, I was elected to spend one whole day riding buses from place to place around the resort and report my findings. (They did, by the way, run on schedule.)

It was experiences like these that have made me an authority on the World. My expertise was not, however, achieved by being escorted through back doors of attractions or bypassing lines, but rather by standing with all the other visitors in hopes of uncovering strategies that would allow readers to avoid the pitfalls many first-timers encounter. On my first visit to the Disney-MGM Studios Theme Park, I waited more than an hour to take the Backstage Studio Tour. While on line with notebook and tape recorder in hand, one of the guests asked me if there was a quiz at the end of the tour. When I explained what I was doing, the gentleman was surprised to find out that I was waiting with the rest of the hordes. How better, I asked him, for me to help people like you than to wait it out?

My first Walt Disney World experience dates back to the World's first spring. In early 1972 my family set out on an adventure to this new "Disneyland in Florida." At that time, there was only one park and, having allowed ourselves four days, we were able to explore most of the Magic Kingdom. Early visitors will remember, too, that many attractions were still under construction at that time. Nonetheless, I fell in love with the place and at the ripe old age of 12 I vowed to return again and again. My second, somewhat less successful visit, took place the June after my college graduation. The crowds and heat combined

to make four good friends turn into arch enemies for a day. The lines seemed endless and we managed to take in just a few attractions during a long and frustrating day. Had I known then what I know now, I could have spared us some of those friendship-testing experiences.

What we've tried to do in designing this book is to keep you and your family from making the same mistakes. This marks the 13th annual edition of this guide, and we've learned a lot about WDW during all those years. Most of all, we know that even the most willing vacation planner needs adequate information in order to prepare an intelligent itinerary. What we hope we've done is to organize all the data necessary for a productive visit into as accessible and comprehensible a format as possible. Anyone who takes the time to read even the outlines of the pages that follow will find an emerging pattern that fits his or her special tastes; for those unwilling to exert even that much effort, we've compiled specific day-by-day itineraries for visits of varying lengths in order to protect you from yourself. In fact, I'm glad to see how many people follow our suggestions for a hassle-free visit. All I have to do is walk around the parks to see who has planned ahead and who has not.

This guidebook owes an enormous debt to the ladies and gentlemen who manage and run Walt Disney World. Despite the designation of *Official Guide*, I want to stress that *the Walt Disney World staff has exercised no veto power whatever over the contents of this book.* What they *have* done is opened their files and explained operations to us in the most generous way imaginable, so that we could prepare the comprehensive appraisals, charts, and schedules that are necessary to help visitors understand the very complex workings of a very complex enterprise.

I daresay there have been times when the Disney folks are less than delighted with some of our opinions or conclusions, yet these statements all remain in the guide. Furthermore, we've been flattered again and again by Disney staff who've commented about how much they've learned about some unfamiliar aspects of Walt Disney World from the material in this guide.

The fact remains that this guide could never have proved as useful as it is without the extremely forthcoming cooperation of Walt Disney World personnel on every level. Both in the park and behind the scenes, they've been the source of the most critical factual data. I can only hope that I'm not omitting any names in thanking Kim Carlson (Operations); Penelope Baker and Barbara Corser (Resorts); Patrice Lynch (Product Packaging); Dwight Dorr (Transportation); Wallace Sears (Publicity); Gene Duncan (Photography), and Mugs Cahill (Creative Services). To Tom Elrod, Bo Boyd, Marty Sklar, Vince Jefferds, Betsy Richman, Charlie Ridgway, John Dreyer, Phil Lengyel, Tom Garrison, Linda Warren, and Diane Hancock, who do so much to make our job easier (and often possible), more thanks for extraordinary help.

No list of acknowledgments would be complete without mentioning Steve Birnbaum, whose spirit continues to infuse every page of this guide.

Lastly, I should point out that every worthwhile travel guide is a living enterprise; that is, this book may be our best effort at explaining how to enjoy Walt Disney World at this moment, but its text is in no way cast in bronze. In each annual revision we expect to refine and expand our material to serve our readers' needs even better.

To this end, no contribution is of greater value to us than *your* personal reaction to what we have written, as well as information about *your* own experiences while you were trying our suggestions. We eagerly and enthusiastically solicit your comments about this guide, and your opinions and perceptions based on your own visit. In this way, we are able to provide the best and most current information—including the actual experiences of individual travelers—and make it more readily available to others. So please contact me at 60 East 42nd Street, Suite 2424; New York, New York 10165.

Have a great visit, and don't forget to write.

Wendy Lefkon

Getting Ready to Go

The key to a successful visit to Walt Disney World is advance planning. This remarkably varied complex is just too vast and diverse to allow a spontaneous visit to be undertaken with notable success—especially when you consider the rapid rate at which it is expanding. That doesn't mean that even the most casual visitors can't have some significant fun, but they may later find a host of opportunities that were missed because of the pressure of time or an absence of information. The primary purpose of this guide is to eliminate that potential frustration.

What follows, then, is intended to provide a sensible scheme for organizing a visit to Walt Disney World, one that will allow the maximum amount of enjoyment and produce the minimum level of frustration and disappointment. One of the very best ways to judge what there is in the World that is most appealing to you is to have a clear idea of all that is available.

(Unless otherwise noted, all phone numbers are in area code 407.)

When To Go

When talk finally turns to the best time to make a trip to Walt Disney World, Christmas and Easter often are mentioned, as well as the weeks that comprise the traditional summer vacation period—especially if there are children in the family. But there also are good reasons to avoid these periods, chief among them is the fact that almost everybody else goes then, and that when Walt Disney World is crowded, it can be very crowded indeed. On the busiest days, visitors may wait more than an hour for admission to some particularly popular attractions—at least twice as long as less crowded times of year.

Considering both the weather and crowd patterns described in the charts that follow, optimal times to visit WDW are September, October, early November, most of December (except Christmas week), the six weeks before and after spring school vacations, and the early part of June.

The period between the end of the Thanksgiving weekend and the week before Christmas stands out as the best time to visit. This is the most festive time at Walt Disney World, and savvy travelers who make their pilgrimage during this time are rewarded with special events featuring holiday parades and fireworks displays, special stage shows, holiday parties, themed dinners, and some of the most spectacular holiday decorations anywhere. And, most importantly, all these extras can be savored at Walt Disney World at one of its least crowded times of the year.

The Magic Kingdom, Epcot Center, and the Disney-MGM Studios Theme Park are all decorated to the nines for the holidays, as is the Disney Village Marketplace. Special events during this period (for which separate admission tickets are required) include Mickey's Very Merry Christmas Party, which takes place several days during early December. The party is held in the Magic Kingdom from 8 P.M. to 1 A.M. and features holiday shows around the park, including the Sparkling Christmas Spectacular, Miss Minnie's Country Christmas, the Country Bear Christmas Special, Tinker Bell's Flight, Mickey's Very Merry Christmas Parade, and a special finale for Fantasy in the Sky fireworks. A complimentary souvenir photograph and button, as well as hot chocolate and Christmas cookies, are included.

Select holiday performances from Mickey's Very Merry Christmas Party also are staged during regular park hours. Be sure to see the nightly tree-lighting ceremony in Town Square in the Magic Kingdom. At Epcot Center there also is a nightly tree-lighting ceremony, plus a character Christmas show, a comedic performance of *A Christmas Carol*, and the Jingle Bell Jubilee. The Disney-MGM Studios Theme Park features several groups who perform holiday music around the park. At the Disney Village Marketplace, a nativity pageant is performed, and the shops are all decorated for the holidays. It's also a great place to shop for last-minute presents.

The best way to take advantage of all there is to see and do at Walt Disney World during this time of year is to book a Jolly Holidays package, available from November 28 through December 18. The packages are available for from two to four nights and include admission to the Jolly Holidays Dinner Show held at the *Contemporary* resort. The show, available only with the packages, features an all-you-can-eat holiday feast with all the trimmings, as a cast of more than 100 singers and dancers, including the Disney characters, perform a festive musical extravaganza. There are holiday receptions at the participating hotels including a turn-of-the-century Christmas at the *Grand Floridian*, a seaside party at the *Yacht Club* and *Beach Club*, a Southwestern Christmas at the *Contemporary*, a Cajun holiday at *Port Orleans*, and a country-inn setting at the *Disney Inn*. Transportation is provided to each of the receptions as part of the packages. The four-night package includes unlimited admission to the Magic Kingdom, Epcot Center, the Disney-MGM Studios Theme Park, and Pleasure Island. For reservations, contact your travel agent or call (407) 827-7200.

Special Events

Inside Walt Disney World

Special festivities are often staged not only to mark holidays, but also to salute special groups by offering discounted admissions to the Magic Kingdom, Epcot Center, and the Disney-MGM Studios Theme Park.

JANUARY: Walt Disney World New Year's Eve Celebration (Dec. 31). There is an extra-large fireworks display over the Magic Kingdom, which is open until 2 A.M. for the occasion. The celebration at the *Top of the World* sells out, despite its relatively high cost. The glass-walled room here provides a fantastic view of the pyrotechnics. Pleasure Island also features a grand celebration.

Resident Salute. Throughout the month, Florida residents pay special low admission prices to enter the Magic Kingdom, Epcot Center, and the Disney-MGM Studios Theme Park. The Florida Resident Salute is held again in May.

APRIL: Easter Sunday. A nationally televised, promenade-style Easter parade helps make this holiday celebration special in the Magic Kingdom, during a very busy time of year. The Magic Kingdom, Epcot Center, and the Disney-MGM Studios Theme Park stay open late during the Easter season.

MAY: Grad Nites. Top rock entertainment is presented, and the Magic Kingdom is open from 11 P.M. to 5 A.M. for graduating high school students who may buy specially priced tickets. Held on three weekends during the month. For details, contact the Grad Nite Office; Box 10000; Lake Buena Vista, FL 32830-1000.

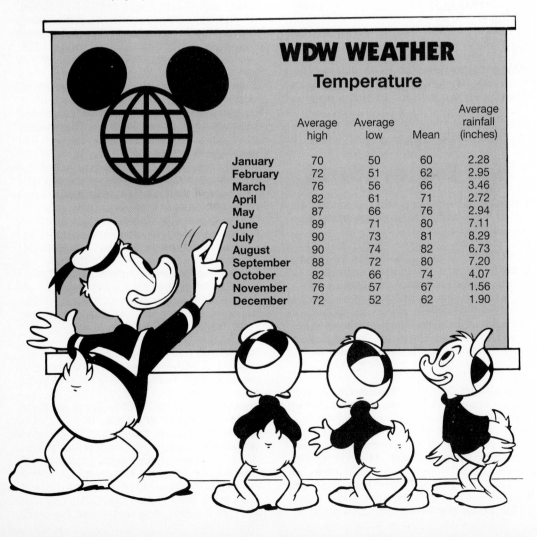

WDW WEATHER

Temperature

	Average high	Average low	Mean	Average rainfall (inches)
January	70	50	60	2.28
February	72	51	62	2.95
March	76	56	66	3.46
April	82	61	71	2.72
May	87	66	76	2.94
June	89	71	80	7.11
July	90	73	81	8.29
August	90	74	82	6.73
September	88	72	80	7.20
October	82	66	74	4.07
November	76	57	67	1.56
December	72	52	62	1.90

JUNE: All-American Wine Festival. More than 75 of America's premier wineries are represented at this annual event. There are seminars on food and wine pairings, a family barbecue, cooking demonstrations, tastings, and other activities. The festival is held at the *Yacht Club* resort.

JUNE–AUGUST: Kids Night Out. A special program for kids of all ages at the Disney Village Marketplace features music, comedians, face painters, jugglers, balloon artists, magicians, a wide variety of shows, and environmental and animal programs.

JULY 4: Fourth of July Celebration. In the evening, fireworks are set off above Cinderella Castle in the Magic Kingdom—as is usual when the park is open until midnight—and over the Seven Seas Lagoon as well. There's the spectacular Illuminations show at Epcot Center featuring music, lasers, and fireworks. This is a very busy time to visit.

OCTOBER: Walt Disney World/Oldsmobile Golf Classic. Top PGA Tour players compete alongside amateurs in this big tourney.
Disney Village Marketplace Boat Show. Central Florida's only in-the-water boat show features the newest lines of watercraft from more than 17 dealers.

NOVEMBER: Festival of the Masters at Disney Village Marketplace. One of the South's best art shows draws exhibitors from all around the country.

Outside Walt Disney World

Several major events in the Central Florida communities around Walt Disney World also are worth a visit.

JANUARY: Orlando; Scottish Highland Games. The sizable Scottish population of the area turns out in force for Highland dancing and bagpipe competitions, as well as such traditional field events as tossing of the caber. Scottish shops also are set up. Scottish-American Society of Central Florida; 1410 North Westmoreland Dr.; Orlando, FL 32804; 422-8226.

FEBRUARY: Daytona; Speed Week. Top names in stock-car racing are on hand at the Daytona International Speedway for one week of competition, culminating in the Daytona 500. Daytona International Speedway; Box 2801; Daytona Beach, FL 32120-2801; 904-253-7223.
Tampa; Gasparilla Pirate Invasion and Parade. Dressed as renegades of the pirate band led by the legendary José Gaspar,

members of a local club sail into Tampa Harbor in a full-size buccaneer ship (accompanied by a flotilla of local boats), claim the city as their own, and then parade through the streets. Among the activities during the subsequent two weeks are another raid, this one on Ybor City—Tampa's historic Latin quarter—and a Spanish bean soup day during which this thick, delectable broth is served (along with Cuban bread and Cuban coffee). An illuminated parade winds up the event. Tampa/Hillsborough Convention and Visitors Association; 111 Madison St., Suite 1010; Tampa, FL 33602-4706; 813-223-1111 or 800-44-TAMPA.
Grant; Grant Seafood Festival. Some 50,000 visitors show up on the third weekend in February to eat fresh Indian River seafood at this huge affair staged by a small community on Florida's east coast. Seafood Festival; Box 44; Grant, FL 32949; 723-6811.
Kissimmee; Silver Spurs Rodeo. This three-day event, held twice a year since 1944 (it's also held in July), draws professional cowboys from all over the United States to compete in bull and bronc riding, steer-wrestling, and barrel racing. Kissimmee-St. Cloud Convention and Visitors Bureau; Box 422007; Kissimmee, FL 34742-2007; 67-RODEO.
Kissimmee; Houston Astros Spring Training. The Astros' training season begins in late February and runs through early April. Osceola County Stadium; Box 422979; Kissimmee, FL 34742-2979; 933-5400.

MARCH: Orlando; Nestlé Invitational. Held annually in mid-March; Arnold Palmer hosts this major PGA Tour event, one of seven in the state of Florida, at the Bay Hill Club. Tournament Office; Bay Hill Club; 9000 Bay Hill Blvd.; Orlando, FL 32819; 876-2888.
Sarasota; Medieval Fair. Hundreds of entertainers from all over the country and abroad join in a human chess match, jousting, processions, singing, and other medieval merriment at the Ringling Museum complex. Everything from the food and drink served (pot pies, giant turkey legs, and ale) to the crafts

sold and the language spoken by participants is authentically medieval. Ringling Museum; 5401 Bay Shore Road; Sarasota, FL 34243; 813-351-8497.

Winter Park; Winter Park Sidewalk Art Festival. Held annually during the third weekend of the month, this display of etchings, pottery, paintings, sculpture, and other artwork and craft items also features concerts, strolling musicians, and a folk sing; it's one of the most prestigious events of its type in the Southeast. The backdrop is a small municipal park full of ancient trees draped with Spanish moss; the town itself is as tony as they come in Central Florida, with an array of chic boutiques and a clutch of first-rate restaurants. Winter Park Sidewalk Art Festival; Box 597; Winter Park, FL 32790; 623-3234.

APRIL: Titusville; Great Indian River Festival. This community near the Kennedy Space Center holds an annual tribute to the celebrated Indian River with a long weekend of arts and crafts, carnival rides, an antique car show, a boat show, live entertainment, food, and the Great Indian River Raft Race, in which only homemade rafts can participate. Titusville Area Chamber of Commerce; 2000 Washington Ave., Drawer 2767; Titusville, FL 32781-2767; 267-3036.

Orlando; Orlando Cubs baseball season. The summer season for this Chicago Cubs farm team begins at Tinker Field in April, and runs through the beginning of September. Tinker Field; 287 Tampa Ave. South; Orlando, FL 32805; 872-7593.

OCTOBER: Kissimmee; Florida State Air Fair. A two-day roster of activities includes aerial acrobatic demonstrations, aeronautical displays, and exhibits of war planes on the ground. Rotary Club of Kissimmee; Box 422185; Kissimmee, FL 34742-2185; 933-7998.

NOVEMBER: Orlando Magic Basketball. One of the NBA's up-and-coming franchises plays 41 home games from November through April at the Orlando Arena. Orlando Arena; One Magic Place; Orlando, FL 32801; 896-2442.

Operating Hours

Hours of operation of the Magic Kingdom, Epcot Center, and the Disney-MGM Studios Theme Park vary from season to season. This fact should figure strongly in decisions on when to visit. For about a third of the year—in May, September, October, parts of November and December, and all of January—the Magic Kingdom is usually open from about 9 A.M. to 7 P.M. Hours are extended to 10 P.M. during Presidents' Week and during spring school breaks; and to midnight for summer and certain holiday periods (Thanksgiving weekend, Christmas, and the two weeks straddling Easter). On New Year's Eve, additional hours are added to the nighttime schedule, keeping the parks open until about 2 A.M.

Epcot Center usually is open from 9 A.M. to 9 P.M.; hours are extended during Thanksgiving weekend, Christmas, Presidents' Week, the two weeks surrounding Easter, and spring school breaks.

The Disney-MGM Studios Theme Park is usually open from 9 A.M. to 7 P.M.; hours are extended to 10 P.M. or midnight during special holiday periods and the summer months.

Guests staying at Walt Disney World resorts can get into the Magic Kingdom an hour before the official opening time on selected days. Information on the exact days this policy is in effect can be found in your hotel room or by asking someone at the resort's Guest Services desk.

Occasionally, during busy periods, the parks may open earlier or close later. Call 824-4321 for up-to-the-minute details.

How Big are the Crowds?

Most visitors to Walt Disney World routinely assume that weekends are by far the busiest days on the property. But with the exception of holidays and holiday weekends, Mondays, Tuesdays, and Wednesdays are actually the most crowded days at the Magic Kingdom. Tuesdays and Wednesdays are more crowded at Epcot Center, and at the Disney-MGM Studios Theme Park Thursdays and Fridays tend to be quite crowded. Sunday mornings rank as the most peaceful time to visit. The chart below offers general information on the density of the crowds during different times of the year. It's very hard to generalize, however, in a property as vast and diverse as Walt Disney World—a crowded day at the Magic Kingdom does not necessarily mean long lines at the Studios—but the chart below does highlight historic trends. Least crowded means that there may be some lines, but by and large most attractions can be visited without much waiting; average

attendance refers to those times when there are lots of people around but the lines are still manageable; and most crowded reflects those times when the lines at the most popular attractions can mean a wait of an hour or more.

LEAST CROWDED	AVERAGE ATTENDANCE	MOST CROWDED
	1st week of January	
2nd week of January through 1st week of February		
	2nd week of February through Presidents' week	
		Presidents' week
	End of February through 1st week of April	
		2nd and 3rd weeks of April
	Last week of April through 1st week of June	
		2nd week of June through 3rd week of August
	Last week of August through Labor Day	
Week after Labor Day until Thanksgiving		
	Thanksgiving week	
Week after Thanksgiving through week before Christmas		
		Christmas through New Year's Day

Planning Ahead

Organizing a trip properly takes time, but almost every traveler finds that the increased enjoyment is well worth the effort. The fact is, that planning can become the most pleasant sort of "armchair" exercise, and kids will enjoy their visit to Walt Disney World all the more if they, too, are involved in the planning process. To aid in that effort, we immodestly recommend our brand-new guide, *Birnbaum's Walt Disney World For Kids, By Kids* ($9.95), a comprehensive look at Walt Disney World from a young person's perspective.

SAMPLE SCHEDULES: It's no exaggeration to say that a visitor could spend three weeks in Central Florida and still not have time to see everything there that's worthwhile. Walt Disney World alone requires every bit of four days just to cover the major attractions, and even that doesn't really allow enough time to take in everything. Just the basic inventory of attractions—the Magic Kingdom, Epcot Center, the Disney-MGM Studios Theme Park, Typhoon Lagoon, Pleasure Island, River Country, Discovery Island, Fort Wilderness, the Village Marketplace—only begins to suggest the broad spectrum of nearly irresistible entertainment opportunities, and we haven't even mentioned six fine golf courses, the beaches, and all the other tempting sports facilities.

The schedules that we suggest here should help put you on the right track—and maybe even keep you there. Deviations from the programs we describe should be based on our "Tips from WDW Veterans" (pages 124, 164, and 178). In general, good sense and normal human stamina dictate that a guest can count on visiting seven or eight attractions per day in the Magic Kingdom, about five pavilions in Epcot Center, and most of the major attractions at the Disney-MGM Studios Theme Park. That leaves some time for shopping, the inevitable lines at some attractions, and some unhurried meals. During less crowded seasons, it may be possible to accomplish significantly more. **Note:** The schedules suggested here are for the periods during the year when extended evening operating hours for the Magic Kingdom, Epcot Center, and the Disney-MGM Studios Theme Park are in effect.

Remember, too, that it's crucial to begin days in the Magic Kingdom, Epcot Center, and the Disney-MGM Studios Theme Park promptly at park opening. It's also wise to recognize that Epcot Center and the Disney-MGM Studios Theme Park frequently open a full half-hour or more before the officially posted time. For guests staying at Walt Disney World resorts, a special program allows admission to the Magic Kingdom one hour before it opens to the general public. Check at Guest Services upon arrival for the exact days of the week that the early bird program is in effect.

One-day visit: There is so much to see and do at WDW that we don't really recommend a visit of this frustratingly short duration. But if that's all the time you've got, first decide which of the three prime areas (the Magic Kingdom, Epcot Center, or the Disney-MGM Studios Theme Park) you want to see, and then study all available material in advance so that you're as familiar as possible with your destination's layout and offerings. Be sure to arrive on the property early and move quickly while you're there. For optimal results, follow our schedules to the letter. **Note:** Because one-day tickets permit visitors to enter *only* one of the three prime park attractions, visitors must concentrate on that park for the day. If you're lodging at a WDW resort, you can purchase a Be Our Guest Pass, good for the length of your stay. It allows unlimited admission to all three parks, River Country, Typhoon Lagoon, Discovery Island, and Pleasure Island.

● If you choose to tour the Magic Kingdom, be in the parking lot at least 45 minutes before the scheduled park opening, so as to be at the Central Plaza end of Main Street at the official opening time. If you're staying at a Walt Disney World resort, take advantage of the early admission program. From the Central Plaza, move rapidly and purposefully from one attraction to the next—first to Space Mountain, then to the Haunted Mansion, Big Thunder Mountain Railroad, Splash Mountain, Tom Sawyer Island, Pirates of the Caribbean, and the Jungle Cruise. Plan on lunching at 11 A.M. to avoid mealtime lines. If time remains after the Jungle Cruise, see the Tropical Serenade and the Swiss Family Treehouse before eating; otherwise go to those attractions after lunch. Then begin making a second trip around the area, stopping at *American Journeys*, *Magic Journeys*, It's A Small World, Peter Pan's Flight, Mickey's Starland, the Main Street Cinema, the shops and entertainment en route, and anything else that catches your eye. (If you are traveling with very young children, your best bet for the morning is to take the Walt Disney World Railroad directly to Mickey's Starland and then visit the Fantasyland attractions.) Then, having made reservations before leaving home, leave the Magic Kingdom about 4 P.M. for the Hoop-Dee-Doo Revue at *Fort Wilderness*. (These reservations can be *very* hard to come by. Even when you call early, there may not be any seats available.)

During busy seasons, when all WDW attractions are open late, it may be possible to follow this dinner show with another visit to the Magic Kingdom, where fireworks and the late installment of SpectroMagic combine to make an evening especially memorable.

During other months (or if you could not get reservations for the Hoop-Dee-Doo Revue), head for the Disney Village Marketplace and spend the evening aboard the *Empress Lilly* in one of its restaurants or lounges, or go to Pleasure Island and have dinner in one of the restaurants there.

● If you choose to spend the day in Epcot Center, arrive approximately one-half hour before the park's official opening and wait at the gate until the turnstiles are unlocked. Then send a member of your party ahead to Earth Station to make a 5 P.M. dinner reservation at one of the special international restaurants in World Showcase or Future World. Pick up an entertainment schedule while there. That done, visit Wonders of Life, The Land, and then Journey Into Imagination in Future World, then head quickly for World Showcase and see *O Canada!* in the Canada Pavilion and *Impressions de France* in the France Pavilion. Then backtrack to *Le Cellier*, in the Canada Pavilion, for lunch around 11:30 A.M. Afterward, enjoy the World Showcase entertainment, see the shows at the American Adventure and Norway, and browse

through the shops in Canada, the United Kingdom, France, Japan, Morocco, Germany, Italy, and Mexico. Then head for Future World to visit The Living Seas (where it's easy to spend at least an hour) before heading for your dining spot at 4:45 P.M. Plan to finish your meal by 6:30 P.M. Spend the time until 7:30 P.M. in the China Pavilion (for one of the last showings of the film there); then head for Future World and see Spaceship Earth, Horizons, and World of Motion. Keep an eye on the time so that you can secure a good spot around World Showcase Lagoon (we recommend the little island between Italy and the American Adventure) to watch the evening's performance of IllumiNations.

● If you opt for the Disney-MGM Studios Theme Park, arrive at the park 45 minutes to an hour before the scheduled opening time. If you'd like to try one of the sit-down restaurants for lunch and/or dinner stop and make reservations when you arrive in the park. Try the *50's Prime Time Café* for some old-time television nostalgia, the *Sci-Fi Dine-In* for some wonderful drive-in theater atmosphere, the *Brown Derby* for a touch more elegance, or *Mama Melrose's* for Italian fare. Once Tower of Terror opens in June of this year, it's bound to be very crowded. If you're up to a freefall, head directly there. Then go to Voyage of the Little Mermaid, Muppet*Vision 3-D, and Star Tours since these three attractions are very crowded later in the day. Check your entertainment schedule and plan to see the next installment of the Indiana Jones Stunt Spectacular. The Animation Building generally opens at 11 A.M., so go there next. Afterwards, go to the Great Movie Ride. Check your entertainment schedule again, and slot in times to see SuperStar Television and the Monster Sound Show (be sure to volunteer to

participate). If small children are along, spend some time at the Honey, I Shrunk the Kids Movie Set Adventure and get autographs from the Teenage Mutant Ninja Turtles. Be sure to browse through the shops along Hollywood Boulevard, taking time to notice all the Studio's small details. At about 5 P.M., head for the Backstage Tour and the Special Effects and Production Tour. After dinner, catch the Beauty and the Beast show (it's particularly wonderful at night) and watch the Sorcery in the Sky fireworks.

Note: The following multi-day schedules are predicated on a late-afternoon arrival at Walt Disney World.

Four-day/five-night visit: This plan is recommended for only the highly energetic, for all the new attractions at WDW make it barely possible to see even the high points during this period. During peak seasons, nothing less than four full days and five evenings will do the trick. Be sure to check (the night before) on required transportation for early morning hours, and allot plenty of extra time for potential delays. On each day, the idea is to make a quick tour of the premises, visiting the major attractions during the least crowded hours of the early morning, then repeat the circuit of the park once again later in the day.

● Before leaving home, try to make reservations for the 5 P.M. seating at the Hoop-Dee-Doo Revue for the evening of the first *full* day of your stay. Then, on the first evening of your arrival at WDW, go directly to Epcot Center (try to arrive before 5 P.M.). Purchase a Four-day Passport. Grab a quick bite in one of the restaurants in CommuniCore East or West, then visit Wonders of Life and the Living Seas. This should take about two hours. Next walk over to Journey Into Imagination, where you should count on spending at least an hour-and-a-half. Be sure to stick around the World Showcase Lagoon for the evening's presentation of IllumiNations, a spectacular outdoor sound, light, laser, and water show.

● On your first full day, have breakfast as early as possible to allow arrival at the Magic Kingdom turnstiles half an hour before scheduled opening—and to be at the Central Plaza end of Main Street at the official opening time. (Remember, if you're staying at a Walt Disney World resort, to take advantage of the special early-admission program.) Follow our outline for a one-day visit to the Magic Kingdom. Then, having reserved in advance, leave the Magic Kingdom at about 4 P.M. to head for the Hoop-Dee-Doo Revue at *Fort Wilderness*. During busy seasons it's possible to follow dinner with a couple of additional hours at the Magic Kingdom to see the fireworks and the late installment of SpectroMagic. During other months (or in the event that Hoop-Dee-Doo Revue reservations were unavailable), head either for Pleasure Island to take in one or more of the unique clubs

and restaurants there, or for dinner at the Disney Village Marketplace.

● On your second full day, arrive at Epcot Center about half an hour before the park's official opening, and wait at the gate until the turnstiles are unlocked. Then go directly to Earth Station to make a 1:30 P.M. lunch reservation at one of the World Showcase restaurants and an 8:45 P.M. dinner reservation (when the park is open late) at another. (Note that guests staying at Walt Disney World resorts and Disney Village Hotel Plaza can make these reservations up to three days in advance. See *Good Meals, Great Times* for details about the reservation procedure and our dining suggestions). That done, take in any major attractions in Future World that you missed on your first evening. Then head for World Showcase and see the American Adventure Show, the film at the Canada Pavilion, the film at the France Pavilion, and the film at the China Pavilion. Save shopping for later in the day, when the attractions are more crowded and the shops are not. The hours between 6 P.M. and your dinner reservation time should be spent seeing any attractions that were missed on your two previous circuits. Skip dessert at your dinner restaurant and instead head for the *Boulangerie Pâtisserie* in the France Pavilion for pastry and espresso. If you couldn't get a reservation in the Epcot Center restaurant of your choice, or if a change of pace is desired, head for Pleasure Island, the Disney Village Marketplace, or the Disney Village Hotel Plaza, where there are many restaurants from which to choose (see *Good Meals, Great Times*).

● On the third full day of your visit, arrive at the Disney-MGM Studios Theme Park 45 minutes to an hour before the scheduled opening. Then follow the schedule outlined in

our one-day visit to the Disney-MGM Studios Theme Park (pages 14 and 15).

Five-day/six-night visit: A stay of this length, while not exactly leisurely, is still the shortest time that can be conscientiously recommended for families with young children, older visitors, or anyone else who wants to visit all the best of Walt Disney World at less than a breakneck pace.

Before visiting, read as much as possible about the WDW attractions and their locations. This is a must because although the pace of this five-day program is slower than that required during a four-day visit, it is still necessary not to waste time in order to cover all the high points. Remember, too, that the first order of business (before leaving home) is to try to make a 5 P.M. reservation for the Hoop-Dee-Doo Revue for the fourth day of your visit.

● On the evening of the day of your arrival, visit Epcot Center and purchase a Five-day Super Duper Pass. Or, for a better value, if you're staying at a Walt Disney World resort, purchase a Be Our Guest Pass at your hotel. Have a quick bite at one of the restaurants in CommuniCore East or West and then proceed as for the first evening of the four-day visit described above.

● On the first full day of your visit, arrive at the Magic Kingdom 45 minutes before the official park opening. *Tony's Town Square* restaurant and the *Crystal Palace* cafeteria on Main Street begin serving early, so have breakfast at one of these eateries and be at the Central Plaza end of Main Street at the park's official opening time. Then begin circumnavigating the park, taking in just the major attractions described for the first morning of a one-day visit.

At about noon, leave the park and head for River Country, Discovery Island, or Typhoon Lagoon. Have lunch and participate in the varied activities offered. Golfers may want to take this opportunity to sample one of the six first class golf courses. Return to the Magic Kingdom at about 5 P.M. and grab a quick bite at the *Tomorrowland Terrace*. Then take another ride on Space Mountain and Splash Mountain. By 8 P.M. head for Main Street to stake a claim to a segment of curb for the 9 P.M. SpectroMagic. Watch the Fantasy in the Sky fireworks after the parade.

● Devote the second day of your visit to Epcot Center. Arrive about half an hour before the official park opening and queue up at the gate. While waiting, choose a restaurant for dinner. When the gates open, send a member of your group to Earth Station to make an early (around 5 P.M.) dinner reservation. Then begin visiting the Future World attractions you missed on your first evening.

Leave Future World at around 10 A.M. and head for World Showcase. First go to France and see the film there, then head to The American Adventure, Norway, and China. Next go to Mexico and have lunch at the pleasant *Cantina de San Angel*. Afterward, reverse the direction of your route around World Showcase, and stop at the pavilions you missed the first time around. Even if you hate shopping, look into Germany's arts-and-crafts and toy shops and Morocco's brass and jewelry bazaars. Also be sure to look in on the entertainers who perform daily around Italy, the puppeteers on the promenade, and the street players at the United Kingdom. For a mid-afternoon snack, stop at the U.K. Pavilion's Tea Caddy, buy a box of crackers or cookies, and then head for the *Refreshment Port* for a cold drink. Then go back to Future World and explore CommuniCore East and the Trans-Center. Remember to allot a full 20 minutes to walk to your dining spot. The uncrowded hours after dinner should be spent visiting any attractions missed on previous circuits.

● On the third full day of your visit, head for the Disney-MGM Studios Theme Park and follow the schedule outlined in the one-day visit. After the fireworks show in the evening, head to Pleasure Island for the shows and/or an evening of dancing. If tired feet prohibit such activity, take in a movie at Pleasure Island's multiplex cinema.

● On the fourth full day of your visit, try one of the character breakfasts (described in *Good Meals, Great Times*) and then head over to the Magic Kingdom and spend the afternoon following our guidelines for the afternoon of a one-day visit. At about 4 P.M. head over to *Fort Wilderness* for the 5 P.M. Hoop-Dee-Doo Revue. Then go to Pleasure Island for some dancing, comedy, or music, or maybe take in a movie at the multiplex cinema next door.

Six-day visit: Follow our program as outlined for the five-day visit. On the sixth day, spend the morning in the one park you most enjoyed. Then leave and have lunch at the *Grand Floridian* resort, the *Polynesian* resort, or the *Disney Inn*, and then spend the afternoon lounging by the pool, playing tennis or golf, or biking. Visit the shops at the Disney Village Marketplace and Pleasure Island. Try a special dinner at *Victoria & Albert's* at the *Grand Floridian* or *Portobello Yacht Club* at Pleasure Island. Then head for one of the clubs at Pleasure Island, or (having reserved in advance) take in one of the dinner shows like the luau at the *Polynesian* resort.

For visits of seven days or longer: In addition to our program described for a six-day visit, a stay of this length allows guests a chance to sample some of the World's other unique offerings. The Walt Disney World Golf Studio can help improve your stroke (see *Sports*); adult visitors with a yen to go behind the scenes can enroll in a Disney Learning Adventure while children 10 to 15 can participate in a Wonders of the World program (see *Everything Else in the World*); Discovery Island offers guided tours that make for a delightful afternoon (see *Everything Else in the World*); or participate in any of the other activities described in our *Sports* and *Everything Else in the World* chapters.

MORE PLANNING TIPS

DO YOU NEED A CAR? Transportation by bus, monorail, and boat within the World gets guests from point to point very efficiently. The bus system is the most extensive form of WDW transportation. Buses are color-coded to make finding your way around fairly simple. Every driver carries copies of a bus schedule which lists which buses go where and how often. Bus schedules also are available at Guests Services desks in the hotels. It's also possible to get to WDW resorts from Orlando Airport without a car—Mears Motor Shuttles operate about every 15 to 25 minutes around the clock, serving on-property hotels, as well as Disney Village Hotel Plaza accommodations, Florida Center hotels, and hotels on U.S. 192. (Call for reservations: 423-5566.) Also, visitors lodging outside the World can usually get to and from WDW via their own hotels' bus service (which most hotels offer). Limos and cabs also are available. But a car is a must for taking in Orlando-area restaurants and attractions outside WDW.

INFORMATION SOURCES: For details about other things to see and do in Central Florida, contact the Florida Department of Commerce; Tourism Division; 126 West Van Buren St.; Tallahassee, FL 32399-2000; 904-487-1462. To find out about the area directly around Orlando, contact the Orlando/Orange County Convention and Visitors Bureau; 7208 Sand Lake Rd., Suite 300; Orlando, FL 32819; 363-5871. For general information about Walt Disney World, write the Walt Disney World Co.; Box 10000; Lake Buena Vista, FL 32830-1000; 824-4321.

Walt Disney World Information/Reservation Center: The best time to make or confirm hotel reservations is *before* you're actually standing at the hotel's front desk. Nobody likes unpleasant surprises on a vacation, so it's wise to have an assured reservation.

Those driving to Walt Disney World can arrange that assurance easily because there is a full-service information facility in Ocala, Florida, at the intersection of Interstate 75 and State Route 200, about 90 miles north of Orlando. Like a welcome center, the facility will help Disney-bound vacationers plan their time, purchase tickets for the Magic Kingdom, Epcot Center, the Disney-MGM Studios Theme Park, and other attractions, and make hotel reservations (or confirm them). And for

those heading home from WDW who forgot to buy enough pairs of mouse ears, the center also offers plenty of Disney souvenirs and character merchandise.

Upon arrival at Walt Disney World, a variety of other information sources is available. First, tune into the WDW radio stations after entering the grounds—1030 on the AM dial inbound to the Magic Kingdom and 810 approaching Epcot Center. (Helpful information is broadcast to guests departing from the Magic Kingdom and Epcot Center on 900.)

Guests at WDW resorts—that is, the *Contemporary* resort, the *Disney Inn*, the *Polynesian* resort, the *Grand Floridian*, the *Caribbean Beach* resort, the *Swan*, the *Dolphin*, the *Yacht Club*, the *Beach Club*, *Port Orleans*, *Dixie Landings*, *Fort Wilderness*, *Wilderness Lodge*, *All-Star Sports* and *All-Star Music* resorts, the *Disney Vacation Club*, and the villas—can tune to Channel 5 on their hotel-room television sets to see a filmed overview of all WDW attractions—a complete orientation tour of the property, which is essential viewing for all first-time visitors. It is broadcast continuously. Guests at Disney Village Hotel Plaza establishments will see a similar program on Channel 7. (The latter gives somewhat more emphasis to the dining rooms and lounges at these lodging places, which, though located on WDW property, are neither Disney-owned nor Disney-operated.) For further information, guests at WDW properties can watch the daily program *Disney Nights*, which provides information about all the nighttime activities available on the property and other useful information, on Channel 10. (This program is not shown outside WDW lodging places.) For additional information, guests at WDW resorts should contact Guest Services. *Fort Wilderness* campers should stop at the Pioneer Hall Information and Ticket Window, call extension 2788, or touch "11" from the phones at the comfort stations located at the center of each campground loop area.

Some hotels off the property—but not all of them—show their own version of the WDW resorts' Channel 5 orientation film; this attempts to give visitors an overview of all Central Florida attractions (WDW among them), rather than concentrating on the World.

Day visitors: All day visitors—that is, those staying off the property, as well as those living in the Orlando area—receive a handout at the Auto Plazas detailing admission prices and other useful information. When purchasing one-day admission media at the Transportation and Ticket Center, at Epcot Center, or at the Disney-MGM Studios Theme Park, guests receive a copy of the Magic Kingdom guide, the Epcot Center guide, or the Disney-MGM Studios Theme Park guide, depending upon which park they have chosen to visit. Guests who purchase multi-day admission

media may receive all three guides upon request. City Hall (in the Magic Kingdom), Earth Station (in Epcot Center), and Guest Services (at the Disney-MGM Studios Theme Park) distribute extra copies of these guides at no charge.

For further information about the World, phone WDW Information at 824-4321.

WHAT TO PACK: Walt Disney World is not so casual that all you need to bring is a bathing suit, but with only a few exceptions, comfortable clothing is the rule. Jackets are required for men for dinner at the *Empress Room* aboard the *Empress Lilly* riverboat; for dinner at *Victoria & Albert's* at the *Grand Floridian* resort; and for dinner at *Palio* at the *Swan*. Everywhere else the dress is very casual. T-shirts and shorts are acceptable during the day. For evening, slacks, jeans, and Bermuda shorts are appropriate. This also is true at the full-service restaurants that are found in the World Showcase pavilions at Epcot Center. Bathing suits are a must, and a spare one is useful, as are the right togs for any other sport you might want to pursue. On the tennis courts, tennis whites are appropriate, though not required. Guests should bring lightweight sweaters even in summer—to wear indoors when the air conditioning gets too frigid. From November through March, warmer clothing is a must in the evening. Always pack something to keep you comfortable should the weather turn unseasonably warm or cool. Especially in summer, lightweight rain gear and a folding umbrella come in handy. Be sure to pack plenty of sunscreen, since even the winter Orlando sun can be brutal.

The most important item of clothing of all? Comfortable, well broken-in walking shoes.

WDW WEDDINGS AND HONEYMOONS

Walt Disney World is the most popular honeymoon destination in the country. Since honeymooners have been flocking to the WDW resorts for many years, a variety of packages are available that cater specifically to newly married couples. The resorts at Walt Disney World offer romantic stretches of white-sand beaches for evening strolls, fine restaurants for candlelit dinners, and a host of activities to rival any Caribbean or Hawaiian destination. Add to that the Magic Kingdom, Epcot Center, the Disney-MGM Studios Theme Park, Pleasure Island, the Disney Village Marketplace, Typhoon Lagoon, River Country, and Discovery Island and it's not hard to see why WDW is number one with honeymooners.

For many years, the folks at Walt Disney World received hundreds of requests from couples who wanted to get married at WDW. And while it's still not possible to take your vows in front of Cinderella Castle, it is possible to celebrate nuptials

at the *Grand Floridian* resort, the *Yacht Club* and *Beach Club*, the *Contemporary* resort, *Disney's Village Resort* or aboard the *Empress Lilly* riverboat.

Weddings at WDW range from very elegant affairs without a hint of Disneyana, to ceremonies in which the bride and groom arrive in Cinderella's coach and Mickey and Minnie are among the guests. The WDW wedding coordinators work with couples to tailor each individual wedding. Among the services offered are wedding gown design, formal-wear rentals, invitations, photographers, hairstyling, manicures, massage, floral arrangements, and musical entertainment.

Wedding specialists also help to arrange accommodations for guests, rehearsal dinners, bachelor parties, and just about any other activities you might require. For additional information about a WDW wedding, call 407-363-6333. For information about honeymoon packages call 407-W-DISNEY.

Reservations

Walt Disney World vacations go most smoothly when details are planned ahead of time. Procrastinators may find no room at the inn, or no space left for a show that they wanted to see. Golf starting times, tennis courts, dinner reservations, and other special affairs also should be reserved in advance.

Central Reservations Office: Many arrangements are handled by the Central Reservations Office (CRO); the phone number is 407-W-DIS-NEY (934-7639). The office is open seven days a week from 8:30 A.M. to midnight.

Thanks to an increase in the number of operators at the CRO, most calls are answered within one minute. Have a pencil and paper close at hand (and your credit card) when calling, to jot down dates and the number of your reservation.

Room reservations: It is important to book accommodations in advance to get your first choice, though the inventory of WDW hotel rooms is so large now, most requests can be satisfied on short notice. It is still necessary, however, to book popular holiday periods well in advance.

Delta Air Lines: As the "Official Airline of Walt Disney World," Delta Air Lines has a substantial number of rooms specifically allocated for its use. Delta is, therefore, a very good means of access to Walt Disney World resort rooms. These rooms are available as part of Delta Dream Vacation packages, which also have the added attraction of saving visitors some money on airfares as well. American Express and Premiere offer similar packages. See page 26 for additional package details.

Reservations for supper seatings, dinner shows, and sporting activities: Some of these are handled by Central Reservations, while others are handled by the individual restaurants and sporting centers. It's always wise to make your plans and reserve your place as far in advance as WDW policy will allow. Just how far in advance may vary depending on where you lodge. (See chart below.)

RESERVATION GUIDE

ACTIVITY	Phone for reservations (area code 407)	Advisability of reservations	*How far in advance can reservations be made?*		
			Guests in WDW hotels/villas	Guests at Hotel Plaza establishments	Guests at off-property hotels
Sports					
Golf starting times— all courses	824-2270	Necessary from February through April; a good idea at other times	30 days	30 days	7 days
Walt Disney World Golf Studio, *Disney Inn*	824-2270	Necessary	..................No limit for any guest..................		
Private golf lessons, *Disney Inn*	824-2270	Necessary	..................No limit for any guest..................		
Private golf lessons, Lake Buena Vista course	824-3741	Necessary	......................Same day only.......................		
Tennis, *Contemporary* resort	824-3578	Suggested	..................24 hours in advance....................		
Tennis, *Grand Floridian*	824-3000 ext. 2134	Necessary	..................24 hours in advance....................		
Tennis lessons, private and group, *Contemporary* resort and Village Clubhouse	824-3578	Necessary	..................No limit for any guest..................		

ACTIVITY	Phone for reservations (area code 407)	Advisability of reservations	How far in advance can reservations be made?		
			Guests in WDW hotels/villas	Guests at Hotel Plaza establishments	Guests at off-property hotels
Trail rides, *Fort Wilderness*	824-2832	Necessary	................Up to 5 days for any guest		
Fishing trips, *Fort Wilderness*	824-2757	Necessary	...............Up to 14 days for any guest		
Good Meals Empress Room, *Empress Lilly* riverboat	828-3900	Necessary	....................30 days		
Lake Buena Vista Club, *Disney's Village Resort*	828-3735	Suggested	....................30 days		
Papeete Bay Verandah, *Polynesian* resort	824-1391	Requested	....................30 days		
Narcoossee's, *Grand Floridian*	824-2383	Suggested	....................30 days		
Flagler's, *Grand Floridian*	824-2383	Suggested	....................30 days		
Ariel's, *Beach Club*	934-3415	Suggested	....................30 days		
Yachtsman Steakhouse, *Yacht Club*	934-3415	Suggested	....................30 days		
Disney Inn restaurant, *Disney Inn*	824-1484	Suggested; available for dinner only	....................30 days		
Epcot Center full-service restaurants	Guest Services (824-8800 Hotel Plaza guests)	Necessary	3 days in advance; from 8 A.M. to 9 P.M.	3 days in advance; from 8 A.M. to 9 P.M.	Available in person only on day of dining
Great Times Hoop-Dee-Doo Musical Revue, Pioneer Hall, *Fort Wilderness*	W-DISNEY (934-7639)	Necessary	Upon receipt of confirmed reservation	45 days*	30 days
Polynesian Luau, *Polynesian* resort	W-DISNEY (934-7639)	Necessary	....................No limit for any guest......................		
Mickey's Tropical Luau, *Polynesian* resort	W-DISNEY (934-7639)	Necessary	....................No limit for any guest......................		
Breakfast à la Disney, *Empress Lilly* riverboat	W-DISNEY (934-7639)	Necessary	Upon receipt of confirmed reservation	45 days*	30 days
Minnie's Menehune Character Breakfast, *Polynesian* resort	824-1391	Suggested	...............30 days		
Sunday Brunch Papeete Bay Verandah, *Polynesian* resort	824-1391	Suggested	...............30 days		

* only if hotel reservations have been made through CRO; otherwise, 30 days

How to Get There

By Car

Here are some suggested routes to WDW from the downtown sections of several metropolitan areas.

Figure on driving 350 to 400 miles a day—a reasonable distance that won't wear you down so much that you can't enjoy your stay.

Atlanta: I-75 south, I-475 south around Macon, I-75 south, Florida's Turnpike south, U.S. 27 south, U.S. 192 east to entrance. Total mileage: 455 miles.

Baltimore: I-95 south, I-495 west and south around Washington, I-95 south, I-295 around Jacksonville, I-95 south, I-4 west, U.S. 192 west to entrance. Total mileage: 916 miles.

Boston: I-90 west, I-84 west, I-91 south, I-95 south, I-287 west, Garden State Parkway south, New Jersey Turnpike south to Delaware Memorial Bridge, I-95 south (through Fort McHenry Tunnel in Baltimore), I-495 west and south around Washington, I-95 south, I-295 around Jacksonville, I-95 south, I-4 west, U.S. 192 west to entrance. Total mileage: 1,346 miles.

Buffalo: I-90 west, I-79 south, U.S. 19 south, West Virginia Turnpike south, I-77 south, I-20 west around Columbia (SC), I-26 east, I-95 south, I-295 around Jacksonville, I-95 south, I-4 west, U.S. 192 west to entrance. Total mileage: 1,209 miles.

Chicago: I-94 south, 80 east, I-65 south, 465 south, I-74 east, I-275 south, I-71 south, I-75 south, I-40 west, I-75 south to Atlanta, 285 west and south, 75 south to Florida's Turnpike south, U.S. 27 south, U.S. 192 east to entrance. Total mileage: 1,200 miles.

Cincinnati: I-75 south, I-40 west, I-75 south, I-475 south around Macon, I-75 south, Florida's Turnpike south, U.S. 27 south, U.S. 192 east to entrance. Total mileage: 911 miles.

Cleveland: I-77 south, West Virginia Turnpike south, I-77 south, I-20 west around Columbia (SC), I-26 east, I-95 south, I-295 around Jacksonville, I-95 south, I-4 west, U.S. 192 west to entrance. Total mileage: 1,098 miles.

Dallas: I-20 east to Shreveport, I-49 south, U.S. 1 south, I-49 south, U.S. 190 east, S.R. 415 south, I-10 east, I-12 east around New Orleans, I-10 east, I-75 south, Florida's Turnpike south, U.S. 27 south, U.S. 192 east to entrance. Total mileage: 1,131 miles.

Detroit: I-75 south, I-285 west and south around Atlanta, I-75 south, I-475 south around Macon, I-75 south, Florida's Turnpike south, U.S. 27 south, U.S. 192 east to entrance. Total mileage: 1,193 miles.

Indianapolis: I-65 south to Nashville, I-24 east to Chattanooga, I-75 south, I-285 west and south around Atlanta, I-75 south, I-475 south around Macon, I-75 south, Florida's Turnpike south, U.S. 27 south, U.S. 192 east to entrance. Total mileage: 985 miles.

Louisville: I-65 south to Nashville, I-24 east to Chattanooga, I-75 south, I-285 west and south around Atlanta, I-75 south, I-475 south around Macon, I-75 south, Florida's Turnpike south, U.S. 27 south, U.S. 192 east to entrance. Total mileage: 873 miles.

Minneapolis: I-94 east to Madison (WI), I-90 east, I-294 south around Chicago, I-90 east, I-65 south, 465 south, I-65 south to Nashville, I-24 east to Chattanooga, I-75 south, I-285 west and south around Atlanta, I-75 south, Florida's Turnpike south, U.S. 27 south, U.S. 192 east to entrance. Total mileage: 1,545 miles.

New York City: Lincoln Tunnel west, New Jersey Turnpike south to Delaware Memorial Bridge, I-95 south (through Fort McHenry Tunnel in Baltimore), I-495 west and south around Washington, D.C., I-95 south, I-295 around Jacksonville, I-95 south, I-4 west, U.S. 192 west to entrance. Total mileage: 1,103 miles.

Philadelphia: I-95 south (through Fort McHenry Tunnel in Baltimore), I-495 west and south around Washington, D.C., I-95 south, I-295 around Jacksonville, I-95 south, I-4 west, U.S. 192 west to entrance. Total mileage: 1,017 miles.

Pittsburgh: I-79 south, U.S. 19 south, West Virginia Turnpike south, I-77 south, I-20 west around Columbia (SC), I-26 east, I-95 south, I-295 around Jacksonville, I-95 south, I-4 west, U.S. 192 west to entrance. Total mileage: 1,016 miles.

Richmond: I-95 south, I-295 around Jacksonville, I-95 south, I-4 west, U.S. 192 west to entrance. Total mileage: 761 miles.

Toronto: Queen Elizabeth Way south, I-190 east, I-90 west, I-79 south, U.S. 19 south, West Virginia Turnpike south, I-77 south, I-20 west around Columbia (SC), I-26 east, I-95 south, I-295 around Jacksonville, I-95 south, I-4 west, U.S. 192 west to entrance. Total mileage: 2,302 miles.

FROM THE AIRPORT

Take Route 528 (known as the Beeline Expressway) west (toward Tampa), to I-4 west until you reach the appropriate Walt Disney World exit. The distance is 28 miles.

AUTOMOBILE CLUBS

Reputable national automobile clubs can offer help with breakdowns en route; insurance that covers personal injury, accidents, arrest, bail bond, and lawyers' fees for defense of contested traffic cases; and travel-planning services—not only advice, but also free maps and route mapping. Programs vary from one club to the next; fees range from about $12 to $75 a year.

Among the leading clubs:

Allstate Motor Club; Customer Service, Box 3094; Arlington Heights, IL 60006-3094; 800-347-8880

American Automobile Association; 1000 AAA Drive; Heathrow, FL 32746-5063; 407-444-7000

Amoco Motor Club; Box 9046; Des Moines, IA 50368; 800-334-3300

Ford Auto Club; Box 224688; Dallas, TX 75222-4688; 800-348-5220

Gulf Motor Club; 6001 North Clark St.; Chicago, IL 60660; 800-633-3224

Montgomery Ward Auto Club; 200 North Martingale Rd.; Schaumburg, IL 60173; 800-621-5151

Motor Club of America; 484 Central Ave.; Newark, NJ 07107; 800-833-3207

United States Auto Club Motoring Division; Box 660460; Dallas, TX 75266-0460; 800-348-5058

OTHER MAPS: Those who don't belong to a club can get free maps from state tourist boards. Also excellent is the Rand McNally *Road Atlas* ($7.95 in bookstores).

By Bus

Relatively few vacationers come to Walt Disney World by bus. But it makes sense to consider this means of transportation if you're traveling just a short distance or have plenty of time, if there are only two or three in your party, or if cost is a major consideration. Bus travel is usually extremely economical.

Greyhound provides frequent direct service into Kissimmee and Orlando. Buses drop arriving passengers off at either 16 North Orlando Avenue in Kissimmee or at 545 North McGruder Boulevard in Orlando. From each of the stops, it's possible to hire a taxi on your own or take one provided by the many area hotels and motels in the area. Check in advance to see if your lodging place offers taxi service. For further information phone Greyhound at 407-843-7720.

Sample Travel Times

Jacksonville, Florida..................about 4 hours
Tallahassee, Florida...................about 8 hours
Atlanta, Georgia ....about 14 hours

By Train

Amtrak serves the Orlando area twice daily from New York City. The trip takes about 21 to 23 hours and costs in the neighborhood of $179 to $221 round trip. En route stops are made in Philadelphia, Washington, D.C., Virginia, North Carolina, South Carolina, and Georgia. (Special discounts are sometimes available; it's a good idea to check.)

Amtrak also offers Auto Train service daily in both directions from Lorton, Virginia, 17 miles south of Washington, D.C., direct to Sanford, Florida, just 25 miles northeast of Orlando. Departure time is 4:30 P.M. and arrival time is 9 A.M. in both directions. The fare is $308 per car, $185 per adult, and $88 for children ages 2 through 15. The fare includes two meals and some entertainment. Sleeping accommodations cost extra. Special off-peak fares are often offered, so be sure to inquire.

For reservations and schedule information, send a self-addressed, stamped envelope to Amtrak Distribution Center; Box 7717; Itasca, IL 60143; or call 800-USA-RAIL.

BY SHIP

Premier Cruise Lines, the "Official Cruise Line of Walt Disney World," has made it possible to combine a three- or four-day ocean cruise to the Bahamas with a Walt Disney World vacation. Travelers can choose to visit WDW before or after they set sail aboard the Star/Ship *Oceanic* and the Star/Ship *Atlantic*. Cruises leave from (and return to) Port Canaveral, only about 45 miles from Walt Disney World. The ships stop at Nassau and Premier's newest destination, Port Lucaya, en route. Premier's packages include three or four days at sea (with all meals), three or four nights' accommodations at a Walt Disney World resort, and a passport allowing admission to the Magic Kingdom, Epcot Center, the Disney-MGM Studios Theme Park, River Country, and Pleasure Island, plus breakfast with the Disney characters. Also included in the package is a rental car for seven days (with unlimited mileage) and a tour of Spaceport, USA, at the Kennedy Space Center or the Astronaut Hall of Fame, just minutes from the ship's dock at Port Canaveral. Air arrangements to Orlando are available as part of the cruise program. For cruise dates and reser-vation information contact your travel agent or call Premier Cruise Lines at 800-327-7113.

By Air

The sleek, multi-million-dollar Orlando International Airport is undergoing yet another expansion in an effort to keep up with the millions of visitors who flock to Central Florida each year. Shuttle trains transport passengers to and from the central terminal. There's a well-stocked shop where arriving and departing travelers can buy T-shirts and other Disney merchandise.

There are more than a dozen airlines offering non-stop flights from all parts of the country. Delta Air Lines alone—the "Official Airline of Walt Disney World"—carries more than three million passengers into Orlando annually, on non-stop flights from 50 cities, direct flights (not including a change of planes), and connecting flights from 150 additional cities. Delta also offers the special Fantastic Flyer® program for kids.

The airline you decide to fly will depend in large part on where you live, when you'll be traveling, and which airline can get you there when you want to go, for the price you want to pay. Remember, direct flights—those whose lure is that they do not include a change of planes—are not always the swiftest way to get from point to point. If your itinerary requires several stops, it is wise to investigate all of the possible connection alternatives.

Discovering the Lowest Airfare

Gone are the days when airlines charged a flat rate to get from point A to point B, so it's more important than ever to shop around.

- Find out the names of all the airlines from your point of departure to your destination, then call them all—more than once if your route is complex. Tell the agent how many people there are in your party, and emphasize that you're interested in economy—if that's the case. The more flexible you can be in your dates and duration of stay, the more money you're likely to save. Fares are usually lowest on competitive, heavily traveled routes.

- Watch the newspapers for ads announcing new short-term promotional fares.
- When it's necessary to change planes en route, it is best to stick with one airline; the agent will know his or her own company's routing—and its discounted fares—better than those offered by other carriers.
- Fly when most other people don't—at night; on weekends on routes that usually serve business travelers; or midweek to and from vacation destinations.
- Plan ahead. Most carriers guarantee their fares—which means that you won't have to pay extra to use a valid ticket even if fares go up. Remember too, that most of the least expensive airfares now assess a penalty for revised flight schedules, and that certain discount fare tickets are nonrefundable.

WHICH AIRLINE FLIES FROM YOUR CITY?

You can fly nonstop to Orlando from about 50 different U.S. cities, on more than a dozen airlines. Schedules change often, and flights may be dropped or new ones added. This was the operative nonstop service at press time:

Atlanta, GA	DL, TW
Baltimore, MD	DL, US
Birmingham, AL	DL, DL*
Boston, MA	DL, NW, UA, US
Charlotte, NC	US
Chicago, IL	DL, AA, KP, TZ, UA
Cincinnati, OH	DL
Cleveland, OH	DL, CO
Columbus, OH	DL, US, HP
Dallas/Ft. Worth, TX	DL, AA
Daytona Beach, FL	DL*, US*
Denver, CO	DL, UA, CO
Detroit, MI	DL, NW
Ft. Lauderdale, FL	DL, DL*, 2S, UA, US*, US, TW, UA*
Ft. Myers, FL	DL, UA*, UA, US*
Freeport, Bahamas	DL*, 7Z
Gainesville, FL	DL*, US*
Hartford, CT/ Springfield, MA	DL, US
Houston, TX	CO
Indianapolis, IN	US, TZ
Jacksonville, FL	DL*, UA, UA*, US*
Kansas City, MO	US
Key West, FL	DL*
Long Island Macarthur, NY	US
Los Angeles, CA	DL, UA
Melbourne, FL	DL*, UA*, US*
Memphis, TN	NW
Mexico City, Mexico	DL, UA, KL
Miami, FL	DL, DL*, UA, UA*, AA, US, US*
Minneapolis/St. Paul, MN	NW
Naples, FL	DL*, US*
Nashville, TN	AA
Nassau, Bahamas	DL, BK, DL*
New Orleans, LA	DL
New York, NY/Newark, NJ	DL, CO, UA, US, TW, KP
Panama City, FL	DL*, US*
Pensacola, FL	DL*, US*
Philadelphia, PA	DL, US
Phoenix, AZ	HP
Pittsburgh, PA	US
Raleigh/Durham, NC	AA
St. Croix, Virgin Islands	DL
St. Louis, MO	TW, US
Salt Lake City, UT	DL
San Francisco, CA	DL, UA
San Juan, Puerto Rico	DL, KW, KP, US, AA
Sarasota/Bradenton, FL	DL, US*, UA, UA*
Tallahassee, FL	DL*, US*
Tampa/St. Petersburg, FL	DL, DL*, UA, HP, UA*
Vero Beach, FL	US*
Washington, DC	DL, US, UA
West Palm Beach, FL	DL, DL*, UA, TW, US*

ABBREVIATIONS—AA: American. BK: Paradise Island. CO: Continental. CS: Florida Air. DL: Delta. DL*: Comair—The Delta Connection. HP: America West. KP: Kiwi. KL: KLM. KW: Carnival. NW: Northwest. TW: Trans World. TZ: American Trans Air. UA: United. UA*: United Express. US: USAir. US*: USAir Express. 2S: Island Express. 7Z: Laker Airways.

SHOULD YOU BUY A PACKAGE?

The sheer number of diverse packages offering vacations in Central Florida is enough to bewilder even the savviest traveler. Still, these packages offer significant advantages. Among them is the opportunity to purchase a vacation that's completely organized in advance, and that will generally cost less than the same transportation, accommodations, and admission elements if they were purchased separately. (A complete Delta Dream Vacation can cost less than just the round-trip economy airfare from certain cities, though the package also may include a hotel room, a rental car with unlimited mileage for a week, and admission to the Magic Kingdom, Epcot Center, and the Disney-MGM Studios Theme Park.)

The main difference among the various package offerings—aside from cost—is the matter of lodging in on-site hotels versus off-property accommodations. Delta Air Lines and American Express packages offer lodgings in Walt Disney World's own on-site hotels, and Walt Disney World itself, along with the Walt Disney Travel Company, offers on-site "Grand Plan," "Admiral Plan," "Disney Deluxe Magic Plan," "Resort Romance," "Resort Magic," "Fort Wilderness Adventure," "Festival Magic," and "Village Magic" packages for visitors staying four or more nights. Many of the Walt Disney World packages are perfect for "top-of-the-line" visitors who don't mind spending a little extra money to obtain a package that includes virtually everything. Some of the packages are designed with a moderate budget in mind. For Walt Disney Travel Company package information call 800-828-0228.

Delta Air Lines packages include the added attraction of low-cost air transportation—plus accommodations at the *Contemporary* resort, *Polynesian* resort, the *Grand Floridian* resort, the villas, *Fort Wilderness*, *Disney Inn*, *Caribbean Beach*, *Yacht Club*, *Beach Club*, *Port Orleans*, or *Dixie Landings*.

Appraising the value of any package depends entirely on your specific needs. The various sections of this book describe the activities and attractions available at Walt Disney World, and once you've determined which of these are most appealing, call Walt Disney World, the airlines that fly between your city and Orlando, or a qualified travel agent to find a package that comes closest to your specific needs. Don't pick a package that includes elements you don't want or won't use; chances are that you'll be paying for them. And remember that while extras like welcoming cocktails sound attractive, their cash value is negligible. Also note that some packages announce as selling points certain services that are available to *every* Walt Disney World guest.

On the other hand, there's real value in certain elements, such as transportation to the Walt Disney World property from the airport and discounts on meals. Some of the packages also include meals with the Disney characters, tennis lessons, golf greens fees, court rentals or boat rentals, and the like.

HOW TO CUT TRAVEL COSTS

Although vacations are not getting any less expensive, scrapping periodic family getaways is no answer. If financial considerations are a primary concern, it's far better to simply prune the vacation budget in three main areas:

Food: Eat hot meals in cafeterias instead of waitress-service restaurants. Visit fancier establishments (if you must) at lunchtime rather than dinner. (The very same entrées usually cost less then.) Carry sandwich fixings and have lunches alfresco when possible. Look for lodging places with kitchen facilities: The savings on food, especially for families at breakfast time, may be more than the extra accommodations expense.

Lodging: The chief rule of thumb here is not to pay for more than you need. Budget chains such as Days Inns and Days Lodges, Susse Chalet Motor Lodges and Inns, Imperial 400 Motor Inns, Passport Inns and Downtowners, Red Roof Inns, Family Inns of America, and Motel 6s can prove economical, though they may not offer many frills. (The best single guide to their whereabouts from coast to coast is the *National Directory of Budget Motels*, revised annually and available for $6.95 including postage from Pilot Books; 103 Cooper St.; Babylon, NY 11702; 516-422-2225.)

If swimming pools and other amenities matter, consider the non-budget chain establishments that have them—but remember that cutoff ages (above which there is a charge for children sharing their parents' room) do vary. Check with the individual hotel for their policy. Get prices for Orlando hostelries in advance, then calculate the exact costs for your whole family.

The *Caribbean Beach* resort, *Dixie Landings*, and *Port Orleans* bring the number of moderately priced hotel rooms on the property to about 5,000. New in 1994 are even more advantageously priced rooms at the *All-Star Sports* and *All-Star Music* resorts. See our *Transportation and Accommodations* chapter for details.

Depending on the number of people in your party, guesthouses and tourist homes may or may not be a good buy. Since these establishments usually levy substantial extra charges for more than two people, regardless of their ages, rooms that are inexpensive for two can prove costly for a family. Consult *Bed & Breakfast, Inns & Guesthouses* published by Lanier ($16.95) for locations and prices. Also look into A&A Bed and Breakfast of Florida (Box 1316; Winter Park, FL 32790; 628-3233). They handle reservations for B&Bs in the WDW area.

Consider sharing accommodations with family or friends. It's often possible to rent a resort condominium or a house large enough to accommodate two families for much less than twice what each would pay for a single conventional hotel room. At Walt Disney World, couples can reap savings by this sort of doubling up—with no loss of privacy and some bonus in space. (See the chart "Rates at WDW Properties" on page 74 for details.) Finally, remember that rooms at Disney hotels have been designed to accommodate up to five guests, with the exception of the *Caribbean Beach* resort, *Port Orleans*, *Dixie Landings*, *All-Star Sports*, and *All-Star Music*, where each room accommodates four.

Transportation: Comparative shopping is vital. Consider transportation needs at your destination, then figure the total transportation cost. Calculate the cost of driving based on your car's mileage, current gasoline prices, the distance you expect to cover, and the cost of accommodations and food en route, then figure what you'll pay by bus, plane, or train. Don't fail to calculate the cost of getting to and from the airport or terminal, and the cost of renting a car (if necessary) in Orlando. And remember that special low fares that are economical for couples can sometimes prove less advantageous for families.

How To Get the Best Photos

There are so many wonderful images glimpsed all over WDW that just about any camera in good working order can capture them for you. Here are some useful hints:

• Don't shoot from closer than 4 feet from your subject, and don't try for a flash picture more than 60 feet away.

• Fill the frame with as much of the prime subject as possible. When shooting people, remember that the larger the subject appears in the picture, the more interesting it will be.

• Don't shoot into the sun. Instead, position yourself so that light is falling directly on your subject—coming from behind you or from the side.

• Flash photography is not permitted inside any WDW attractions.

• Check the camera's batteries and battery contacts regularly.

• Use film that is fresh. When purchasing film, check the expiration date stamped on the bottom of the box. Keep film cool.

• Keep the camera clean. Blow dust off the lens and then wipe it with a soft tissue.

• When taking movies or using videotape cameras, note that they'll be more effective if you pick a theme such as "A Walk Down Main Street," "A Stroll Through France," or the like. Pan very slowly and smoothly.

• If you suspect that your camera isn't functioning correctly, visit the Camera Center on the east side of Main Street near Town Square in the Magic Kingdom; the Camera Center near Spaceship Earth or Cameras and Film at Journey Into Imagination at Epcot Center; or The Darkroom at the Disney-MGM Studios Theme Park.

Rental cameras: Thirty-five-millimeter and video cameras are available for rental at the Camera Center in the Magic Kingdom; at the Camera Center in Epcot Center near Spaceship Earth and Cameras and Film at Journey Into Imagination; and at The Darkroom at the Disney-MGM Studios Theme Park. The 35mm cameras cost $5 per day to use plus a $100 refundable deposit and video cameras cost $40 per day with a $600 refundable deposit. The required deposits can be charged to American Express, Visa, or MasterCard. Similar cameras are also available at Magicam at the *Royal Plaza* hotel.

Film processing: Two-hour processing is available at the Magic Kingdom, Epcot Center, the Disney-MGM Studios Theme Park, at the resorts, and the Disney Village Marketplace wherever there is a Photo Express sign. Film is processed right on the premises.

WHERE TO BUY FILM

THE MAGIC KINGDOM

Main Street—Camera Center; Emporium
Adventureland—Zanibar Shell Co.
Frontierland—Frontier Trading Post
Liberty Square—Heritage House
Fantasyland—Royal Candy Shoppe;
    Kodak Kiosk
Tomorrowland—Mickey's Star Traders

EPCOT CENTER

Future World—All merchandise locations
    (best stock at the Camera Center)
World Showcase—At least one shop
    in each pavilion (film is often stashed
    under the counter)

THE DISNEY-MGM STUDIOS THEME PARK

The Darkroom
Crossroads of the World
Movieland Memorabilia

THE HOTELS

Contemporary resort—Concourse
    Sundries & Spirits
Disney Inn—Gifts and Sundries
Polynesian resort—News from
    Civilization
Grand Floridian—Sandy Cove; M. Mouse
    Mercantile
Caribbean Beach—Calypso Trading Post
Yacht Club—Fittings and Farings
Beach Club—Atlantic Wear Gifts
Port Orleans—Jackson Square Gifts
Dixie Landings—Fulton's General Store
Disney Vacation Club—Conch Flats
    General Store
Wilderness Lodge—Wilderness Lodge
    Mercantile

FORT WILDERNESS

Settlement and Meadow Trading Posts

DISNEY VILLAGE MARKETPLACE

Guest Services, just outside You & Me Kid

PLEASURE ISLAND

Music Legends

TYPHOON LAGOON

Singapore Sal's

Hints on Traveling with Children

Tell youngsters that a Walt Disney World vacation is in the works and the response is apt to be nothing less than overwhelming—and the journey to the park is likely to be fraught with "Are-we-there-yets?" recurring like a stuck record. Before leaving home be sure to pick up a copy of our brand-new guide, *Birnbaum's Walt Disney World For Kids, By Kids* ($9.95). It's filled with information about Walt Disney World from a kid's perspective.

En route: Certain ploys can quiet this refrain a bit. Get older children involved in planning every leg of the trip, and set up a series of intermediate goals to which they can look forward. Younger children can anticipate discovering the contents of a pint-size suitcase packed with familiar games and toys, plus a few surprises.

In addition, it's smart to take along snacks to keep things peaceful when stomachs start rumbling and food is miles away. Above all, and especially if the trip is by car, take it easy, and allow time for plenty of breaks en route.

Those who fly should schedule travel during off-peak hours, when the chances are better that empty seats will be available. When the plane is taking off and landing, babies should be given bottles, pacifiers, or even thumbs to promote swallowing and clear ears; a piece of gum or hard candy will provide the same relief for a small child. Newborn babies should not be taken aloft, since their lungs may not be able to adjust easily to the altitude. For finicky young eaters, request special meals when reserving seats. As the "Official Airline For Kids," Delta features the Fantastic Flyer® program for children ages 2 through 12. On every Delta flight, kids receive a complimentary Mickey Mouse visor with an enrollment card and a copy of the *Fantastic Flyer* magazine featuring games, puzzles, and prizes. Be sure to ask the flight attendant for details.

Budget watchers should pay careful attention to motel rate structures (see page 27 for ideas) when reserving accommodations. Also, some motels charge for cots, while others might bring them in at no charge. Note that some hostelries outside the World *seem* a lot less expensive than the WDW resorts—until the actual costs for everything for a whole family are computed. Sometimes airfares that sound inexpensive actually cost more for a family; sometimes air packages cut costs. The key is to check carefully.

At Walt Disney World: This vacationland ranks among the easiest spots on earth for traveling families with children. Older youngsters don't need to be driven around, and the general supervision is such that kids are hard pressed to get into trouble. All the resorts, plus *Fort Wilderness* and the Villa Recreation Center at the villas, have at least a small room full of pinball machines and video games, much to the satisfaction of kids of all ages; the one at the *Contemporary* resort is positively vast. And all the hotels have playgrounds; the ones at the *Polynesian* resort, *Dixie Landings*, and *Caribbean Beach* get high marks from children.

And the *Polynesian* resort, the *Grand Floridian*, the *Contemporary* resort, the *Yacht Club*, the *Beach Club*, the *Swan*, and the *Dolphin* have child-care facilities. In-room babysitters can be summoned to all resort hotels and villas; contact the Guest Services desk. And there also is a center known as KinderCare, which accepts one-year-olds through four-year-olds. For details and availability, phone 827-5444.

There is not any cause for excessive hand-holding inside the Magic Kingdom, Epcot Center, or the Disney-MGM Studios Theme Park; with older youngsters, it's enough to establish a specific meeting place and a meeting time (allowing a little latitude, just in case). If there are younger children along, it's not a bad idea to stop at City Hall or the Baby Center next to the Crystal Palace to pick up a special name tag to facilitate a reunion in case the family gets separated. Name tags also are available at Earth Station and the Baby

Services at Epcot Center, and at Guest Services at the Disney-MGM Studios.

At the Magic Kingdom, families traveling with small children will want to know about the "kid switch" policy. At attractions with age and/or height restrictions, a parent who waits with a young child while the other parent rides the attraction can go right on when the first parent comes off. If lines are long this can save a lot of time, so be sure to ask the attendant.

Aunt Polly's Landing on Tom Sawyer Island in the Magic Kingdom is a good bet for lunch; while adults in the party are sipping lemonade, the kids can be bouncing across the Barrel Bridge and exploring every nook and cranny on the island. *Lumiere's Kitchen* in Fantasyland also is a good spot for lunch. The *Sci-Fi Dine-In* and the *50's Prime Time Café* at the Studios are good choices for kids as well.

Strollers are available for rent for a nominal fee (small deposit required) at Strollers—Wheelchairs on the east side of Main Street at the entrance to the Magic Kingdom; at Epcot Center at the Stroller and Wheelchair Rentals Shop on the east side of the Entrance Plaza and at the International Gateway; and at Oscar's at the Disney-MGM Studios Theme Park. If your stroller disappears, as often happens while you're inside an attraction, a replacement may be obtained at Space Port (the shop of contemporary decorative gifts) in Tomorrowland; at the Trading Post in Frontierland; at Tinker Bell's Treasures in Fantasyland; at the World Traveler Shop at the International Gateway and the Germany Pavilion in Epcot Center; and at Oscar's at the Disney-MGM Studios Theme Park. Stroller renters should be aware that guests only have to pay once a day for a stroller. If you rent one in the Magic Kingdom in the morning and plan to spend the afternoon in Epcot Center, just keep the receipt and present it for a free stroller at Epcot Center.

Baby Services at the Magic Kingdom, Epcot Center, and the Disney-MGM Studios Theme Park can be helpful in many ways to parents with young children. There are low-lighted rooms with comfortable rocking chairs and love seats for nursing mothers, and cheerful feeding rooms. Highchairs, bibs, and plastic spoons also are available. The baby centers have facilities for changing infants, preparing formulas, and warming bottles. Disposable diapers and nurser bags, pull-on rubber pants, baby bottles with nipples, formula (Similac, Isomil, and Enfamil), teethers, pacifiers, prepared cereal, juices, and strained and junior baby food in a limited selection are available for sale on the spot at a nominal cost. The decor is soothing; the atmosphere is such that it seems a million miles away from the Magic Kingdom, Epcot Center, or the Disney-MGM Studios Theme Park. A stop for diaper changing makes a good break for child and parent alike. Changing areas are available in most women's and some men's restrooms as well. Hours at the baby centers vary, so check at City Hall, Earth Station, or Guest Services.

A variety of other baby-care supplies can be purchased at Baby Services in Epcot Center, Strollers—Wheelchairs on Main Street, and Oscar's Super Service at the Disney-MGM Studios Theme Park. Disposable diapers are sold, though not displayed, in the Emporium on Main Street in the Magic Kingdom, at Baby Services near the *Odyssey* restaurant at Epcot Center, and at Baby Services in the Guest Services Building at the Disney-MGM Studios Theme Park.

Lost children: The security forces inside the Magic Kingdom, Epcot Center, and the Disney-MGM Studios Theme Park are far more careful than the happy appearance of things indicates. This is a welcome thought on those rare instances when a child suddenly disappears or fails to show up on schedule. If this happens to you, check the lost children's logbooks at Baby Services or at City Hall in the Magic Kingdom; at Earth Station or Baby Services behind the *Odyssey* restaurant in Epcot Center; or at Guest Services at the Disney-MGM Studios Theme Park. Every Disney employee knows where they are—and what to do if a lost-looking child suddenly starts to call for his or her mommy. There are no paging systems in the parks, but in very serious emergencies an all-points bulletin can be put out among employees. The staff at the Guest Services windows at the entrances to Epcot Center, the Magic Kingdom, and the Disney-MGM Studios also may have information about lost children.

Helpful Hints

Hints For Older Travelers

Walt Disney World can overwhelm an elderly traveler not accustomed to unfamiliar places; Epcot Center encompasses significant distances, and the Magic Kingdom and the Disney-MGM Studios Theme Park can be disorienting because of the profusion of sights and sounds, nooks and crannies. The heat, particularly in summer, also can be hard to take. Yet with the proper planning and precautions, all of WDW can be just as delightful for older visitors as for kids. Here are a few suggestions:

● Join a tour. Surprisingly enough, not many companies offer tours to WDW specifically designed for older travelers. However, the following firms offer private guides to take guests through the parks: Florida Convention Services (1244 West Landstreet Rd.; Orlando, FL 32824; 407-856-6400 or 800-356-7891) has private guides and charges $20 per hour (four-hour minimum, plus admission for the guide). Suntoast Destination Management (6149 Chancellor Dr., Suite 700; Orlando, FL 32809; 407-859-0027 or 800-827-0028) can provide uniformed guides for either $20 per hour (four-hour minimum plus admission for the guide) or $200 for the entire day (including admission) at WDW.

● Inside the Magic Kingdom and Epcot Center group tours—among the best buys in the World—are offered by Guest Services. These four-hour guided walks provide an introduction to the parks; the price is $5 and includes the services of a guide and visits to various attractions. Admission to the parks is an additional cost. For details and availability, phone 560-6233.

● Schedule visits for off-peak seasons and hours when the crowds will not be overwhelming and discouraging. Also, note that special values are available to Florida residents during Resident Salute Days on selected non-peak dates in the winter. Call 824-4321 for details.

● Read all Walt Disney World literature carefully before arrival so that things are familiar.

● In the parks, don't be timid about asking for directions or advice. Disney employees are always happy to help out.

● Eat early or late, to avoid mealtime crowds. In the Magic Kingdom, stop in more sedate restaurants such as the *Crystal Palace*, *Tony's Town Square* restaurant, or *King Stefan's* in Cinderella Castle. Or take the monorail to the still calmer *Polynesian* resort, the *Contemporary* resort, or the *Grand Floridian*, to lunch in one of the full-service restaurants there. In Epcot Center, the *Odyssey* restaurant in Future World is an especially restful counter service spot for lunch. At the Disney-MGM Studios Theme Park, the *Hollywood Brown Derby* offers a relaxing sit-down meal.

● Don't try to save money by scrimping on food. Traveling takes energy, and only a good meal can provide it.

● Protect yourself from the sun. Always wear a hat, and don't stint on the sunscreen. (And remember to cover your legs, which are easily sunburned by light rays reflected from pavements.)

● Don't become overheated. Take frequent rest stops in the shade, and get out of the mid-afternoon heat by stopping for a snack in an air conditioned restaurant. Avoid standing in line at Frontierland's Big Thunder Mountain Railroad and at Fantasyland's 20,000 Leagues Under the Sea in midafternoon; parts of these queues are unprotected from the sun and can be very hot. In Epcot Center, spend the hot midafternoon hours in the TransCenter in the World of Motion, in CommuniCore East and West, or Wonders of Life or the Sea Base Alpha exhibit at The Living Seas in Future World and avoid the uncovered outdoor queues at all the Future World pavilions and at World Showcase attractions like *O Canada!*, *Impressions de France*, and El Rio del Tiempo. Don't underestimate the distances at Epcot Center; you may need to walk as much as two miles in the course of a day. If taken slowly and in short increments, this is not too ominous. But if you are not strong enough to cover that distance, be sure to rent a

HINTS FOR SINGLE TRAVELERS

Walt Disney World does not exactly attract the young swinging singles crowd, so those on the lookout for romantic encounters probably would do better elsewhere. But those who travel alone for the freedom and the fun of it can have as enjoyable a time at Walt Disney World as they would anywhere else.

WDW employees are generally a friendly and entertaining lot; chatting with a painter about the perpetual repainting of Main Street woodwork, talking to the animal keepers on Discovery Island, or discussing life abroad with one of the young World Showcase employees born and educated in the country the pavilion represents, a single traveler usually learns more about the ways of the World than any group member. Other visitors who might be encountered in the course of a day are away from their own home base as well, and are apt to be just that much less standoffish.

Pleasure Island has clubs, bars, restaurants, and shows that can prove to be fertile meeting places. In addition to the other Walt Disney World guests, lots of folks from the Orlando area also patronize the Pleasure Island establishments.

Single women traveling alone will not find the bars and lounges at Walt Disney World hotels off limits. The same relaxed atmosphere prevails in the *Rose & Crown Pub* in the United Kingdom Pavilion and the *Matsu No Ma* lounge in Japan, both in the World Showcase area of Epcot Center. Another good way to meet people (albeit a somewhat older crowd) is to sign up for one of the Guest Services' Guided Walking Tours of the Magic Kingdom or Epcot Center. The *Biergarten* in World Showcase's Germany Pavilion and the Teppanyaki dining rooms in Japan's

Mitsukoshi restaurant are especially convivial since several parties are seated together at one large table. River Country, Typhoon Lagoon, and the hotel swimming pools and beaches also are good places for meeting people.

A note for budget watchers: Rates at all WDW resort hotels and those at Disney Village Hotel Plaza, and at some others in the Orlando area, are the same whether one or two persons occupy a room. Similarly, the villas are priced per unit, regardless of the number of people who sleep there.

wheelchair at the outset of your visit. The buses that circumnavigate World Showcase Lagoon and the launches that make regular crossings can help you cover the distances—but only when there are no long queues. It is better to walk between pavilions, resting frequently en route, than to wait 15 or 20 minutes for a ride in a bus or boat.

● Above all, don't push yourself. Half the fun of Walt Disney World—the part that younger travelers often miss—is just sitting under a tree on a park bench, watching the people go by.

Lost Adults

Occasionally, traveling companions do get separated in the press of the crowds or someone may fail to show up at an appointed meeting spot. So it's good to know that Guest Services maintains message books at City Hall in the Magic Kingdom. In Epcot Center, messages are handled by the Guest Services hosts and hostesses staffing Earth Station. At the Disney-MGM Studios Theme Park, messages are can be left for fellow travelers at the Guest Services building.

Hints for Travelers with Disabilities

Walt Disney World gets high marks among travelers with disabilities because of the attention that has been paid to their special needs. Special parking is available for guests visiting the Magic Kingdom, Epcot Center, and the Disney-MGM Studios Theme Park; get directions at the Auto Plazas upon entering. From the Transportation and Ticket Center (TTC), the Magic Kingdom is accessible either by ferry or by monorail (though the former is preferable, since the slant of the ramp to the monorails makes holding a wheelchair a bit taxing when there are any waiting lines at all). All WDW monorail stations are accessible to wheelchairs except the one at the *Contemporary* resort, which can be reached only by escalator. Special vans, with motorized platforms that lift wheelchairs inside, are available too. To request one, day guests should inquire at the Guest Services window at the TTC, at Epcot Center Entrance Plaza, in City Hall in the Magic Kingdom, Earth Station at Epcot Center, or Guest Services at the Disney-MGM Studios Theme Park. Resort guests should contact Guest Services in their hotel. Count on at least 20 minutes between the request and pick-up.

In the Magic Kingdom, wheelchairs are available for rent at Strollers—Wheelchairs on the right-hand side of the souvenir area, just past the turnstiles. In Epcot Center, the rental area is just inside the turnstiles on the left as you enter. Oscar's Super Service rents wheelchairs at the Disney-MGM Studios Theme Park. The *Guidebook for Guests with Disabilities* will prove beneficial throughout your visit and may be obtained at wheelchair rental locations, City Hall in the Magic Kingdom, Earth Station in Epcot Center, and Guest Services at the Disney-MGM Studios Theme Park. The guidebook describes the accessibility of all WDW attractions. The guidebook also is available by mail. Send a written request to Walt Disney World Guest Letters; Box 10,000; Lake Buena Vista, FL 32830. Most restrooms in the parks have extra-wide cubicles with wall bars for people in wheelchairs. Furthermore, most attractions are accessible to guests who can be lifted to and from their chairs with the assistance from a member of their party, and many can accommodate guests who must remain in their wheelchairs at all times.

Epcot Center, the Disney-MGM Studios Theme Park, and all WDW resort hotels are easily explored by wheelchair. All the WDW resorts have accommodations for guests with disabilities, with the exception of the *Disney Inn*. At the villas some two-bedroom units are accessible to wheelchairs and some are not; the best bets are the planned-for-the-purpose units facing the Lake Buena Vista golf course. In River Country and at Typhoon Lagoon, life jackets are available for travelers with disabilities.

For guests who are visually impaired, a tape recorder and cassette that describes the Magic Kingdom, Epcot Center, and the Disney-MGM Studios Theme Park in terms of smells and sounds is available. A small refundable deposit ($25) is required for recorder use. Service dogs are permitted in the parks. In Epcot Center, personal translator units that amplify attraction sound tracks for the benefit of guests who are hearing impaired are available at Earth Station. There is a $4 rental fee and a $40 deposit is refunded upon the return of the unit. Guests also are required to present a major credit card when renting. Guests who use telecommunications devices for the deaf (TDDs) can call 827-5141 for WDW information. TDDs are available for guest use at City Hall in the Magic Kingdom, Earth Station in Epcot Center, Guest Services at the Disney-MGM Studios Theme Park, and at all the resorts. There is no charge for use of the TDDs.

Tours: The Society for the Advancement of Travel for the Handicapped (347 Fifth Ave., Suite 610; New York, NY 10016; 212-447-7284) has a number of member travel agents who are knowledgeable about tours for travelers with disabilities and can help arrange individual and group tours. Send a self-addressed stamped envelope and $3 to receive a copy of their listings. Among the organizations that sponsor trips for travelers with disabilities and offer tours to WDW are Flying Wheels Travel; Box 382; Owatonna, MN 55060 (800-535-6790) and Evergreen Travel Services; 4114 198th SW, Suite 13; Lynnwood, WA 98036 (800-435-2288). These organizations also can arrange trips for individuals.

Local Assistance: Friends of the Family (7380 Sand Lake Road; Orlando, FL 32819; 856-7676 or 800-945-2045) offers free referrals for travelers with disabilities visiting Cen-

tral Florida. They can help with everything from transportation information to nursing and medical care. They also provide helpers to push wheelchairs for $15 per hour or $150 for a full day.

Traveling by car: Hertz, Avis, and National all have a limited quantity of hand-control cars for rent in the Orlando area; it's a good idea to call well in advance to reserve them.

Traveling by plane: Airlines have not always been as helpful in dealing with travelers with disabilities as they are now. Occasionally, vacationers can go into the aircraft in their own chair—provided the chair is narrow and the plane's aisles are wide; more often, travelers transfer to a narrower airline chair at the door of the aircraft, while their own chair is sent down to the luggage compartment. Passengers in wheelchairs are usually preboarded and then deplaned after other passengers. If you are not taking your own wheelchair along and have a tight connection to make, be sure to advise the airlines' attendants well in advance. Similarly, if a passenger wishes to utilize an airline's wheelchair at a connecting point or destination, that wheelchair service should be ordered at the time that flight reservations are being made.

Allow plenty of time to make all your arrangements, and don't fail to alert all airline personnel to your special needs.

Policies on motorized wheelchairs vary, depending on the airline and the type of chair; check with carriers in advance. Service dogs are always allowed aboard aircraft (though some carriers may require them to be muzzled), but arrangements should be made at the

time reservations are made so that a bulkhead seat may be requested.

Traveling by train: Whether riding with or without reservations, it's wise to phone in advance to arrange for one of the special seats that Amtrak maintains for travelers with disabilities. Wheelchairs are available at major Amtrak stations, some 500 in all, including Orlando. Cars have special seats and specially equipped bathrooms and sleeping compartments; older equipment also has been refurbished to accommodate travelers with disabilities. Passengers who are visually impaired or have other disabilities get a 25 percent discount on one-way tickets, though companions must pay full fare. Service dogs may ride with passengers at no extra charge.

Battery-powered, standard-size wheelchairs are permitted in coaches. Fuel-powered and oversize chairs must be stored in the baggage car for the duration of the trip. Always be sure to phone the train stations and reservations center well before your departure date to arrange for any special facilities or services you may need.

Traveling by bus: Greyhound has implemented plans that allow vacationers with disabilities and a companion (to help with boarding and disembarking) to travel together on a single adult ticket. Greyhound carries nonmotorized folding wheelchairs at no additional charge. Some motorized wheelchairs are accepted.

And remember to plan in advance. Allow extra time, and at each portion of the trip, inform air, bus, train, and hotel personnel of your special needs.

Other Information

BARBERS: The most amusing place to get a haircut is the old-fashioned Harmony Barber Shop (824-6550), tucked away at the end of the flower-filled cul-de-sac just off the west side of Main Street in the Magic Kingdom; the Disney books on hand are terrific, and the "Dapper Dans," the park's own barbershop quartet, can often be heard here. Moustache cups and other nostalgic shaving items are for sale.

Outside the Magic Kingdom, visit the Captain's Chair on the third floor of the *Contemporary* resort (824-3411), the Alii Nui Barber Shop on the first floor of the Great Ceremonial House at the *Polynesian* resort (824-1400), and the Periwig Salon at the *Yacht Club* and *Beach Club* (934-3260).

BEAUTY SHOPS: Shampoos, sets, coloring, waving, manicures, and pedicures are available at the Pretty Wahine Beauty Shop in the *Polynesian* resort (824-1396), the American Beauty Shoppe on the third floor of the *Contemporary* resort (824-3413), the Periwig Salon at the *Yacht Club* and *Beach Club* (934-3260) the Ivy Trellis at the *Grand Floridian* (824-2581), and the Niki Bryan shops at the *Dolphin* (934-4250) and the *Swan* (934-1375).

CAR CARE: Auto and travel club members probably will want to call their local club-sponsored towing service in the event of problems. The Disney Car Care Center (824-4813), located on Floridian Way near the Magic Kingdom Auto Plaza, has a service garage which is open Mondays through Fridays from 7 A.M. to 6 P.M. Emergency road service and gas are available from the Car Care Center during park operating hours. Though routine maintenance work is probably best done by mechanics who know your car well—before leaving home—the Disney Car Care Center is a good place for gas and repairs in a pinch. Disney personnel here will chauffeur guests to their day's WDW destination, and arrange for later pickup when requested.

It's also reassuring to know that WDW breakdowns don't mean disaster. All WDW roads are patrolled constantly by security vehicles equipped with radios which can be used to call for help.

RELIGIOUS SERVICES: A variety of religious services are held around Walt Disney World.

Protestant: 9 A.M. on Sundays at Luau Cove at the *Polynesian* resort.

Catholic: 8 A.M. and 10:15 A.M. on Sundays at Luau Cove at the *Polynesian* resort. Call Holy Family Catholic Church (876-2211) for specific information, or check with Guest Services at any of the Disney hotels.

The closest Catholic church off the property is Mary, Queen of the Universe Shrine, 2½ miles north of Lake Buena Vista on the I-4 service road. Call 239-6600 for mass times. In Orlando, there are services at St. James Cathedral (215 North Orange Ave.; 422-2005) at 4 P.M. and 6 P.M. on Saturdays and on Sundays at 7:30 A.M., 9 A.M., 10:30 A.M., noon (in Spanish), and 6 P.M.

In Kissimmee, there are services at the Holy Redeemer Catholic Church (1603 North Thacker Ave.; 846-3700) on Saturdays at 4 P.M., 6 P.M., and 7:30 P.M. (in Spanish), and on Sundays at 7:30 A.M., 8:45 A.M., 10:30 A.M., noon, and 6 P.M. Daily masses are said at 7:30 A.M. and 9 A.M., and at 5:30 P.M. Mondays through Thursdays during Lent.

Jewish: Conservative services are at 8:15 P.M. on Fridays and 9 A.M. on Saturdays at the Congregation Ohev Shalom (5015 Goddard Ave.; 298-4650) in Orlando. Reform services are at 8:15 P.M. on Fridays (7:30 P.M. on the first Friday of every month) and 10:30 A.M. on Saturdays at the Congregation of Liberal Judaism (928 Malone Drive; 645-0444).

MAIL

Postcards are for sale at many spots in the resorts and around the Magic Kingdom, among them Main Street Book Store on the west side of Main Street. Postage stamps can be purchased at all the Disney resorts, at City Hall in the Magic Kingdom, near the lockers at Epcot Center, at the Guest Services desk at the Disney-MGM Studios Theme Park, and at Guest Services at the Disney Village Marketplace. The old-fashioned, olive-drab mailboxes that punctuate Main Street are no longer official U.S. post boxes, but letters can be mailed there for pickup by Disney employees and subsequent transportation to the Lake Buena Vista post office. Postmarks read "Lake Buena Vista," *not* "Walt Disney World." All window services are available at the Lake Buena Vista post office, including postal money order and stamp sale, registry, and certification. The post office is located at the Crossroads of Lake Buena Vista shopping center.

Mail may be addressed to guests c/o their hotel at Walt Disney World; Box 10000; Lake Buena Vista, FL 32830-1000.

Don't forget to arrange for mail at home to be held by the post office.

LOST AND FOUND: The extensive indexing system maintained by Walt Disney World's Lost and Found department is impressive, especially when a prize possession turns up missing, whether it's false teeth or a camera. (Both have been lost in the past; the dentures were never claimed.) If you lose (or find) something, report it on the proper forms at City Hall, at the Guest Services window on the east end of the Transportation and Ticket Center, at the Epcot Center Entrance Plaza, Earth Station, the Guest Services desks at the Disney-MGM Studios Theme Park, in the first floor lobby at the *Contemporary* resort, or the main lobbies at the *Polynesian* resort, the *Disney Inn*, the *Grand Floridian*, the *Caribbean Beach*, *Yacht Club*, *Beach Club*, *Port Orleans*, *Dixie Landings*, *Wilderness Lodge*, *All-Star Sports*, *All-Star Music*, and the *Disney Vacation Club*; at *Fort Wilderness*, phone ext. 7-2726 from a comfort station telephone; from outside the campground, phone 824-2726; at Walt Disney World Village, phone 828-3384.

Items lost in the Magic Kingdom can be claimed on the day of the loss at City Hall, and thereafter at the main Lost and Found station at the Transportation and Ticket Center. Articles found at Epcot Center remain at the Epcot Center Lost and Found for one day before being delivered to the main Lost and Found. At the Disney-MGM Studios Theme Park, claim or report lost items at the Guest Services building on the day of your visit. To report lost items after your visit, call 824-4245.

Articles not claimed by the owner may be claimed by the finder—an added incentive for visitors to turn over valuable items to Lost and Found.

POCKET PAGERS: Two types of devices are available to WDW guests to signal a telephone call or message. They are available at all WDW hotels, Fort Wilderness Outpost, the villa reception center, and the *Royal Plaza*.

DISNEY DOLLARS: Available in one-, five-, and ten-dollar denominations. Disney Dollars are accepted at all Magic Kingdom, Epcot Center, and Disney-MGM Studios Theme Park restaurants, shops, and food stands, and at all WDW resorts.

DRINKING LAWS: In Florida, drinking is legal at 21. There are many bars and lounges all over the World; minors are permitted to accompany their parents, but are prohibited from sitting or standing at the bar. There's no drinking in the Magic Kingdom (where even the piña coladas are nonalcoholic), but alcoholic beverages are available at restaurants in Epcot Center, the Disney-MGM Studios Theme Park, Pleasure Island, and the Disney Village Marketplace.

By the bottle: Liquor is sold in full-size and mini bottles at Village Spirits at the Disney Village Marketplace, at Trader Jack's on the second floor of the Great Ceremonial House at the *Polynesian* resort, at Gifts and Sundries in the lobby at the *Disney Inn*, at Concourse Sundries & Spirits in the *Contemporary* resort, and at Calypso Trading Post at the *Caribbean Beach* resort. Liquor also may be purchased from room service at the *Polynesian* resort, the *Contemporary* resort, the *Disney Inn*, the *Grand Floridian* resort, the *Yacht Club*, and the *Beach Club*.

LOCKERS: There are coin-operated lockers underneath the Main Street Railroad Station in the Magic Kingdom and at two locations at the Transportation and Ticket Center—next to Lost and Found on the west end and beside the bus parking lot on the east side. Lockers are also available at Epcot Center at the Bus Information Center in the bus parking lot, in an area to the right of Earth Station as you face World Showcase Lagoon, and at International Gateway in World Showcase. At the Disney-MGM Studios Theme Park, lockers can be found next to Oscar's near the main entrance. Cost is 50¢ per use for the regular size, 75¢ for the larger ones. Items too big to fit into the latter can be checked at the Guest Services windows at the TTC, at City Hall inside the Magic Kingdom, in the package pickup area or in the storage area at Epcot Center, and at Guest Services at the Disney-MGM Studios Theme Park. Be aware that lockers are available for use at your own risk. It is not recommended that valuable items be stored in lockers.

MEDICAL MATTERS

For travelers with chronic health problems, it's a good idea to carry copies of all prescriptions and to get names of local doctors from hometown physicians. However, Walt Disney World is equipped to deal with many types of medical emergencies. In the Magic Kingdom, next to the Crystal Palace, there's a First Aid Center staffed by a registered nurse; there is another at Epcot Center, located in the *Odyssey* restaurant complex. At the Disney-MGM Studios Theme Park, the First Aid Center is in the Guest Services building at the main entrance. For resort guests, as well as guests staying at other area hotels, a service known as HouseMed is available. Call 648-9234 and a physician will report directly to the guest's room. Medications can be dispensed by the visiting physician. The service is available 24 hours a day. HouseMed also operates the MediClinic, located at the intersection of I-4 and 192. It's open daily from 9 A.M. to 9 P.M., and transportation is available from all WDW First Aid Centers, resorts, and area hotels. Serious emergencies can be reported to the nearby Sand Lake Hospital, 351-8550.

The most common malady? Not sensitive stomachs upset by rides, but simple *sunburn*. So be forewarned. Wear a hat, and slather on sufficient sunblock or sunscreen, especially during the spring and summer.

For diabetics: Walt Disney World resorts provide refrigeration services for insulin; the villas and the *Fort Wilderness* homes have their own refrigerators.

Prescriptions: The Buena Vista Walk-In Medical Center (828-3434) offers shuttle service from the First Aid Center and Epcot Center. The clinic is open daily from 9 A.M. to 8 P.M. for basic medical, diagnostic, and treatment services for non-critical injuries and illnesses. A pharmacy, Turner Drugs (828-8125), is located next door to the clinic and is open 9 A.M. to 8 P.M. daily. Delivery to any WDW resort hotel can be arranged. The Gooding's supermarket at the Crossroads shopping center also has a pharmacy.

MONEY

Cash, traveler's checks, personal checks, American Express (the official credit card of WDW), MasterCard, and Visa are accepted as payment for all admission media. Checks must bear your name and address, be drawn on a U.S. bank, and be accompanied by the proper identification—a valid driver's license and a current major credit card such as American Express, Visa, Master-Card, Diners Club, or Carte Blanche. Fast-food restaurants in the Magic Kingdom, Epcot Center, and the Disney-MGM Studios Theme Park operate on a cash-only basis.

For charges at sit-down restaurants and shops inside the theme parks, however, and for all other charges throughout Walt Disney World, American Express, Visa, and MasterCard credit cards are accepted. WDW resort guests may use the WDW resort IDs that each member of a party receives upon check-in to cover purchases in shops, lounge and restaurant charges, and recreational fees incurred inside WDW. At the Magic Kingdom, Epcot Center, and the Disney-MGM Studios Theme Park, guests can use IDs to charge meals at table-service restaurants. These cards are not valid for charges made past check-out time on the last day of the guest's stay.

Automatic Teller Machines: ATMs are located at the Sun Bank on Main Street in the Magic Kingdom, at the entrances to the Disney-MGM Studios and Epcot, at Pleasure Island, and at the Disney Village Marketplace.

Sun Bank: This institution (which has an old-fashioned branch on Main Street inside the Magic Kingdom, a branch in Epcot Center to the left of the turnstiles as you enter, one in Walt Disney World Village, and one at the Crossroads shopping center) can:

● Give cash advances on MasterCard and Visa credit cards, with a $50 minimum in amounts as large as a guest's credit limit will permit.

● Cash and sell traveler's checks and provide refunds for lost American Express and Bank of America traveler's checks.

● Cash personal checks of up to $1,000 for American Express cardholders upon presentation of their cards (part payable in cash and the rest in American Express traveler's checks).

● Cash personal checks for up to $25 upon presentation of a driver's license and a major credit card.

● Help with wire transfers of money from a guest's own bank to the Sun Bank branch.

The Sun Bank branches in the Magic Kingdom and Epcot Center are open from 9 A.M. to 4 P.M. daily; phone 828-6101 or 827-5200, respectively, for further information. The Sun Banks in Walt Disney World Village and at the Crossroads shopping center are open from 9 A.M. to 4 P.M. on weekdays (until 6 P.M. on Thursdays); drive-in teller windows are open from 8 A.M. to 6 P.M. on weekdays; phone 828-6100.

Traveler's checks: Even the most careful of vacationers occasionally loses a wallet, and traveler's checks can take the sting out of that loss. Which type a traveler should buy is not so much a function of which is most easily refunded (because in the U.S., and at Walt Disney World in particular, all the major traveler's check offerers can come through with emergency funds in a pinch), but which costs less. It's a good idea, therefore, to look for special promotions by banks at home in the months preceding a vacation, and check to see which of the five major brands—American Express, MasterCard, Visa, Citicorp, and Bank of America—are available free.

Don't fail to sign checks in the proper place as soon as they are purchased. And stash the receipt bearing the check numbers in a separate place from the checks themselves, along with one piece of identification such as a duplicate driver's license or a spare credit card. These will speed the refund process should your checks get lost.

Foreign currency exchange: This can be done at the Guest Services windows at all three parks, or at City Hall, Earth Station, or, from 9 A.M. to 4 P.M. daily, the Sun Bank in Town Square inside the Magic Kingdom or at the Epcot Center branch. Currency can be exchanged at WDW resorts, except the *Disney Inn*, at other times. The Sun Banks at Walt Disney World Village and at the Crossroads shopping center also exchange foreign currency.

SHOPPING FOR NECESSITIES: Almost all everyday needs can be satisfied right on the property. Concourse Sundries & Spirits in the *Contemporary* resort, Village Gifts & Sundries on the second floor of the *Polynesian* resort, Gifts and Sundries in the lobby of the *Disney Inn*, Sandy Cove at the *Grand Floridian*, Calypso Trading Post at the *Caribbean Beach* resort, Fittings and Fairings at the *Yacht Club*, Atlantic Wear and Wardrobe at the *Beach Club*, Jackson Square Gifts and Desires at *Port Orleans*, Fulton's General Store at *Dixie Landings*, Conch Flats General Store at the *Disney Vacation Club*, Wilderness Lodge Mercantile at *Wilderness Lodge*, the shops at *All-Star Sports* and *All-Star Music*, Daisy's Garden at the *Dolphin*, Disney Cabana at the *Swan*, and the Meadow and Settlement Trading Posts at *Fort Wilderness* all stock a limited number of brands of a wide variety of toiletries; a broader selection is available at the Disney Village Marketplace at the Gourmet Pantry. In addition, a number of over-the-counter health aids, plus many other useful items, can be purchased in the Books and Records section of the Emporium on Main Street in the Magic Kingdom; they're kept behind the counter, so it's necessary to ask for the supplies you want. Aspirin and suntan

lotion also are available at Mickey's Star Traders in Tomorrowland.

Gooding's supermarket, at the Crossroads of Lake Buena Vista Shopping Center near Hotel Plaza, has a large pharmacy department.

In Epcot Center, sundries are available in at least one shop in each of the World Showcase pavilions and at all the retail outlets in Future World (except the Kodak camera sales kiosk at Journey Into Imagination).

At the Disney-MGM Studios Theme Park, sundries are available at the Crossroads of the World and Movieland Memorabilia shops.

Reading matter: Newspapers, magazines, bestsellers, and paperbacks are available in a limited selection at Concourse Sundries & Spirits in the *Contemporary* resort, at News from Civilization on the first floor at the *Polynesian* resort, at Gifts and Sundries in the lobby at the *Disney Inn*, Sandy Cove at the *Grand Floridian*, Calypso Trading Post at the *Caribbean Beach* resort, Fittings and Fairings at the *Yacht Club*, Atlantic Wear and Wardrobe at the *Beach Club*, Meadow and Settlement Trading Posts at *Fort Wilderness*, Jackson Square Gifts and Desires at *Port Orleans*, Fulton's General Store at *Dixie Landings*, Conch Flats General Store at the *Disney Vacation Club*, Wilderness Lodge Mercantile at *Wilderness Lodge*, the shops at *All-Star Sports* and *All-Star Music*, Daisy's Garden at the *Dolphin*, Disney Cabana at the *Swan*, and at Gourmet Pantry at the Disney Village Marketplace. Most carry the daily papers from Orlando and Miami, *The Wall Street Journal*, and, on Sundays, *The New York Times* and *The Chicago Tribune*.

The Emporium in the Magic Kingdom has children's books. Epcot Center offers an interesting selection as well. Books related to the themes of Future World pavilions are available in the Centorium and at Epcot Outreach. In World Showcase, the United Kingdom's Toy Soldier and Der Bücherwurm in Germany stock children's books.

Comic books and magazines are available at Lakeside News at the Disney-MGM Studios Theme Park. Books on the subject of animation are on sale at the Animation Gallery.

PETS

No pets (other than service dogs) are allowed in the Magic Kingdom, Epcot Center, the Disney-MGM Studios Theme Park, or at the WDW resorts. Travelers who bring pets along can lodge them in one of four attractive air conditioned Pet Care Kennels: near the Transportation and Ticket Center; to the left of the Epcot Center Entrance Plaza; at the Disney-MGM Studios Theme Park entrance; and at the *Fort Wilderness* campground entrance, next to a huge field where pet owners can take their animals out for a run. In busy seasons, it's best to arrive before the 9 A.M. to 10 A.M. morning rush hour. Be sure to note that the kennels close an hour after the Magic Kingdom, Epcot Center, and the Disney-MGM Studios Theme Park.

Bears, cougars, and ocelots have all been accommodated by the WDW kennels, and exotic pets may be accepted—if a bit reluctantly. However, owners themselves must put the more unusual animals into the kennel's cages; and snakes, rabbits, birds, turtles, hamsters, and other animals unsuited (because of size) to cat- and dog-size cages must be accompanied by their own escape-proof accommodations.

WDW resort guests and guests at Disney Village Hotel Plaza may board their pets overnight in the TTC Kennel or until 8 P.M. in the *Fort Wilderness* kennel. Cost is about $7 for overnight stays, including food; $4 for a day stay, with one feeding. Only pets of WDW resort guests may board overnight.

Never leave pets in your car. It is against the law in Florida.

Also, bring along your pet's certificate of vaccination, since Florida law requires proof of immunization for animals involved in biting incidents.

Outside Walt Disney World: A number of hotels in the Orlando and Kissimmee area permit pets. For specific information phone the Orlando/Orange County Convention and Visitors Bureau; 363-5800.

TIPPING: Walt Disney World is not one of those places where bellmen stick out their hands even before they put down your luggage. Instead, they seem genuinely glad to help out. Oddly enough, this pleasant attitude seems to discourage tipping at the same time it arouses the sentiments that make most travelers want to reach for their wallets.

Lack of ostentatious need does not mean that tips are any less valued at WDW than they would be at any other good resort hotel—the standard 50¢ to $1 per bag is appropriate for lugging luggage. Gratuities of 15 percent to 18 percent are also customary at full-service restaurants all over WDW. At the posh *Empress Room*, a service charge of 20 percent of the food and drink bill is automatically added.

Gratuities are not required in fast-food restaurants or at the attractions, but in the beauty shops, it's usual to leave a tip of about 15 percent of the total bill.

Cabdrivers in the Orlando area expect a 15 percent tip. Baggage handlers at bus and train stations and at the airport expect at least 50¢ per bag.

TELEPHONE: The folks at home can reach resort guests at the following numbers (all are in area code 407):

Contemporary:	824-1000
Disney Inn:	824-2200
Polynesian:	824-2000
Grand Floridian:	824-3000
Wilderness Lodge:	824-3200
Caribbean Beach:	934-3400
Swan:	934-3000
Dolphin:	934-4000
Yacht Club:	934-7000
Beach Club:	934-8000
Village Resort:	827-1100
Port Orleans:	934-5000
Dixie Landings:	934-6000
Disney Vacation Club:	827-7700
All-Star Sports:	939-5000
All-Star Music:	939-6000
Fort Wilderness:	824-2900

Public telephones in the Orlando area and in Walt Disney World cost 25¢.

TIME AND WEATHER PHONE: In the Orlando area, the number is 646-3131.

Transportation and Accommodations

The popularity of Walt Disney World has made the region around Orlando one of the world's major tourism and commercial centers, and everything from a state-of-the-art airport to an efficient network of highways brings visitors to the area by the millions.

There's no doubt, however, that confusion about getting to and around the Walt Disney World region is pervasive and may be exceeded only by the dilemma concerning which specific sort of accommodation is most appropriate for a given family's needs.

Just the accommodations facilities that are operated by Walt Disney World itself range from futuristic high-rise towers to treehouses buried deep in piney woods. In between are resorts echoing images of the South Pacific, old Florida, the Caribbean, New England, and Louisiana, and efficient trailer-type facilities in an almost perfectly maintained campground. And that doesn't include villas that provide extraordinary space and luxury, at surprisingly affordable prices, or studio, one-, two-, and three-bedroom homes that can be purchased through a unique vacation ownership system. What follows should help any traveler sort out all the available options and preferences on the Walt Disney World property, as well as describing a broad range of possibilities that exist outside the WDW gates.

(Unless otherwise noted, all telephone numbers are in area code 407.)

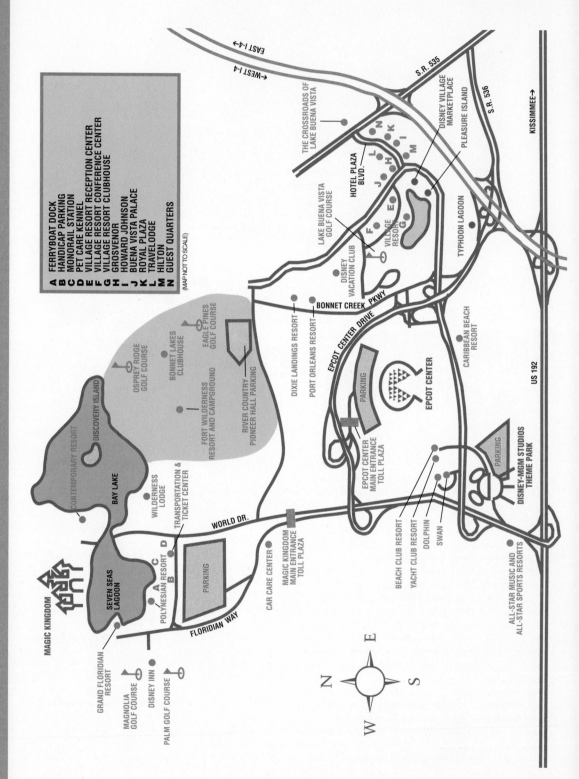

A FERRYBOAT DOCK
B HANDICAP PARKING
C MONORAIL STATION
D PET CARE KENNEL
E VILLAGE RESORT RECEPTION CENTER
F VILLAGE RESORT CONFERENCE CENTER
G VILLAGE RESORT CLUBHOUSE
H GROSVENOR
I HOWARD JOHNSON
J BUENA VISTA PALACE
K ROYAL PLAZA
L TRAVELODGE
M HILTON
N GUEST QUARTERS

(MAP NOT TO SCALE)

MAGIC KINGDOM

SEVEN SEAS LAGOON

GRAND FLORIDIAN RESORT

MAGNOLIA GOLF COURSE

DISNEY INN

PALM GOLF COURSE

FLORIDIAN WAY

POLYNESIAN RESORT

TRANSPORTATION & TICKET CENTER

WILDERNESS LODGE

CONTEMPORARY RESORT

BAY LAKE

DISCOVERY ISLAND

OSPREY RIDGE GOLF COURSE

BONNET LAKES CLUBHOUSE

EAGLE PINES GOLF COURSE

FORT WILDERNESS RESORT AND CAMPGROUND

RIVER COUNTRY PIONEER HALL PARKING

PARKING

CAR CARE CENTER

WORLD DR.

MAGIC KINGDOM MAIN ENTRANCE TOLL PLAZA

DIXIE LANDINGS RESORT

PORT ORLEANS RESORT

BONNET CREEK PKWY

EPCOT CENTER DRIVE

DISNEY VACATION CLUB

LAKE BUENA VISTA GOLF COURSE

VILLAGE RESORT

HOTEL PLAZA BLVD.

THE CROSSROADS OF LAKE BUENA VISTA

EAST I-A →
← WEST I-A

S.R. 535

DISNEY VILLAGE MARKETPLACE

PLEASURE ISLAND

S.R. 536

TYPHOON LAGOON

EPCOT CENTER MAIN ENTRANCE TOLL PLAZA

PARKING

EPCOT CENTER

CARIBBEAN BEACH RESORT

BEACH CLUB RESORT

YACHT CLUB RESORT

DOLPHIN

SWAN

DISNEY-MGM STUDIOS THEME PARK

PARKING

ALL-STAR MUSIC AND ALL-STAR SPORTS RESORTS

US 192

KISSIMMEE →

N
E
S
W

Getting Oriented

Orlando, the Central Florida city of over 165,000 residents, is the municipality with which Walt Disney World is most closely associated. It is not, however, the closest urban community to WDW. That distinction belongs to Kissimmee, a far smaller community of 27,000 people, located just southeast of WDW. Many motels are located here, though there are far more in Orlando proper, to the north.

Most of the area's better restaurants are found in Orlando, or in adjacent communities like Winter Park (on its northeastern extremity), Maitland (east of Winter Park), and Altamonte Springs (east of Maitland).

ORLANDO-AREA HIGHWAYS: The most important Orlando traffic artery is I-4, which runs diagonally through the area from southwest to northeast, cutting through the southern half of Walt Disney World. It then angles on toward Orlando and Winter Park, ending near Daytona Beach at I-95, which runs north and south along the coast. All the city's other important highways intersect I-4. From south to north, these include U.S. 192 (aka Irlo Bronson Memorial Highway), which takes an east-west course that crosses the WDW entrance road and leads into downtown Kissimmee on the east; S.R. 528 (aka the Bee Line Expressway), which shoots eastward from I-4; S.R. 435, also known as Kirkman Road, which runs north and south and intersects International Drive, where many motels catering to WDW visitors are located; U.S. 17-92-441 (aka Orange Blossom Trail), which runs due north and south, paralleling Kirkman Road on the east; and S.R. 50 (aka Colonial Drive), which runs due east and west.

WALT DISNEY WORLD ROADS: The 43-square-mile tract that is Walt Disney World is roughly rectangular. I-4 runs through its southern half from southwest to northeast; there are three highway exits leading to WDW. The first Disney exit (number 35) is marked "S.R. 535/Lake Buena Vista," and should be used by guests heading for Disney Village Hotel Plaza, the villas, the Disney Village Marketplace, and the Crossroads shopping center. The second exit (number 26B), marked "Epcot Center/Disney Village," should be taken by guests going to Epcot Center, Typhoon Lagoon, Pleasure Island, the *Caribbean Beach* resort, the *Swan, Dolphin, Yacht and Beach Club, Port Orleans, Dixie Landings, All-Star Music* and *All-Star Sports* resorts, and *Disney Vacation Club.* It also is a good alternate route to the Disney Village Marketplace and the Disney-MGM Studios

GETTING AROUND WDW

The internal transportation system at Walt Disney World is quite extensive, and always is being revised to serve the ever-increasing number of attractions and accommodations. The Magic Kingdom bus entrance means that guests traveling on WDW transportation can bypass the TTC when going to the Magic Kingdom. All bus stops are clearly marked, and guests staying at WDW hotels receive detailed information about transportation options upon checking in. Also, all bus drivers carry a color-coded listing of bus routes.

Theme Park. The third exit (number 27) is marked "192/Magic Kingdom," and leads to the Magic Kingdom, the Disney-MGM Studios Theme Park, the *Contemporary* resort, the *Polynesian*, the *Disney Inn*, the *Grand Floridian*, *Wilderness Lodge*, *Fort Wilderness*, and River Country.

There also are a number of roads *inside* the World. In some cases, it is possible to drive from place to place on them. Bus transportation also is provided between most points, and is available without charge to most guests. At the northernmost end of WDW, an elevated monorail train operates along a circular route, making stops at the *Polynesian*, the *Grand Floridian*, the *Contemporary* resort, and at the Magic Kingdom and the TTC; a separate extension of the monorail system also goes to Epcot Center. Motor launches and cruisers from the *Contemporary* resort and the Magic Kingdom call at *Fort Wilderness* and Discovery Island.

TRANSPORTATION ID REQUIREMENTS

Within WDW there are several different types of identification and/or admission media that are required for use of the various forms of transportation. This list explains what sort of card, ticket, or Passport permits use of each:

- WDW resort identification card allows a guest unlimited use of any part of the WDW transportation system (including buses, monorails, and watercraft).
- Disney Village Hotel Plaza hotel identification card allows unlimited use of the bus transportation system.
- Valid one-day Magic Kingdom ticket permits a guest to use the ferries and monorails running between the TTC and the Magic Kingdom entrance. (**Note:** Valid one-day Epcot Center or Disney-MGM Studios Theme Park tickets do not allow guests to use the WDW transportation system.)
- Four-day Super Passes, Five-day Super Duper Passes, Be Our Guest Passes, and Annual Passports allow guests use of the WDW transportation system.
- River Country, Discovery Island, and Pioneer Hall tickets allow guests the use of buses from the TTC, watercraft from the *Contemporary* resort, and watercraft from the Magic Kingdom to and from River Country, Discovery Island, and Pioneer Hall. Guests with these tickets also may take buses from the *Polynesian* resort and *Contemporary* resort to the TTC and then transfer to other buses. For further information call 824-4321.

A WDW Transportation Ticket ($2.50) allows unlimited use of all WDW transportation systems for one day.

Accommodations

Orlando and its environs literally have tens of thousands of hotel and motel rooms. Few of these, however, whether inside or outside the World, are of a design much beyond the predictable Anywhere, USA motel/modern decor, usually with two standard double beds, plush carpeting, simulated-wood paneling, a color television set, and private bathroom.

The biggest differences among accommodations seem to be in the power of the showers, the sizes and thicknesses of the towels, the dimensions of the rooms and the bathrooms, the furnishings, the recreational facilities, the landscaping of the surrounding grounds, and the locations.

Basically, Walt Disney World-area accommodations fall into two main categories: those located within the boundaries of WDW and those outside the property. Rates are generally higher at WDW addresses than at most other motels in the area (with the exception of the new *All-Star Sports* and *All-Star Music* resorts slated to open this June), but the convenience is so much greater and the additional benefits available to an on-property guest so extensive—guaranteed park admission even when parks are full, free use of WDW transportation, closed-circuit TV announcing WDW events, early admission to the Magic Kingdom during certain periods, and the best possible access to Guest Services personnel—that the extra expense is not at all unreasonable. Resort guests, for instance, can make dinner reservations at Epcot Center and Disney-MGM Studios Theme Park restaurants one to three days in advance by telephone, a considerable convenience. They also can reserve tee-off times on the golf courses up to 30 days in advance, and assure places at most of the dinner shows as soon as their on-property room reservations are confirmed. They have access to all transportation within the World. The benefits for guests are so extensive that you should be wary of anyone who encourages you to stay elsewhere for reasons other than a major difference in price.

You also should be aware that accommodations on the WDW grounds are divided into several areas, including the Magic Kingdom resorts, Epcot resorts, Studio resorts, the Village resorts, *Fort Wilderness*, and Disney Village Hotel Plaza hostelries.

Locations of the off-site properties are quite scattered. The closest to WDW are located on S.R. 535 in Lake Buena Vista. Others are located in Kissimmee, along U.S. 192 (which runs east and west) intersecting the WDW entrance road, and along International Drive (off S.R. 435 at the Orlando city limits). The U.S. 192 establishments are closer to the WDW main entrance—usually only a few miles away, depending on the individual hostelry. International Drive, some ten miles from the WDW main gates, has an extensive array of lodging places, restaurants, and other attractions. Its proximity to still more of the same in Orlando, just a few miles farther north, constitutes an additional lure.

In choosing a place to stay, decide first just how much you want to spend. If your budget permits, try to get a reservation at one of the on-site properties. Remember that there are Disney accommodations in varying price ranges. If not, select accommodations outside the World based on your budget and on the guidelines given in this section.

Remember, when examining rate sheets for the best buy for your family, check the cut-off age at which children accompanying you (and staying in the same room) will be billed as extra adults. Those with large families should note that the Disney villa-type accommodations, which may seem more expensive at first glance, actually can prove less costly in the long run—by eliminating the necessity of securing an additional hotel room and providing cooking facilities that can mean big savings on meals.

Walt Disney World Resort Properties

With the addition of moderately priced rooms at the *Caribbean Beach* resort, *Port Orleans*, and *Dixie Landings*, and the even less expensive rooms that will open at the *All-Star Sports* and *All-Star Music* resorts in June of this year, we find it difficult to recommend staying off the property. Additionally, reservations are generally easy to obtain, even on short notice, since there are now more than 14,000 rooms on the property.

In general, rooms at the *Contemporary* resort, the *Polynesian* resort, the *Disney Inn*, the *Grand Floridian* resort, *Wilderness Lodge*, the *Yacht Club*, and the *Beach Club* are quite large and can accommodate up to five guests in a single room without difficulty. Rooms at the *Caribbean Beach*, *Port Orleans*, *Dixie Landings*, the *Swan*, the *Dolphin*, *All-Star Sports*, and *All-Star Music* resorts accommodate up to four people. Many rooms have patios or balconies. And considering the incredibly high occupancy rate, it's astonishing that things look so fresh. Even the rooms without views have views, if only across the gardens.

The villa accommodations, which can accommodate larger groups, are particularly good for families, especially those who want to cook some of their own meals "at home." The vacation homes at the *Disney Vacation Club* also are good for families. Unsold accommodations at the *Disney Vacation Club* are available as hotel rooms. At *Fort Wilderness* resort there are both campsites and fully equipped Wilderness Homes set on 780 acres of quiet woods.

The WDW hotels in this section are broken down into five groups: Magic Kingdom resorts; Village resorts; Epcot resorts, Studio resorts, and *Fort Wilderness*. The hotels, rooms, and facilities are described in detail. Restaurants are mentioned here, but are described at length in the *Good Meals, Great Times* chapter. Note that all restaurants at WDW resorts are nonsmoking, as are all public spaces with the exception of lounges.

Magic Kingdom Resorts

CONTEMPORARY RESORT

Watching the monorail trains disappear into this hotel's enormous, 15-story, A-frame tower never fails to amaze first-timers. The sleek trains look like long spaceships docking as they slide inside, or the sight may bring to mind the story of Jonah being swallowed by the whale. (Note that guests who use a wheelchair cannot board the monorail here, but they can at the *Polynesian* resort or at the *Grand Floridian* resort.)

Passengers, for their part, are impressed by the cavernous lobby, with its tiers of balconies and, at its center, designer Mary Blair's huge 90-foot-high, floor-to-ceiling tile mural depicting Indian children, stylized flowers, birds, trees, and other scenes from the Southwest. (Look carefully and you may be able to spot the five-legged goat.)

This imposing establishment has more than 1,050 rooms in its Tower and the two Garden Wings that flank it on either side. There are seven shops, three restaurants, two snack bars, two lounges, a large convention space, a marina, a beach, a health club, and more. The larger of the hotel's pair of swimming pools, measuring a generous 20-by-25 meters, is a delight for lap swimmers. And the

Fiesta Fun Center—a vast room full of pinball and other electronic games that's open around the clock—is lively even until the wee hours of the morning.

A concierge package is available for guests who choose to stay in the hotel's 14th-floor suites. Special services include special check-out service, complimentary continental breakfast in the morning and wine, beer, and hors d'oeuvres at night, and nightly turndown service. The telephone number of the *Contemporary* resort is 824-1000.

ROOMS: The hotel's guestrooms are almost evenly apportioned between the Tower and the North and South Garden Wings. Rooms in the Tower boast views of Bay Lake or the Magic Kingdom, and cost more than the rooms in the Garden Wings. All rooms can accommodate up to five (plus one additional child under three). Some units have king-size beds; the rest have two queens, and all rooms have a day bed. Adjoining and/or connecting rooms may be requested, though they can't be guaranteed. Rooms for guests with disabilities and nonsmoking rooms also are available. Bathrooms in the *Contemporary* resort are well laid out. Not only are they large, but they also have double sinks and a bathtub with a shower head (some even have a separate shower stall). There also is a variety of elegant suites available that accommodate from 7 to 12 people.

MEETING AND CONVENTION SPACE: A large convention center is located in a separate building attached by covered bridge to additional space on the second floor of the tower. The external building space features 82,495-square-feet of meeting space, including a 42,300-square-foot Grand Ballroom. There also are 15 breakout rooms. The 11,968-square-foot Ballroom of the Americas, at the north end of the Tower's second floor accommodates up to about 1,400 seated theater-style, or about 1,000 for a banquet. It can be divided into two smaller rooms, each with a capacity of about half the above numbers. The 8,777-square-foot Grand Republic Ballroom holds slightly fewer people; it can be split into three rooms ranging in size from 1,024 to 4,290 square feet. In addition, there are five other rooms nearby of 800 to 1,160 square feet each; and on the 15th floor there are two others measuring 697 square feet and 1,247 square feet. Both have wonderful panoramic views of the Magic Kingdom.

WHERE TO EAT: The hotel's two restaurants are located on the Grand Canyon Concourse on the fourth floor, and there are snack spots beside the marina and in the first-floor Fiesta Fun Center.

    Contemporary Café: On the Grand Canyon Concourse. Features a character breakfast buffet daily and a bountiful, all-you-can-eat international buffet dinner every evening; one of the World's best buys. No reservations.

    Concourse Grill: On the Grand Canyon Concourse. Breakfast, lunch, and dinner are served here. Traditional favorites are available and a new light menu focuses on nutrition, preparation techniques, and freshness.

    Fiesta Fun Center Snack Bar: On the first floor; serves light fare 24 hours a day.

WHERE TO DRINK: The no-liquor policy in the Magic Kingdom notwithstanding, it's easy to enjoy a drink at Walt Disney World.

    Outer Rim Cocktail Lounge: On the Grand Canyon Concourse, overlooking Bay Lake. Serves appetizers, cocktails, and specialty drinks. Open from 3 P.M. to 11 P.M.

Sand Bar: Beside the marina, serving a variety of mixed drinks. The specialty here is a nifty piña colada made with ice cream. Open during peak seasons only.

ROOM SERVICE: A wide range of offerings suitable for breakfast, lunch, dinner, and snacks can be ordered 24 hours a day; consult room service menus for serving times. It's a good idea to pre-order room service breakfasts the night before, using the card hanging from the doorknob. For other meals, count on phoning in an order 30 to 45 minutes before you want to be served. When the food arrives, it comes with a smile and, in the morning, with a newspaper.

WHAT TO DO: All by itself, the *Contemporary* resort boasts more activities and recreational facilities than many large resorts.

Boat rentals: Sailboats, flote boats, as well as the zippy little motorcraft known as Water Sprites, are all available for rent at the *Contemporary* resort marina, near the beach. (See *Sports* for details.)

Tennis: This is WDW's major tennis center. There are six courts, three backboards, and instruction (private or group lessons) available. For court reservations, call 824-3578.

Waterskiing: Boats with driver and skis can be hired at the hotel marina. (For details, see *Sports*.)

Swimming: There are two pools here, the big 20-by-25-meter main pool, and the round splash pool, deep in the center and shallow on the outside. A toddler's pool is located near the North Garden Wing, and swimming is permitted in the roped-off area of Bay Lake beside the beach. The bottom is delightfully sandy. (For hours, see *Sports*.)

Fitness: The Olympia Health Club has Nautilus equipment, stair climbers, rowing machines, bicycles, sauna, lockers, and massage by appointment.

Volleyball: Nets are set up on the beach.

Children's program: The Mouseketeer Clubhouse is open from 4:30 P.M. to midnight for children three to nine years of age. The cost is $4 per hour for the first child; $2 per hour for each additional child. There is a four-hour maximum stay. Reservations are necessary; call 824-3038. A playground in located near the North Garden Wing.

Fiesta Fun Center: On the first floor of the hotel, this is one of the World's great indoor recreational facilities, the biggest and most varied of all the Disney hotels' mechanical gamerooms, boasting everything from skee ball to air hockey, and all the other favorites of the pinball-and-electronic-games-playing set—worth at least a look.

Movies: Two different Disney movies are shown each evening in the theater at the Fiesta Fun Center. A good place to get off your feet.

Shopping: The fourth-floor Grand Canyon Concourse is home to several first class shops. The Fantasia Shop sells kids' stuff and Walt Disney-themed merchandise (china figurines of Mickey Mouse, Minnie, the Cheshire Cat, the Mad Hatter, the White Rabbit, Pluto, and company; T-shirts and sweatshirts; and stuffed animals). Concourse Sundries and Spirits, next door, has a selection of newspapers, magazines, books, snack foods, and liquor—just what's needed for a cocktail party on your terrace. On the opposite side of the Concourse, the Contemporary Woman offers a range of good-quality women's clothing (and plenty of bathing suits) in all price ranges, and the adjoining Contemporary Man stocks casual clothes and beachwear.

The adjacent Kingdom Jewels, Ltd. displays men's and women's jewelry from around the globe. Bayview Gifts carries souvenirs, gifts, and fresh flowers.

The Bay 'n' Beach shop at the marina sells suncare products, beach toys, and character souvenirs. The Racquet Club, at the North Garden Wing, has tennis equipment, men's and women's tennis fashions, and tennis shoes. Racquet restringing also is available here.

TRANSPORTATION: The *Contemporary* resort is connected to the Transportation and Ticket Center (TTC) and the Magic Kingdom by the monorail trains, which glide into the hotel every 10 or 15 minutes from 7 A.M. until two hours after the official park closing time. Board just above the Grand Canyon Concourse, inside the atrium area of the Tower. The monorails stop at the *Polynesian* resort (from which point you can board a bus to the *Disney Inn*), the Magic Kingdom, the *Grand Floridian* resort, and the TTC. From the TTC, Epcot Center can be reached by bus or by another monorail, and the Disney-MGM Studios Theme Park can be reached by bus.

Watercraft also travel regularly from the marina to *Fort Wilderness* and Discovery Island.

POLYNESIAN

The *Polynesian* resort is as close an approximation to the real thing as Walt Disney World's designers could create. The vegetation is as lush as anywhere in the World; the architecture reeks of the tropics; and the atmosphere is more subdued than that of even the relatively placid *Disney Inn*. *Aitea-Peatea*, promises the hotel's motto: "There will be another day tomorrow just like today." Here, that's a pleasant thought.

The mood is set by a three-story-high garden that occupies most of the lobby. To call the construction at the center a fountain is to do it a grave injustice; it's more like a waterfall. The water cascades over craggy volcanic rocks. Coconut palms tower over 250 square feet of some 75 different species of tropical and subtropical plants—1,500 anthuriums, banana trees, ferns, gardenias, orchids, and other greens. The climatic conditions are nearly perfect, so that everything is verdant year-round.

The structure that contains this mass of greenery, the so-called Great Ceremonial House, is the central building in the *Polynesian* resort complex. The front desk, the shops, and most of the restaurants are located here. Flanking the Great Ceremonial House on either side are 11 two- and three-story "longhouses" named for various Pacific islands. These structures house the resort's 853 rooms. The fact that the monorail stops at this resort makes it a very convenient place to stay; in fact, it's just a couple of minutes' ride to the Magic Kingdom. But because the accommodations are scattered around the property, and because the hotel is not quite as large as the *Contemporary* resort, things seldom feel as hectic, and the *Polynesian* resort has a loyal following among returning Walt Disney World visitors.

The *Polynesian* resort also offers a special concierge service called King Kamehameha. The amenities are similar to those on the "suite" floor at the *Contemporary* resort: free valet parking, special check-in and check-out service, complimentary juice and coffee in the morning, soft drinks and snacks in the afternoon, and a special concierge on duty from 8 A.M. to 9 P.M. The special *Polynesian* resort rooms are located on the lagoon side of the Tonga, Samoa, Moorea, and Bali Hai (exclusively suites) longhouses, and are the most expensive rooms in the hotel. The telephone number of the *Polynesian* resort is 824-2000.

ROOMS: The rooms all have a patio, and most have a view of either the Seven Seas Lagoon or one of the swimming pools; those in the Oahu, Moorea, and Pago Pago longhouses are the largest. All have two queen-size beds and a day bed, and all rooms can accommodate five (plus a sixth under age three). Adjoining rooms may be requested, though they cannot be guaranteed. (The Oahu and Pago Pago longhouses have rooms specially equipped for guests with disabilities.) There also are nonsmoking rooms available.

Suites are all located in the Bali Hai longhouse, and accommodate from four to six. Some have a king-size bed in the bedroom and two queen-size beds in the parlor.

WHERE TO EAT: Some of the more interesting Walt Disney World eating spots are located at the *Polynesian* resort.

Papeete Bay Verandah: On the second floor of the Great Ceremonial House, *Papeete Bay Verandah* serves sit-down dinners daily (with entertainment), a Minnie Mouse breakfast buffet Mondays through Saturdays, and a massive brunch buffet on Sundays. The room is large and open, and offers fine views across the Seven Seas Lagoon all the way to

Cinderella Castle. After dark, a Polynesian combo entertains quietly. Reservations are requested for breakfast, dinner, and Sunday brunch; phone 824-1391.

Coral Isle Café: On the second floor of the Great Ceremonial House, around the corner from *Papeete Bay Verandah*. This standard coffee shop (with South Seas decor) serves the usual assortment of breakfast items, plus a WDW specialty, banana-stuffed French toast, each morning, and does a booming business at lunch and dinner. A good bet when you want a no-fuss meal.

Captain Cook's Snack and Ice Cream Company: Located on the lobby level of the Great Ceremonial House, this is a good spot for continental breakfasts and for sandwiches, snacks, and ice cream during the day.

Snack Isle: Most guests discover this snack bar on their way to the gameroom or the East Pool—to which it is extremely convenient. Pizza, sandwiches, snacks, and continental breakfast also are served.

WHERE TO DRINK: The resort's Polynesian theme has inspired a whole raft of deceptively potent potables like Seven Seas (fruit juice, grenadine, orange curaçao, and rum), Chi Chis (a standard piña colada made with vodka instead of rum), and WDW piña coladas (which include orange juice in addition to rum, pineapple, and coconut cream). There's even a special *Polynesian* resort non-alcoholic treat—the pink Lei-Lani, a delicious orange juice and strawberry mixture.

Barefoot Bar: Adjoining the Swimming Pool Lagoon.

Tambu Lounge: Cozy and clublike, this lounge adjoins the *Papeete Bay Verandah*. A good spot for quiet conversation, with entertainment nightly.

ROOM SERVICE: A variety of specialties is available. It's a good idea to fill out the order card and place it on the doorknob outside your room before going to sleep.

WHAT TO DO: A wide range of activities is available at the *Polynesian* resort, just as at the *Contemporary* resort.

Boat rentals: Several types of sailboats, speedy little Water Sprites, pedal boats, and flote boats are available for rent at the *Polynesian* resort marina. Waterskiing excursions also can be arranged.

Swimming: There are two main pools here, the elliptical East Pool, in the shadow of the Oahu, Tonga, Hawaii, Bora Bora, and Maui longhouses, and the larger free-form Swimming Pool Lagoon, closer to the marina and the beach. This pool is framed by a large cluster of boulders that forms a water slide much beloved by youngsters; to get to the ladder that takes you to the top, you must duck underneath a waterfall. Toddlers have their own shallow areas in both *Polynesian* resort pools. Swimming also is permitted in the roped-off areas of the Seven Seas Lagoon (when there's a lifeguard on duty).

Children's program: The Neverland Club is a supervised evening activity program for children ages 3 to 12. The program operates between 5 P.M. and midnight. The cost is $7 per hour and there is a three-hour minimum. Required reservations can be made by calling 824-2170. The *Polynesian* playground features an assortment of apparatuses for climbing, swinging, and sliding.

Gameroom: Moana Mickey's Fun Hut has a small assortment of the latest video games and is located alongside the *Snack Isle*.

Shopping: News from Civilization, on the first floor of the Great Ceremonial House, is the only place in Walt Disney World where you can buy a grass skirt, and for that reason alone it's worth a peek, though most of the other merchandise there—with the exception of items with the hotel logo—is of the utilitarian variety—daily newspapers, magazines, tobacco, film, suncare products, and gifts. Robinson Crusoe, Esq., right nearby, sells casual sportswear and swimwear for men, while the Polynesian Princess stocks an assortment of brightly colored resort fashions, bathing suits, and hot-weather accessories for women. Kanaka Kids stocks children's resortwear and accessories. Upstairs, Village Gifts sells souvenirs, toys, fashions, and miscellaneous items; Trader Jack's Grog Hut has food, liquor, wine, beer, and other fixings for an impromptu party.

TRANSPORTATION: The *Polynesian* resort is located right on a monorail line and the entrance is on the second floor of the Great Ceremonial House. Buses, which circulate between the *Polynesian* resort, the *Disney Inn*, and the Transportation and Ticket Center, stop at the traffic island in front of the hotel. From the TTC, Epcot Center is accessible by monorail or by bus, and the Disney-MGM Studios, Typhoon Lagoon, the Marketplace, and Pleasure Island can be reached by bus. Launches leave from the *Polynesian* dock for the Magic Kingdom and the *Grand Floridian* resort.

GRAND FLORIDIAN

At the turn of the century, Standard Oil magnate Henry M. Flagler saw the realization of his dream: The railroad he had built to "civilize" Florida had spawned along its right-of-way an empire of grand hotels, lavish estates, prominent families, and opulent lifestyles. High society blossomed in winter, as the likes of John D. Rockefeller and Teddy Roosevelt put up at the *Royal Poinciana* in Palm Beach, enjoying the sea breezes from the oceanside suites.

The *Royal Poinciana* later burned to the ground, and Florida's golden era faded with the Depression. But nearly a century after Flagler first made Florida a fashionable resort destination, Walt Disney World opened a grand hotel—a 900-room Victorian structure, with gabled roofs and carved moldings—on 40 acres of Seven Seas Lagoon shorefront, between the Magic Kingdom and the *Polynesian* resort.

Like its late 19th-century predecessors, the *Grand Floridian* boasts abundant broad verandas, ceiling fans, intricate latticework and balustrades, turrets, towers, and red-shingle roofs. White-sand beaches hold the promise of clambakes. And yet, it has all the advantages of 21st-century living—air conditioning and monorail service. With five restaurants, two lounges, one snack bar, four shops, an arcade, a child-care facility, a swimming pool, a children's activity area, a health club, and a marina, the *Grand Floridian* is not only a grand hotel but a complete resort.

The main building houses a 14,800-square-foot Grand Lobby, a palatial space soaring five stories to a ceiling of stained glass domes, glittering chandeliers, and ornate metal scrolls. Potted palms and an aviary decorate the sitting area; an open-cage elevator carries guests to the shops and restaurants on the second floor. The turn-of-the-century theme is apparent everywhere, from the Edwardian costumes worn by the staff to the shop displays, from the restaurants to the room decor. The telephone number of the *Grand Floridian* resort is 824-3000.

ROOMS: The accommodations are quite luxurious, with rooms decorated as they might have been a century ago: soft moss greens and salmon pinks, printed wall coverings, armoires and light-wood furnishings, marble-topped sinks, ceiling fans, and Victorian woodwork. The main building houses 65 concierge rooms and 11 suites; five lodge buildings, each four and five stories high, 623 standard rooms, 161 slightly smaller "attic" chambers, and 10 suites. Most rooms are about 400 square feet, and include two queen-size beds, plus a day bed, to accommodate up to five people. Many rooms have terraces. Suites include a parlor, plus one, two, or three bedrooms; most of the 15 honeymoon rooms, located on the second, third, fourth, and fifth floors, enjoy wonderful views. In the main building, access to the upper three concierge/suite levels is restricted to guests occupying rooms on those floors only, by private elevator. On the third floor, the concierge desks offer such personalized services as reservations and information. The fourth floor features a quiet seating area where continental breakfast and evening refreshments are served. Rooms equipped for guests with disabilities and nonsmoking rooms are available.

MEETING AND CONVENTION SPACE: A convention center with 27,037 square feet of meeting space is available at the *Grand Floridian*. The Grand Ballroom measures 18,216 square feet and there are eight breakout rooms with a total of 8,821 square feet. The Business Center offers clerical assistance including typing and copying.

WHERE TO EAT: Most of the restaurants and lounges are on the first two floors of the main building.

Gasparilla Grill and Games: A snack bar on the Windsor Level (first floor), offers light items for breakfast, lunch, and dinner, plus video games.

Grand Floridian Café: Its peaches-and-cream color scheme and veranda-like feel make this the best place to get a quick, sit-down breakfast. Lunch and dinner also are available. Located on the first floor.

1900 Park Fare: A buffet restaurant on the first floor, festively decorated with carousel horses, plenty of plants, and Big Bertha—the carnival organ. Breakfast and dinner with the characters are served.

Flagler's: The largest of the hotel's restaurants, seating 285, features Italian cuisine complete with singing waiters and waitresses and strolling musicians. Open for breakfast and dinner. Alcazar Level (second floor).

Victoria & Albert's: Also on the second floor, but much smaller than *Flagler's*, is the hotel's finest restaurant, named after the former queen and prince consort of England. Elegant meals are served to no more than 56 guests; service is refined and diligent. Jackets are required for men and reservations are a must.

Narcoossee's: Octagon-shaped and open-beamed, this seafood restaurant and bar has a romantic shoreline location. Broiled, steamed, sautéed, and smoked fresh seafood characterize the menu, cooked in an open kitchen.

Garden View Lounge: Windsor Level, with a view of the hotel's lush, landscaped pool and garden area. Afternoon tea is served at this pleasant spot.

WHERE TO DRINK: While guests staying on the concierge floors or in suites all have their own wet bars, other guests will find lounges on the first and second floors of the main building.

Mizner's Lounge: Named after the eccentric, wildly prolific architect who defined much of the flavor of Palm Beach County, this bar is on the Alcazar Level.

Summerhouse: The only bar serving the pool and beach.

ROOM SERVICE: A wide assortment of items is available. For the best breakfast service, fill out the card on your doorknob before going to sleep.

WHAT TO DO: The *Grand Floridian* offers all the recreational facilities of a typical beach-side resort—and much more.

Tennis: There are two clay courts available for play. Reservations are required; phone 824-2433.

Volleyball and croquet: Equipment for these activities is available at the Captain's Shipyard marina.

Boat rentals: All manner of watercraft—sailboats and Water Sprites—are available for rent at the Captain's Shipyard marina.

Swimming: In addition to the 275,000-gallon swimming pool outside the main building, the hotel has its own white-sand beach along the Seven Seas Lagoon.

Children's program: The Mousekeeter Club is a supervised children's program for kids three to nine years of age. It's open from 4:30 P.M. to midnight. The cost is $4 per hour for the first child and $2 per hour for each additional child. There is a four-hour maximum. Reservations are required; phone 824-2985.

Fitness: St. John's, open to *Grand Floridian* guests only, offers an exercise room with state-of-the-art equipment, steamrooms, locker facilities, and massage. For massage reservations call 824-2433.

Gameroom: The *Gasparilla Grill and Games* on the first floor of the main building features a video arcade.

Shopping: On the first floor (Windsor Level) of the main lodge is Summer Lace, a women's apparel shop, and Sandy Cove, where guests may purchase gifts and sundries. One floor up at the Alcazar Level is Commander Porter's, a men's shop; M. Mouse Mercantile is the character shop.

TRANSPORTATION: The *Grand Floridian* is connected to the Transportation and Ticket Center (TTC) and the Magic Kingdom by monorail. The monorail entrance is located outside the hotel under an awning on the second floor. From the TTC, Epcot Center is accessible by WDW's other monorail, or via a bus. The Disney-MGM Studios Theme Park can be reached by bus. Launches leave from the dock for the Magic Kingdom and the *Polynesian* resort.

DISNEY INN

The *Disney Inn* has a Snow White theme. Guestrooms have dividers separating the sleeping area from the section with a sofa and table to give each room more of a mini-suite feel. There is a quilt on each bed, the furniture is light oak, and the floral accents add to a basic country feeling. The *Disney Inn* also has a pleasantly relaxed atmosphere—more akin to that of the villas. But the *Disney Inn* is more convenient to the main activities of Walt Disney World since buses make the short trip between the *Disney Inn*, the *Polynesian* resort, and the Transportation and Ticket Center every 15 minutes. The *Disney Inn*'s telephone number is 824-2200.

ROOMS: These are located in two 3-story wings behind the lobby area. All have patios or balconies and views of woods, the golf courses, the courtyard, or the pool; can accommodate up to five (plus a sixth under age three); and have two queen-size beds and a sleep sofa. (No king-size beds are available here.) There are no special room provisions for guests with disabilities, but the hotel is accessible to all visitors. One suite also is available. Nonsmoking rooms are available.

MEETING AND CONVENTION SPACE: A small meeting can be accommodated in the 1,024-square-foot Summer Room.

WHERE TO EAT: There is one full-service restaurant and a couple of snack spots.
  Disney Inn Restaurant: One of the most relaxed spots in the World for a meal. The menu focuses on "American cuisine," featuring a variety of unique salads, sandwiches, and entrées for lunch and dinner. There's also a children's menu.
  Diamond Mine: A snack spot offering sandwiches, burgers, salads, soft drinks, coffee, and beer.
  Sand Trap Food Cart: Poolside food cart for drinks, sandwiches, and hot dogs.

WHERE TO DRINK: The *Back Porch Lounge*, adjoining the *Disney Inn* restaurant, is a light and airy spot that's lovely for drinks, snacks, and sandwiches.

ROOM SERVICE: The full menu from the *Disney Inn* restaurant is available through room service. Allow 30 to 45 minutes for delivery, and for the most prompt breakfast service, be sure to put the order card on the doorknob outside your room the night before.

WHAT TO DO: The *Disney Inn* is landlocked, so when you decide to go boating, you've got to head for the *Contemporary* resort or the *Polynesian* resort. But there are plenty of other activities.
  Swimming: The *Disney Inn* has two swimming pools and a kiddie pool at Happy's Hollow. For beach action, head for the *Polynesian* resort.
  Tennis: There are two courts tucked away behind the hotel. These are open from 8 A.M. to 10 P.M. daily, and are lighted for night play. (For more information, and for details about court reservations, see *Sports*.)
  Fitness: The Magic Mirror exercise room features Nautilus machines, aerobics classes, exercise bicycles, a treadmill, and weights.
  Children's playground: The Wee-Bits Play Yard is located in Happy's Hollow near the kiddie pool.
  Gameroom: The Mine Arcade is located on the lobby level in the guestroom area.
  Golf: There are two par-72, Joe Lee-designed, championship courses—the tree-dotted Magnolia, to the north of the hotel, which plays from 5,414 (women's) to 7,190 (championship) yards; and, south of the hotel, the Palm, ranked by *Golf Digest* magazine among the United States' top 100 courses—shorter and tighter, with more wooded fairways and nine water hazards, playing from 5,398 to 6,957 yards. Each course has its own driving range. Oak Trail, a nine-hole, 2,913-yard walking course, occupies a 45-acre corner near the Magnolia. (See *Sports* for additional details.) Proper golf attire is required. If shorts are worn, they must be Bermuda length.
  Shopping: The Pro Shop stocks men's and women's golf and tennis togs and gear, some emblazoned with Mickey Mouse and Minnie Mouse emblems. Gifts and Sundries sells souvenirs, books and magazines, daily newspapers, liquor, tobacco, film, toiletries, and a little bit of a lot of other things.

TRANSPORTATION: Buses make regular trips from the *Disney Inn* to the *Polynesian* resort and then on to the Transportation and Ticket Center (TTC). To get to the Magic Kingdom or the *Contemporary* resort, it's quickest to take the monorail from the second-floor lobby at the *Polynesian* resort; to get to the Disney Village Marketplace, Epcot Center, or the Disney-MGM Studios Theme Park, stay on the bus until you get to the TTC, and then change for the bus marked for those areas. To get to *Fort Wilderness*, change to a bus marked *Fort Wilderness*.

WILDERNESS LODGE

A combination of the spirit of the early American West and the feeling of the National Park Service lodges built in the early 1900s is what *Wilderness Lodge* is all about. The hotel is slated to open in June 1994. Inspired by the arts and crafts movement, the National Parks lodges architecturally unified the elements of the unspoiled wilderness parks, kept harmony with nature, and incorporated the culture of Native Americans.

The resort is situated between the *Contemporary* resort and *Fort Wilderness*. Guests arrive along a winding road shaded by pines. The lobby is in an eight-story, log-structured building. Massive bundled log columns support a series of trusses. Four large chandeliers with torch-cut iron bands featuring silhouettes of Indians and buffalo are topped with glowing tepees. Two authentic Northwest Coast totem poles, soar 55 feet on each side of the lobby. There also is a stone fireplace and an intricately detailed, multi-colored floor that recall Northwest Indian designs. Six levels of corridors surround the lobby providing access to guestrooms, sitting and reading areas and porches. There are 38 rooms equipped for guests with disabilities and nonsmoking rooms also are available. *Wilderness Lodge's* telephone number is 824-3200.

ROOMS: The 760 guestrooms are located in a U-shaped building. Most rooms have two queen-size beds, a writing table with two chairs, and a balcony with another table and chairs. There are some rooms with one queen-size bed and a bunk bed. The bathroom is a comfortable size with a separate vanity area with double sinks. The fixtures are designed to look like pewter. The cream-colored wallpaper has a border with an Indian motif and the curtains are a traditional plaid. The quilted bedspreads are very colorful and the buffalo lamps complete the theme.

WHERE TO EAT: The American West theme is carried out with flair in the hotel's two restaurants.

Artist Point: Decorated with artwork representing the painters who first chronicled the Northwest landscape, this fine dining spot features wild game as well as traditional items.

Whispering Canyon Café: A traditional family-style coffee shop is open for all-day dining. The cowboy silhouette cutouts are great for picture-taking.

Roaring Fork: Light snacks are available at the hotel's arcade.

WHERE TO DRINK: Two spots are available for a relaxing break.

Territory Lounge: Located between the *Whispering Canyon Café* and *Artist Point*, this spot honors the survey parties who led the move westward.

Trout Pass: The poolside bar features a variety of specialty drinks.

ROOM SERVICE: A wide selection of items is available through room service. Breakfast can be ordered by placing the card on the outside doorknob before going to bed.

WHAT TO DO: A resort unto itself, there are many activities to pursue.

Swimming: The themed pool actually begins in the lobby where it is a hot spring. From there, water flows out of the building into Silver Creek, a quiet, contemplative setting in the upper courtyard. The creek widens as it develops into a rushing, roaring waterfall and then widens again into the swimming area that looks as if it was carved from rockscape. A kiddie pool, hot and cold spas, and an Old Faithful-style geyser round out the design.

Boat rentals: A variety of watercraft can be rented for a trip around Bay Lake.

Bicycling: Bicycles can be rented for a ride around the resort. Other paths lead to *Fort Wilderness* and River Country.

Children's program: The Cubs Den is a supervised program for kids ages 3 to 12. There is an innovative playground near the pool.

Gameroom: The Roaring Fork features about 50 of the latest games to keep kids occupied for hours.

Shopping: Necessities and sundries as well as a line of clothing with the *Wilderness Lodge* logo are available at Wilderness Lodge Mercantile. A selection of Disney-character merchandise is featured as well.

TRANSPORTATION: Boats go to the Magic Kingdom from the dock behind the hotel. Buses make the trip to all other parts of the World including Epcot Center, the Disney-MGM Studios Theme Park, Typhoon Lagoon, and the Disney Village Marketplace. It's also possible to bicycle to *Fort Wilderness* and River Country.

Epcot Resorts

CARIBBEAN BEACH

This colorful hotel is set on 200 acres southeast of Epcot Center and near the Disney-MGM Studios Theme Park. The hotel is composed of five brightly colored "villages" surrounding a 42-acre lake. Each village is identified with a different Caribbean island— Martinique, Barbados, Trinidad, Aruba, and Jamaica—and features cool pastel walls, white railings, and vividly colored metal roofs. There are 2,112 rooms in all, making the *Caribbean Beach* resort one of the largest hotels in the United States.

The villages consist of a cluster of two-story buildings, a swimming pool, a guest laundry, and a lakefront stretch of white sandy beach. Guests check in at the Custom House, a reception building that immediately projects the feeling of a tropical resort. Decor, furnishings, and staff costumes all reflect the Caribbean theme. Old Port Royale, a complex located near the center of the property, evokes images of an island market. Stone walls, pirates' cannons, and tropical birds and flowers add to the atmosphere. The area houses the resort's six counter-service restaurants, two shops, a gameroom, and a lounge. The port opens onto a lakeside recreation area which includes a pool with waterfalls and slides; the main beach; the Barefoot Bay Bike Works and Boat Yard, where watercraft and bicycles can be rented; a 1.4-mile promenade around the lake that's perfect for biking, walking, or jogging; and Parrot Cay Island, an area with a playground, and a wildlife walk. The telephone number at the *Caribbean Beach* resort is 934-3400.

ROOMS: Rooms are located in two-story buildings in each island village. A typical 300-square-foot room has two double beds and can sleep up to four. The rooms here are a bit smaller than the standard rooms at the other Disney hotels, but the bathrooms are comfortable and fine for a family of up to four. The rooms are decorated in softer tones than the colors found on the exterior. The furniture is white oak, and bedspreads are pink and blue pastels. Each room has a mini-bar and a coffeemaker. Rooms equipped for travelers with disabilities and nonsmoking rooms are available.

One note for the budget-conscious: all the rooms here are identical in terms of size and comfort, and the only difference between the most and least expensive is the view.

WHERE TO EAT: The six counter-service restaurants are located in Old Port Royale. A 500-seat common area serves all diners.

Cinnamon Bay Bakery: Freshly baked rolls, croissants, pastries, ice cream, and other treats are available.

Port Royale Hamburger Shop: Hot sandwiches and burgers are on the menu.

Wok Shop: A variety of Chinese items, including egg rolls, sweet and sour chicken, and spicy lo mein are served.

Montego's Deli: Soups, salads, and cold sandwiches are offered.

Bridgetown Broiler: Chicken fajitas, taco salads, and grilled chicken are among the menu items.

Royale Pizza & Pasta Shop: Very good pizza by the slice or the pie and a variety of hot and cold pasta dishes are available.

WHERE TO DRINK: The tropical, Caribbean theme is carried out in a pair of specialty drinking spots.

Captain's Hideaway Tavern: Tropical drinks, wine, beer, and traditional cocktails are served at this 200-seat lounge at Old Port Royale. Prime ribs, baked chicken, and crab legs are served from 5 P.M. to 10 P.M.

Banana Cabana: Drinks and snacks are available at this poolside spot.

WHAT TO DO: There are many recreational opportunities.

Boat rentals: Sailboats, toobies (oversize tires with zippy motors), and pedal boats are available for rent at the Barefoot Bay Bike Works and Boat Yard for use on the resort's 42-acre lake.

Swimming: Each village has its own pool and the main pool features waterfalls and slides in a Caribbean-themed setting.

Children's playground: A lovely playground is on Parrot Cay Island, across the footbridge from the Barefoot Bay Bike Works and Boat Yard. Playgrounds are also located on the Barbados, Martinique, and Trinidad beaches.

Jogging: The 1.4-mile promenade around the lake is perfect for a morning jog.

Gameroom: Goombay Games features a selection of electronic games at Old Port Royale.

Shopping: Calypso Trading Post, at Old Port Royale, stocks a large selection of character merchandise and sundries. The Calypso Straw Market features items with the *Caribbean Beach* resort logo and a variety of island-themed goods.

Bicycling: Bikes can be rented at the Barefoot Bay Bike Works and Boat Yard.

Nature walks: Walks are conducted at Parrot Cay Island.

TRANSPORTATION: The *Caribbean Beach* resort is served by the Walt Disney World bus system. Buses go directly to Epcot Center and the Disney-MGM Studios Theme Park. Other routes lead to the Disney Village Marketplace, Pleasure Island, Typhoon Lagoon, and the Magic Kingdom.

YACHT CLUB AND BEACH CLUB

The New England seaside exists at Walt Disney World in the form of the *Yacht Club* and its sister the *Beach Club* next door. (The rooms and restaurants in each hotel differ—and we describe them separately—but since the two adjacent properties share most activities, meeting spaces, and transportation options, we've combined the "What to Do," "Meeting and Convention Space," and "Transportation" sections.)

YACHT CLUB

Situated just west of Epcot Center, the hotels, designed by noted architect Robert A. M. Stern, are set around a 25-acre lake. The *Yacht Club's* design evokes images of the New England seashore hotels of the 1880s. Guests enter the five-story, oyster-gray, clapboard building along a wooden-planked bridge. Hardwood floors, millwork, and brass enhance the nautical theme. A lighthouse on the pier serves as a beacon to welcome guests back to the hotel from WDW attractions. The telephone number for the *Yacht Club* resort is 934-7000.

ROOMS: The 635 rooms are spacious and decorated in a nautical motif. The furniture is white and the headboards on the two queen-size beds were designed to incorporate small ship's wheels. The carpeting is blue and the

Special Room Requests

The Central Reservations Office (W-DISNEY—934-7639) can accept requests for a particular view or location, but although they will try to accommodate guest requests, they cannot guarantee that they will be able to fulfill every wish.

drapes and bedspreads are blue and dusty rose. The bathrooms are large, with double sinks outside. Mirrors are silver trimmed with brass. Each room has a color TV set, ceiling fan, mini-bar, a table (complete with checkerboard top), and two chairs. Chess and checker sets are provided. There are rooms equipped for guests with disabilities and nonsmoking rooms are available.

WHERE TO EAT: The yachting theme also dominates the hotel's restaurants.

Yachtsman Steakhouse: Select cuts of aged beef are the specialty of the house. Fresh seafood and poultry also are available.

Yacht Club Galley: The buffet breakfast is bountiful. Breakfast, lunch, and dinner are available from an à la carte menu.

WHERE TO DRINK: The lounges here offer a variety of specialty drinks in settings with a nautical feel.

Crew's Cup Lounge: The place to try assorted beers shipped in from the world's seaports. Located next to the *Yachtsman Steakhouse*.

Ale and Compass Lounge: This lobby lounge features specialty coffees and drinks until 11 P.M. to help welcome guests back from a long day in the parks.

ROOM SERVICE: A wide variety of menu items is available. For best breakfast service, put the order card on your doorknob before turning in for the night.

BEACH CLUB

Beach is the operative word at the *Beach Club*, which is approached along an entrance drive flanked by palm trees. A patterned walkway leads past a croquet court to beachside cabanas on the white-sand shore. Guests are met by hosts and hostesses dressed in colorful beach resort costumes of the 1870s. The telephone number at the *Beach Club* resort is 934-8000.

ROOMS: The 580 rooms are spacious and reflect a beach motif. The wallpaper is seafoam green and the curtains and bedspreads are white and seafoam green with a border of mauve beach umbrellas. The room layouts are similar to those at the *Yacht Club*, and each room features a ceiling fan, double sinks, two queen-size beds, a hairdryer, and a wall-mounted makeup mirror. There are rooms equipped for guests with disabilities and nonsmoking rooms are available.

WHERE TO EAT: The sea plays an important role in the restaurants here.

Ariel's: Named for the heroine of *The Little Mermaid*, fresh mesquite-grilled seafood is the specialty of the house. There also are items for landlubbers.

Cape May Café: An indoor clambake is held here each night. Guests dine within earshot of the sizzling, crackling pit from which clams, lobster, shrimp, and chicken are extracted. A character breakfast is served daily. No reservations are accepted.

WHERE TO DRINK: The two lounges provide a very relaxing respite.

Martha's Vineyard Lounge: Selections from American and international vineyards are featured at this lounge adjacent to *Ariel's*.

Rip Tide Lounge: The lobby lounge features a variety of California wines, wine coolers, and other frosty concoctions. The bar is open until 11 P.M.

ROOM SERVICE: A large variety of options is available from room service. For the quickest breakfast service, place the order card on your doorknob before going to bed.

AT THE YACHT CLUB AND BEACH CLUB

Hurricane Hanna's Grill: Burgers, hot dogs, sausages, and other snacks are served at this spot at Stormalong Bay. A full bar also is located here, and poolside beverage service is available.

Beaches and Cream Soda Shop: A classic American soda fountain, where sodas, shakes, malts, and oversize sundaes are the prime lures. The other specialty is the Fenway Park Burger, served as a single, double, triple, or homerun.

MEETING AND CONVENTION SPACE: A mid-size meeting facility is shared by the two resorts, and complements the design of the *Yacht Club*. There is a separate entrance which has a porte cochere with a gambrel roof that evokes the feel of a coach house. The interior of the meeting space is reminiscent of a grand, turn-of-the-century New England town meeting hall. The Grand Harbour Ballroom is 36,004 square feet and can accommodate up to 2,800 guests. There also is the Asbury Hall (8,228 square feet) and other adjacent meeting and function rooms. All the audio and visual equipment is state of the art, and a business center is located in the pre-function area. As with all WDW resorts, meeting planners have all the Disney resources at hand to help arrange parties, banquets, and events.

WHAT TO DO: There is enough to do right at this resort to fill an entire vacation.

Boat rentals: Pedal boats, sailboats, toobies, flote boats, and Water Sprites are available for rent at the Bayside Marina.

Swimming: The centerpiece of the dual resort is Stormalong Bay, a three-acre, 750,000-gallon pool that's really a mini water park. There is a lagoon expressly for relaxed bathing, and another "active" lagoon with whirlpools, jets, and rising sands. Adjacent to the main pool is a sunken ship where guests can enjoy a variety of unique water slides. There also is a quiet pool at the far end of each hotel. Note that the pools are open to *Yacht Club* and *Beach Club* guests only.

Fitness: The Ship Shape Health Club is located in the area between the two resorts, and features exercise machines, aerobics classes, sauna, spa, steamroom, and massage rooms. The health club is open to *Yacht Club* and *Beach Club* guests only and you must be over 13 to use the facilities.

Tennis: There are two lighted tennis courts on the *Beach Club* side of the resort. Rental equipment is available at the Ship Shape Health Club.

Gameroom: Lafferty Place Arcade, located in the central area, has about 60 video games and pinball machines.

Children's program: The Sandcastle Club, for children 3 to 12, is available from 4:30 P.M. to midnight. Cost is $4 per hour for the first child; each additional child is $2 per hour. Reservations are required; call 934-8000. A variety of toys, children's videos, games, and Apple computers are on hand to keep children entertained. Milk and snacks also are served.

Croquet: A grass court has been set up on the *Beach Club* side. Equipment is available free at the health club.

Volleyball: A court is located in the sand on the *Beach Club* side. Equipment is free at the health club.

Beauty/barber shop: The Periwig salon for men and women is located in the central area.

Shopping: At the *Yacht Club*, Fittings and Fairings Clothes and Notions is an all-purpose shop offering nautical fashions, character merchandise, and sundries. At the *Beach Club*, Atlantic Wear and Wardrobe Emporium features a similar selection of goods (albeit with a beach theme).

TRANSPORTATION: *Yacht Club* and *Beach Club* guests walk or use a tram that goes to the nearby Epcot Center entrance (beside the France Pavilion). Buses and watercraft go to the Disney-MGM Studios Theme Park. Buses also go to the Magic Kingdom, Pleasure Island, the Disney Village Marketplace, Typhoon Lagoon, and the Transportation and Ticket Center. From the TTC transfer to other buses to that go to River Country and *Fort Wilderness*.

SWAN

The exterior of this 758-room waterfront hotel, operated by Westin, is painted a sun-washed coral beneath rolling waves of turquoise. The guestrooms are encased in a striking 12-story main building and two 7-story wings. And just in case the shape and color of the buildings weren't distinctive enough, two 45-foot swan statues sit atop the resort at either end of the main building. By the way, the statues each weigh about 28,000 pounds. (The *Swan* faces its sister property, the *Dolphin*, across Crescent Lake. Both hotels were designed by noted architect Michael Graves as prime examples of what has come to be known as "entertainment architecture.") The telephone number at the *Swan* is 934-3000.

ROOMS: The corridors outside the guestrooms feature patterned carpets and murals on the walls that carry the wave theme through from the exterior design. Inside, the rooms are decorated in corals and turquoises, and feature such whimsical touches as lamps in the shapes of birds and pineapples painted on the outside of the dressers. In-room safes, clock radios, cable television, voice mail telemessaging, mini-bars, hairdryers, bathrobes, and daily newspaper delivery are among the amenities. There also are 45 concierge rooms on the 11th and 12th floors, and 64 suites. Rooms equipped for guests with disabilities and nonsmoking rooms are available.

MEETING AND CONVENTION SPACE: Along with its sister *Dolphin*, the two hotels make up the Southeast's largest convention-resort complex. Details about the vast conference center can be found in the data describing the *Dolphin*. At the *Swan* itself, there are 54,300 square feet of meeting space, including the 23,064-square-foot *Swan* Ballroom. A total of 31 meeting and breakout rooms also are available, as are seven hospitality suites and a spacious and elegant boardroom. The hotel can provide all necessary audiovisual equipment, and convention planners have access to all the areas and attractions at WDW.

WHERE TO EAT: An Italian restaurant and a seafood spot are among the eateries.

Palio: A pleasant Italian bistro featuring veal specialities, homemade pasta, and brick-oven pizza. There are tasty daily specials and live entertainment.

Garden Grove Café: This 24-hour eatery features a greenhouse atmosphere, and serves a variety of fresh seafood and steaks daily at lunch and dinner. A buffet breakfast with the characters is held twice weekly. Breakfast is served every day. A glassed-in pastry kitchen allows guests to witness the creation of some of the delicious baked goods.

Splash Grill: A poolside café serving breakfast, lunch, dinner, and snacks. A full-service bar also is located here.

WHERE TO DRINK: An unusual Japanese lounge is located here.

Kimonos: The Oriental decor helps make this lounge a pleasant place for a drink. Sushi is served in the evenings.

Lobby Court Lounge: Drink service is available in the vast lobby.

ROOM SERVICE: Available 24 hours a day, featuring an extensive all-day dining menu.

WHAT TO DO: A variety of activities are offered and some are shared by both the *Swan* and the *Dolphin*.

Boat rentals: A variety of boats is available for rent on the white-sand beach between the *Swan* and the *Dolphin*.

Swimming: A large rectangular pool, ideal for lap swimming, is located on the shore of Crescent Lake. There also is a themed grotto located near the *Dolphin*.

Fitness: A small health club, offering exercise equipment and aerobics classes, is located near the pool.

Children's program: Camp Swan, open to children 3 to 12, offers supervised activities from 4 P.M. to midnight. The cost is $5 per hour for the first child and $3 per hour for each additional child. Dinner, ordered through room service, is extra.

Tennis: There are eight lighted tennis courts shared by the *Swan* and *Dolphin*.

Gameroom: A small gameroom is located near the pool.

Shopping: Disney Cabanas features men's and women's fashions, character merchandise, and sundries. Located in the lobby.

TRANSPORTATION: Guests at the *Swan* ride trams to Epcot Center's entrance near the France Pavilion. They also can walk to Epcot. Watercraft make the trip to the Disney-MGM Studios Theme Park. Buses go to the Magic Kingdom, Pleasure Island, the Disney Village Marketplace, Typhoon Lagoon, and the Transportation and Ticket Center. From the TTC, other buses run to River Country and *Fort Wilderness*.

DOLPHIN

A 27-story triangular tower rises from a 14-story main building, a part of the hotel's design that was honored by *Progressive Architecture* magazine. There are four guest-room wings, nine stories each, that stretch out to the shores of Crescent Lake. The exterior of the *Dolphin* complements the *Swan* in color scheme though its exterior walls feature a mural of banana leaves. And not to be out-done by its neighbor, two 55-foot-tall dolphin statues sit atop the hotel. A lush, tropical setting has been created, and a lovely waterfall cascades down the face of the triangle into a series of seashells and on into a large shell-shaped pool supported by smaller dolphin statues. The telephone number at the *Dolphin* is 934-4000.

ROOMS: The 1,510 rooms, including 140 suites, are decorated in a lighthearted fashion, with lamps in the shape of palm trees and colorful bedspreads and curtains. All feature a clock radio, mini-bar, voice mail telemessaging, cable television, a vanity dressing area, and daily newspaper delivery. Concierge rooms are located in the main building. There are rooms equipped for guests with disabilities and nonsmoking rooms are available.

MEETING AND CONVENTION SPACE: The *Dolphin's* enormous conference center has its own entrance, and also is accessible from the hotel lobby. There is a total of 202,295 square feet of meeting space. The 55,903-square-foot Hemisphere Ballroom is the largest hotel ballroom in Florida and the second largest hotel ballroom in the country. There also are 28 meeting rooms, a boardroom, a 51,275-square-foot exhibit hall, and other smaller, conference spaces available. The hotel staff can provide all necessary audiovisual equipment and access to the entire Walt Disney World attraction and entertainment inventory.

WHERE TO EAT: There are several restaurants from which to choose.

Harry's Safari Bar and Grill: Grilled beef, poultry, and seafood are served here.

Sum Chows: A blend of Oriental dishes is served in an elegant atmosphere.

Ristorante Carnivale: As its name suggests, a festival atmosphere prevails at this Italian dining spot. Regional dishes are the specialties. There also is a Sunday character brunch buffet.

Coral Café: Bountiful buffets at breakfast and dinner, as well as à la carte selections for breakfast, lunch, and dinner.

Tubbi Checkers Buffeteria: A 24-hour cafeteria with a little flair. The checkerboard design makes this a pleasant place for a quick meal. There also is a convenience store here with snacks and baby-care items.

Dolphin Fountain: Homemade ice cream in some unusual flavors is the specialty here. Huge sundaes, waffle cones, and an assortment of cakes and pies also are offered as well as burgers and sandwiches.

Cabana Bar Grill: This poolside spot serves burgers, sandwiches, yogurt, and fruit for a nice break from the sun. There also is a full bar with specialty drinks.

WHERE TO DRINK: It's not too tough to find an interesting spot for a drink here.

Copa-Banana: The tabletops are shaped like slices of fruit, and a variety of hors d'oeuvres make this a pleasant place for a drink. Live entertainment is featured nightly.

Harry's Safari Bar: Pull up a stool and enjoy the tropical atmosphere and drinks.

Carnivale Bar: Patrons at the bar at *Ristorante Carnivale* can enjoy the festival atmosphere here.

ROOM SERVICE: Available 24 hours a day. For prompt breakfast service, program your selections on the special television channel.

WHAT TO DO: There are many activities at this resort.

Boat rentals: Several types of watercraft are available for rent on the beach, just past the Grotto Pool.

Swimming: An enormous rectangular pool is perfect for laps. The Grotto Pool lies just beyond, with bridges, mountains, connecting pools, and an entertaining waterslide.

Fitness: A branch of Body by Jake (run by television fitness guru Jake Steinfeld) is located near the pool. State-of-the-art equipment is available, as are personal trainers. There are aerobics classes (including water aerobics), a sauna, steamroom, massage, and whirlpool.

Children's program: Camp Dolphin offers two programs, one for kids ages 3 to 5 and another for kids ages 6 to 12. A lifetime membership in Camp Dolphin costs $35. Hourly rates are $5 per child. The program for 3- to

5-year-olds runs from 3 P.M. to 5 P.M. A dinner club from 5 P.M. to 8 P.M. is $15 for members and $20 for nonmembers. The program for the 6 to 12 group runs from 2 P.M. to 6 P.M. The dinner club operates from 6 P.M. to 10 P.M. and costs $20 for members and $25 for nonmembers.

Gameroom: A gameroom is located near *Tubbi Checkers Buffeteria*.

Shopping: Daisy's Garden is the place to find character merchandise and sundries. At Brittany Jewels, a large selection of Cartier and other name-brand jewels is available. Indulgences allows chocolate lovers a chance to sample some tasty concoctions. Signatures of Fashion offers resortwear for men and women.

TRANSPORTATION: *Dolphin* guests ride a tram to Epcot Center's entrance near the France Pavilion. Guests also can walk to Epcot. Watercraft make the trip to the Disney-MGM Studios Theme Park. Buses go to the Magic Kingdom, Pleasure Island, the Disney Village Marketplace, Typhoon Lagoon, and the Transportation and Ticket Center. At the TTC, it's possible to catch other buses to River Country and *Fort Wilderness.*

Village Resorts

PORT ORLEANS

This 1,008-room resort is an evocation of the historic French Quarter of New Orleans. Starting at the entrance gate, with its wrought-iron portal and overgrown landscape, the appeal of the Delta City surrounds arriving guests. The entry drive leads to the heart of the city, which is Port Orleans Square. The central building, The Mint, was based on an original turn-of-the-century mint where farmers would go to trade their harvest for "Dixes." A dix was a ten-dollar bill, and when the farmers said they were going to get their Dixes, they probably didn't know they had coined a phrase. The Mint houses the hotel's check-in facilities, the guest services desk, a shop, the food court, an arcade, and the restaurant. It has a vaulted ceiling, and the check-in desks are designed as old-fashioned bank-teller windows. The mural behind the check-in counter features a Mardi Gras street scene, and was painted by a Connecticut artist in three parts, each shipped to Orlando separately. The musical notes in the mural are the notes to "When the Saints Come Marching In." The telephone number at *Port Orleans* is 934-5000.

ROOMS: The guestrooms are located in seven 3-story buildings (with elevators) and each can accommodate four people. Each room has two double beds and some king-size beds are available. The rooms are a bit smaller than the standard rooms at the more expensive Disney hotels, but they are comfortable for a family of up to four. The photographs on the walls were donated by Disney cast members, and the captions explain their history. The buildings are painted in different colors including cream, pink, blue, purple, and yellow, with wrought-iron railings of varying designs around each building. About half of the rooms have doors connecting to the room next door. Connecting rooms can be requested, but they cannot be guaranteed. The rates are based on the room's view. The least expensive rooms overlook parking areas, the mid-range overlook gardens, and the most expensive offer water views.

WHERE TO EAT: There is one sit-down restaurant with waitress service, and four counter-service restaurants in the Sassagoula Floatworks and Food Factory. A 300-seat common area serves food-court customers.

Bonfamilles Café: The name of this waitress-service eatery comes from the Disney movie *The Aristocats*. Steaks, seafood, and Creole cooking highlight the dinner menu. Breakfast also is served.

Preservation Pizza Company: Freshly baked pizza from gleaming stainless steel ovens, fresh pasta, and other Italian specialties are on the menu at this stand.

King Creole Broiler: Fresh spit-roasted chicken with red beans and rice and other traditional Creole dishes are featured here.

Basin Street Burgers and Chicken: A variety of burgers and batter-fried chicken are available.

Jacques Beignet's Bakery: Fresh beignets, a delectable New Orleans tradition, are the attraction here. Hand-dipped and soft-serve ice cream also are on the menu.

Sassagoula Pizza Express: Hand-tossed pizza, salads, desserts, and soft drinks can be delivered directly to guestrooms.

WHERE TO DRINK: The New Orleans theme is carried through in the hotel's watering holes.

Scat Cat's Club: A traditional bar featuring a light menu of hors d'oeuvres and entertainment.

Mardi Grogs: The poolside bar serves a variety of specialty drinks during pool hours. Popcorn, hot dogs, and ice cream also are available.

WHAT TO DO: A special pool is the highlight of the recreational opportunities here.

Bike rentals: Bicycles are available for rent at the Port Orleans Landing.

Boat rentals: Pedal boats, rowboats, canopy boats, and flote boats are available for rent at the Port Orleans Landing.

Swimming: Doubloon Lagoon is a pool built around a serpent that, as the legend goes, is still lingering underground. His tail can be seen jutting up in spots along the walkways, and the water slide is actually the serpent's tongue. The shower at the pool has an alligator's head, and there is a large clam shell where an alligator band serves as the centerpiece of a fountain. Note that the pool is open to *Port Orleans* guests only.

Gameroom: South Quarter Games is located at Port Orleans Square. It features state-of-the-art video and arcade games.

Shopping: Jackson Square Gifts and Desires located at Port Orleans Square features Disney character merchandise, clothing featuring the *Port Orleans* logo, and sundries.

TRANSPORTATION: Buses go to Epcot Center, the Magic Kingdom, the TTC, the Disney-MGM Studios Theme Park, Typhoon Lagoon, Pleasure Island, and the Disney Village Marketplace. Water launches also make the trip to *Dixie Landings*, Pleasure Island and the Disney Village Marketplace.

DIXIE LANDINGS

The city feel of *Port Orleans* gives way to the rural South upriver at *Dixie Landings*. The resort is divided into "parishes." Closest to the "city," guestrooms are found in Mansion homes; further upriver are the Bayou rooms with a more rustic feel. The guest registration area, "Dixie Landings," is located in a building designed to resemble a steamship. When guests check in, they are booking passage on the steamboat. The food court and restaurant are located in Colonel's Cotton Mill. Fultons General Store is in *Dixie Landings*. The telephone number at *Dixie Landings* is 934-6000.

ROOMS: The 2,048 Mansion and Bayou guestrooms are the same size, and each features two double beds (some king-size beds are available). The Magnolia Bend Mansion rooms are situated in sprawling, elegant manor homes with stately columns and grand staircases. The Alligator Bayou rooms are in rustic, weathered-wood buildings with tin roofs that are tucked among trees and bushes native to the area. These rooms surround Ol' Man Island, a three-and-one-half-acre recreational area with a pool, a playground, and a fishing hole. Decorative touches in the rooms include wood and tin armoires and pedestal sinks with brass fittings. The beds have hickory bedposts and

quilted bedspreads. The rooms are a bit smaller than the standard rooms at the more expensive Disney hotels, but they are comfortable for a family of up to four.

WHERE TO EAT: The food court and sit-down restaurant are designed to resemble a cotton mill. There is a 30-foot working water wheel outside the building that powers a real cotton press located inside the food court.

Boatwright's Dining Hall: A 200-seat, waitress-service establishment serving Cajun specialties from the rural South and traditional American specialties. The restaurant is modeled after a boatmaking warehouse. Breakfast also is served.

Acadian Pizza 'n' Pasta: Fresh pizza with a variety of toppings, pasta dishes, and calzones are on the menu at this food court location.

Bleu Bayou Burgers and Chicken: Fried and grilled chicken and an interesting assortment of burgers are the offerings here.

Cajun Broiler: Spit-roasted chicken, pork, and dishes native to Louisiana Cajun country are available at this food court stand.

Riverside Market and Deli: This convenience store stocks snack foods, soda, salads, sandwiches, beer, and wine.

Southern Trace Bakery: Pastries, freshly baked breads, and sticky buns are the specialties here.

Sassagoula Pizza Express: Hand-tossed pizza, salads, desserts, and soft drinks can be delivered right to guestrooms.

WHERE TO DRINK: The two lounges each possess a certain degree of charm.

Cotton Co-Op: Situated in a room designed as a cotton exchange, this lounge features specialty drinks and some light hors d'oeuvres and live entertainment.

Muddy Rivers: The poolside bar serves specialty and traditional drinks plus hot dogs, popcorn, and ice cream during pool hours.

WHAT TO DO: A wide variety of activities awaits visitors here.

Swimming: There are five pools set among the parishes of the resort. In addition, Ol' Man Island is a three-and-a-half-acre recreation center featuring a themed pool, spa, children's wading pool, a playground, and a fishing hole stocked with a variety of fish for catch and return. Note that Ol' Man Island and the pools are open to *Dixie Landings* guests only.

Boat Rentals: A variety of watercraft are available for rent at Dixie Levee.

Jogging: The walkways between the various accommodations have been designed for joggers.

Gameroom: The Medicine Show Arcade is located in the Dixie Landings building and features a small selection of video games.

Bicycling: Bicycles of all types can be rented at the Dixie Levee.

Shopping: Fulton's General Store also is in the Dixie Landings building and stocks Disney character merchandise, clothing with the *Dixie Landings* logo, as well as sundries.

TRANSPORTATION: Buses go to the Magic Kingdom, Epcot Center, the TTC, the Disney-MGM Studios Theme Park, Typhoon Lagoon, Pleasure Island, and the Disney Village Marketplace. *Port Orleans*, the Disney Village Marketplace, and Pleasure Island also can be reached aboard the Sassagoula River Cruise.

DISNEY'S VILLAGE RESORT

The area near the Disney Village Marketplace is dotted with exceptionally attractive villa-type accommodations, many fitted out with fully equipped kitchens and many other extras and amenities. Some may cost more than individual guestrooms at the conventional Disney hotels, but they accommodate more people as well. For families of more than five (who might otherwise need to rent an extra hotel room), this is the most economical way to stay hereabouts. Smaller families generally can come out at least even by cooking some of their own meals (especially breakfast) in their villa. Accommodations for guests with disabilities are available in the Club Suites and the Fairway Villas. Nonsmoking accommodations are available in the Club Suites.

Aside from the delights of having lots more space, the villas are exceptionally quiet and secluded; the pace is definitely more relaxed and the atmosphere very low-key. They are conveniently located with respect to Epcot Center, the Disney-MGM Studios Theme Park, Disney Village Marketplace, Pleasure Island, and Typhoon Lagoon. The telephone number at the villas is 827-1100.

TYPES OF VILLAS: There are five major types of villas. All have either full kitchens or wet bars with small refrigerators. Check-in

and check-out for all guests takes place at the Reception Center near the Vacation Villas.

One- and two-bedroom Vacation Villas: These accommodations are located about five minutes' walk from the Lake Buena Vista Club. They are pleasantly straightforward in feeling and decor, and have cathedral-height living room ceilings. One-bedroom units can accommodate four; there's a king-size bed in the bedroom and a Sico bed in the living room. Two-bedroom units, which can accommodate up to six, have a king-size bed in the loft bedroom, a king-size bed in the second bedroom, and a Sico bed in the living room.

The Villa Center near these villas is the main recreation area. In addition to the 50-by-30-foot swimming pool, there are a spa, a laundry, snack bar, an arcade with electronic games and pinball machines. Another swimming pool, this one measuring 65-by-30 feet, is located closer to the Disney Village Marketplace.

One-bedroom Club Suites: These are located slightly northeast of the Vacation Villas. There are 316 regular Club Suites and eight Deluxe Club Suites. The smallest one-bedroom units are roughly L-shaped, with a special sitting area (equipped with a wet bar) that is just far enough removed from the sleeping area (with its two queen-size beds) that business travelers who invite their colleagues in for a nightcap don't feel as if they're entertaining in the bedroom. While the layout was drawn up with special attention to the needs of those attending conferences at the Walt Disney World Conference Center, it works equally well in providing families with a bit more space and privacy than they get in the standard rooms at the WDW resort hotels. (The single disadvantage for families is the size of the bathrooms—small.) Note that these

units, which cost about the same as rooms at the resort hotels, do not have full kitchens—only a small refrigerator, a sink, a microwave oven, and a coffeemaker.

For the largest accommodations here, ask for a Deluxe Club Suite, which sleeps six and includes a Jacuzzi. These units have two queen-size beds upstairs and a day bed downstairs.

There are two pools on opposite sides of the lake, and the Club Suite Villa Center offers a pool, a spa, and an arcade.

Fairway Villas: These cedar-sided, slant-roofed units, located near the first, second, eighth, and ninth fairways of the Lake Buena Vista Golf Course, are among the World's most spacious and attractive accommodations, with cathedral ceilings, rough-hewn walls, large windows, contemporary-styled furniture, and an overall feeling that there's lots of elbow room. There is a queen-size bed in one bedroom, two double beds in the other, and a double Sico bed in the living room. They can sleep eight, plus there's room for a crib.

Treehouse Villas: Guests who lodge in one of these octagonal houses-on-stilts, scattered along a barbell-shaped roadway at the western edge of the resort, go to sleep to a cacophony of crickets and wake up to a chorus of birds. You're literally in the woods, alongside some of the winding WDW canals, and you feel a million miles from the rest of the WDW property and all its hubbub. Upstairs is the small (but modern) kitchen, the living room (where the televison set and a sleep sofa are located); two bedrooms (each with a queen-size bed) and two bathrooms; the whole floor is surrounded by a deck where you can eat or just sit and look out into the trees. Downstairs, there's a bedroom with a double bed and a utility room equipped with a washer and dryer. The canals offer some of the World's best fishing, mainly for bass, and the roadways—shady, flat, and untrafficked

information, see the chart "Rates at WDW Properties" on page 74.)

WHERE TO EAT: The *Lake Buena Vista Club* restaurant, located in the Disney Village Clubhouse, caters to guests staying in these accommodations. Breakfast, lunch, and dinner are served. Other breakfast options include the *Empress Lilly* character breakfast; the Gourmet Pantry (which opens at 9:30 A.M.); or *Chef Mickey's Village* restaurant, all at the Disney Village Marketplace. There also are abundant breakfast facilities at the nearby hotels in Disney Village Hotel Plaza. For lunch and dinner, the selections are even broader. (See *Good Meals, Great Times* for more details.) The *Lake Buena Vista Club Snack Bar* located next to the Pro Shop features breakfast items, hot dogs, sandwiches, soft drinks, and beer. It's open from 7 A.M. to 3 P.M. daily.

Groceries: The Gourmet Pantry stocks staples of all sorts, as well as delicacies from around the globe, and good meat, poultry, and fresh vegetables. Purchases can be delivered to your villa at no charge; if you won't be home to receive them, arrangements may be made for the delivery person to be let in so that perishables can be stashed in the refrigerator. It's also possible to order by phone. Touch "31" on your room telephone (before 1 P.M.), or dial 828-3886 when calling from someplace other than your villa. There also is a Gooding's supermarket located at the Crossroads of Lake Buena Vista shopping center.

as they are—are terrific for jogging. The nearest swimming pool is the one in the Treehouse area.

Grand Vista Suites: This quartet of ultra-luxurious homes—originally designed as model homes for a development project that has been abandoned for the moment—are available for rent. Bed-turndown service and daily newspaper deliveries are provided, refrigerators are stocked with staples when you arrive, and the furnishings are all first class. A golf cart and bicycles are included in the price of the suites. (For complete price

WDW CONFERENCE CENTER

This sleek cedar creation is located on the banks of Club Lake at the Village resort villas. It was designed expressly with small- and medium-size meetings and seminars in mind, and may be one of the most innovative structures of its type in existence. (Larger meetings are accommodated at the *Contemporary* resort, the *Grand Floridian*, the *Swan*, and *Dolphin* hotels. The *Yacht Club* and *Beach Club* also have meeting facilities. See individual hotel entries for details.) Four large rooms, each with its own light, sound, and projection systems, can be combined in a wide assortment of configurations, the largest comprising 6,500 square feet, to seat 505 theater-style.

Rearview projection screens can be supplemented by audiovisual equipment rented from Disney's own extensive equipment pool. In addition, technicians are available to record meetings, set up sound and lighting systems, and edit and splice film and tape. All rooms are extremely attractive; the chairs are comfortable enough for all-day sitting; and despite the fact that you're just a 15-minute ride from the Magic Kingdom, Epcot Center, and the Disney-MGM Studios Theme Park, the whole facility has a relaxed atmosphere.

Meeting planners often choose one of several popular theme parties, each performed by an all-Disney cast. Anyone with a penchant for playing impresario (and the funds to pay the piper) can concoct a special affair with the aid of the vast WDW talent pool. Arrangements can be made for meeting guests to take advantage of just about everything in the WDW vacation inventory. Account managers can even set up tennis and golf tournaments. For information about WDW meetings and conventions, contact Walt Disney World Sales; Box 10000; Lake Buena Vista, FL 32830; 407-828-3200.

Swimming: There are six pools and spas around the villas—two near the Vacation Villas (one at the Villa Center, the other close to the shores of the Buena Vista Lagoon), the third at the Lake Buena Vista Club, the fourth and fifth on opposite sides of the lake at the Club Suites, and the sixth at the Treehouses.

Tennis: There are three courts, bordered by the woods and a section of the golf course, at the Lake Buena Vista Club (open 8 A.M. to 10 P.M. daily; lighted for play after dark). Racquets can be rented for a nominal fee; you must buy your own balls. (For fee information, see *Sports*.)

TRANSPORTATION: Buses go to Epcot Center, the Disney Village Marketplace, the Disney-MGM Studios Theme Park, and the Magic Kingdom. These circulate through the Villa areas, making pickups at bus stops located at regular intervals along the roadways; they arrive every 15 to 20 minutes.

Another option: A $30-a-day electric golf cart can get you from your villa to the Disney Village Marketplace or the Lake Buena Vista Club. Or rent a bike. Either can be rented at the Villa Center.

DISNEY VACATION CLUB

The *Disney Vacation Club* offers the opportunity to own a real estate interest in a Disney resort. For a one-time purchase price and annual dues, members receive an allotment of vacation points to use for stays at the resort, which features studio, one-, two-, or three-bedroom units on the Disney property overlooking the Lake Buena Vista Golf Course.

In addition, members can exchange their points for stays at more than 200 premium resorts worldwide, including other Walt Disney World, Disneyland, and Euro Disney properties. Vacation homes not occupied by members are available for nightly rental.

WHERE TO DRINK: For liquid refreshment, head for the *Lake Buena Vista Club Lounge*, inside the *Lake Buena Vista Club* restaurant. At the Disney Village Marketplace there are the lively *Baton Rouge Lounge* aboard the *Empress Lilly*, *Cap'n Jack's Oyster Bar*, and the *Village Lounge*. Or try Pleasure Island's clubs: *Mannequins*, the *Neon Armadillo*, *Rock & Roll Beach Club*, *8TRAX*, the *Comedy Warehouse*, or the *Adventurers Club*. (For details about these, see *Everything Else in the World*.)

ROOM SERVICE: Touch "15" on your room telephone for room service at the villas.

WHAT TO DO: In addition to boating, shopping, and fishing at the Disney Village Marketplace, and shopping at Pleasure Island (discussed in more detail in *Sports* and *Everything Else in the World*), you also can enjoy a variety of activities in and around the villas themselves.

Biking: The meandering, relatively untrafficked, and scenic roads around the villas, not to mention the eight miles of bike paths there, can make for an enjoyable hour or two of pedaling. Two-wheelers are available for rent at the Reception Center. (See *Sports* for fees.)

Gameroom: Small arcades with electronic games and pinball machines are located at the two Villa Centers.

Golf: The par-72 Lake Buena Vista course plays from 5,176 to 6,829 yards, and is one of the shorter of the Disney courses. Some of the fairways are bordered by Fairway Villas and the Treehouses; others by *Dixie Landings* and *Port Orleans*. Most of the back side of the course meanders through the *Disney Vacation Club* and offers plenty of hazards and one island green. Practice greens, a driving range, and golf lessons are available, along with top-quality rental clubs and shoes. Proper golf attire is required. (For fees and starting information, see *Sports*.)

The homes are designed in a Key West theme with color schemes of seafoam green and mauve. The *Vacation Club* has the feel of a resort community and all the amenities that go with resort life.

Membership in the *Disney Vacation Club* is valid until the year 2042. From now until the end of 1999, any members booking a vacation home also get free admission to the Magic Kingdom, Epcot Center, and the Disney-MGM Studios Theme Park for the duration of their stay. There also are discount golfing and dining programs available to members, as well as other exclusive benefits.

A presentation describing all the details of club membership is offered at the Commodore House. The telephone number at the *Disney Vacation Club* is 827-7700.

HOMES: There are studio (known as deluxe rooms), one-, two-, and three-bedroom units available. The deluxe rooms consist of a large bedroom with two queen-size beds, a table and chairs, and a small kitchenette with a small refrigerator, microwave oven, coffeemaker, and sink. The bathrooms are spacious. The larger units feature a king-size bed in the master bedrooms, two queen-size beds in the other bedrooms, a large living room with a queen-size sofa bed, a dining room with a table and chairs, a full-size kitchen equipped with everything one could imagine from dishes, glasses, silverware, napkins, and towels to pots and pans, cooking utensils, and even napkin rings. There is a full-size refrigerator, dishwasher, coffeemaker, and toaster. There is a VCR hooked up to the living room television set. The bathroom has two separate rooms with an extra-large whirlpool tub and a sink in one room and an oversize shower, a sink and vanity, and the toilet in the other. There is a terrace off the living room and bedroom and ceiling fans in each room as well. Deluxe rooms and one-bedroom units sleep 4 people; two-bedroom units sleep 8 people; three-bedroom homes can accommodate up to 12 people. Some homes are equipped for guests with disabilities. Nonsmoking homes also are available.

WHERE TO EAT: *Olivia's* serves an assortment of Key West favorites plus some more traditional items for breakfast, lunch, and dinner. There is a Winnie The Pooh character breakfast every Wednesday. *Good's Foods to Go* offers snacks. There also are grills and picnic tables available. Guests also can make a short boat journey to the Disney Village Marketplace. Pizza delivery is available from *Dixie Landings* from 5 P.M. to midnight.

WHERE TO DRINK: The *Gurgling Suitcase* near the main pool serves an assortment of specialty drinks and traditional cocktails, wine, beer, and soft drinks.

WHAT TO DO: An activities director is on hand to schedule events for guests and members alike.

Tennis: There are two lighted courts located near the main pool.

Swimming: The main pool is located behind the Hospitality House. A children's wading pool and play area is designed to resemble a giant sandcastle. There are additional pools around the resort.

Boat rentals: Hank's Rent 'N Return has several types of boats available for a ride on Trumbo Canal. Hank's also has equipment for volleyball, shuffleboard, and tennis.

Fitness: The exercise room features Nautilus equipment, sauna, and massage.

Shopping: Conch Flats General Store stocks groceries, books, magazines, suncare products, and Disney character merchandise.

Gameroom: The Electric Eel Arcade is located in the Hospitality House.

Conch Flats Community Hall: Table tennis, board games, playing cards, a large-screen television set, complimentary video rentals, nightly movies, and planned activities are all on hand at the Community Hall.

TRANSPORTATION: Buses go to Epcot Center, the Magic Kingdom, the TTC, the Disney-MGM Studios Theme Park, Typhoon Lagoon, Pleasure Island, and the Disney Village Marketplace. Water launches also make the trip to Pleasure Island and the Disney Village Marketplace.

Studio Resorts

ALL-STAR SPORTS AND ALL-STAR MUSIC RESORTS

The first Disney entry into the economy-priced hotel market, the *All-Star Sports* and *All-Star Music* resorts are being built in three phases. The first phase consisting of 400 rooms will be complete in June of this year. The second phase consisting of another 3,440 rooms will be complete in May 1995 and the third phase of 1,920 rooms is slated for future development.

The themes at the resorts are startlingly obvious. The first two sections will be designated as *All-Star Sports* and *All-Star Music* resorts. Each segment consists of ten buildings devoted to each of five sports and five kinds of music. The outside of the buildings at the sports hotel are decorated to carry out the themes of tennis, football, surfing, baseball, and basketball. At the music hotel, the five sections represent rock and roll, calypso, Broadway tunes, country and western, and jazz. Each building will feature an oversize symbol at the main entrance, plus other decorative icons at either end of the building. For example, at the *Center Court* (tennis), a giant referee's chair sits at the main entrance. There are tennis racquets and tennis balls all around and giant tennis ball cans are at the stairways at either end of the hotel. Over at the *Rock Inn*, the entranceway is decorated with a giant jukebox. Other icons include huge speakers, guitars, and microphones. Each hotel has a Commercial Center that houses the check-in facilities. A retail shop, a large arcade, and a food court also are located in this central structure. The telephone number at the *All-Star Sports* resort is 939-5000; the telephone number at the *All-Star Music* resort is 939-6000.

ROOMS: The guestrooms are rather small, measuring 260 square feet, compared with the rooms at the *Caribbean Beach*, *Port Orleans*, and *Dixie Landings*. which are 314 square feet. Each room has two double beds (with the exception of rooms designed for travelers with disabilities, which have one king-size bed), a vanity area with a single sink, a separate bathroom, a closet bar and shelf, an armoire, and a small table with two chairs. Nonsmoking rooms also are available.

WHERE TO EAT: Each hotel has its own food court featuring about five stands including hamburgers, barbecue, Italian food, a bakery, and a convenience store. There is a common seating area and a central beverage bar.

WHERE TO DRINK: There are no lounges at the *All-Star* resorts, however, there is a bar at each of the main pools.

WHAT TO DO: Swimming takes first priority at these resorts.

Swimming: Each hotel has two pools and one kiddie pool. At the *All-Star Sports* resort, one pool is designed to look like an ocean for surfers and the other pool is shaped like a baseball diamond. At the *All-Star Music* resort, one pool is shaped like a guitar and the other like a piano.

Children's playground: There is one playground at each hotel designed with an appropriate theme in mind.

Gameroom: Each hotel has a large arcade featuring about 90 games.

Shopping: A retail shop is located in each Commercial Center. Magazines, books, suncare products, character merchandise, and sundries are available.

TRANSPORTATION: Buses make pick-ups at designated spots around the resorts and make the trips to the Magic Kingdom, Epcot Center, the Disney-MGM Studios Theme Park, Typhoon Lagoon, and the Disney Village Marketplace.

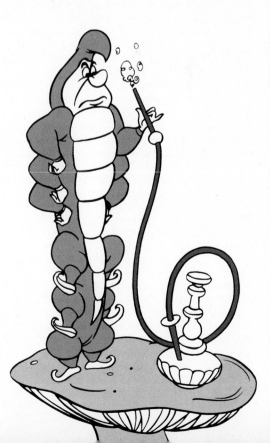

Fort Wilderness Resort and Campground

The very existence of this 780-acre, canal-crossed expanse of cypress and pine, laced by pleasant blacktop roadways, always surprises visitors who come to WDW expecting to find the theme parks and nothing more. If they've heard about *Fort Wilderness* at all, they often confuse it with the Magic Kingdom's Frontierland section.

But the *Fort Wilderness* atmosphere is relaxed and not at all frenetic. In one corner, a group of kids may be battling it out at tetherball, and on the playing fields there are often a couple of energetic touch football games in progress. In the mornings, the campground smells sweetly of dew-dampened pines, then of frying bacon. In the evening, the warmth and stillness of the afternoon give way to dinnertime bustle, and fish and steaks are thrown onto grills as next-door neighbors organize get-togethers. Later on, groups of kids gather alongside the trading posts or at Pioneer Hall, where the *Fort Wilderness* electronic-games-and-pinball arcade is located. *Fort Wilderness* also has a marina and a beach, a nature trail, and a number of waterways where fishing, canoeing, and pedal boating are popular; these and other recreational possibilities make *Fort Wilderness* one of the livelier places to be in WDW. An expansion project added the Meadow Recreation Complex, located in the area behind the Meadow Trading Post. It features two lighted tennis courts, a swimming pool, an arcade, and a snack bar.

You can enjoy the *Fort Wilderness* experience even if you don't have your own camping gear. Among the total of 1,192 campsites, there are 408 air conditioned Wilderness Homes available for rent, complete with kitchen utensils, dishes, linens, color television wired for cable, daily maid service, and enough other amenities that the woods all around are the only reminders of the fact that you're camping out. The cost is comparable to that of some of the more expensive of the rooms at the resort hotels. (But those don't have kitchens and so don't offer the money-saving option of cooking some of your vacation meals "at home.") The telephone number for the *Fort Wilderness* resort is 824-2900.

CAMPSITES: *Fort Wilderness* has 784 campsites, ranging in length from 25 to 65 feet, spaced throughout 20 camping loops. Some of them are set up for tent campers, and most of the rest are rented to trailer campers. Each site has a 110/220-volt electric outlet, barbecue grill, and picnic table. Most offer a sanitary-disposal hookup; all loops have at least one comfort station equipped with restrooms, private showers, an ice machine, telephones, and a laundry room. The per-site fee allows for occupancy by up to ten people.

The various campground areas are designated by numbers. The 100, 200, 300, 400, and 500 loops are the closest to the beach, the Settlement Trading Post, and Pioneer Hall. The 1500, 1600, 1700, 1800, 1900, and 2000, loops are farthest away from the beach and many other *Fort Wilderness* activities, but they are quieter and more private.

WILDERNESS HOMES: It used to be that the 408 Wilderness Homes at *Fort Wilderness* were taken only by people who wanted hotel rooms and couldn't get a reservation. Now—mainly as a result of good word-of-mouth—almost every booking is specifically requested. Lodging here provides all the advantages of villa accommodations—with woodsy surroundings to boot.

There are two types of homes. One model sleeps four adults and two children, with a bedroom at one end with a double bed and a bunk bed, plus a separate vanity area. There's a spacious living room with a pull-down bed and a paddle fan. The other trailers sleep four, with a double bed in the bedroom and a pull-down bed in the living room. Both types come equipped with pots and pans, dishes, and all the basic kitchen equipment, plus a color TV set and a complete bathroom. The bathroom is not the sort of makeshift setup you might expect, but instead compares favorably to, say, a bathroom in the villas. There are eight Wilderness Homes equipped for travelers with disabilities. Nonsmoking trailers are available.

Note: No extra camping equipment is allowed on the site; all guests must be accommodated in the rental trailer. (For complete price information, see the chart "Rates at WDW Properties" on page 74.)

WHERE TO EAT: Most people cook their own meals. Groceries and supplies are available at the Meadow and Settlement Trading Posts (open from 8 A.M. to 10 P.M. in winter, to 11 P.M. in summer). Sandwiches, fruit, ice cream, and chips are available there for carry-out; you can eat them at your own site, on the beach, or at tables just outside River Country. A Gooding's supermarket is located at the Crossroads of Lake Buena Vista shopping center across from the Disney Village Hotel Plaza.

When you want to go out, there's the *Trail's End Buffeteria*, an informal, log-walled, beam-ceilinged cafeteria inside Pioneer Hall, where home-style fare for breakfast, lunch, and dinner is served. Beer and sangría also are available. *Crockett's Tavern*, also inside Pioneer Hall, serves breakfast in the morning and cocktails, unique appetizers, steaks, ribs, and chicken in the evening. A children's menu is available.

Snacks: Down on the shores of Bay Lake, the *Beach Shack* offers snacks and sodas. Snack foods also are available at the Meadow and Settlement Trading Posts.

Pizza: Served nightly at the *Trail's End Buffeteria* inside Pioneer Hall from 9 P.M. to 11 P.M. on weekdays and 9 P.M. to midnight on weekends, along with soft drinks and beer.

WHERE TO DRINK: Full meals, beer, wine, and cocktails are served at *Crockett's Tavern* in Pioneer Hall. Snacks also are offered and there is nightly entertainment. If you have a car, make the short drive to the *Empress Lilly* riverboat restaurants, or the many clubs at Pleasure Island, or *Cap'n Jack's* or the *Village Lounge* at the Disney Village Marketplace.

FAMILY ENTERTAINMENT AFTER DARK: The Hoop-Dee-Doo Musical Revue is presented three times nightly at 5 P.M., 7:15 P.M., and 9:30 P.M.; reservations are required and are so hard to come by that they need to be made well in advance through the WDW Central Reservations Office (W-DISNEY—934-7639). Cancellations do occur, however. WDW resort guests who can't get a reservation can present themselves at the Pioneer Hall Ticket Window before the show and tables available due to cancellations will be given out.

There's also a nightly campfire program held at the center of the campground, near the Meadow Trading Post. A sing-along (featuring Chip and Dale) and Disney movies and cartoons are the main goings-on (free). At 9:45 P.M., you can see the Electrical Water Pageant—a procession of waterborne floats, during which an assortment of sea creatures

1½-mile-long Wilderness Swamp Trail. All of these activities are described in detail in *Everything Else in the World* and *Sports*. There are two gamerooms: Davy Crockett's Arcade in Pioneer Hall and Daniel Boone's Arcade at the Meadow Trading Post.

River Country, a major attraction in its own right, with a separate admission charge, also is located at *Fort Wilderness*. The features of this watery playground—a WDW must, right along with the Magic Kingdom, Epcot Center, and the Disney-MGM Studios Theme Park—are discussed in detail in *Everything Else in the World*.

TRANSPORTATION: Buses circulating at seven-minute intervals provide transportation within the campground, while buses and watercraft connect *Fort Wilderness* to the rest of the World. To get to the *Contemporary* resort or the Magic Kingdom, watercraft (which have regular departures from the *Fort Wilderness* marina) provide the most efficient transportation during their operating hours. At other times, and to get to Disney Village Marketplace, take a bus from the *Fort Wilderness* bus stop, near the Settlement Trading Post and Pioneer Hall, to the Transportation and Ticket Center. This bus operates at regular intervals. Change to another bus for the Disney Village Marketplace, the Disney-MGM Studios Theme Park, and Epcot Center; the Monorail from the TTC to the *Contemporary* resort, the *Polynesian* resort, or the *Grand Floridian* resort; or a bus from the *Polynesian* resort to the *Disney Inn*.

is outlined in a galaxy of tiny colored lights. This also can be viewed from the *Fort Wilderness* beach; don't miss it. (For more details, see *Everything Else in the World* and *Good Meals, Great Times*.)

WHAT TO DO: There are more on-site activities at *Fort Wilderness* than at almost any other area in the World. There are two tennis courts in the area, and Osprey Ridge and Eagle Pines golf courses are very close by.

There are two heated swimming pools and a 315-foot-long, 175-foot-wide beach for swimming in Bay Lake. You can rent tandems and other two-wheelers at the Bike Barn for afternoon bicycle excursions or as reliable transportation around the campground. Visits to the Petting Farm and the horse barn near *Fort Wilderness* are amusing. Boating is popular; rentals are available at the marina. Canoes and pedal boats can be hired at the Bike Barn. Pony rides are available for $2 per ride from 9 A.M. to 5 P.M. Basketball, checkers, electric-cart rentals, fishing (on your own in the canals or on organized morning or afternoon angling excursions), horseback riding (on guided trail rides), horseshoes, tetherball, volleyball, and waterskiing also are available. Or you can just go out for a stroll along the

Practical Matters

The Walt Disney World hotels and villas have some important operating procedures that first-time guests don't always take seriously—much to their later dismay.

Deposit requirements: Deposits equal to one night's lodging (or campsite rental) are required within 21 days of the time that a reservation is made. Personal checks, traveler's checks, cashier's checks, and money orders are acceptable forms of payment. To have deposit charges billed to an American Express, Visa, or MasterCard account, send your card number, its expiration date, the bank number (for Visa and MasterCard), and your signature. Deposits will be fully refunded if you cancel your reservation at least 48 hours before your scheduled arrival. Reservations are canceled if deposits are not received by the 21-day deadline. (Reservations booked less than 30 days prior to arrival will receive special instructions for deposits.)

Check-in and check-out times: While not unique in the Orlando area, the early check-out time (11 A.M. at all WDW lodging places) is almost invariably too early for most WDW guests, while the late check-in times (1 P.M. at the campsites, 3 P.M. in the resort hotels, 4 P.M. in the villas) are often painfully late. Guests can, however, pre-register, purchase Passports, and head for the parks. Luggage can be stored at the resorts.

Payment methods: Hotel bills may be paid with American Express, Visa, and MasterCard credit cards, with traveler's checks or cash, and with personal checks. Checks must bear the guest's name and address, be drawn on a U.S. bank, and be accompanied by proper identification—that is, a valid driver's license or a government-issued passport.

WDW ID Cards: Issued on arrival at WDW-owned resorts, these unprepossessing little squares are among resort guests' most valuable possessions while in WDW. They entitle you to:

- Theme park admission if you've purchased a Be Our Guest Pass.
- Unlimited transportation by bus, monorail, and watercraft.
- Use of many of the roadways within Walt Disney World.
- Charge privileges: The cards may be used to cover purchases if you've left a credit card imprint with your hotel (up to certain account limits) in shops, lounges and restaurants, and recreational fees incurred anywhere in WDW. At the Magic Kingdom, Epcot Center, and the Disney-MGM Studios Theme Park, guests may use their IDs to charge meals at full-service restaurants and in shops but not at fast-food outlets or food carts.

Note: ID cards are valid for use of the transportation facilities through the end of the last day of your stay, but are not valid for charging past your check-out time. Also note that guests at the *Swan* and *Dolphin* hotels may not charge meals at restaurants outside their hotel to their rooms. Other restrictions may apply. Read the information on the cards carefully when checking in.

Rates at WDW Properties

CALL W-DISNEY (934-7639) FOR RESERVATIONS

	Charge for single or double occupancy		Room capacity	Types of beds
	Season*	Off-season		
Contemporary Resort				
Rooms–Garden Wings	$205-$245	$190-$225	5, plus 1 additional occupant under age 3	2 queen beds and 1 day bed; Some king beds available
Rooms–Tower	$270-$310	$250-$290		
Suites	$705-$2,240	$645-$2,240	7 to 12	Most have 2 queen beds and 2 sleep sofas
Polynesian Resort				
Rooms	$210-$325	$195-$280	5, plus 1 additional occupant under age 3	2 queen beds and a day bed; no cots available
Suites (in Bali Hai longhouse)	$520-$3,175	$520-$3,175	4 to 6	King beds in bedroom and usually 2 queen Sico beds in parlor
Caribbean Beach Resort				
Rooms	$89-$117	$89-$117	4	2 double beds
Grand Floridian Resort				
Rooms–Standard	$265-$345	$245-$320	4 to 5, plus 1 additional occupant under age 3	2 queen beds and 1 day bed
Rooms–Concierge	$450-$465	$430-$440		
Suites	$520-$1,720	$480-$1,700	4 to 10	King beds in bedroom and 1 or 2 day beds
Disney Inn				
Rooms	$200-$225	$185-$205	5, plus 1 additional occupant under age 3	2 queen beds and a sleep sofa; no king beds available
Suites	$360-$960	$360-$915	Up to 7	2 queen beds and 2 sleep sofas; no cots available
Yacht Club and Beach Club Resorts				
Rooms–Standard	$220-$290	$205-$270	5	2 queen beds and 1 day bed
Rooms–Concierge	$375-$385	$355-$365	5	
Suites	$390-$995	$370-$995	5 to 10	Most have king beds in bedroom and 2 sleep sofas
Port Orleans				
Rooms	$89-$119	$89-$121	4	2 double beds
Dixie Landings				
Rooms	$89-$119	$89-$121	4	2 double beds
Wilderness Lodge				
Rooms	$164-$195	$149-$180	4	2 queen beds or 1 queen bed and 1 bunk bed
Swan				
Rooms–Standard	$260-$295	$235-$285	4	2 queen beds
Rooms–Concierge	$330	$325	4	
Suites	$350-$1,650	$325-$1,650	5 to 10	Various configurations

	Charge for single or double occupancy		Room capacity	Types of beds
	Season*	**Off-season**		
Dolphin				
Rooms–Standard	$239-$319	$209-$289	4	2 double beds or 1 king bed
Rooms–Concierge	$350	$319	4	
Suites	$525-$2,400	$450-$2,400	5 to 10	Various configurations
All-Star Sports and All-Star Music Resorts				
Rooms	$69-$79	$69-$79	2 to 4	2 double beds or 1 king bed
Disney Vacation Club				
Deluxe Room (studio)	$205	$190	4	2 queen beds
One-bedroom	$260	$240	4	1 king bed in bedroom; queen sleep sofa in living room
Two-bedroom	$365	$345	8	1 king in master bedroom; 2 queens in second bedroom queen sleep sofa in living room
Grand Villa	$755	$755	12	1 king bed in master bedroom 2 queen beds in 2 other bedrooms; queen sleep sofa in living room
Villa Accommodations				
Club Suite	$200	$185	4	2 queen beds
Deluxe Club Suite	$290	$270	6	2 queen beds upstairs; 1 sleep sofa downstairs
Vacation Villas (one bedroom)	$270	$250	4	1 king bed in bedroom; Sico bed in living room
Vacation Villas (two bedrooms)	$320	$300	6	King beds in each bedroom; Sico bed in living room
Treehouses	$355	$335	6	1 queen bed in each bedroom, plus double bed in downstairs bedroom
Fairway Villas	$375	$355	8	1 queen bed in 1 bedroom; 2 double beds in the other, 1 Sico bed in living room
Grand Vista Suites	$750-$825	$750-$825	8	1 king; 2 queens and 2 twins; or 1 king and 2 queens
Fort Wilderness Homes	$195	$180	6	1 double bed in bedroom; and bunk beds in bedroom

Campsites: Preferred loops 700 and 1,400 with full hookups ($52 per night; $49 off-season); all other loops with full hookups ($47 per night; $43 off-season). Sites without hookups are $40; $35 off-season. Check-out is at 11 A.M., check-in at 1 P.M.

Check-in time for the hotels is 3 P.M., except at the villas and the *Disney Vacation Club* where check-in time is 4 P.M. Check-out time is 11 A.M. for all hotels.

* Season refers to: December 21, 1993 through January 1, 1994; February 13, 1994 through April 16, 1994; and June 11, 1994 through August 13, 1994. All other dates are considered off-season, however, this designation in no way reflects park attendance.

The prices listed here were correct at press time, but the rates do change, so be sure to double check with the hotels before finally setting your vacation budget.

The seven hotels here—*Grosvenor* resort, *Travelodge*, *Royal Plaza*, *Howard Johnson*, *Buena Vista Palace*, *Guest Quarters Suite* resort, and the *Hilton*—occupy a unique position among non-Disney-owned Orlando-area accommodations. They are designated as "official" hotels and are actually located inside the boundaries of Walt Disney World, within walking distance of the Disney Village Marketplace and Pleasure Island. Their guests enjoy certain privileges similar to those of guests at WDW-owned properties such as bus transportation directly to the Magic Kingdom, the TTC, to Epcot Center, and to the Disney-MGM Studios Theme Park, and the opportunity to make reservations for dinner shows before bookings are accepted from the general public. Guests also can use the tennis and golf facilities at the Lake Buena Vista Club. WDW Central Reservations (W-DISNEY—934-7639) can take your bookings for Disney Village Hotel Plaza properties (they're also included in several Walt Disney Travel Co. and Delta Air Lines packages).

GROSVENOR: The 629 rooms are located in a white 19-story tower and two wings. The decor is British Colonial, with pale greens, peaches, and pinks evoking a Caribbean feel. Each room has a VCR, refrigerator-bar, and a coffeemaker. Current movies are available for rent at *Crumpets Café*. Restaurants include *Baskerville's*, highlighted by a Sherlock Holmes museum, which serves breakfast and dinner buffets. There's seasonal entertainment at *Crickets* lounge and bar, and continental breakfasts, snacks, and lighter fare are available at *Crumpets Café* 24 hours a day. Two lighted tennis courts, handball and shuffleboard courts, a basketball court, a volleyball court, two heated pools, a children's pool, a playground, and a gameroom also are available. The 17,000 square feet of meeting space here can accommodate up to 1,200 people for meetings or banquets. Additional conference rooms of varying sizes, a reception center, and two boardrooms are ideal for break-out sessions and seminars. The hotel's sales and convention staff can arrange for all necessary audiovisual equipment as well as for food and entertainment. Rates range from $115 to $160 for two, year-round ($10 for cots). There are several rooms accessible to guests with disabilities. Nonsmoking rooms are available. *Grosvenor*; 1850 Hotel Plaza Blvd.; Lake Buena Vista, FL 32830; 828-4444 (800-624-4109).

TRAVELODGE: This tri-arc hotel-tower has 325 spacious rooms and suites. All rooms have either one king-size or two queen-size beds, color TV set, AM/FM radio, and private balconies offering very pretty views of Walt Disney World Village. The gameroom, pool, and playground are appreciated by youngsters. *Traders* restaurant serves breakfast and dinner. The *Parakeet Café* serves pizza and snacks. *Toppers* nightclub on the 18th floor

Hotel Plaza

offers a panoramic view of Walt Disney World. Small meetings can be accommodated in the 2,044 square feet of meeting space. Poolside receptions can be arranged for up to 150 people, and all audiovisual equipment and themed parties can be handled by the *Travelodge* sales staff. Rates start at $99 (no additional charge for children under 17 sharing parents' room; $10 for rollaways). There are two rooms for travelers with disabilities. Nonsmoking rooms also are available. *Travelodge*; 2000 Hotel Plaza Blvd.; Box 22205; Lake Buena Vista, FL 32830; 828-2424 (800-348-3765).

ROYAL PLAZA: Offers 396 rooms in a 17-story high rise and two-story garden-style wings. Each room has its own balcony or patio, a VCR, and safe deposit box. There also are ten suites available, including two celebrity suites, the Burt Reynolds and the Barbara Mandrell. For on-site recreation, there's a heated pool, a spa, a gameroom, shuffleboard courts, four lighted tennis courts, a tanning salon, and men's and women's saunas. The *Plaza Diner*, a 24-hour family-oriented restaurant, features a nostalgic American menu. *Intermissions* lounge features a midnight to 2 A.M. happy hour and the *Giraffe* is a popular spot that features top-40 music video entertainment and attracts an energetic young local crowd (many of them Disney employees). A barbershop, beauty salon, a one-day film-developing service, and the Magicam video camera rental kiosk also are available on the premises. The *Royal Plaza* specializes in smaller meetings of fewer than 300 people. There's 12,000 square feet of space in 12 flexible meeting rooms, plus additional hospitality suites. Special events at the Magic Kingdom, Epcot Center, and the Disney-MGM Studios Theme Park can be arranged, and other Disney-related entertainment is available. Depending on the season and the floor, rates range from $95 to $150. Room rates apply for up to four in a room using existing beds. There are ten rooms specially equipped for travelers with disabilities. Nonsmoking rooms also are available. *Royal Plaza*; 1905 Hotel Plaza Blvd.; Lake Buena Vista, FL 32830; 828-2828 (800-248-7890).

HOWARD JOHNSON: This establishment features 323 guestrooms located in a 14-story tower and a 6-story annex building. Tower rooms surround an atrium lounge and waterfall and are reached by glass-walled elevators. There are three heated pools, one designed for toddlers; a playground, and a gameroom. The exercise room features Nautilus equip-ment. There is a *Howard Johnson* restaurant on the premises. The conference center with 2,304 square feet of meeting space can accommodate up to 200 people. The sales staff will customize a menu, provide audio-visual equipment, arrange exclusive "Behind the Scenes" seminars, and set up entertainment and appearances by the Disney characters. Five special rooms are equipped with wider doors and grab rails for guests with disabilities. Nonsmoking rooms also are available. Rates range from $95 to $165 year-round (no additional charge for children under 18; $15 for cots). *Howard Johnson*; Box 22204; 1805 Hotel Plaza Blvd.; Lake Buena Vista, FL 32830; 828-8888 (800-223-9930).

BUENA VISTA PALACE: The largest of the Disney Village Hotel Plaza properties is actually a cluster of towers (one of them is 27 stories) boasting mirrored, multifaceted facades, and a contemporary interior. Every one of the 1,028 rooms (including suites) has its own private patio or balcony, ceiling fan, air conditioning, and remote-control color TV set. There are 36 Crown Level concierge rooms which include special services and amenities. Many rooms and suites provide a view of Epcot Center's Spaceship Earth. All rooms have two telephones—one with voice mail at bedside and one in the bathroom. Three guestrooms have hot tubs. There are two swimming pools, a kiddie pool, a health spa, three lit tennis courts, and a huge gameroom. Summer Kid Stuff is an organized recreational program for children ages 5 to 17. It is available June through August and during Christmas and Easter school vacations. The hotel also features 24-hour room service, Disney-run gift and sundry shops, and a self-service laundry. There also is a salon for men and women. Eating spots include the *Watercress Café & Bake Shop*, for counter-service baked goods and deli items; *Arthur's 27*, an award-winning rooftop dining room that offers an ambitious menu; *Arthur's Wine Cellar in the Sky* stocks 800 bottles and features a private dining room (reservations essential); and the *Outback* restaurant, which features fresh seafood and Black Angus steaks. It is

accessible via a glass-enclosed private elevator. The adjacent *Laughing Kookaburra Good Time Bar* offers live entertainment and 99 brands of beer from around the world. Unfortunately, noise from these restaurants tends to flow through the atriums and penetrate the solid oak doors, so if serenity and silence matter to you, choose accommodations in either the 5-story tower or the 27-story tower, neither of which has an atrium. This large convention facility has more than 90,000 square feet of meeting space. There are 40 meeting rooms, 127 suites, and 9 break-out rooms. The Conference/Exhibition Hall offers 23,000 square feet of exhibit space; the Empire Ballroom, 18,125 square feet; and the Great Hall, 16,530 square feet. A special entrance and check-in facilities are available for convention guests, and a staff of professional meeting coordinators, banquet managers, and caterers is on hand to help plan any function. Disney-theme entertainment also can be arranged. Rooms range from $145 to $254 per night (no charge for children under 18). There are 12 rooms equipped for guests with disabilities. Nonsmoking rooms also are available. *Buena Vista Palace*; 1900 Buena Vista Dr.; Lake Buena Vista, FL 32830; 827-2727 (800-327-2990).

HILTON: Located directly across the street from the Disney Village Marketplace, this hotel features a state-of-the-art digital telephone system that adjusts air conditioning, contacts the valet, room service, and operators with just the touch of a button. The 813 rooms are tastefully decorated in mauve, peach, and earth-tone color schemes. Each has a coffeemaker and mini-bar. The hotel is set on 23 acres and features a total of nine restaurants and lounges. The *American Vineyards* offers American regional cuisine; *County Fair* serves breakfast, lunch, and dinner; and the *Rum Largo Pool Bar & Café* offers hamburgers, salads, sandwiches, and tropical drinks. The *County Fair Terrace* features outdoor dining. A branch of the *Benihana* Japanese steakhouses is on the premises. Recreational activities include two lighted tennis courts, two heated swimming pools, and a spa. Guests traveling with children will appreciate the Youth Hotel, a hotel-within-a-

hotel that has been designed to accommodate children from 4 to 12 years of age. There is a video room and play area, as well as scheduled recreational activities supervised by a trained staff. The cost is $5 for the first child and $1 for each additional child. The *Hilton* also provides a separate entrance for convention and meeting guests. A total of 52,000 square feet of space is available. The facilities are very flexible and can accommodate up to 2,350 people. There are 21 meeting rooms, and the two ballrooms measure 11,850 square feet and 18,101 square feet, respectively. Special Disney-related functions can be arranged. Rates range from $165 to $240, with the higher prices prevailing for rooms on the higher floors. There are 48 rooms designed for travelers with disabilities. Nonsmoking rooms also are available. *Hilton* at Walt Disney World Village; 1751 Hotel Plaza Blvd.; Lake Buena Vista, FL 32830; 827-4000 (800-782-4414).

GUEST QUARTERS: A seven-story structure, located across from the Crossroads shopping center, contains 229 suites (including 12 designed for guests with disabilities), each of which measures 643 square feet and has a living room and a separate bedroom. Each suite can sleep up to six people. Amenities include two remote-control color television sets, plus a small TV set in the bathroom, a wet bar, a refrigerator, a coffeemaker, and an optional microwave oven. Recreational facilities include a heated pool with a whirlpool, a pool bar, a gameroom, a children's play area, and an exercise room. There's one restaurant, the *Parrot Patch*, where diners can enjoy meals indoors or outdoors on a terrace. A two-story tropical bird aviary adds to the atmosphere. There's also an ice-cream parlor and a snack bar by the pool. There is one meeting room here which can accommodate from 10 to 50 people, and is ideal for small business get-togethers, board meetings, or seminars. Though the facility is small, all services, from audiovisual equipment to themed entertainment, can be arranged. Rates run from $139 to $235. Nonsmoking rooms also are available. *Guest Quarters Suite* resort; 2305 Hotel Plaza Blvd.; Lake Buena Vista, FL 32830; 934-1000 (800-424-2900).

Lake Buena Vista Accommodations

MARRIOTT'S ORLANDO WORLD CENTER:
This is one of Florida's largest hotels, with 1,503 guestrooms located in a 27-story, Y-shaped tower. The hotel is situated on nearly 200 landscaped acres and is surrounded by an 18-hole, Joe Lee-designed golf course. The atrium lobby offers a sampling of exotic plants, including Sabal palms, banana trees, and jade plants. Waterfalls, museum-quality 16th- and 17th-century Chinese artifacts, and a couple of lounges make the lobby a very pleasant place to linger. The guestrooms have peach and mauve tones, and the wicker furniture reinforces the tropical theme. Each room has a single sleep sofa and a choice of two double beds or one king-size bed. There are 3 heated swimming pools (plus one indoors), 12 lighted tennis courts, a health club, a beauty parlor and barbershop, a gameroom, and several retail shops. The enormous hotel also has five full-service restaurants, including *Mikado's*, a Japanese steakhouse; two snack bars; and three lounges. The Lollipop Lounge, a children's program for kids ages 5 to 12, operates from 4 P.M. to midnight. The convention facilities are appropriately vast with 143,000 square feet of meeting space, all located on one level. Rates range from $124 to $184; $250 to $2,000 for suites. There are rooms equipped for travelers with disabilities. Nonsmoking rooms also are available. *Marriott's Orlando World Center*; 8701 World Center Drive; Orlando, FL 32821; 239-4200 (800-228-9290).

GRAND CYPRESS: The *Hyatt Regency Grand Cypress*, a $110-million hotel, is the centerpiece of the 1,500-acre resort. Directly adjacent to the Disney Village Hotel Plaza area and just three miles from Epcot Center, the 18-story building is T-shaped with three wings of guestrooms off the 200-foot atrium lobby. There are 750 rooms (74 are suites), and each has air conditioning, a ceiling fan, color television, and one king-size or two double beds. The 11th and 17th floors have been designated the Regency Club, and guests receive a complimentary breakfast buffet and the convenience of a concierge. (There are also three concierges in the lobby to assist hotel guests.) There's a half-acre, free-form swimming pool with 12 waterfalls and a 45-foot water slide. The 21-acre lake is a perfect place to try out one of the sailboats, sailboards, canoes, or pedal boats available for rent. The tennis complex features 12 courts, and there are racquetball and volleyball areas as well. There also are a children's playground, walking and jogging trails, a health club, and an equestrian center. The 45 holes of Jack Nicklaus-designed golf stand out among the facilities. The superb original course features two Scottish-style shared greens, grassy dunes, and elevated tees. This course is open to guests of the hotel and the villas, and the greens fee will set you back $100 ($70 in the summer). The Grand Cypress Academy of Golf offers two-, three- and four-day programs, which allow golfers to practice situations encountered during a regular round.

The *Grand Cypress* offers space for meetings ranging from small executive sessions to large conventions of up to 2,500 people, with a total of 57,000 square feet of space.

The hotel has five restaurants and three lounges, plus a poolside bar. There are 12 guestrooms designed for guests with disabilities. Nonsmoking rooms are available. Rates range from $175 to $450; suites begin at $450.

There are 146 luxurious rooms at the *Villas of Grand Cypress*, situated around the fairways. There are hotel rooms called Club Suites and one-, two-, three-, and four-bedroom villas. Each villa includes a full kitchen, master suites with private bath and dressing rooms, cathedral ceilings, tile floors, and large picture windows. Some feature a bi-level floor plan with fireplaces, balconies, and patios. The *Grand Cypress* Executive Meeting Center offers meeting space for up to 200 participants. Decks and terraces offer a dramatic lakeside view and fine spots for evening gatherings. Rates range from $150 to $280 for club suites and $225 to $1,120 for villas. *Hyatt Regency Grand Cypress*; One Grand Cypress Blvd.; Orlando, FL 32836; 239-1234 (800-233-1234); *Villas of Grand Cypress*; One North Jacaranda; Orlando, FL 32836; 239-4700 (800-835-7377).

HOLIDAY INN SUNSPREE—LAKE BUENA VISTA: Specializing in family travel, this hotel is located about one-and-a-half miles from the Disney Village Marketplace. The 507 guestrooms all have a mini-kitchen with a refrigerator, microwave oven, and a coffeemaker. There also are VCRs in all rooms and tape rentals are available in the lobby (or guests can bring their own). Most of the rooms have two queen-size beds; some king-size beds are available. Camp Holiday is a free supervised activity program for children ages 2 to 12. The hours are 5 P.M. to 10 P.M., and guests can leave the property and take along a beeper ($5 rental) so they can be reached. There also is a complimentary day-time Castle Childcare Center. There is one pool, two spas, a kiddie pool, and a playground. There also is a fitness center. There are two restaurants. *Maxine's* serves a buffet for breakfast and dinner, along with an à la carte menu. *Pinky's Deli and Mini-Market* is a self-serve restaurant where guests can eat in or carry out. The deli stocks a wide variety of items which can be cooked in the guestroom kitchens. Free scheduled transportation to WDW is provided. Four rooms are equipped for guests with disabilities. Nonsmoking rooms are available. Rates are $79 to $160. *Holiday Inn SunSpree—Lake Buena Vista*; 13351 S.R. 535; Lake Buena Vista, FL 32830; 239-4500 (800-FONMAXX).

HOWARD JOHNSON PARK SQUARE INN: One of several properties located in the Vista Centre, where there are a number of shops and restaurants and a miniature golf course. It's just a few minutes' drive to the Disney Village Marketplace. There are 222 guestrooms and 86 suites. The rooms are standard, with two double beds, and the bathrooms are a nice size for the price range. Suites feature a microwave oven and a refrigerator. Recreational activities include two heated pools, a spa, a kiddie pool and children's playground, and a gameroom. The *Courtyard Café* serves a buffet breakfast and an à la carte dinner. Complimentary shuttles are provided to the parks. Room rates range from $65 to $105; suites run from $80 to $130, depending on the season. There are 60 rooms equipped for guests with disabilities. Nonsmoking rooms also are available. *Howard Johnson Park Square Inn*; 8501 Palm Parkway; Box 22818; Lake Buena Vista, FL 32830; 239-6900 (800-635-8684).

EMBASSY SUITES: The 280 suites at this hotel each have a spacious bedroom with either a king-size bed or two double beds; a separate living room with a queen-size sofa bed; dining and kitchen area with a microwave oven, refrigerator, coffeemaker with free coffee and tea; and an extra-large bathroom with two sinks. There also are two remote-control color television sets with cable and in-room movies, and a VCR. There is one restaurant and a deli for lighter fare. The suite price includes a buffet breakfast daily. There also are complimentary evening cocktails from 5:30 P.M. to 7:30 P.M. Recreational amenities include an indoor/outdoor pool, a lighted tennis court, basketball and volleyball courts, a fitness course, and a children's playground. Supervised children's activities are available. There are six rooms equipped for guests with disabilities. Nonsmoking rooms are available. Rates range from $145 to $250, depending on location, season, and view. *Embassy Suites*; 8100 Lake Ave.; Lake Buena Vista, FL 32836; 239-1144 (800-25-SUITE).

DOUBLETREE CLUB: The 167 rooms here are decorated in seafoam green and mauve, and feature either two double beds or a queen-size bed with a single sleep sofa. The bathrooms are small and have only one sink. There is one restaurant, where a buffet breakfast is served for $5 for adults and $3 for children under 12, making this hotel a particularly good value. There's free transportation to WDW, one heated pool, a gameroom, laundry facilties, a kids' playroom, and an exercise room. There are three rooms equipped for guests with disabilities. Nonsmoking rooms are available. Rates range from $69 to $135, depending on the season. *Doubletree Club*; 8688 Palm Parkway; Lake Buena Vista, FL 32836; 239-8500 (800-228-2846).

RADISSON INN: Also located at the Vista Centre, the 200 guestrooms are more spacious than average, but the bathrooms are quite small. Each room has two double beds, a table and two chairs, and most have a fully stocked mini-bar and a balcony. There's a nicely landscaped heated pool with a 25-foot waterslide. There's also a spa, a small playground, a gift shop, and a gameroom. The *Café Flamingo* serves breakfast. There is a complimentary shuttle to WDW. There are ten rooms equipped for travelers with disabilities. Nonsmoking rooms are available. Rates range from $69 to $130, depending on the season. *Radisson Inn*; 8686 Palm Parkway; Lake Buena Vista, FL 32830; 239-8400 (800-333-3333).

COMFORT INN: This very large property is more of a motel than a hotel. The 640 rooms are basic, with two double beds and very small bathrooms. There is one restaurant, two pools (one heated), a gameroom, and gift shop. Free transportation to WDW is provided. Up to three children under 12 eat free when accompanied by two adults. Several rooms are designed for guests with disabilities. Nonsmoking rooms are available. Rates are very reasonable: $39 to $69, depending on the season. *Comfort Inn*; 8442 Palm Parkway; Lake Buena Vista, FL 32830; 239-7300 (800-999-7300).

U.S.-192 Accommodations

The motels along this four-lane divided highway (this stretch of 192 is also known as Irlo Bronson Memorial Highway), which intersects I-4 in the community of Kissimmee, are closer to the WDW main gate than those along Orlando's International Drive, but the area itself is far less attractive. Still, the accommodations here can't be faulted for convenience, and on stays of short duration, that may be a consideration.

HOLIDAY INN—MAIN GATE EAST: Situated three miles from the WDW main gate, this 670-room property has undergone a multi-million dollar renovation. The rooms feature mini-kitchens equipped with microwave ovens, a refrigerator, and a coffeemaker. There also is a VCR in each room. There are two Olympic-size swimming pools, a kiddie pool, two playgrounds, a lighted tennis court and two Jacuzzis. The children's program, Camp Holiday, is a free supervised activity program for children ages 3 to 12. The hours are 8 A.M. to midnight, and guests can leave the property and take along a beeper (for a nominal charge) so they can be reached. The People's Choice Lobby Food Court has six eateries, plus the *Vineyard Café*, where children 12 and under eat free when accompanied by an adult. Three rooms are equipped for travelers with disabilities. Nonsmoking rooms are available. Rates are $56 to $126. *Holiday Inn—Main Gate East*; 5678 Irlo Bronson Memorial Highway; Kissimmee, FL 34746; 396-4488 (800-366-5437).

HYATT ORLANDO: The closest non-Disney-owned resort to the WDW main gate is this large hotel, with some 924 rooms grouped in four clusters of buildings so complexly arranged that it takes some people a couple of days to find their way around. Each guestroom has a color TV set, AM/FM radio, and in-room movie capacity. And there are three tennis courts and a 1.3-mile jogging-and-exercise trail right on the property. The gameroom here stands out, even in a town full of terrific competitors. Each of the four clusters has its own medium-size heated swimming pool and whirlpool, a kiddie pool, and an innovative playground. There are three restaurants and a lounge. Shuttle service to WDW is available for $6 per person. Rates range from $79 to $144. Facilities for travelers with disabilities are available. Nonsmoking rooms are available. *Hyatt Orlando*; 6375 West Irlo Bronson Memorial Highway; Kissimmee, FL 34746; 396-1234 (800-544-7178; or in Florida, 800-331-2003).

KING'S: There are a handful of nonchain establishments on U.S.-192 as you head toward downtown Kissimmee and away from Walt Disney World. This 122-room establishment is among the better ones. Its small rectangular pool sits on the shore of a lake, and rowboats can be borrowed at the motel office (or you can fish from the dock). In addition to standard motel rooms, efficiencies accommodating up to six also are available. Many units have lake views. Rates are reasonable: $30 to $60 for rooms; $50 to $75 for efficiencies. Two rooms are designed for travelers with disabilities. Nonsmoking rooms and efficiencies are available. *King's*; 4836 West Irlo Bronson Memorial Highway; Kissimmee, FL 34746; 396-4762 (800-952-5464).

KNIGHT'S INN: The royal purple, crushed-velvet bedspreads in many rooms of this establishment (down the road from the *Holiday Inn—Main Gate East*) may take some getting used to, but this small hostelry offers a good choice of rooms—standard two double-bed ones; efficiency apartments (fitted out with a bed, a sofa bed, and a completely furnished kitchen); and two royal rooms (equipped with just one bed and a sofa). Nonsmoking units are available in double rooms. The pool is small, but everything is on one story, and you can park right outside your door. Complimentary continental breakfast is served daily. Rates are $40 to $50 for two (no charge for children under 18 sharing their parents' room). The rooms with kitchens are only $3 more. Some rooms are equipped for travelers with disabilities. *Knight's Inn*; 2880 Poinciana Blvd.; Kissimmee, FL 34746; 396-8186 (800-843-5644).

RAMADA RESORT MAIN GATE: Attractive landscaping makes this 391-room establishment, just west of I-4, another very pleasant spot. There are two medium-size heated swimming pools—rectangular to make for good lap swimming, an exercise room and sauna, a pair of lighted tennis courts, and a gameroom. The *Café Terrace* serves family-style breakfasts and dinners daily. Children under ten eat free when accompanied by an adult. There also is a lounge and a deli. Rates are about $50 to $95, depending on the season; rates for the hotel's two suites are $410. Free shuttle service is available to Walt Disney World. The hotel has seven rooms for guests with disabilities. Nonsmoking rooms are available. *Ramada Resort Main Gate*; 2950 Reedy Creek Blvd.; Kissimmee, FL 34746; 396-4466 (800-365-6935).

SHERATON LAKESIDE INN: Located west of I-4 (not far from the *Ramada*), this property has 651 rooms arranged in several buildings around two good-size trapezoidal swimming pools, an L-shaped one, and along the shores of Black Lake, where guests go pedal boating (though swimming is not permitted). Two playgrounds are located poolside, and there are four tennis courts and a good miniature golf course as well. There is a supervised children's program free to hotel guests: Herbie's Kid's Club is open to children ages 5 to 12. There are two restaurants and a lounge. The *Corner Market Deli* is open from 6:30 A.M. to midnight. At the *Greenhouse Restaurant Buffet*, children ten and under eat breakfast and dinner free when accompanied by an adult. The cost, about $82 to $121 per couple (no charge for children under 18), is lower than at the *Hyatt Orlando* and the WDW hotels, and there are enough amenities to make this a fairly good deal. There is a free shuttle to Walt

Disney World. Wide doors and ramps make most of the hotel accessible to travelers in wheelchairs. There also are 17 rooms equipped for guests with disabilities. Nonsmoking rooms are available. *Sheraton Lakeside Inn*; 7769 West Irlo Bronson Memorial Highway; Kissimmee, FL 34747; 239-7919 (800-848-0801).

CAMPING OUTSIDE WALT DISNEY WORLD

The lush, cypress-hung woods of WDW's *Fort Wilderness* are not duplicated at any other Orlando-area campground. But not everyone can get a reservation at *Fort Wilderness*, and in any case, not everyone wants to spend the money. If you fall into one of these groups, consider some of the other local campgrounds. Most offer planned activities, swimming pools, hot showers, and other amenities.

PORT O' CALL: This campground is big, with some 490 sites, and it has an expansive list of activities and facilities: fishing, shuffleboard, a playground, a gameroom, a laundry, evening entertainment (during the winter), and a large heated swimming pool, very much like the one at WDW's own *Polynesian* resort. And you can't beat the location, just four miles east of the main gates. But there's not much shade. Rates are about $18 for two adults and children under 12 during the summer; $25 during the winter; $2 per additional adult per night, including all hookups. Tenters are welcome and pay $16.65. *Port O' Call*; 5195 West Irlo Bronson Memorial Highway; Kissimmee, FL 34746; 396-0110 (800-327-9120, or 800-432-0766 from Florida).

YOGI BEAR'S JELLYSTONE: There are two Yogi Bear campground locations in the WDW area: 8555 West Irlo Bronson Memorial Highway; Kissimmee, FL 34746 (239-4148; 800-776-YOGI) and 9200 Turkey Lake Rd.; Orlando, FL 32819 (351-4394; 800-776-YOGI). The two sites offer similar facilities including a swimming pool and a miniature golf course. Free shuttle service to WDW is available. Rates are $18 for tents without hookups; $23 for water and electricity; and $25 for full hookups. Winter rates are slightly higher. Rates are for two adults and any children under 18. Additional adults cost $3 each per night.

International Drive Accommodations

Many of the best-known motel chains are represented along International Drive, and many restaurant chains also have branches. Most of the facilities on nearby Sand Lake and Kirkman roads are clustered close to their intersections with International Drive. The city's more interesting restaurants are too far away to reach on foot, however, and the cost of shuttle transportation for a family of four is so close to that of renting a car that it seems pointless not to do so.

It's also worth noting that the distance to the WDW main gates from here (you have to figure an hour from the parks to your hotel swimming pool) is such that leaving the WDW for a rest at your hotel—a good idea, especially in the heat of summer—is not always practical unless the parks are open late and you can muster the energy to go early, stay for a few hours, and then return after dinner to savor the nighttime delights of the parks for a few hours more. This takes stamina; young children may not always have it. The traffic along International Drive tends to be very heavy all day, so be sure to add an extra 15 minutes to any schedule.

The area is, however, one of the livelier places to lodge outside WDW. It also is relatively accessible to downtown Orlando (10 to 15 minutes' drive away), and Winter Park (about 20 minutes from parking space to parking space), where there are more than a dozen interesting little shops and nearly as many intriguing restaurants.

A selection of some of the more attractive properties (in a variety of price ranges) follows.

CLARION PLAZA: Adjacent to the Orange County Convention Center, this 810-unit hotel offers oversize guestrooms. In addition to a heated outdoor pool and Jacuzzi, there are a gameroom and two restaurants, including a 24-hour bakery and deli. A babysitting service is available. There is an extensive business center with 60,000 square feet of meeting space. More than 200 rooms are wheelchair accessible and 12 rooms are fully equipped for travelers with disabilities. Nonsmoking rooms are available. Rates range from $99 to $125 for doubles; $200 to $620 for suites. *Clarion Plaza*; 9700 International Dr.; Orlando, FL 32819-8144; 352-9700 (800-366-9700).

DELTA ORLANDO: This lively, 800-room establishment just a block from Universal Studios has facilities for meetings of up to 1,000, but the family trade wasn't forgotten either, and the place is as bright and cheery and appealing as any in the area, especially considering the price. Rooms are arranged in four 4-story buildings. There are three swimming pools—two small round ones and another that is shamrock-shaped (but large enough for swimming laps)—and they all have plenty of palm trees and chairs. There are two tennis courts that are lighted for night play and nine holes of miniature golf. There also are two kiddie pools, three hot tubs, and two saunas. There are three restaurants and a sports bar. Wally's Kids' Club is a children's activity center free to hotel guests. The somewhat secluded location, inside a complex of hotels where the roads are little used, off busy Kirkman Road, makes for good (if unshaded) jogging. The children's playground is nothing out of the ordinary. Doubles are $69 and up, depending on the season (no additional charge for children under 18; $10 per cot; no charge for cribs). This is considerably less than the *Twin Towers* complex nearby, which does a big convention business. (The *Howard Johnson* nearby has some rooms that are less expensive than any offered at the *Delta*, and if price is a prime consideration, it is your best bet.) Pet owners can bring small animals inside. There are 12 rooms equipped for travelers with disabilities. Nonsmoking rooms are available. *Delta Orlando*; 5715 Major Blvd.; Orlando, FL 32819; 351-3340 (800-634-4763).

HOLIDAY INN INTERNATIONAL DRIVE: This 650-room property's 13 tropically landscaped acres are occupied by six buildings— a 14-story tower, a 5-story annex, and four other buildings 2 stories high. There is a free-form pool with a sun deck, a playground, an excellent gameroom that looks appropriately space age, and shuffleboard and volleyball

courts. There are two restaurants where kids under 12 eat free when accompanied by an adult, plus the pleasant *Coral Key Bar & Grille*. Some rooms have a microwave oven, a refrigerator, and a coffeemaker. All rooms have clock radios. Twelve special rooms for travelers with disabilities are available. Nonsmoking rooms are available. Rates for doubles in the hotel are about $99 to $139 (no charge for children 18 and under; rollaways $10). *Holiday Inn International Drive*; 6515 International Dr.; Orlando, FL 32819; 351-3500 (800-465-4329).

ORLANDO MARRIOTT: Located at the corner of Sand Lake Road and International Drive, near the exit to I-4, this is one of the choicest of the lodging spots outside the World. The *Marriott* has three heated outdoor pools—one quite large and dogleg-shaped, another barbell-shaped and relatively small, and the third, Olympic-size—four lighted tennis courts, and a health club. There are three restaurants, including the *Marmalade Tree*, a 24-hour snack bar and *Illusions*, a nightclub and lounge. The 1,076 smartly decorated guestrooms and three suites are arranged in some 16 two-story, peach-colored, stucco-walled "villas" scattered around grounds that are handsomely landscaped with ferns, palms, and other kinds of tropical vegetation. (You'll even find some lagoons, canals, and waterfalls.) Rooms can be opened up to form spacious quarters with one or two bedrooms, living room (or third bedroom), two or three baths, and a kitchenette. Rates are $115 to $155 for doubles. Suites are $250 to $375. Nine rooms specially designed for travelers with disabilities are available. Nonsmoking rooms are available. *Orlando Marriott*; 8001 International Dr.; Orlando, FL 32819; 351-2420 (800-421-8001).

PEABODY ORLANDO: The only sister property to the famed *Peabody* hotel in Memphis, this imposing 27-story, 891-room hostelry is International Drive's most luxurious establish-

ment. Facilities include a double Olympic-size pool, four lighted tennis courts, tennis lessons, a pro shop, a health club with personal trainers, a fitness trail, a gameroom, and aerobics classes. There's also a Children's Hotel on the pool level where adult supervision is provided for the pool, gameroom, and reading room. Then there are the famous *Peabody* ducks, which every morning at 11 A.M. waddle from a private elevator into the enormous lobby, down the red carpet, then settle into a marble fountain—a spectacle that continues to attract hotel guests and locals. They waddle back at about 5 P.M. Each guestroom has a hairdryer, a small television set in the bathroom, nightly turn-down service, and daily newspaper delivery. *Dux* (where no duck is served) is the hotel's signature restaurant. There are two other restaurants as well. The meeting facilities are vast with 54,000 square feet of meeting space. Rates run $180 to $240; $375 to $1,300 for suites. There are 27 rooms specially designed for travelers with disabilities. Nonsmoking rooms are available. *Peabody Orlando*; 9801 International Drive; Orlando, FL 32819; 352-4000 (800-732-2639).

RAMADA FLORIDA CENTER: Comparable to the *Marriott* (described above), this 396-room establishment has a restaurant where kids under 12 eat free with the purchase of an adult meal, and a deli, two large swimming pools (one of them Olympic-size and under an open-air pavilion), a well-kept (but hardly huge) gameroom with about a dozen machines, and a large convention center. This means a certain amount of hubbub that may not appeal to all family vacationers, but the hotel itself is quite pleasant. Rates are $55 to $95; $120 to $350 for suites. No charge for up to three children under 18 sharing accommodations with parents. Cribs and rollaway beds are free, and there are 13 rooms specially designed for travelers with disabilities. Nonsmoking rooms are available. *Ramada Florida Center*; 7400 International Dr.; Orlando, FL 32819; 351-4600 (800-327-1363).

SHERATON WORLD: Particularly attractive and situated off by itself, well south of Sand Lake Road and just a stroll from Sea World, this 800-room establishment has three good-size, heated swimming pools, two children's pools, a gameroom, five lighted tennis courts, a fitness center, supervised children's activity program, and a miniature golf course. The surrounding area is ideal for early-morning jogging. Guestrooms feature a coffeemaker. There also are a restaurant, a deli, and a lounge. There are 41 rooms suitable for travelers with disabilities. Nonsmoking rooms are available. Rates are reasonable: $69 to $125 (no charge for youngsters under 18 when accompanied by an adult). *Sheraton World*; 10100 International Dr.; Orlando, FL 32821; 352-1100 (800-325-3535).

Miscellaneous Accommodations

The following establishments are located outside the U.S.-192 and International Drive areas. Each has appealing features that make it stand out among Orlando-area hostelries.

EMBASSY SUITES: Located near the Convention Center, this establishment features an eight-story atrium with a waterfall and piano lounge, where complimentary breakfast is served in the morning and complimentary cocktails are served between 5 P.M. and 7 P.M. Each of the 246 suites includes a bedroom, living room with a fold-out sofa, dressing area, bathroom, and wet bar, microwave oven, and refrigerator. Guests receive a complimentary deluxe buffet breakfast as well. Recreational facilities include an indoor/outdoor pool, whirlpool, steamroom, sauna, and an exercise center. There are 16 suites equipped for guests with disabilities. Nonsmoking rooms are available. Rates are $99 to $160. *Embassy Suites*; 8250 Jamaican Court; Orlando, FL 32819; 345-8250 (800-327-9797).

GRENELEFE: Located some 22 miles from the WDW main gate, this 1,000-acre resort is a fine destination in its own right with its three 18-hole golf courses, 20 tennis courts, golf and tennis instruction programs, lakefront marina, beach, pools, saunas, Jacuzzis, and 1.7-mile-long fitness course. *Grenelefe* is primarily of interest to those who want to add a visit to Walt Disney World to the beginning or end of a vacation in a country clublike atmosphere that is less oriented to the family trade than WDW's own resorts—not to mention lots less frenetic. The 950-odd rooms here are located in clusters of buildings scattered along winding drives facing the fairways of the golf courses; some are like standard hotel rooms, with two double beds, while one- and two-bedroom parlor suites with fully equipped kitchens also are available. The program of golf instruction is interesting: All instruction includes videotape analysis. Private lessons and golf school including a daily playing lesson are available. There are three restaurants and a lounge. Five rooms are equipped for travelers with disabilities. Nonsmoking rooms are available. Rates range from $95 to $365 for hotel rooms and suites, depending on the season. *Grenelefe Golf and Tennis Resort*; 3200 S.R. 546; Haines City, FL 33844-9732; 813-422-7511 (800-237-9549).

HARLEY OF ORLANDO: Lodging in downtown Orlando puts vacationers close to some of the more interesting local restaurants, and the *Harley*—one of the best among the Greater Orlando-area hotels—is the establishment of choice. You're only a few minutes' drive from Winter Park—a fact best appreciated when, at the end of a long day of sightseeing, you can have a late meal there. And you're only a couple of minutes from *Rosie O'Grady's*, a lively Orlando nightspot. On the other hand, you are not quite as close to Walt Disney World. But driving the 17 miles or so to the WDW main gate early in the day is not difficult. Adults traveling without children will especially enjoy the atmosphere at this hotel, which is one of the few in the Orlando area that doesn't cater primarily to a family crowd. The *Café on the Park*, the hotel's restaurant, is lovely, with its tropical decor and its fine view out over Lake Eola and the municipal fountain at its center. The hotel's swimming pool, which shares the view, also is an especially relaxing place to be. And the guestrooms' handsome decor warrants special mention. Rates are $55 to $85. Some rooms are equipped for travelers with disabilities. Nonsmoking rooms are available. *Harley Hotel of Orlando*; 151 East Washington St.; Orlando, FL 32801; 841-3220 (800-321-2323).

HYATT REGENCY ORLANDO INTERNATIONAL AIRPORT: This 446-room hotel is located right in the Orlando International Airport's main terminal. The lobby has a huge atrium, and there is a full-service business center, a fitness center, a swimming pool, a state-of-the-art amphitheater, and soundproof guestrooms with either indoor balconies or oversize outdoor balconies. *McCoy's* is a transportation-themed restau-

rant and there also is an Italian restaurant. There are 23 rooms equipped for travelers with disabilities. Nonsmoking rooms are available. Rates range from $99 to $195. *Hyatt Regency Orlando International Airport*; 9300 Airport Blvd.; Orlando, FL 32127; 825-1234 (800-233-1234).

LANGFORD: Set on its own tree-shaded grounds, this esteemed 218-room hotel is just off the beaten path in the ritzy community of Winter Park. The Park Avenue shopping district is a block away, but the hubbub of commerce (what little hubbub is allowed in the exclusive shops there) never reaches the guests at *Langford*—even those lounging by the side of the Olympic-size pool. There also is a health spa. It has a dining room, the *Bamboo Room*, which features live entertainment and opportunities for ballroom dancing. Rates are $65 to $75 a night for a single; $75 to $85 for a double. *Langford*; 300 East New England Ave.; Winter Park, FL 32789; 644-3400.

OMNI INTERNATIONAL: A striking, mirrored glass structure, seemingly gift wrapped with a red stripe around its upper floors (the same mirrored glass, but in red), this is a 15-story, 290-room hotel in downtown Orlando. Facilities include a large pool with sundeck and whirlpool, a fitness center, and privileges at a nearby golf course and a tennis and racquetball club. All guestrooms have color television sets with cable hook up, AM/FM clock radios, desks, and at least two phones. There are two restaurants and *Ozone*, one of Orlando's most popular nightspots, is located here. Rates range from $109 to $154; $194 to $594 for suites. There are 68 rooms specially equipped for guests with disabilities. Nonsmoking rooms are available. *Omni International*; 400 West Livingston St.; Orlando, FL 32801; 843-6664 (800-THE-OMNI).

PARK PLAZA: Orlando's closest approximation of a cozy country inn occupies a prominent location on Park Avenue in Winter Park. The guestrooms don't quite measure up to the lobby, but with their thick carpet, subdued color scheme, and polished wooden moldings, they're attractive enough—particularly the two-room suites ($150 nightly), with a sitting area and balcony. Smaller rooms, more suitable for one, could be cramped for two; they're available with parkside views and balcony at $125 nightly or without the view for $85. Continental breakfast in your room is included in the rates. No children under five are permitted—but this is not basically set up for families because of the size of the rooms and bathrooms. (There is an elevator, but there are not any rooms specially designed for travelers with disabilities.) The distance from Walt Disney World, a 45-minute drive or so, makes it a good choice only for those who don't plan to spend a great deal of time in the World. *Park Plaza*; 307 Park Ave. South; Winter Park, FL 32789; 647-1072 (800-228-7220).

SONESTA VILLA RESORT ORLANDO: Something a little different in the Orlando area, this complex features 369 one- and two-bedroom villas. Each beautifully decorated villa features a living room, dining room, one or two bathrooms, and a fully equipped kitchenette. The complex is set on 97 acres facing 300-acre Sand Lake. The hotel offers two tennis courts, 11 whirlpool spas, a swimming pool, health club, three playgrounds, a gameroom, and a free supervised children's program for kids ages 4 to 12. Resort guests also have golf privileges at nearby courses (Cypress Creek, International Golf Club, and Orange Tree). There is one restaurant, a lounge, a gift shop, and meeting space. There's full maid service daily. Rates for a one-bedroom villa are $98 to $145; two-bedroom units are $170 to $285 depending on the season. One two-bedroom villa is equipped for guests with disabilities. *Sonesta Villa Resort Orlando*; 10000 Turkey Lake Rd.; Orlando, FL 32819; 352-8051 (800-SONESTA).

STOUFFER ORLANDO: Located directly across the street from Sea World, this $86-million hotel offers 780 guestrooms and has been designed as a convention facility with a total of 185,000 square feet of meeting space. Each guestroom has individual climate controls, color TV set, clock radio, wet bar, and either two double beds or one king-size bed. One-bedroom suites have a parlor, wet bar, a pull-out sofa, and conference table. The rooms are built around a 65,000-square-foot atrium and are reached by seven glass-enclosed elevators. There are four restaurants, a 24-hour deli, plus a poolside snack bar and two lounges. Recreational facilities include a swimming pool, a Jacuzzi, five lighted tennis courts, a health club, and a professionally staffed children's center. There are 39 rooms equipped for guests with disabilities. Nonsmoking rooms are available. Rates are $159 to $245; $318 to $567 for suites. *Stouffer Orlando*; 6677 Sea Harbor Dr.; Orlando, FL 32821; 351-5555 (800-327-6677).

SHORT-TERM RENTALS

Apartment, condominium, and bed-and-breakfast accommodations can be arranged locally. For availabilities, write Orlando/Orange County Convention and Visitors Bureau; 7208 Sand Lake Road, Suite 300; Orlando, FL 32819; 363-5800.

The Magic Kingdom

The Magic Kingdom is the most special part of the World. Few who have visited it are disappointed, and even the most blasé travelers manage a smile. The sight of the soaring spires of Cinderella Castle, the gleaming woodwork of the Main Street shops, and the crescendo of music that follows the parades never fail to have their effect. Even when the crowds are large and the weather is hot, a visitor who has toured this wonderland dozens of times still can look around and think how satisfying this place is for the spirit.

But the delight that most guests experience upon their first sight of the Magic Kingdom can quickly disappear when disorientation sets in. There are so many nooks and crannies, so many bends to every pathway, and so many sights and sounds clamoring for attention that it's too easy to wander aimlessly and miss the best that the Magic Kingdom has to offer. So we earnestly suggest that you study this chapter before you make your own visit.

Every land has a theme, which is carried through from the hosts' and hostesses' costumes to the food served in the restaurants, the merchandise in the shops, and even the design of the trash bins. Thousands of details contribute to the overall effect; recognizing these touches makes any visit more enjoyable.

And during the next few years at the Magic Kingdom, expect to see a new CircleVision film and a complete Tomorrowland refurbishment.

Magic Kingdom

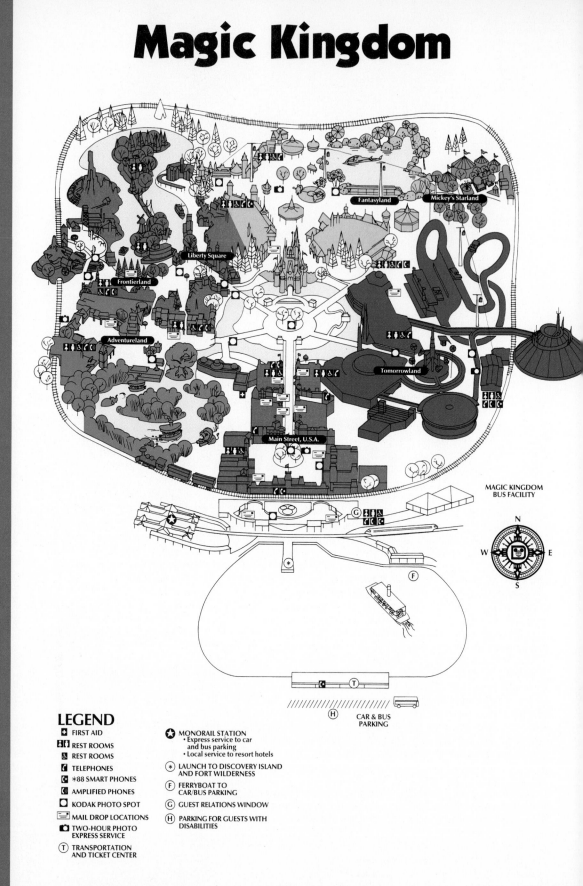

Fantasyland

Mickey's Starland

Liberty Square

Frontierland

Adventureland

Tomorrowland

Main Street, U.S.A.

MAGIC KINGDOM
BUS FACILITY

CAR & BUS
PARKING

N
W · E
S

LEGEND

➕ FIRST AID

🚻 REST ROOMS

♿ REST ROOMS

📞 TELEPHONES

📞 *88 SMART PHONES

📞 AMPLIFIED PHONES

◻ KODAK PHOTO SPOT

✉ MAIL DROP LOCATIONS

📷 TWO-HOUR PHOTO
EXPRESS SERVICE

Ⓣ TRANSPORTATION
AND TICKET CENTER

✪ MONORAIL STATION
• Express service to car
and bus parking
• Local service to resort hotels

✳ LAUNCH TO DISCOVERY ISLAND
AND FORT WILDERNESS

Ⓕ FERRYBOAT TO
CAR/BUS PARKING

Ⓖ GUEST RELATIONS WINDOW

Ⓗ PARKING FOR GUESTS WITH
DISABILITIES

HOW TO GET TO THE MAGIC KINGDOM

From the *Contemporary* resort, the *Polynesian* resort, and the *Grand Floridian* resort: The monorail is the easiest way to go.

From the *Disney Inn*: Take the bus in front of the hotel to the *Polynesian*, walk through the lobby to the second floor, then to the monorail boarding area.

From the *Yacht Club* or *Beach Club* resorts: Take the bus directly to the Magic Kingdom.

From *Port Orleans* and *Dixie Landings*: Take the bus directly to the Magic Kingdom.

From the *Caribbean Beach* resort: Take the bus directly to the Magic Kingdom entrance.

From the *Dolphin* or *Swan* hotels: Take the bus directly to the Magic Kingdom entrance.

From *Wilderness Lodge*: Take the bus or the boat directly to the Magic Kingdom.

From the *Disney Vacation Club*: Take the bus directly to the Magic Kingdom entrance.

From the villas: Board a bus at one of the stops located throughout the villa area and take it to the Magic Kingdom.

From *Fort Wilderness*: Buses make the trip from the campground to the Magic Kingdom; depending on the location of your campsite, it may be more convenient to take the boats at the dock.

From the *All-Star Sports* and *All-Star Music* resorts: Take the bus directly to the Magic Kingdom.

From the Disney Village Marketplace: Take the bus directly to the Magic Kingdom.

From Epcot Center: Take the monorail to the Transportation and Ticket Center (TTC), then transfer to the other monorail or ride a ferry.

From the Disney-MGM Studios Theme Park: Take the bus to the TTC, then transfer for a ferry or the monorail.

From the hotels at Disney Village Hotel Plaza: Take the bus directly to the Magic Kingdom.

From Orlando or Kissimmee: Follow the signs for Walt Disney World on I-4, take the Magic Kingdom turnoff (exit 27), and proceed to the Auto Plaza. Go straight ahead and then turn left into the parking lots. Grayline and Rabbit shuttle buses serve most hotels, but the per person charges are so high relative to the low local car rental rates that it usually makes economic sense to drive. Many of the hotels in the area offer free shuttle service to WDW.

GETTING IN: One of Walt Disney's greatest personal disappointments was the fact that the citrus groves that originally rimmed the Disneyland site in Anaheim, California, soon gave way to unsightly commercial development. Finally, only the berm rimming the park protected it from surrounding eyesores. When planning Walt Disney World, he pledged to prevent a repeat of that situation and set the Magic Kingdom some four miles from the nearest public highway.

From the Walt Disney World exit off highway I-4, it's four miles to the Auto Plaza, from there it's under a mile to the main entrance complex known as the Transportation and Ticket Center (TTC). Even then, Magic Kingdom visitors have not completed their journey: There remains a five-minute ride by ferry across the manmade Seven Seas Lagoon, or a slightly shorter trip by monorail around its shore. Each section of the trip—the drive from the I-4 exit to the Auto Plaza and then to the parking lot, then the lake crossing—serves to heighten the suspense, and by removing guests from the workaday world, to prepare them for the visual delights to come.

TRANSPORTATION COSTS: Parking in the Magic Kingdom lots costs $4 (free to guests at WDW resorts, upon presentation of their ID cards). To ride the bus between Disney Village Hotel Plaza and the Transportation and Ticket Center, and to board the bus between Disney Village Marketplace and the Transportation and Ticket Center, it is necessary to show an ID card from a Hotel Plaza establishment or a WDW resort; all multi-day Passports also provide free use of the buses.

WHEN TO ARRIVE: Especially during the busy summer and holiday seasons—when the highways leading to the Auto Plaza can look like a Los Angeles freeway during rush hour, and when there are long queues at WDW monorails and ferries—it's advisable to plan on reaching the park by 7:30 A.M. or 8 A.M. Eat breakfast at your hotel—or wait and eat inside the park. Or if this just seems too early, wait until later—about 1 P.M.—or even later than that during the seasons when the park is open late. During less congested periods, when the park closes at 7 P.M., plan to arrive around 10 A.M.

PARKING: After passing through the Auto Plaza, drive straight ahead and bear left for the parking lots. Parking attendants will direct you to a spot in one of a dozen areas. Each lot is named for a Disney character—Daisy, Donald, Sneezy, Bashful, Grumpy, Happy, Goofy, Pluto, Chip & Dale, Minnie, Sleepy, and Dopey. Minnie, Sleepy, and Dopey are within walking distance of the TTC; other lots are served continuously by tractor-drawn trams that make periodic stops to pick up and discharge passengers.

Before leaving your car, check the name of your section and your aisle number; there is a spot for noting this information on the back of your parking ticket. Roll up all windows and lock all doors. Also, do not leave any pets in the car! It is against the law in Florida. The Pet Care Kennel—it's air conditioned, far more comfortable for the animal, and far safer—is conveniently located right at the TTC.

Guests who leave the park at midday for their hotels should keep their parking tickets; the tickets are good for re-entry to the parking area throughout the day. Also remember that to re-enter the parks on the same day, you must have your valid ticket or Passport *and* a hand stamp.

FERRY VS. MONORAIL: Once you've bought your admission ticket or Passport and made your way through the TTC turnstiles, it's necessary to decide whether to travel to the Magic Kingdom by ferry or by monorail. (The bus loading area at the Magic Kingdom itself means that guests using WDW transportation can bypass the TTC entirely.) For guests arriving by car or tour bus, the monorails make the trip in a bit less than the five minutes required by the ferries—but the latter often will get you there more quickly during the busier seasons, because long lines can form at the monorails; most people simply don't make the short extra walk to the ferry landing. When there's no line for the monorail, it's your best choice.

Vacationers who use wheelchairs should note that while the monorails are accessible, the ramp leading to the boarding area is a bit steep.

MONEY MATTERS: WDW resort guests who buy their Passports at WDW resorts may charge them to their rooms by using their resort ID cards. At the TTC, cash, traveler's checks, personal checks, MasterCard, Visa, or American Express cards are accepted as payment for all admission media; personal checks must be imprinted with your name and address and must be accompanied by a driver's license and a major credit card (that is, American Express, Visa, MasterCard, Diners Club, or Carte Blanche).

American Express, Visa, and MasterCard are accepted at sit-down restaurants and for merchandise. Traveler's checks and WDW resort identification cards also are accepted. No credit cards are accepted at fast-food eating spots. You must pay in cash or use traveler's checks.

Guests also may want to purchase Disney Dollars, available in one-, five-, and ten-dollar denominations. Disney Dollars are accepted at all Magic Kingdom, Epcot Center, and Disney-MGM Studios Theme Park restaurants, shops, and food stands, and at all WDW resorts. They can be redeemed for greenbacks at any time. Many visitors, however, take at least one home as a souvenir. When purchasing tickets or passports at Walt Disney World ticket locations, guests can request Disney Dollars as change.

ADMISSION: Tickets and Passports are available for one, four, and five days. The Disney organization defines a ticket as admission for one day only; other forms of admission media (for longer periods) are called Passports. One-day tickets may be used at the Magic Kingdom, Epcot Center, or the Disney-MGM Studios Theme Park, but not at more than one site on the same day. Four-day Super Passes and Five-day Super Duper Passes can be used at the Magic Kingdom, Epcot Center, and the Disney-MGM Studios Theme Park on the same day; unlike one-day tickets, they also include unlimited use of the transportation system inside Walt Disney World. The Five-day Super Duper Pass also allows admission to River Country, Typhoon Lagoon, Discovery Island, and Pleasure Island for a seven-day period beginning with the first use of the pass. Guests staying at Walt Disney World resorts can purchase a Be Our Guest Pass valid for the length of their stay. The Be Our Guest Pass offers savings over the Four-Day Super Passes and Five-Day Super Duper Passes, and includes unlimited admission to the Magic Kingdom, Epcot Center, the Disney-MGM Studios Theme Park, Pleasure Island, Typhoon Lagoon, River Country, and Discovery Island for the duration of your stay. Cash, traveler's checks, personal checks (with proper ID), American Express, Visa, and MasterCard can be used to pay for all admission media. Multi-day Passports do not have to be used on consecutive days. **Note:** Old multi-day World Passports are *not* accepted for admission to Disney-MGM Studios Theme Park.

Passports may be purchased at the TTC and at many local resorts and hotels, including WDW establishments. Passports also may be purchased at a branch of The Disney Store or through the Disney Catalog by calling 800-237-5751.

Passports by mail: Send a check or money order payable to Walt Disney World Company in the exact amount plus $2 for handling to:

Walt Disney World;
Box 10030; Lake Buena Vista, FL 32830-0030
Attention: Ticket Mail Order

Remember to include your return address. Allow at least four to six weeks for ticket requests to be processed.

Guided tours: Three- to four-hour guided walking tours of the Magic Kingdom are available (except during some peak seasons). These include the services of a guide and admission to attractions during your tour of all lands in the Magic Kingdom. These tours are terrific for first-time visitors, especially those without a great sense of direction, and the cost is quite reasonable ($5 for adults and $3.50 for children, in addition to the applicable price of admission media). For details call Guest Services (560-6233) or inquire at the Transportation and Ticket Center.

ADMISSION PRICES*

ONE-DAY TICKET
(Restricted to use in the Magic Kingdom only.)

Adult $ 35.90
Child** $ 28.50

FOUR-DAY SUPER PASS
(Valid in all three parks for four days and includes use of WDW transportation system.)

Adult $126.70
Child** $ 99.25

FIVE-DAY SUPER DUPER PASS
(Valid in all three parks for five days, includes use of WDW transportation system, and allows admission to Typhoon Lagoon, River Country, Discovery Island, and Pleasure Island for up to seven days from the first use of the Super Pass.)

Adult 186.15 $174.30
Child** 151.10 $138.40

BE OUR GUEST PASS
(Available to WDW resort guests only. Valid in all three parks, Typhoon Lagoon, Pleasure Island, Discovery Island, and River Country for the duration of stay and includes unlimited use of WDW transportation system.)

Length of Stay	Adult	Child**
3 nights/4 days	$139.44	$109.87
4 nights/5 days	$162.67	$128.84
5 nights/6 days	$183.80	$145.76
6 nights/7 days	$201.76	$160.57
7 nights/8 days	$213.37	$170.09
8 nights/9 days	$223.87	$178.51
9 nights/10 days	$234.42	$186.96
10 nights/11days	$244.98	$195.41

The cost of an **ANNUAL PASSPORT** is $200.60 for adults and $174.25 for children; renewals are $179.40 for adults and $153.05 for children.

Note: Multi-day Passports need not be used on consecutive days.

These prices were correct at press time, but may change during 1994.

*The prices quoted include sales tax.
**3 through 9 years of age

The Lay of the Lands

Not long ago, one Magic Kingdom visitor spent an entire day in Tomorrowland, thinking it was the full extent of the place. To avoid having a similar experience, it's essential to understand the lay of all the lands before you arrive on Main Street.

There are seven sections, or "lands," in the Magic Kingdom—Main Street, U.S.A.; Adventureland; Frontierland; Liberty Square; Fantasyland; Mickey's Starland; and Tomorrowland. The monorail stations and ferry docks at which all guests arrive are just outside the Magic Kingdom gates; just inside them is Town Square, at the head of Main Street, which runs straight to Cinderella Castle. The area in front of the Castle is known as the Central Plaza, or, more aptly, the Hub. It is surrounded by small canals, the Hub Waterways, which are crossed by bridges to enter each of the lands. The first bridge to your left goes to Adventureland; the next, to Liberty Square and Frontierland. On your right, the first bridge heads to Tomorrowland, the second to Fantasyland and Mickey's Starland. The end points of the avenues lead-

ing to the lands are linked by a roadway that is roughly circular, so that the layout of the Magic Kingdom resembles a wheel. All of the attractions, restaurants, and shops are arranged in various buildings along the rim of the wheel and along its spokes.

In theory, it couldn't be simpler; in practice, it's only too easy to get confused because of the many bends and curves in the pathways, the many entrances to each shop and restaurant, and the somewhat angular placement and architecture of many of the buildings. But if you keep mental notes of your own route, losing your bearings becomes fairly difficult. If you still manage to get confused, however, any park employee can help set you straight.

A note on north, south, east, and west: When you stand at the Magic Kingdom entrance and face Cinderella Castle, you're looking north. Main Street is straight ahead, with Fantasyland and Mickey's Starland beyond the Castle. Adventureland, Liberty Square, and Frontierland are to the west. Tomorrowland flanks the Hub on the east.

Main Street, U.S.A.

This is the Disney version of turn-of-the-century small-town Main Streets all over the country—freshly painted, full of curlicued gingerbread moldings and pretty details, and with its baskets of hanging plants and genuine-looking gaslights, a showplace both in the bright light of high noon and after nightfall, when the tiny lights edging all of Main Street's rooflines are flicked on.

What's particularly amazing is that all the variety of furbelows and frills that a real, growing Main Street would have enjoyed have been assimilated into the Disney version. Most of the structures along the thoroughfare are given over to shops, and each one is different, from the wallpaper and layout of displays to the flooring materials, the style of chandeliers, and even the lighting level. Some emporiums are big and bustling, others are relatively quiet and orderly; some are spacious and airy, others are cozy and dark. Floors are made of black-and-white tile or of wide oak planks set in with wooden pegs; some are covered with Victorian-patterned carpets. Where wallpaper is used, it is striped, or gaudily flowered; in contrast, some walls are paneled in subdued mahogany or oak. The effect is far more sophisticated than first-time visitors probably would have imagined, and it doesn't really matter that some of the "wood" is fiberglass.

Inside and outside, maintenance and housekeeping are superb. White-suited sanitation workers patrol the street to pick up litter and quickly shovel up any droppings from the horses who pull the trolley cars from Town Square to the Hub. The pavement, like all in the Magic Kingdom, is washed down every night with fire hoses. There's one crew of maintenance workers whose sole job is to change the little white lights around the roofs; another crew devotes itself to keeping the woodwork painted. As soon as these people have worked their way as far as the Hub, they start all over again at Town Square. Epoxy, acrylic, and other varieties of paints are used, depending on the area to be painted. The greenish, horse-shaped cast-iron hitching posts are repainted 20 times a year on the average—and totally scraped down each time. It's no wonder the professional painters who visit here marvel at the quality of work they see.

Visitors from outside the United States find all these details so fascinating that it takes them a good deal longer than the 40 minutes spent by the average guest to get from one end of Main Street to the other. There are only four real "attractions" along Main Street, and they are relatively minor compared to the really big deals such as Tomorrowland's Space Mountain and Frontierland's Big Thunder Mountain Railroad and Splash Mountain. But each and every shop has its own quota of merchandise that is meant as much for fun and show as for sale—the monster masks at the House of Magic, for instance, or the large Hummel figurines at Uptown Jewelers. It's also entertaining to stand and watch the host or hostess demonstrating tricks at the House of

Magic and the cooks stirring up batches of peanut brittle at the Confectionery. The windows at the Emporium also are worth a look.

While walking along the street, note the names on the second-story windows. Above Crystal Arts are the names of Roy Disney, Walt's brother, and Patty Disney; above the Shadow Box, that of Dick Nunis, Chairman of Walt Disney Attractions. Above the House of Magic are the names of Ted Crowell, WDW's former Vice President of Facilities Support, who, among other things, was responsible for maintenance and for the World's own electric generating plants, and John de Cuir, the Disney artist in charge of the production of the paintings filmed for The Hall of Presidents show. Card Walker, the "practitioner of Psychiatry and Justice of the Peace" mentioned nearby, is the company's former Chairman of the Executive Committee. Other names, as well as those on signs elsewhere in the Magic Kingdom, also are those of real people connected with the company.

Finally, some advice: Before heading toward the Castle, stop at City Hall and inquire about the times and places where live entertainment is scheduled to take place all around the park that day and night. Also, do your shopping in the early afternoon, rather than at day's end when the shops are normally jammed; purchases can be stored in lockers under the Walt Disney World Railroad's depot or, in the case of very large items, behind the desk at City Hall.

PENNY ARCADE: Scarcely a motel in the area lacks its blipping, bleeping, squeaking room full of electronic games; the one at the *Contemporary* resort ranks among the largest in the country. The Magic Kingdom also has its gameroom—but here on Victorian Main Street, in addition to the modern machines, there are authentic old-time games—a Kiss-O-Meter, tests of strength, and an antique football game.

In addition, in the center of the front section of the arcade, there are a number of machines that show very early "moving pictures"—that is, stacks of cards on a roller that can be turned to flip the cards and thereby "animate" the images they contain. There are two types of viewing devices—Mute-o-scopes, first introduced around 1900, whose rollers must be turned by hand, and Cail-o-scopes, developed about a decade later, which are turned automatically. Both of these are worth your while. Most stories here are comedies; the humor is broad and slapstick—good for at least a smile (if not a roar) and as an amusing

comment on the changing ideas about what tickles a funny bone. On the Cail-o-scopes, there are such stories as *Yes, We Have No Bananas*, in which a suitor slips on a banana peel and is ridiculed; *Tough Competition*, in which sailors come to blows over a pretty girl; *Texas Rangers*, where the good guy lassoes the robber; and *Run Out of Town*, in which one unfortunate man has paint dumped on him, falls into a manhole, is knocked over by a car, sits on a freshly painted bench, and knocks over a paint bucket—all in a single day. During *A Raid On A Watermelon Patch*, two fellows do and are discovered. *Oh Teacher* concerns the antics of a teacher's pest. *Brigitte On A Bike* shows a real sourpuss taking a tumble; it might be subtitled, "Or The Trials of Riding in a Long Skirt." Particularly interesting is *Captain Kidd's Treasure*, in which a pirate lass shows knees, bare arms, and ankles. The display of skin—which would rate a solid *G* today—must have looked very risqué three-quarters of a century ago.

Among the Cail-o-scopes, the best is probably *Expecting*, which is a funny cartoon about people waiting. Some of the others also are worth a peek—and the cost is only a penny.

While you're looking, you can be pumping the big coin-operated antique PianOrchestra against the Arcade's south wall; its ringing tones almost block out the clatter and clacks of the pinball and electronic games machines (at least when it's not out of order; it's as temperamental as a prima donna, and even the ministrations of the resident musical-instrument caretaker can't always keep it singing). Before leaving, also note the paintings that hang on the walls. They depict a roadster race, the Wright Brothers and an early flying machine, a Victorian-era amusement arcade, and a rural Illinois river valley scene. All of these were created for the film that precedes the chief executives' roll call in Liberty Square's Hall of Presidents.

MAIN STREET CINEMA: The beauty of this prominent attraction on Main Street is that most vacationers bypass it in their rush to get to Space Mountain in Tomorrowland or Pirates of the Caribbean in Adventureland, or other thrill-a-minute attractions. Yet on a steamy summer afternoon—when everyone else is standing in line for these blockbusters—this air conditioned theater is a fine place to relax. Vintage Disney cartoons are shown simultaneously. *Steamboat Willie* is featured. It is the first sound cartoon, in which a little mouse named Mickey, making his film debut, meets Minnie and then makes beautiful music on (among other instruments) a cow's udder, a feat that drew one of the film's biggest laughs at the time of its November 1928 release. (By the way, Mickey was originally scheduled to be named Mortimer, but Mrs. Disney convinced Walt to make the change.)

WALT DISNEY WORLD RAILROAD: The best introduction to the layout of the Magic Kingdom, the 1 1/2-mile 15-minute journey on this rail line is as much a must for the first-time visitor as it is for railroad buffs. For the former, it offers an excellent orientation, as it passes through Adventureland and Frontierland and skirts Fantasyland, Mickey's Starland, and Tomorrowland. The 1928 steam engine happens to be exactly the same age as Mickey Mouse. Aficionados of railroadiana may remember that Disney himself was among their number and perhaps, during the early years of television, saw films of him circling his own backyard in a one-eighth-scale train, the *Lilly Belle*, named for his wife. The Walt Disney World Railroad also has a *Lilly Belle* among its quartet of locomotives. All of these were built in the United States around the turn of the last century and later were taken down to Mexico to haul freight and passengers in the Yucatan, where Disney scouts found them in 1969. The United Railways of Yucatan was using them to carry sugarcane.

Brought north once again, they were completely overhauled, and even the smallest parts were reworked or replaced. New boilers and fiberglass cabs were built, along with new tenders and tanks. (The cast-iron wheels, side rods, frames, and parts of the hardware, however, are original.) Originally designed to burn coal or wood, then converted by the Mexi-

cans to use oil, they now consume diesel fuel—considerably less dirty than either of the former fuels.

The *Lilly Belle* is a Mogul-type engine, with two small front wheels and six drive wheels, while the *Roy O. Disney* is an American Standard eight-wheeler (with four small wheels forward and four drive wheels), and the *Walter E. Disney* and the *Roger E. Broggie* (named for a Disney Imagineer who shared Walt Disney's enthusiasm for antique trains) are both ten-wheelers, with four small forward wheels and six large drive wheels.

MAIN STREET VEHICLES: A number of these can be seen traveling up and down Main Street—horseless carriages and jitneys patterned after turn-of-the-century vehicles (but fitted out with Jeep transmissions and special mufflers that make the putt-putt-putting sound); a spiffy scarlet fire engine, which can be seen in the Firehouse adjoining City Hall when not in operation; and a troop of trolleys drawn by Belgians and Percherons, two strong breeds of horses that once pulled plows in Europe. These animals—aged between six and ten, weighing in at about a ton each, and shod with plastic (easier on their feet)—pull the trolley the length of Main Street about two dozen times during each of their three to four working days; afterward, they're sent back to their homes at the barn at the *Fort Wilderness* campground.

CINDERELLA CASTLE

Just as the courtly little mouse named Mickey stands for all the joy and merriment in the whole of Walt Disney World, the many-spired Cinderella Castle, childhood's storybook castle made real, represents the hopes and dreams of those youthful years when anything seems possible.

This Castle is different from Disneyland's Sleeping Beauty Castle: Measuring some 180 feet in height, the Florida castle is more than 100 feet taller; and with its slender towers and lacy filigree work, it's also more graceful, taking its inspiration not only from the architecture of 12th- and 13th-century France, the country where Charles Perrault's classic fairy tale originated, but also from the mad Bavarian King Ludwig's castle at Neuschwanstein, and from the designs prepared some three decades ago for the motion picture version of Perrault's story—and the imaginations of a whole troupe of creative Disney Imagineers who have collectively spent several lifetimes turning fantasies into reality.

Unlike real European castles, this one is not made of granite, but of steel beams, fiberglass, and some 500 gallons of paint. There are no dungeons underneath it, but rather service tunnels for the Magic Kingdom's day-to-day operations. In the Castle's upper reaches there are broadcast facilities, security rooms, and the like; toward the top, there's the apartment originally meant for members of the Disney family (but never occupied).

When mounting the curving staircase to *King Stefan's Banquet Hall*, the parapet-level restaurant, or when passing through the Castle's main gateway—or as seen by night from the *Contemporary* resort's observation deck, with fireworks exploding all around those slender towers—the Castle looks as if it had come straight out of some never-never land of make-believe.

The mosaic murals: The elaborate murals in the five panels beneath the Castle's archway-entrance rank as one of the true wonders of the World. Measuring some 15 feet high and 10 feet wide, these creations of the Disney artist Dorothea Redmond, crafted by the mosaicist Hanns-Joachim Scharff, tell the familiar story of a little cinder girl, a hard-hearted stepmother, two ugly step-

sisters, a fairy godmother, a pumpkin transformed, a handsome prince, a certain glass slipper, and one of childhood's happiest happily-ever-afters, using a million bits of Italian glass in some 500 different colors, plus real silver and 14-karat gold. The renderings of the step-sisters and of the many small woodland animals are particularly faithful to images from the Disney film; but every passerby has favorite sections. Don't fail to stop and look.

Coats of arms: The one above the Castle on the north wall belongs to the Disneys. Others belonging to assorted Disney executives hang in the waiting hall just inside the door to *King Stefan's*; the hostess keeps a book behind the desk that details which belong to whom, for any interested party to see. Some of the same names show up as on the second-story windows of the Main Street shops.

Adventureland

Adventureland seems to have even more atmosphere than the other lands. That may be a result of its neat separation from the rest of the Magic Kingdom, by the bridge over Main Street on the one end, and by a gallerylike structure where it merges with Frontierland on the other; or possibly it's because of the abundance of landscaping. There are Canary Island date palms, the small Cape Sable palms, as well as pygmy date species, and more. On the Adventureland Bridge alone, visitors will see Cape honeysuckle from South Africa, flame vines from Mexico, bougainvillea from Brazil, Chinese hibiscus, hanging sword ferns, spider plants, and Australian tree ferns, to name just a few.

As for the architecture, even though it derives from such diverse areas as the Caribbean, Polynesia, and Southeast Asia, there's a strong sense of being in a single place, a nowhere-in-particular that is both exotic and distinctly foreign, smacking of island idylls and tropical splendor. Shops offer imports from India, Thailand, Hong Kong, Africa, and the Caribbean islands. The *Adventureland Veranda* serves food cooked in the Magic Kingdom's most exotic style (never mind that it's simple Chinese fare).

Strolling away from Main Street, there is the sound of the beating of drums, the squawk of a couple of parrots, the regular boom of a cannon. Paces quicken. And the wonders soon to be encountered do not disappoint.

TROPICAL SERENADE: The first of the Audio-Animatronics attractions, the one that laid the foundation for attractions such as "Great Moments With Mr. Lincoln" at the 1964-1965 New York World's Fair, this one, introduced at Disneyland in 1963, features four emcees—José, Michael, Pierre, and Fritz—plus some 225 birds, flowers, and tiki god statues singing and whistling up a tropical storm with such animation that even the most blasé folks can't help but smile.

PIRATES OF THE CARIBBEAN: One of the very best of the Magic Kingdom's adventures, this cruise through a series of sets depicting a pirate raid on a Caribbean island town is a Disneyland original added to WDW's Magic Kingdom, in revised form, because of popular demand. Here there are flowerpots that explode and mend themselves, drunken pigs whose legs actually twitch in the porkers' soporific contentment, chickens that look for all the world like the real thing (even when seen at close range); the observant will note that the leg of one swashbuckler, dangled over the edge of a bridge, is actually hairy.

Each pirate's face has remarkable personality, and the rendition of "Yo-Ho-Yo-Ho"—the attraction's theme song—makes what is actually a rather brutal scenario into something that comes across as good fun. Before entering the queue area, be sure to stop and give a nod to the parrot, dressed in the pirate costume, near the Pirates of the Caribbean sign.

SWISS FAMILY TREEHOUSE: "Everything we need right at our fingertips" was how John Mills, playing the father in Disney's 1960 rendition of the classic novel *Swiss Family Robinson*, described the treehouse that he and two of his three sons constructed to house the family after the ship transporting them to America was wrecked in a storm. When given a chance—several adventures later—to leave the island, all but one son decided to stay on. That decision is not hard to understand after a tour of the Magic Kingdom's version of the Robinsons' banyan-tree home. This is everybody's idea of the perfect treehouse, with its many levels and many comforts—patchwork quilts, lovely mahogany furniture, candles stuck in abalone shells, even running water in every room. (The system is ingenious.)

The Spanish moss draping the branches is real; the tree itself—unofficially christened *Disneyodendron eximus*, which translates roughly as "out-of-the-ordinary Disney tree"—was constructed by the props department. Some statistics: The roots, which are con-

crete, poke 42 feet into the ground; and some 800,000 leaves and flowers (vinyl) grow on 600-odd branches, which stretch some 90 feet in diameter. "Boy, Dad sure went out on a limb for that one," quipped a Disney prop worker's son on hearing of his father's task.

JUNGLE CRUISE: Inspired in part by the 1955 documentary *The African Lion*, this ten-minute cruise adventure is one of the crowning achievements of Magic Kingdom landscape artists for the way it takes guests through landscapes as diverse as a Southeast Asian jungle, the Nile valley, the African veldt, and an Amazon rain forest. Along the way, passengers encounter zebras and giraffes, impalas, lions, vultures, and headhunters; they see elephants bathing and tour a Cambodian temple—and listen to the amusing spiel delivered by the skipper. For most passengers, this is all just in fun. Gardeners, however, are especially impressed by the variety of species coexisting in such a small area. To keep some of the more sensitive of subtropical specimens alive, 100 gas-fired heaters and electric fans concealed in the rocks pump hot air into the jungle at the rate of 25 million BTUs per hour when temperatures fall to 36° F. This adventure, which is best enjoyed by daylight, is one of the Magic Kingdom's most popular attractions, and it does tend to be crowded from late morning until late afternoon, so plan accordingly.

THE MAGIC KINGDOM

Frontierland

With the Rivers of America lapping up at its borders and Big Thunder Mountain rising toward the rear, this re-creation of the American Frontier encompasses the area from New England to the Southwest, from the 1770s to the 1880s. Hosts and hostesses wear denim, calf-length cutoffs, long skirts, or similar garb. Additionally, the shops, restaurants, and attractions have unpainted barn siding or stone or clapboard walls, and outside there are a few of the kind of wooden sidewalks down which Marshal Matt Dillon used to stride.

Near *Pecos Bill Café*, the landscape seems desertlike (even on humid summer days), with mesquite providing shade and Peruvian pepper trees nearby; the latter's twisted branches boast clusters of bright-red berries in fall and winter. Jerusalem thorns blossom with sweet-smelling yellow flowers in the spring. Century plants and Spanish bayonets also can be seen. Farther down the Frontierland avenue, slash pines provide some shade, along with other evergreens of a variety known as cajeput, which can be recognized by its spongy, light-colored bark and white flowers.

DIAMOND HORSESHOE JAMBOREE: The half-hour-long show presented in this re-creation of a western dance hall saloon is the kind of thing that makes sophisticated folk laugh in spite of themselves. The jokes range from corny to absolutely preposterous, yet seldom fall flat, thanks to the enthusiastic, energetic efforts of the talented crew of singers and dancers who perform here several times each day. Reservations are necessary, and must be made in person at the reservation podium outside Disneyana Collectibles on Main Street on the morning of the day of the performance. Since they are dispensed on a first-come, first-served basis, it's essential to show up within an hour of park opening. Those who arrive too late may be able to snag a cancellation by showing up at the door a half hour or so before seating time, which is 45 minutes before the entertainment begins; but you can't count on it.

FRONTIERLAND SHOOTIN' ARCADE: Silver bullets have given way to infrared beams at the completely electronic shooting arcade. Genuine Hawkins 54-caliber buffalo rifles have been refitted, and when an infrared beam strikes any of the 97 reactive targets, a humorous result is triggered. The arcade is set in an 1850s town in the Southwest Territory. Gun positions overlook Boothill, a town complete with bank, jail, hotel, and cemetery. Struck tombstones rise, sink, spin, or change their epitaphs; hit the cloud and a ghost rider gallops across the sky; a bull's-eye on a gravedigger's shovel causes a skull to pop out of the grave. Sound effects—howling coyotes, creaking bridges, and the shooting guns—are created by a digital audio system. Note that Passports do *not* include use of the arcade, and there is an additional charge here.

COUNTRY BEAR JAMBOREE: An occasional determined sophisticate will remain impervious to the charms of this country-and-western hoedown in Frontierland's big stone-walled Grizzly Hall. But most guests, with the exception of the 10-to-18 crowd, call it one of the Magic Kingdom's best attractions. Ostensibly concocted by one Ursus H. Bear after an especially inspiring hibernation season, it is performed mainly by a cast of close to 20 life-size Audio-Animatronics bruins, with results more believable than almost anywhere else in the park, outside the Hall of Presidents. Henry, the debonair, seven-foot-tall master of ceremonies, introduces the Five Bear Rugs (a C&W plinking group made up of Zeke, Zeb, Ted, Fred, and Tennessee); a big-bodied, tiny-headed pianist named Gomer; the girthy Trixie, the Tampa Temptation, sings "Tears Will Be the Chaser for Your Wine"; Teddi Barra floats down from the ceiling crooning "He Doesn't Know the Heart He's Breakin'"; Bubbles, Bunny, and Beulah, in sweet harmony, sing "All the Guys that Turn Me On Turn Me Down"; and assorted other bruins, including Terrence, the shank shaker; Wendell, the overbearing baritone; Liver Lips McGrowl; and Big Al, one of the few Audio-

Animatronics figures with a following great enough to create a demand for his image on postcards and stuffed animals.

Since the Country Bear Jamboree is a popular attraction, lines can get quite long during busy periods. They usually seem longer than they are, however, and it's worth noting that huge bunches of people are admitted together so that once a line starts moving, it dwindles fast. Seats in the rear of the house are just as good as seats toward the front, if not a little better.

TOM SAWYER ISLAND: This small landfall in the middle of the Rivers of America has hills to scramble up, a working windmill, Harper's Mill, with an owl in the rafters and a perpetually creaky waterwheel, and a pitch-black (and scary) cave.

There are oaks, pines, and sycamores here, red maples and elms, and a number of small plants—dwarf azaleas; firethorn, an evergreen shrub that sprouts bright-red berries in December; Brazilian pepper trees, which also grow berries at the end of the year; and American holly plants, which acquire their masses of berries in fall. Dirt paths wind this way and that, and it's easy to get disoriented, especially the first time around. There also are two bridges—an old-fashioned swing bridge and a so-called barrel bridge, which floats atop some lashed-together steel drums. When one person bounces, everybody lurches—and all but the most chicken-hearted laugh. Both bridges can easily be missed, so keep your eyes peeled and ask for directions if the path eludes you.

Across the bridge is Fort Sam Clemens, where there is a guardhouse in which the figure of a ratty-looking drunk is Audio-Animatronically snoring off his last bender, accompanied by a mangy-looking dog, chickens, and a pair of horses. On the second floor of the fort, there are close to a dozen air guns for youngsters to trigger into ceaseless cacophony. This area offers a fine view across the Rivers of America to Big Thunder Mountain Railroad. Keep poking around and you'll find the twisting, dark, and occasionally scary escape tunnel out of the fort. Walk along the pathway on the banks of the Rivers of America, and you're back at the bridges.

The whole island seems as rugged as backwoods Missouri, and probably as a result, it actually feels a lot more remote than it is, enough to be able to provide some welcome respite from the bustle of the Magic Kingdom. One particularly pleasant way to pass an hour here is over lemonade and a sandwich on the porch at *Aunt Polly's Landing*. While adults in the party are giving their feet some rest, watching the sternwheelers plying the Rivers of America, kids can go out and burn up some more energy. Restrooms are located at the main raft landing. Note that this attraction closes at dusk.

SPLASH MOUNTAIN: As its name implies, guests are escorted on a waterborne journey through brightly painted backwoods swamps and bayous, down waterfalls, and, finally, over the top of a steep spillway, hurtling them from the peak of the mountain to a briar-filled pond five stories below. Splash Mountain is based on the animated sequences in Walt Disney's 1946 film, *Song of the South*. The scenery is very entertaining and there is a storyline that follows Brer Rabbit through a variety of exploits as he tries to reach his "laughing place." It's tough for a first-timer to take in all the details, since the tension of waiting for the big drop is all-consuming.

There are three tame watery drops during the course of the trip, all leading up to the big fall—a 52-foot drop at a 45-degree angle at a top speed of 40 miles per hour—the steepest flume in the world. It is a bit terrifying at the top but once back on the ground it seems most riders can't wait for another trip. (Even though you may get drenched!) By the second or third time around, it's possible to relax and enjoy the interior design and also to take in the spectacular views of the Magic Kingdom from the top of the mountain.

Splash Mountain's designers not only borrowed the attraction's characters and color-saturated settings from *Song of the South*, they also included quite a bit of the film's Academy Award-winning music. As a matter of fact, the song in the attraction's finale, "Zip-A-Dee-Doo-Dah," has become something of a Disney anthem over the years.

Note that you must be at least 42 inches tall to ride Splash Mountain.

BIG THUNDER MOUNTAIN RAILROAD:
This attraction, located partly inside the 197-foot-high redstone mountain that pokes into the sky behind the Tom Sawyer Island rafts landing, is something of a cross between Tomorrowland's Space Mountain (an honest-to-goodness roller coaster) and Adventureland's Pirates of the Caribbean (a tame but very exciting and scenic boat tour). As any true coaster buff could tell you, this three-minute ride is a relatively mild one, despite the posted warnings; the thrills are there, but the experience is not so extreme that you'll be left with a determination never to subject yourself to it again. The pleasant rush of adrenaline that comes with some of the swoops and curves, as well as the attractive scenery along the 2,780 feet of track, gives most visitors the opposite reaction. There are the bats, the phosphorescent pools and waterfalls, and best of all, Tumbleweed, the flooded mining town (best seen to your left during one of the uphill climbs). There are some 20 Audio-Animatronics figures here—including real-looking chickens, donkeys, possums, a goat, a longjohn-clad resident spinning through the flood in a bathtub, and a rainmaker whose name is Professor Cumulus Isobar. Careful observers will note a party still going on in a not-yet-sunken second-story room of a saloon, whose weathered look (like that of some other sections of the Magic Kingdom) derives from a judicious mixture of plant food and paint. The $300,000 worth of real antique mining equipment sprinkled around the attraction's 2 1/2 acres—an ore-hauling wagon, a double-stamp ore crusher, a wooden mining flume, and an old ball mill used to extract gold from ore—were picked up at auctions all over the Southwest, at something less than bargain prices, since the high price of gold and the resulting profitability of small-scale mining operations had boosted demand by genuine miners themselves. As with Pirates of the Caribbean, every trip yields new sights, and even a second or third trip in a matter of days is as amusing as the first time.

The summit of the mountain, whose name refers to an old Indian legend about a certain sacred mountain in Wyoming that would thunder whenever white men took out its gold, is entirely Disney-made. It was in the planning for some 15 years and under construction for 2, and required some 650 tons of steel, 4,675 tons of cement, and 16,000 gallons of paint; hundreds of rockmakers contributed, applying multiple coats of cement and paint, throwing stones at the mountain, kicking dirt on it, and banging on it with sticks and picks to make the whole thing resemble the rocks of Monument Valley, Utah—that is, as if Mother Nature herself had created it. Design was largely by Tony Baxter, a Disney Imagineer who started his career with a job at a Disney ice cream parlor while in high school. (His name now can be seen on one of the doors in the unloading and boarding area.) The area inside the mountain that does not house the tunnels of the ride itself is occupied by the machinery that makes the ride go—pumps, electronic equipment, and part of the computer that runs the show. The total cost was about $17 million, which, give or take a few million, was as much as it cost to build all of California's Disneyland in 1955. Incidentally, that park's version of the attraction, which opened in 1979, is similar, but lacks the flash-flood scene and a few other details. You must be at least 40 inches tall to ride.

Note on timing: Certain aspects of the ride are more convincing after dark. Optimally, you should experience it first at night, then have a second go-round by the light of day. Since the trip is extremely popular, plan to take it in during the 9 P.M. running of SpectroMagic (in season), or just before park closing, when the lines are generally shorter. By day, go during the early morning hours.

Liberty Square

The transition between Frontierland on one side and Fantasyland on the other is so smooth that it's hard to say just when you arrive, yet ultimately there's no mistaking the location. The small buildings are clapboard or brick and topped with weather vanes; the decorative moldings are Federal or Georgian in style; the glass is sometimes wavy, and there are flower boxes in shop windows, brightly colored gardens, neatly trimmed borders of Japanese yew, and masses of azaleas in a number of varieties—George Tabor azaleas, which blossom white and pink in March and May; redwing-hybrid Kurume azaleas, which boast red blossoms in winter; southern charms, which from February to April turn rosy pink; and more. There are a number of good shops, most notably the Yankee Trader, and Olde World Antiques; plus two of the park's most popular attractions—The Haunted Mansion and The Hall of Presidents—and the *Liberty Tree Tavern*, one of the few Magic Kingdom restaurants to offer table service, and one of just three to take reservations. Liberty Square also is home of one of the most delightful nooks in all the Magic Kingdom—the small, secluded area just behind the Silversmith Shop. There are tables with umbrellas, plenty of benches, and big trees to provide shade—and the sound of the crowds seems a million miles away.

THE LIBERTY TREE: Not an attraction per se, this live oak (*Quercus virginiana*)—which recalls trees all over the colonies, on which the Sons of Liberty used to hang lanterns after the Boston Tea Party of 1773—was found on the southern edge of WDW's 27,400 acres, and then moved to its present site in one of the more complex of the Magic Kingdom's landscaping operations. Since the tree was so large (weighing an estimated 35 tons, with a root ball that measured some 18 by 16 by 4 feet around), lifting it by cable was out of the question—the cable would have sliced through the bark and into the trunk's tender cambium layer, injuring the tree. Instead, two holes were drilled horizontally through the sturdiest section of the trunk; the holes were fitted with dowels, and a 100-ton crane lifted the tree by these rods, which were subsequently removed and replaced with the original wood plugs. Unfortunately, the wood plugs had become contaminated, and a serious infection set in and rotted out a portion of the inside of the trunk. To save the tree, the plugs again were removed, the holes were filled with cement, the diseased areas were cleaned out, and a young *Quercus virginiana* was grafted onto the tree at its base, where it grows even today. Careful observers will be able to spot the plugs and the portions of the trunk that were damaged. The 13 lanterns hanging on the branches represent the 13 original states.

THE HALL OF PRESIDENTS: This is not one of those laugh-a-minute attractions, like Pirates of the Caribbean or the Country Bear Jamboree; it's long on patriotism and short on humor. But the detail certainly is fascinating. After a film (presented on a sweeping 70-mm screen) discusses the importance of the Constitution from the time of its framing through the dawn of the Space Age, the curtain goes up on what some guests have mistakenly called the "Hall of Haunted Presidents." A portion of today's Hall of Presidents presentation derives from the Disney-designed Illinois Pavilion's presentation, "Great Moments with Mr. Lincoln" from New York's 1964–1965 World's Fair.

At the Magic Kingdom show, Lincoln's remarks are prefaced by a roll call of all 42 American presidents, through Bill Clinton. Each chief executive responds with a nod; careful observers will note the others swaying and nodding, fidgeting, and even whispering to each other during the proceedings.

Costumes were created by two famous film tailors who were coaxed out of retirement. Not only are the styles those of the period in which each president lived, but so are the tailoring techniques and the fabrics. Some had to be specially woven for the purpose. Each figure has at least one change of clothes, and jewelry, shoes, hair texture, and even George Washington's chair are all re-created exactly as indicated by the results of careful research using paintings, diaries, newspapers, and government archives. Perceptive viewers should be able to see the braces on Franklin Delano Roosevelt's legs. The effect is so lifelike that the figures look almost real, even at close range.

The paintings in the waiting area outside the hall are just a few of the 85 created for the pre-roll call film—in the style of the period during which the event depicted took place—by a dozen artists working under the direction of the Academy Award-winning artist John De Cuir. Other paintings can be seen in Main Street's City Hall and Penny Arcade, and Liberty Square's *Liberty Tree Tavern* and *Columbia Harbour House*.

THE HAUNTED MANSION: Visitors who expect to get the daylights scared out of them inside this big old house, modeled on those built by the Dutch in the Hudson River Valley in the 18th century, will be a tad disappointed. In deference to the number of small children and other easily frightened souls who tour the Magic Kingdom every day, the most terrifying parts were expunged and a pleasant voiceover keeps things from getting too serious. Even then, the experience that's left is among the Magic Kingdom's best. Special effect is piled upon special effect, and just when you think you've seen it all, there's something new: the raven who appears over and over again; bats eyes on the wallpaper; the plaque that reads "Tomb, Sweet Tomb"; the suit of armor that comes alive; the horrible transparent specter in the attic; the terrified cemetery watchman and his mangy mutt; the ghostly teapot pouring ghostly tea; the difficult-to-identify flying objects above the image in the crystal ball.

In the portrait hall (which you enter after passing through the mansion's front doors), it's amusing to speculate: Is the ceiling moving up—or is the floor descending? It's one way here, and the other way at the Haunted Mansion in California's Disneyland.

At both places, one of the biggest jobs of the maintenance crews is not cleaning up, but keeping things nice and dirty. Since each mansion's attic is littered with some 200 trunks, chairs, dress forms, shovels, harps, rugs, and assorted other knickknacks, it requires a good deal of dust. This is purchased from a West Coast firm by the five-pound bagful and distributed by a device that looks as if it were meant to spread grass seed. Local legend has it that enough has been used since the park's 1971 opening to bury the mansion. Cobwebs are bought in liquid form and strung up by a secret process.

When waiting to enter, note the amusing inscriptions on the tombstones in the overgrown cemetery.

LIBERTY SQUARE RIVERBOAT: The *Richard F. Irvine*, built in drydock at WDW and named for a key Disney designer, is a real steamboat. Its boiler turns water into steam, which is then piped to the engine, which drives the paddle wheel that propels the boat. It is not the real article in one respect, however: It moves through the half-mile-long, seven-foot-deep Rivers of America on an underwater rail. The ride is more pleasant than thrilling, but it's good for beating the heat on steamy afternoons. En route, a variety of props create a sort of Wild West effect: moose, deer, cabins on fire, and the like. (Best seats are in front or rear and center, so that you can see both riverbanks equally well.)

The trees framing the entrance to Riverboat Landing, which bear crinkly blossoms of bright red most of the year, are crepe myrtles.

MIKE FINK KEEL BOATS: Named for a riverboat captain who lived from 1770 to 1823 and once met up with Davy Crockett, the pair of squat, oddly shaped Mike Fink Keel Boats—*Bertha Mae* and the *Gullywhumper*—also traverse the Rivers of America. Since they take in the same scenery as the Liberty Square Riverboat (from a different angle), you wouldn't want to do both in the same day. Note that this attraction closes at dusk.

Mickey's Starland

A stage show starring Mickey Mouse, Bonkers, and characters from "Goof Troop," "Tale Spin," and "Dark Wing Duck," the popular Disney afternoon cartoons, is ranked by youngsters as WDW's best attraction. Adults will find it entertaining as well. The best way to get to Mickey's Starland is aboard the Walt Disney World Railroad.

Mickey's house is here, with his balloon-tired car and Pluto's doghouse out front. Once inside, visitors see Mickey's bedroom; a radio plays some old Disney song favorites in the den; the television set shows the "Mickey Mouse Club"; and in the memorabilia room, photos of Mickey with Walt and other celebrities cover the walls.

From Mickey's house, guests head for the pre-show area, which is the entrance to Mickey's Magical TV World. The walls are lined with brightly colored cubes and individual Disney character cutouts. The screen looks like a large television set and guests are entertained by clips from cartoons that are featured in the live show ("Goof Troop," "Dark Wing Duck" "Bonkers," and "Tale Spin.")

The countdown to showtime continues on the screen, and then Mickey Mouse appears to invite guests to enter his Magical TV World. The tunnel leading to the theater is brightly painted, and TV set cutouts are placed along the way. Mickey Mouse and his hostess sing a theme song and introduce the guest stars.

After the live show, guests are lead into the Mickey Mouse Club Funland tent, where they are surrounded by a colorful cartoon version of a city skyline. An interactive video area allows guests to see themselves on TV screens, and there is a variety of activities waiting just outside the exit doors. A walkway features shops that offer interactive audio experiences. The Popcorn Shop, for example, has boxes out front that pop when opened. The firehouse features a working siren and rotating light activated when guests push the right button. In addition, Mickey's Walk of Fame replicates Hollywood's star Walk of Fame. In these stars, however, are several Disney characters, and when guests step on the stars they hear the character's voice.

Guests have the opportunity to greet and meet Mickey Mouse at the Hollywood Theater, and have their picture taken with him.

In the outdoor area of Mickey's Starland, Mickey's Treehouse and Minnie's Doll House offer opportunities for climbing, exploring, and having an all-around good time. There's Grandma Duck's Farm, where children can get up close to some extremely cuddly baby animals. Guests also can see Minnie Moo, a white cow that happens to have black spots in the shape of mouse ears on its side. A photograph of the cow was sent by its owner and Walt Disney World purchased it. When the cow is not touring, she lives at Grandma Duck's Farm. There's also a maze, called the Mouskamaze, where topiary shrubs and trees create a not-too-confusing path for children. Drink, cookie, and ice cream carts are located all around the outdoor area.

Guests leave Mickey's Starland along a path guarded by topiary trees and shrubs that have been pruned into many shapes, including Disney characters. The path leads directly to Fantasyland, so the transition is a smooth and pleasant one.

Fantasyland

size moving platform measuring 60 feet in diameter, plus several stationary chariots. During the Disney refurbishing, these were removed, and many were replaced with additional horses made of fiberglass. Also, the original horses' legs, which were arranged in a rather decorous pose, were ingeniously rearranged to make the steeds look like real chargers. (Careful examination seems to reveal some of the cracks by which this change was effected.) Also, for the wooden canopy above the horses, Disney artists hand-painted 18 separate scenes (each measuring about two by three feet) with images of the little cinder girl from Charles Perrault's fairy tale and Disney's 1950 film. Additionally, the original mechanical wooden parts were replaced by metal ones; the thick layer of paint that had obscured some of the finer points of the original carving was stripped away, and the horses were repainted. The painting alone required about 48 hours per horse. All the horses are white, Disney spokespeople say, because all the riders are good guys!

While waiting to mount the carousel's steeds it's worthwhile to take the time to study the animals carefully. One is festooned with yellow roses, another carries a quiver of Indian arrows, and yet another sports a portrait of Eric the Red on its back. No two are exactly alike. The band organ, which plays favorite music from Disney Studios (such as the Oscar-winners "When You Wish Upon A Star," "Zip-A-Dee-Doo-Dah," and "Chim-Chim-Cheree"), was made in one of Italy's most famous factories.

MAD TEA PARTY: The theme of this ride—in a group of oversize pastel-colored teacups that whirl and spin as wildly as many carni-

Walt Disney called this a "timeless land of enchantment," and his successors term it "the happiest land of all"—and it is, for some. Although it's not precisely a kiddieland, it is the home of a number of rides that are particularly well liked by children. The nursery-song cadences of "It's A Small World" appeal to them, as do the bright colors of the trash baskets, the flowers, and the tentlike rooftops; and they delight in the fairy-tale architecture and ambience, reminiscent of a king's castle courtyard during a particularly lively fair. Fantasyland also is one of the most heavily trafficked areas of the park. Parents of younger children should note that many of the attractions are dark and in some cases the special effects may be too intense for small children.

CINDERELLA'S GOLDEN CARROUSEL: Not everything in the Magic Kingdom is a Disney version of the real article. This carousel, discovered at the now-defunct Maplewood, New Jersey, Olympic Park, was built for the Detroit Palace Garden Park (also long gone) by Italian-born woodcarvers of the Philadelphia Toboggan Company back in 1917. That was the end of the golden century of carousel-building that began around 1825 (when the Common Council of Manhattan Island, New York, granted one John Sears a permit to "establish a covered circus for a Flying Horse Establishment"). "Liberty"—as the Philadelphia Toboggan Company's red, white, and blue creation was called during that patriotic era—originally featured 72 horses on an over-

vals' Tubs of Fun—derives from a scene in the Disney studio's 1951 production of Lewis Carroll's novel *Alice in Wonderland*. During the sequence in question, the Mad Hatter hosts a tea party for his un-birthday. Unlike many of the other rides in Fantasyland, this attraction is not strictly for younger children; the 9-to-20 crowd seems to like it best. Be sure to note the soused mouse that pops out of the teapot at the center of the platform full of teacups.

DUMBO, THE FLYING ELEPHANT: This is purely and simply a kiddie ride—though personages as varied as Romanian gymnast Nadia Comaneci and Muhammad Ali have loved it. The character of the flying elephant was developed for the 1941 film release of *Dumbo*, one of the shortest of Disney's animated features and one of the best, starring a baby elephant born with inordinately large ears and an ability to fly that is discovered after he accidentally drinks from a bucket of champagne. The mouse that sits atop the mirrored ball in the middle of the circle of the ride's flying elephants is the faithful Timothy Mouse, who in the film becomes Dumbo's manager after the circus folk who had once laughed at the flying elephant hire him to be a big star.

MAGIC JOURNEYS: This spectacular 18-minute, 70mm 3-D motion picture (it used to play at Journey Into Imagination in Epcot Center), which guest's view wearing purple-rimmed polarized eyeglasses, is one of the largest-format films of this type. It also is remarkably realistic: when the screen fills with apple blossoms or a kite heads right at the audience, nearly everyone in the theater reaches out; when lightning strikes, people jump back in fright.

To get dramatic results like these, Disney cameramen developed a system of 3-D photography, which some observers have called the most precise and versatile in existence today. Two synchronized cameras are used, one for each of the images that each visitor's eyes see. The amount of depth that the viewer perceives is determined by the distance between the cameras and the direction in which they are aimed. The Disney system offers greater-than-ever control over both of these variables.

PETER PAN'S FLIGHT: The inspiration for this attraction was the Scottish writer Sir James M. Barrie's play about the boy who wouldn't grow up, which appeared as a Disney movie in 1953. Riding in flying versions of Captain Hook's ornate ship—which are suspended from an overhead rail once they leave the boarding area—visitors swoop and soar through a series of scenes that tell the story of how Wendy, Michael, and John get sprinkled with pixie dust and, heading for "the second star to the right and straight on till morning," fly off to Never-Never-Land with Tinkerbell; and meet Princess Tiger Lily, the evil Captain Hook, his jolly-looking sidekick Mr. Smee, and the crocodile—who has already made off with one of Hook's hands and is on the verge of getting the rest of him as you sail out into daylight. As in the movie, one of the most beautiful scenes—one that makes this attraction a treat for adults as well as for smaller folk—is the sight of nighttime London, dark blue and speckled with twinkling yellow lights, complete with the Thames, Big Ben, London Bridge, and vehicles that really move on the streets. The song that accompanies the trip is "You Can Fly, You Can Fly, You Can Fly" by Sammy Cahn and Sammy Fain.

SNOW WHITE'S ADVENTURES: This attraction near the carousel retells the scary part of the Grimm Brothers' fairy tale, which Walt Disney made into the world's first full-length animated feature in 1938. Though basically a ride for kids, Snow White's Adventures features two skeletons and plenty of spooky darkness; also, the wicked witch—evil, long-nosed, and practically toothless—appears more than once with such suddenness and menace that some youngsters can be really frightened. At the end, the hag dumps a rock on the passengers; the stars you see are among the attraction's best special effects.

MR. TOAD'S WILD RIDE: Wild in name only, this attraction is based on the 1949 Disney release *The Adventures of Ichabod and Mr. Toad*, which itself derives from Kenneth Grahame's classic novel *The Wind in the Willows*. It seems that a gang of weasels has tricked that memorable man-about-town Mr. J. Thaddeus Toad into trading the deed to his ancestral mansion for a stolen motorcar. In the attraction, flivvers modeled on this very car take guests zigging and zagging along the road to Nowhere in Particular, through dark rooms painted in neon colors and illuminated by black lights where the redoubtable Mr. Toad is trying to get out of the scrape. In the process, you crash through a fireplace, narrowly miss being struck by a falling suit of armor, go hurtling through haystacks and barn doors and into a coop full of squawking chickens, then ride down a railroad track on a collision course with a huge locomotive. Some of this is scary enough that some children end up momentarily frightened. By and large, though, this is for kids.

SKYWAY TO TOMORROWLAND: Entered from near Peter Pan's Flight, this aerial tram transports guests one-way to Tomorrowland. En route it's possible to see the clear aquamarine pool traversed by Captain Nemo's ship, the striped tent tops of Cinderella's Golden Carrousel, Tomorrowland's Grand Prix Raceway, and the not-so-wonderful rooftops of the buildings where many Magic Kingdom adventures actually take place. This attraction is best boarded at its Tomorrowland terminus, where the lines are usually slightly shorter. Guests with disabilities who are able to leave their wheelchairs can take a round-trip ride from the Fantasyland station.

IT'S A SMALL WORLD: Originally created for New York's 1964–1965 World's Fair, with a tunefully singsong melody written by Richard M. and Robert B. Sherman (the Academy Award-winning composers of the music for *Mary Poppins*, among other Disney scores), this favorite of young children and senior citizens involves a boat trip through several large rooms where stylized Audio-Animatronics dolls—wooden soldiers, cancan dancers, balloonists, chess pieces, Tower of London guards in scarlet beefeater uniforms, bagpipers and leprechauns, gooseherds, little Dutch kids in wooden shoes, Don Quixote and a goatherd, yodelers and gondoliers, houri dancers, dancers from Greece and Thailand, snake charmers, Japanese kite flyers, hippos, giraffes, frogs, hyenas, monkeys, elephants, hip-twitching Polynesians, surfers, and even dolphins—sing and dance to a melody that will run through your head for hours after you float out of their wonderland. Of the two queues that are usually found here, the one to the left is almost always shorter.

20,000 LEAGUES UNDER THE SEA: Jules Verne, on whose novel Disney based the 1954 release that provides the theme for this attraction, described the Machiavellian Captain Nemo's ship as an undersea monster, with headlights that appeared as eyes in the dark water. The 61-foot-long, 58-ton, 38-passenger crafts that ply the beautiful, blue Fantasyland lagoon are far too handsome to fit the description, but—at least on the outside—they bear a remarkable resemblance to the craft piloted by the nefarious Nemo toward Vulcania. In the course of the trip, visitors tour an 11½ million-gallon pool filled with sea grass, kelp, giant fishes, clams, seahorses, coral, icebergs, and rock formations fashioned of fiberglass, plastic, steel, stucco, and epoxy paint. The ship's course passes by the lost continent of Atlantis and under a rather attractive "polar ice cap"; as in the film, passengers listen to Nemo playing the organ, and endure an attack by a giant squid. The special effects aren't the Magic Kingdom's best, and the queues outside move rather slowly—so don't line up unless it's not busy.

Incidentally, the nautical flags above the entrance—which now spell out the word "Leagues" in the attraction's name—read S-E-U-G-A-E-L when the park first opened. A Navy visitor pointed out the mistake. The queue area is done up with Disney-made rocks, which are meant to resemble the volcanic boulders that would have been found on Nemo's Vulcania. The area also is graced with a large Senegal date palm and a southern magnolia, which were so heavy that the ceiling of the Magic Kingdom basement down below had to be specially reinforced to support them. The cliffs into which the submarines disappear, on the far side of the lagoon, conceal the backstage area where much of the scenery is set up; a better view of the layout is available from the Skyway above.

Tomorrowland

With its vast expanse of concrete, Tomorrowland offers a picture of the future that is a little less than wonderful, since the architecture looks a bit too much like yesterday's version of tomorrow. As Disney planners have discovered, it isn't easy to portray a future that persists in becoming the present. Tomorrowland will be getting a facelift during the next five years. New attractions will include Alien Encounter, designed by George Lucas.

SPACE MOUNTAIN: Rising to a height of over 180 feet and extending some 300 feet in diameter, this gleaming white steel and concrete cone (shaped vaguely like Japan's Mount Fuji) houses an attraction that most people call a roller coaster. Actually, it bears the same sort of resemblance to the traditional thrill ride as the Magic Kingdom does to the garden variety of theme park. It's the Disney version—a roller coaster and then some. While the 2-minute-and-38-second ride does not exactly duplicate a trip into outer space, there are some truly phenomenal and quite lovely special effects— shooting stars and strobelike flashing lights among them; and the whole ride takes place in an outer space-like darkness that gets progressively inkier—and scarier—as the journey progresses. The six-passenger rockets that roar through this blackness attain a maximum speed of just over 28 miles per hour. Just how terrifying this actually is to any given passenger depends on his or her level of tolerance. In general, the Space Mountain trip seems to inspire in lovers of thrill rides an immediate desire to go again; it's just wild enough to send eyeglasses, purses, wallets, and even an occasional set of false teeth plummeting to the bottom of the track, so be sure to find a safe place for your possessions before the ride starts. It's also turbulent enough to upset the stomachs of those so unwise as to ride it immediately after eating—but not so harrowing that passengers shake and weakened knees persist for more than a minute or two

after "touchdown." Those in a quandary about whether or not to line up can get a preview from the WEDway PeopleMover described below; and those who decide to pass after hearing the shrieks and the clatter of the cars from the queue area have their own exit.

After experiencing the space journey, it's interesting to note some statistics: The mountain itself—which occupies a ten-acre site and contains 4,508,500 cubic feet, enough to accommodate a small skyscraper—is composed of 72 pre-stressed concrete beams cast nearby, then hoisted into place by mammoth cranes. Each rib weighs 74 tons, and measures 117 feet in length and, in width, 4 feet at the top and 13 feet at the bottom. With the work lights on, the interior of Space Mountain looks humdrum and almost commercially common, with its tangled array of track and supporting scaffolding. Some of the shooting stars are produced quite simply, by aiming a beam of light at a mirrored globe; and legend has it that the meteors visible to guests in the queue area are actually projections of chocolate chip cookies! The whole ride is controlled by a computer and is monitored on a board full of dials and a battery of closed-circuit television screens by Disney hosts and hostesses sitting in a control room (whose eerie blue glow is another striking feature of the queue area). As a result, any guest caught acting in an unsafe manner can be warned, and the ride stopped, if necessary. Children under seven years old must be accompanied by an adult; guests under 44 inches tall are not permitted to ride; and as the many signs at the attraction warn, "You Must be in Good Health, and Free from Heart Conditions, Motion Sickness, Back or Neck Problems, or Other Physical Limitations" to ride. It also is suggested that expectant mothers pass up the trip. Presented by Federal Express.

RYCA 1/DREAM OF A NEW WORLD: The moving sidewalk that takes guests out of Space Mountain also carries them past a

futuristic mining colony on the planet RYCA. Far more interesting are the broadcast systems (they cost $70,000 to $80,000 each) that allow guests to see themselves on television—in living color.

SKYWAY TO FANTASYLAND: This aerial cable car takes guests from Tomorrowland to a point near Peter Pan's Flight in Fantasyland. The trip takes five minutes, and the cable car—built by Von Roll, Ltd., of Bern, Switzerland, then shipped to Miami and on to Orlando—is notable for being the nation's first conveyance of its type able to make a 90-degree turn. If you're going to ride the Skyway, this is the place to get on: The lines at the Fantasyland end are usually slightly longer.

STARJETS: Towering high over Tomorrowland, this is purely and simply a thrill ride and ought to delight anyone who loves Space Mountain, but doesn't necessarily want to get in line all over again.

MISSION TO MARS: After a preflight briefing in a room styled to look like Mission Control, and a narration by an Audio-Animatronics flight engineer who looks just like the father in the Carousel of Progress family, guests enter a round cabin for a simulated trip to Mars that was developed in cooperation with NASA. Seats tilt and shake, sub-audible sound waves are sent out, and oversize speakers let out great roars and hisses that sound like a washing machine during the spin cycle; corny though the idea is, the realization is okay. The attraction is located opposite *American Journeys* (described below). Films screened during the flight, some developed from photos taken during the Mariner Nine space program, show a section of Mars's surface called

Mariner Valley and its 40-mile-wide Olympus Mons, the universe's largest-known volcano. The best viewing for this show is from the third and fourth rows.

WEDWAY PEOPLEMOVER: Boarded near the StarJets, these small, five-car trains move at a speed of about ten miles per hour along close to a mile of track, alongside or through most of the attractions in Tomorrowland. If you have any doubts about riding Space Mountain, a trip on the PeopleMover—which travels through the queue area inside and offers a view of the rockets as they hurtle through the darkness—will probably help you decide. Just as important, from an intellectual standpoint, is the fact that the WEDway PeopleMover shows off an innovative means of transportation: It is operated by a linear induction motor that has no moving parts, uses little power, and emits no pollution.

CAROUSEL OF PROGRESS: First seen at New York's 1964–1965 World's Fair and moved here in 1975, this 22-minute show features a number of tableaux starring an Audio-Animatronics family, and demonstrates the improvements in American life that have resulted from the use of electricity.

CIRCLEVISION 360 *AMERICAN JOURNEYS*: This 21-minute film, the first attraction on the far right just over the Tomorrowland Bridge, is a travel film like few others. Instead of showing only what's in front, it also lets viewers see what's behind and to either side. *American Journeys* was in the planning and production stages for four years. The crews trekked across the country from the Statue of Liberty to the ice floes of Glacier Bay, Alaska, with a 700-pound rig consisting of nine cameras mounted so that they point up into a cir-

cle of mirrors. For one scene the crew placed the cumbersome camera rig atop a steam locomotive in the Colorado Rockies; in another the rig was attached to the bottom of a helicopter for a fly through Monument Valley, Utah; and the first-ever underwater CircleVision scenes were done off the Florida coast using a custom-designed enclosure. This footage is shown in the big theater by an equally innovative arrangement of nine projectors, nine 20-by-30-foot screens, and 12 channels of sound reproduced through nine different speakers, plus six others, affixed to the ceiling, which carry the narration. Consequently, the experience is really impressive (and a few of the flight scenes are realistic enough to make some guests airsick). The journey includes stops at Mount St. Helens, just two days after it erupted in 1980; a ship-carver's workshop in Mystic, Connecticut; a bluegrass musical performance in Norris, Tennessee; Dodger Stadium in Los Angeles; and Cape Canaveral, Florida, for the launching of Space Shuttle *Columbia*. The grand finale is a spectacular fireworks display at the Statue of Liberty. The attraction can accommodate up to 3,100 people an hour, so don't be discouraged if you see a crowd outside; it disappears every 20 minutes or so. This is generally one of a handful of spots where the queues on a busy afternoon are the least discouraging. Note that there are no seats in the theater.

GRAND PRIX RACEWAY: The little cars that *vroom* down the four 2,260-foot-long tracks at this attraction opposite the Tomorrowland Terrace provide most of the background noise in Tomorrowland—and that's another grim thought about the future. Older kids and teenagers love the ride and will spend as many hours driving the Mark VII-model gasoline-powered cars as they can; one 87-year-old grandmother comes here just to watch. Like true sports cars, the vehicles—which cost about $6,000 each—have rack-and-pinion steering and disc brakes; unlike most sports cars, these run on a track. Nonetheless, even expert drivers have a hard time keeping them going in a straight line until the technique is mastered: Just steer all the

way to the right, or all the way to the left, and you've got it made. One lap around the track takes about four minutes, and the cars (which are manufactured by a Disney company called MAPO, short for Mary Poppins) can travel at a maximum speed of about seven mph. You must be at least 52 inches to drive the cars alone. Presented by Goodyear.

DREAMFLIGHT: A whimsical look at the adventure and romance of flight—as seen through the eyes of a child—awaits guests at this Tomorrowland attraction. A mixture of two- and three-dimensional media combine with special effects and digitally produced stereo music to take visitors on an entirely delightful journey. The attraction opens with a scene from a giant pop-up book, in which mankind's first attempts at flight are humorously depicted. Three-dimensional aircraft are used in a variety of scenes from the early days of flight. A barnstorming flying circus segment features a man and woman, each standing on a wing and keeping up a tennis match. The next segment highlights a 70mm live-action film, produced in the Northwest exclusively for this attraction, in which stunts are performed to the oohs and ahs of the audience. A wing walker does acrobatic feats, another stuntman out on a wing comes within five feet of the ground to pick up a ribbon, and a plane comes out of a barrel roll and sets down on a lake, all to the thrilled delight of onlookers.

From the world of barnstorming, guests make the transition to the age of commercial aviation. A full-size segment of an M-130 Flying Boat, a popular plane during the late 1930s, is on view. An elegant dining room (particularly by today's standards) is displayed as monitors allow glimpses of the faraway places the M-130 made accessible. In one scene, two dancers perform outside a Japanese temple garden; in another, the sun sets over Paris as a flower merchant packs up his blossoms on the steps of Montmartre. Next stop on the 4½-minute journey is the jet age, in its most pure form. Guests actually ride through a real engine. Digitally prepared graphics and special effects re-create the rotation of the turbine in a realistic fashion.

In another 70mm film segment, visitors get that "you are there" feeling as they speed down a runway and fly off towards space. The moon, backlit by the sun, provides the lighting for some spectacular views over canyons, valleys, and flat terrain, where the suggestion of cities of the future are depicted. The finale features another pop-up book measuring 16 feet tall and 11 feet wide showing contemporary London and New York.

If this journey fuels the desire to travel, Delta is prepared to fulfill it. Brochures, ticket information, and flight schedules are available at the Delta counter at the *Contemporary* resort. Presented by Delta Air Lines.

Shops in the Magic Kingdom

No one travels all the way to the Magic Kingdom just to go shopping. But as many a first-time visitor has learned with some surprise, shopping is one of the most enjoyable pastimes there. Donald Duck key chains and Mickey Mouse lapel pins, Alice in Wonderland dresses for little girls, Walt Disney World sweatshirts, and other Disney souvenir items make up a large portion of the merchandise you see on display.

But the Magic Kingdom's boutiques and stores stock much more than just Disneyana, and it's possible to buy antiques and silver-plated tea services, escargot holders and cookbooks, mock pirate hats and toy frontier rifles, 14-karat gold charms and filigreed costume jewelry in Main Street shops that also sell magic tricks, film, and peanut brittle. In Adventureland, you can buy imported items from around the world—handcarved elephant statues from Africa, inlaid marble boxes from India, batik dresses from Indonesia, and much more. Shops stock items that complement the themes of the various lands (and so, in Tomor-

rowland, one finds contemporary wall hangings and futuristic-looking table lamps). Every store offers a selection of items from the inexpensive to the costly: In Tinker Bell's Treasures in Fantasyland, for instance, kids can beg for a $5 windup toy after requests for the larger-than-life-size $350 stuffed animals are denied. At Uptown Jewelers on Main Street, a three-foot-high Hummel figurine costs thousands of dollars. And in many shops, you can watch craftsmen at work—peanut brittle being poured in the Main Street Confectionery, a glass blower in Main Street's Crystal Arts, and the like.

Consequently, there's no need to spend a fortune to have a good time. Budget-watchers should note, though, that the temptation to nickel-and-dime yourself into penury is very strong, and you need to be careful. It's a good idea to set a spending limit for each member of your party in advance—and try to stick to it.

MAIN STREET
East Side

WHEELCHAIRS—STROLLERS: Just after the turnstiles into the Magic Kingdom, to the right as you face Cinderella Castle. A limited number of strollers and wheelchairs are available on a first-come, first-served basis, and assorted souvenirs may be purchased.

THE CHAPEAU: This Town Square shop is the place to buy Mouseketeer ears and have them monogrammed, and to shop for visors, strawhats, derbies, top hats, and other headgear. The shop sells decorated ladies' hats—fun to try on, if not necessarily worth the investment.

DISNEYANA COLLECTIBLES: Located next to *Tony's Town Square* restaurant. Limited edition Disney plates, cels from Disney movies, and other collectibles are sold here.

KODAK CAMERA CENTER: Gleaming glass-fronted mahogany cases show off the Canon, Minolta, Pentax, Nikon, and other 35mm, instant-load, quick-developing cameras for sale at this high-ceilinged shop near Town Square. Film and other photo supplies also are available, and very minor repairs can be made. Cameras, including RCA Video Camcorders, are available for rent (a deposit is required).

MAIN STREET CONFECTIONERY: Delicious chocolates are available in this old-fashioned pink-and-white paradise. A delight at any time of day, but especially when the cooks in the shop's glass-walled kitchen are pouring peanut brittle onto a huge tabletop to cool, and the candy is sending up clouds of scent that you could swear were being fanned right out into the street. Some 18 to 20 batches are made each day. The sweet product is for sale in small bags, along with pastilles, jelly beans, marshmallow crispies, nougats, mints, and dozens of other nemeses for a sweet tooth. When your stomach is growling, this is a good place to grab a snack.

UPTOWN JEWELERS: Fine china and other gift items—china birds and figurines, swans, china flowers, Dresden and Lladro figurines, and all manner of pretty teacups, Disney character figurines—priced from $3.50 to $3,500—are the stock-in-trade of this airy establishment. The most expensive item, at last look, was a giant Hummel statue, depicting ruddy-cheeked peasant children in an apple tree; at least peek at it, even if it is a bit rich for most pocketbooks. There's also a selection of good-quality and costume jewelry. One counter stocks wonderful souvenir charms in 14-karat gold and sterling silver: Tinkerbell, Cinderella Castle, and the Walt Disney World logo (a globe with mouse ears). Clocks and watches in all shapes and sizes, not to mention Mickey Mouse watches in a variety of configurations, are available here. There are clocks for the kitchen and clocks for the living room, clocks with chimes and clocks without them, alarm clocks for bedside tables and others for travel, digital watches and watches with hands, and even some pocket watches and a Mickey Mouse telephone. Purchases can be shipped on request. Presented by Lorus.

DISNEY & COMPANY: The wallpaper at this shop on Center Street (the cul-de-sac just off Main) is Victorian and the woodwork elaborate; and old-fashioned ceiling fans twirl slowly overhead. This character shop offers sweatshirts and T-shirts, hats and bags, pens and pencils, stuffed animals, and other items. The selection is not as vast as the Emporium, but neither is Disney & Company quite so overwhelming.

MARKET HOUSE: An old-fashioned spot, with pretzels, pickles, honey, and all kinds of tea and snack items arranged in oak cases. The floors are oak and pegged, the lighting comes in part from brass lanterns, and in one corner there's a real old-fashioned hand-crank telephone. Tobacco products also are available, and very attractive souvenir matchbooks are handed out with each purchase.

THE SHADOW BOX: Watching Rubio Artist Co. silhouette cutters snip black paper into the likenesses of children is one of Main Street's more fascinating diversions, and there's always a crowd on hand—some folks waiting their turn, some just inspecting the progress and the results. Framed silhouettes cost $4.

CRYSTAL ARTS: Cut-glass bowls and vases, urns and glasses, plates and shelves glitter in the mirror-backed glass cases of this high-ceilinged, brass-chandeliered emporium. An engraver or a glassblower is always at work by the bright light flooding through the big windows. Presented by the Arribas Brothers.

West Side

NEWSSTAND: No newspapers are sold in the Magic Kingdom—even at its Newsstand, which is opposite the Stroller Shop, to your left as you face Cinderella Castle, just after you've passed through the turnstiles at the entrance to the Magic Kingdom. Character merchandise and souvenirs are for sale. The selection is fairly limited, but you can usually pick up items you've forgotten during your travels through the rest of the park.

THE EMPORIUM: Framed by a two-story-high portico, this Town Square landmark, the Magic Kingdom's largest gift shop, stocks a little bit of everything—stuffed animals and toys, an array of dolls, sundries, film, and more. Everyone seems to have an armload of Walt Disney World T-shirts and sweatshirts, towels and handbags, Mouseketeer ears and other hats, and various items emblazoned with Mickey, Minnie, or Walt Disney World logos. The cash registers almost always seem to be busy, especially toward the end of the afternoon and before park closing. It's a good place to

souvenir-shop, though, since it's only a few steps from lockers (under the train station) where purchases can be stowed. Don't forget to note the window displays, which usually feature Audio-Animatronics displays ranging from themes of the season to the most recent Disney movie.

HARMONY BARBER SHOP: The setting is quaint and old-fashioned, worth a peek even if you've no need for a trim. Nostalgic shaving items and moustache cups are for sale.

DISNEY CLOTHIERS: Disney-character merchandise has always been popular, as evidenced by the number of T-shirts, Mickey Mouse ears, wristwatches, and sweatshirts sold each year. This shop caters to fashion-conscious shoppers with a love for Disney gear. There is a vast array of men's, women's, and children's clothing and accessories, all of which incorporate Disney characters in some way. There are men's golf shirts with a small Mickey Mouse embroidered on the pocket, and satin-look jackets with Mickey (as the sorcerer's apprentice in *Fantasia*) embossed on the back. Hats, ties, exercise clothing, and dress shirts round out the adult selections. Children's items include socks, suspenders, tops, pants, and bathing suits.

HOUSE OF MAGIC: Magicians can make ordinary playing cards simply disappear, balls pass through cups, water pour out of a jug that looks empty, coins pass through solid sheets of rubber, and a wand turn into two silken handkerchiefs. Some believers can produce coins from thin air, or pour the milk from a whole pitcher into a thimble. This Main Street shop sells the kinds of magician's tools that can turn everyday travelers into magicians, along with party-joke items such as phony arm casts, slimy reptiles, and similar stuff.

MAIN STREET BOOK STORE: Books about the art of Walt Disney are the focus of this boutique. Also available here are greeting cards, wrapping paper, and pretty party items, including paper plates, napkins, and tablecloths.

ADVENTURELAND

TRADERS OF TIMBUKTU: This shop is in a marketlike complex in the plaza opposite the Tropical Serenade, and displays a fine selection of the sort of handsome (but inexpensive) trinkets that travelers find while visiting the erstwhile Dark Continent—carved wooden giraffes and antelopes, ethnic jewelry (including carved bangles, malachite, and elephant-hair jewelry), dashikis, and khaki shirts.

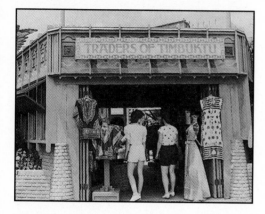

BWANA BOB'S: A whimsical and colorful hut full of the critters you may have just seen on the Jungle Cruise or at the Tropical Serenade.

TIKI TROPIC SHOP: Hawaiian and tropical clothing, short sets, shoes, and jewelry are featured at this establishment located near Traders of Timbuktu, opposite the exit of *Sunshine Tree Terrace*.

ELEPHANT TALES: A variety of women's and men's clothing with a safari theme are featured at this shop. Women's accessories and safari plush toys also are available.

ISLAND SUPPLY: This tropical surf shop features a vast assortment of surfing clothing and accessories. Colorful T-shirts, baggies, sharks' teeth jewelry, and even surfboard wax can be found here.

CARIBBEAN PLAZA

LAFFITE'S PORTRAIT DECK: Hidden away near the Plaza del Sol Caribe, you can have an 8-by-10 portrait taken as you dress up as swashbucklers and pirate maids amid what look to be pieces of eight and chests brimful of pearls and precious jewels. It's amusing just to stand and watch other guests lining up to say "cheese."

HOUSE OF TREASURE: The only spot in the Magic Kingdom that sells pirates' hats, this swashbuckler's delight adjoins Pirates of the Caribbean on the west and stocks piratical merchandise—toy rifles and brass dolphins, a Pirate's Creed of Ethics printed on parch-

ment, Jolly Roger flags, rings, old-looking maps, pirate dolls, sailing-ship models, ships in a bottle, and eye patches. There's as much for adults as for youngsters.

THE GOLDEN GALLEON: A low-ceilinged, tile-floored shop full of golden treasures—handsome nautical items, brass schooners, ships' wheels, and replicas of racing yachts—not to mention nautical and resort ready-to-wear fashions for men and women as well as comfortable, casual shoes.

PLAZA DEL SOL CARIBE: Located next to the Pirates of the Caribbean, this market sells candy and snacks, a variety of strawhats (including colorful oversize sombreros), piñatas, pottery, straw bags, ready-to-wear clothes, and artificial flowers.

FRONTIERLAND

FRONTIER TRADING POST: Stock your chuck wagon with venison chili, wild boar meat, and buffalo. Or outfit a youngster like a true child of the Great Frontier: Cowboy hats or feathered headdresses and moccasins, hefty brass belt buckles, sleeve garters, sheriff's badges, gold nugget and turquoise jewelry, and reproduction pistols and rifles should do the trick. Also available are western items like tom-toms, peace pipes, plastic toy horses, and forts. Film and sundries are in stock, too.

TRAIL CREEK HAT SHOP: Hats of all descriptions (though the specialties of the house are western styles), plus feathered hatbands and leather goods are on sale. It's tucked away near the arcade leading to Adventureland, between the ornamental Frontierland stockade, alongside the *Diamond Horseshoe*.

PRAIRIE OUTPOST & SUPPLY: Clothing and decorative gifts and items from the American Southwest are the specialties of the house.

BRIAR PATCH: Cuddly creatures from the *Song of the South* are featured at this shop near the exit to Splash Mountain. Country crafts and an unusual line of Disney character merchandise round out the offerings.

FRONTIERLAND WOOD CARVING: The spot for personalized, wood-carved gifts. Presented by Rubio Artist Co.

BIG AL'S: Located along the river, this is a good place to acquire leather goods, harmonicas, rock candy, and a fine assortment of six-shooters.

LIBERTY SQUARE

OLDE WORLD ANTIQUES: One of the first of the Liberty Square shops that visitors pass after crossing the bridge from the Hub area in front of Cinderella Castle, this little, lace-curtained emporium stocks real antiques—hutches, drop-leaf tables, and assorted decorative items in brass, pewter, copper, mahogany, oak, and pine—as well as some reproductions. Other unique treasures from the past include jewelry and clothing. Prices run into thousands of dollars, and bargains are nowhere to be found, but every item is in tip-top condition and tagged with a description of its origin, so the browsing is good. Both perfumes created to order and name-brand fragrances are available here.

HERITAGE HOUSE: Among the early American reproductions that predominate in the stock of this store next to The Hall of Presidents, youngsters may go for the parchment copies of famous American documents, while homeowners might snap up pewter plates and candlesticks, creweled items, wooden candlesticks and pepper mills, busts of the presidents, souvenir spoons, mugs in early American motifs, wrought-iron knickknacks, or lovely enameled paintings of clipper ships.

YANKEE TRADER: No first-time visitor to the Magic Kingdom would expect to be able to buy stoneware soufflé dishes and espresso makers, cast-iron muffin tins and escargot holders. But this shop, immediately to the right after you turn into the lane leading to the Haunted Mansion, is crammed like a too-small kitchen cabinet with just these kitchen items, and more: cookie cutters and choppers, graters and spatulas, french-fry slicers, wooden-handled whisks, egg timers, and wall plaques made of dough, to name just a few of the sorts of things available here. There also are displays of Smuckers' jams and jellies in more varieties than any supermarket shopper would have imagined existed. Cookbooks also are for sale—not only the old favorites like *Joy of Cooking*, but also unusual volumes of historic recipes. The store is located near the archway-entrance to Fantasyland. Presented by Smuckers.

ICHABOD'S LANDING: This small shop, situated next to Mike Fink's Keel Boats, gives guests on their way to the Haunted Mansion a taste of things to come with a stock of horrific monster masks and assorted ghoulish goodies (in a more limited selection than at Main Street's House of Magic).

SILVERSMITH: The sign above the entrance to this tiny shop adjoining Olde World Antiques (just next to the Liberty Square bridge to the Hub) reads "J. Tremain, Prop." That refers to the main character in the 1957 Disney film of the Esther Forbes novel about a silversmith's apprentice who joins the Boston Tea Party and helps hang the lights on the Liberty Tree during America's colonial days. At this low-ceilinged, plank-floored establishment, antique-looking cabinets display tongs and teaspoons, Revere-style bowls, tea sets, silver-coated roses, candelabras, and more—all in sterling or silver plate.

FANTASYLAND

THE KING'S GALLERY: Situated inside Cinderella Castle, near the entrance to *King Stefan's Banquet Hall*, this shop is one of the Magic Kingdom's best. The walls are dark and the ceilings beamed, and the stock includes large tapestries, suits of armor, unicorns of all sizes, decorative boxes, cuckoo clocks, Spanish-made swords, German beer mugs with lids, chess sets, and more—very little of it at rock-bottom prices. Also here, practiced artisans demonstrate the art of Damascening, a form of metal-working originated by the inhabitants of Damascus in the sixth century A.D.; it is mastered today by only a handful of specialized craftsmen around the world. Painstakingly, these skilled workers dip steel pendants into acid to create tiny pores, then use a combination of sterling silver and 24-karat gold wire to outline butterflies and other designs onto the acid-blackened steel.

MICKEY'S CHRISTMAS CAROL: A wide selection of Christmas items, including treetop dolls and souvenir ornaments, is available at this location year-round.

WHERE TO EAT IN THE MAGIC KINGDOM

A complete listing of all Magic Kingdom eateries—full-service restaurants, fast-food emporiums, snack shops, and food vendors—are found together with all other WDW eating spots in the *Good Meals, Great Times* chapter.

SHOPPING AWAY FROM THE PARKS

MAIL-ORDER MICKEY: T-shirts, Mouseketeer ears, stuffed animals, and many other souvenir items can be ordered through the Disney Catalog. Phone 800-237-5751 to receive one.

THE DISNEY STORES: Located in malls all around the country, these shops offer a wide selection of merchandise comparable to the WDW character shops.

THE MAD HATTER: Another place to buy Mouseketeer ears and other souvenir hats and have your name embroidered on them on the spot. This shop was named for the Mad Hatter, who held the tea party for his un-birthday in Disney's 1951 film version of Lewis Carroll's classic *Alice in Wonderland*.

TINKER BELL'S TREASURES: One of the more wonderful boutiques in the Magic Kingdom, and a fine toy store by any standards. For sale are stuffed animals, miniature model cars and trucks, character patches, windup toys and wooden toys, bar soap emblazoned

ROYAL CANDY SHOPPE: This souvenir stand next to *Lumiere's Kitchen* sells assorted Disneyana, including Mickey Mouse back scratchers, key chains, and stuffed animals, plus a selection of jelly beans, peppermint sticks, Tootsie Rolls, lollipops, and other hard candy.

KODAK KIOSK: A convenient location to buy film and other photo supplies.

INFORMATION: Features whimsical, colorful, plush, stuffed characters and toys.

MICKEY'S STARLAND

MICKEY'S STARLAND TENT: "Disney Afternoon" merchandise and Mickey Mouse character memorabilia are among the items available here.

TOMORROWLAND

MICKEY'S STAR TRADERS: One of the best places in the Magic Kingdom for Disney-themed items.

SKYWAY STATION SHOP: A small spot tucked away near the Tomorrowland terminus of the Skyway to Fantasyland; great for Disney souvenirs.

SPACE PORT: Sells the kind of contemporary decorative gifts that teens and preteens seem to love: futuristic toys, games, jewelry, watches, clothing, and other such items. This is one of the Magic Kingdom's most popular shops.

SPACE PLACE: This small shop features a variety of souvenir hats.

with Disney scenes, Mickey and Minnie toys and clothing, Alice in Wonderland dresses, Snow White dresses (with Dopey on the skirt), and a positively marvelous array of Madame Alexander dolls. A must.

THE ARISTOCATS: Most of the lands have one store that specializes in Disney souvenirs; this stone-walled, vaguely Gothic shop slightly to the northeast of Cinderella Castle is Fantasyland's spot for Donald and Mickey key chains, sweatshirts and T-shirts, china Disney figurines, salt-and-pepper shakers, Minnie tote bags, tennis balls with a Mickey logo, and more.

WHERE TO BUY RAIN PONCHOS

The show doesn't stop just because of a storm. Instead, shops all over the Magic Kingdom stock ponchos to outfit guests who have left their own back home, at their hotel, or in the car. Among them are:

Main Street:	The Emporium
Adventureland:	Tiki Tropic Shop
Frontierland:	Frontier Trading Post
Fantasyland:	Tinker Bell's Treasures, Information, Mad Hatter, AristoCats
Tomorrowland:	Mickey's Star Traders, Skyway Station Shop, Space Place

Happenings and Live Entertainment

Walt Disney World is constantly adding new live shows to its repertoire, so before heading down Main Street, check at City Hall to get times for special Magic Kingdom happenings, as well as a schedule of entertainment at the resorts, the Disney Village Marketplace, Epcot Center, the Disney-MGM Studios Theme Park, and Pleasure Island. Others may be encountered serendipitously in the course of the day, and occasionally shows scheduled for a given place or time may be changed or canceled at the last minute—but more often than not, the shows proceed as planned.

DAPPER DANS: Likely to be encountered while you're strolling down Main Street. This barbershop quartet, its members clad in strawhats and striped vests, tap dance and let one-liners fly during their short four-part harmonic performances. Occasionally, they bring out their set of bamboo organ chimes.

WALT DISNEY WORLD BAND: This concert band performs during the morning every day in Town Square, and on occasion at the Fantasy Faire stage in Fantasyland.

REFRESHMENT CORNER RAGTIME PIANO: The pianist here tickles the ivories of a snow-white upright daily at this centrally located hamburgers-and-hot dogs restaurant.

FANTASY IN THE SKY: Even those rare recalcitrant souls who resist fireworks displays as though they were other people's home movies have little quarrel with this spectacular show, which is presented nightly when the park is open until 10 P.M. or later. The 150-odd shells that were mortarized over a 15-minute period when the program was first introduced are now ignited in a period of just 4 minutes—a rate of one shell every 2 seconds. The big symmetrical starburst shells are generally Japanese-made, while the ones whose explosions look as if they had been poured from a pitcher (with a concentrated area of particularly vivid color at the center) are manufactured in England.

ALL-AMERICAN COLLEGE MARCHING BAND: Featuring college students from around the country. Performs throughout the Magic Kingdom weekdays in the afternoon and early evening. Part of a 12-week summer program.

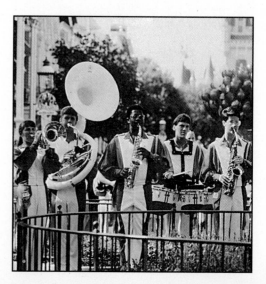

AFTERNOON PARADE: Each day at 3 P.M. a spectacular parade wends its way down Main Street.

SWORD IN THE STONE CEREMONY: Children are appointed king or queen of the realm by pulling the magical sword, Excalibur, from the stone in front of Cinderella's Golden Carrousel. Merlin the Magician presides over this ceremony.

KIDS OF THE KINGDOM: During the summer and Easter seasons, this group performs every day in the Castle Forecourt, in a show featuring lively singing and dancing to classic Disney tunes—plus appearances by Disney characters such as the portly Winnie the Pooh and Mickey Mouse himself.

FLAG RETREAT: Usually around 5:10 P.M., a small band and color guard march into Town Square, take down the American flag that flies from the flagpole there, then release a flock of snowy homing pigeons symbolic of the dove of peace. Watch carefully lest you miss them: As one wag quipped, these are union pigeons; they flap away toward their lofthome (behind the Castle) practically before you can say "Cinderella." The whole flight takes just 20 seconds. Some trivia: The carts in which the birds are transported are fashioned from authentic peddlers' carts bought in England for the 1971 Disney film *Bedknobs and Broomsticks*.

J. P. AND THE SILVER STARS: Play familiar tunes on the instruments so well known in the Caribbean islands, steel drums—oil barrels whose sides have been cut to a foot or less from the bottom (which itself has been pounded hollow). On a stage near Adventureland's Pirates of the Caribbean.

THE DIAMOND HORSESHOE JAMBOREE: A dance hall such as might have been found in 19th-century Missouri. Five times a day, there's a lively old-time show with can-can dancers. Reservations are required; to get them, appear in person at the reservation podium outside Disneyana Collectibles on Main Street shortly after park opening.

RHYTHM RASCALS: This group plays specialty songs and comic ditties from the Roaring Twenties on washboards and banjos, usually on Main Street.

SPECTROMAGIC

Since its premier during Walt Disney World's 20th anniversary celebration, this parade has gotten rave reviews and has taken its place among WDW's must-sees. Even avid fans of the Main Street Electrical Parade (which was, by the way, shipped to Paris to be presented at Euro Disneyland) won't be disappointed with this display. SpectroMagic borrows from the prismatic holographic industry, military lighting developments, electroluminescent and fiber-optic technologies, plus light-spreading thermoplastics, clouds of underlit liquid nitrogen, smoke, and some old-fashioned twinkling lights. The spectacle is choreographed to music composed just for the parade and is heard over 204 speakers generating 72,000 watts of power.

Approximately 100 miles of fiber-optic cable and threads are conduits for shimmering lights that create everything from the strands of "hair" on King Triton's beard to the giant hibiscus blooms and daisy petals. Some 600,000 miniature lights chase in wild patterns, moving in perfect concert with sound effects and music. Goofy's xylophone keys dance with light at his touch. Mickey's cape transforms in a 24-step cascade of color sweeping from shoulder height to the base of the float and upward to 17 feet above his head.

SpectroMagic is a marvel of the computer age. Approximately 30 mini-computers are used and the audio is stored digitally on state-of-the-art microchips. A sequence of electronic triggers activates the visual effects and audio effects.

There are two SpectroMagic parades nightly during busy seasons. Spectro-Magic follows the traditional WDW parade route and of all the spots along the way, the single best vantage point is the very center of the platform of the Walt Disney World Railroad's depot. From there, it's possible to see the parade circling Town Square, and then follow it as it makes its way down Main Street. Unfortunately, only a couple of seats here have views that are not obstructed by trees.

The next-best viewing point is from the curbs on either side of Main Street. It's very crowded here, and you must claim your foot of curb as much as an hour before the parade (particularly for the busier 9 P.M. running).

If you hate crowds, head for *Pecos Bill Café*; park yourself on one of the restaurant's stools right next to the parade route.

Note that the 9 P.M. parade is always more crowded than the one at 11 P.M.

Holiday Doings

EASTER SUNDAY: A holiday promenade helps make this holiday extra special.

FOURTH OF JULY CELEBRATION: The busiest day of the summer—and with reason: There's a double-size fireworks display, whose explosions light up the skies not only above Cinderella Castle, but also over the Seven Seas Lagoon.

CHRISTMAS: A Christmas tree—a real Douglas fir that is as perfect among trees as Main Street is among small-town thoroughfares—goes up in Town Square, and the entire Magic Kingdom is decked out as only Disney can do it. There also are special Christmas parades, shows, and carolers. The crowds, of course, are thick. But the scenery is beautiful, and the weather is fine (if chilly)—so it's no wonder that some veteran Magic Kingdom lovers call this the very best time of year.

NEW YEAR'S EVE CELEBRATION: With nearly 93,000 people streaming through the gates of the theme park, New Year's Eve Day of 1980 hosted the biggest crowd in Magic Kingdom history. And though the visitation rate was a little higher than in years past, it has always been true that on December 31, the throngs are practically body to body. For a celebration, that's fun. (On an introductory visit, it could be less delightful; first-timers take note.) There is a double-size fireworks display, and the Main Street holiday decorations (including that almost surrealistically perfect Christmas tree presiding over Town Square) are still up. There's plenty of nip in the air as the evening wears on, so dress accordingly.

WHERE TO FIND THE CHARACTERS

The characters appear next to City Hall throughout the day. A queue has been set up to allow each guest a turn to meet the characters and perhaps have a photo taken. But the best place to see the characters is at Mickey's Starland where Mickey, Goofy, Bonkers, Baloo, Louie, and Dark Wing Duck are on hand for a spectacular show. At the Hollywood Theater there, Mickey is available for photo opportunities.

Tips From WDW Veterans

- Study up before you arrive in the Magic Kingdom so that you're familiar with the layout and the things to see and to do in the park. Special services are occasionally available to guests during slack seasons, so be sure to peruse any printed information you find in your room.

- Allow plenty of time so that you can sample the Magic Kingdom in small bites. Trying to see it all in a day (or even just two) is like eating a rich ice cream sundae too quickly.

- Try to visit the park on a weekend in summer—and any day but Mondays, Tuesdays, or Wednesdays year-round.

- Start out early. Most people arrive between 9:30 A.M. and 11:30 A.M., when the roads approaching the Auto Plaza and the parking lots are jammed. If you're coming at Easter, Christmas, or in summer, plan to arrive before 8:30 A.M., or wait until nightfall, when things are less crowded. Be at the gates to the Magic Kingdom when they open, have breakfast at *Tony's Town Square* restaurant or the *Crystal Palace*, then be at the end of Main Street when the rest of the park opens.

- Organize your visit so that you don't hop around from area to area, for that wastes time. Plan to eat early or late; before 11 A.M. or after 2 P.M., and before 5 P.M. or after 8 P.M.

- At busy times on busy days, take in the following not-so-packed attractions:

Main Street:	Walt Disney World Railroad, Main Street Cinema
Liberty Square:	Liberty Square Riverboat
Tomorrowland:	Mission to Mars, WEDway PeopleMover, Carousel of Progress, Dreamflight, CircleVision 360 *American Journeys*

- Break up your day. Go to Typhoon Lagoon or River Country (admission included in a Five-day Super Duper Pass or a Be Our Guest Pass), or head back to your hotel, if it's not too far, for some swimming. Be sure to have your hand stamped and hold on to your Passport and your parking stub.

- Shop on Main Street in the early afternoon, not at day's end, when everybody else goes. Besides, the stores are good places to escape the afternoon heat.

- Many attractions have two lines. Before getting into the one on the right-hand side, look at the one to your left. Most of the time it will be less crowded, since most Magic Kingdom visitors automatically head for the one on the right.

- Wear your most comfortable shoes: You'll be spending a lot of time on your feet. (Note that no bare feet are permitted in the Magic Kingdom.)

- Don't take food into the Magic Kingdom. (There are, however, picnic facilities and lockers at the TTC.)

- If your party decides to split up, set a fixed meeting place and time that can't be confused. Avoid meeting in front of Cinderella Castle, since this area can become congested during showtimes and parades.

- If you have arranged to meet members of your group somewhere, don't get into a queue as the meeting time approaches.

Useful Stops

Cash: The Sun Bank, located in Town Square next to City Hall. Open seven days a week, from 9 A.M. to 4 P.M.

Baby-care needs: The Magic Kingdom Baby Services, at the Hub end of Main Street, next to the *Crystal Palace*, is the best source. This is a good area for nursing mothers. Check at City Hall for operating hours. Disposable diapers and other infant items also are available on request at many shops.

Strollers: For rent at the Wheelchairs—Strollers, located to the right in the souvenir area near the turnstiles at the entrance to the Magic Kingdom.

Haircuts: At the Harmony Barber Shop on Center Street, the flower-filled cul-de-sac off the west side of Main Street. The barber chairs are heavy, curlicued metal, like the cash register—the real McCoy.

Postcards and stamps: The Emporium on the west side of Main Street is the prime source for postcards; stamps are sold at City Hall.

Mailboxes: Located up and down Main Street. An elaborate polished brass one can be found near the entrance to Disney Clothiers, Ltd. Postmarks read Lake Buena Vista, *not* Walt Disney World.

Epcot Center

Imagine a typical world's fair, with the requisite number of pavilions devoted to nations from all around the world, and others depicting the advanced state of modern technology. Got all that?

Now imagine that same world's fair as the creators of the Magic Kingdom would have built it, using every skill and resource at their considerable command, not to mention the investment of about one billion dollars. You now have some small inkling of what Epcot Center is all about.

Walt Disney suggested the idea back in October 1966. "Epcot will be an experimental prototype community of tomorrow that will take its cue from the new ideas and new technologies that are now emerging from the creative centers of American industry." It would never be completed, he said, but would "always be introducing and testing and demonstrating new materials and systems."

There are two "entertainment worlds" that comprise Epcot Center— Future World and World Showcase. The former examines complex and often controversial concepts, such as energy and transportation, in ways that suddenly make them seem not only comprehensible but also downright irresistible. In the latter, the nations of the Earth are portrayed in all their variety, with extraordinary devotion to detail

During the next several years, there are plans for a new pavilion in Future World that will be devoted to space exploration, and the addition of a new thrill ride in World Showcase called Mount Fuji.

World Showcase

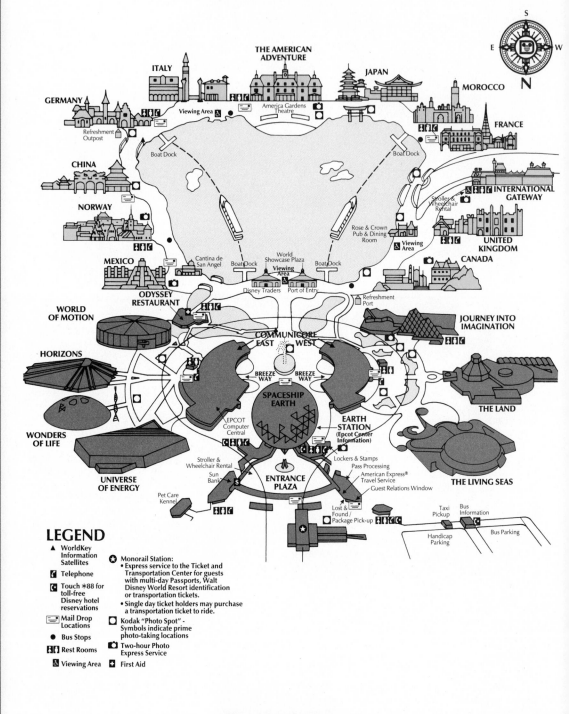

THE AMERICAN ADVENTURE

ITALY

JAPAN

GERMANY

MOROCCO

Viewing Area

America Gardens Theatre

FRANCE

Refreshment Outpost

CHINA

Boat Dock

Boat Dock

INTERNATIONAL GATEWAY

Stroller & Wheelchair Rental

NORWAY

Rose & Crown Pub & Dining Room

UNITED KINGDOM

Viewing Area

MEXICO

Cantina de San Angel

Boat Dock

World Showcase Plaza

Boat Dock

CANADA

Viewing Area

Disney Traders   Port of Entry

Refreshment Port

ODYSSEY RESTAURANT

WORLD OF MOTION

COMMUNICORE EAST   WEST

JOURNEY INTO IMAGINATION

HORIZONS

BREEZE WAY   BREEZE WAY

SPACESHIP EARTH

THE LAND

EPCOT Computer Central

EARTH STATION
(Epcot Center Information)

WONDERS OF LIFE

Stroller & Wheelchair Rental

Sun Bank

ENTRANCE PLAZA

Lockers & Stamps
Pass Processing
American Express® Travel Service
Guest Relations Window

THE LIVING SEAS

UNIVERSE OF ENERGY

Pet Care Kennel

Lost & Found / Package Pick-up

Taxi Pickup

Bus Information

Handicap Parking

Bus Parking

LEGEND

▲ WorldKey Information Satellites

☎ Telephone

☎ Touch *88 for toll-free Disney hotel reservations

✉ Mail Drop Locations

● Bus Stops

🚻 Rest Rooms

👁 Viewing Area

✚ First Aid

⊛ Monorail Station:
  • **Express service to the Ticket and Transportation Center for guests with multi-day Passports, Walt Disney World Resort identification or transportation tickets.**
  • Single day ticket holders may purchase a transportation ticket to ride.

☐ Kodak "Photo Spot" - Symbols indicate prime photo-taking locations

📷 Two-hour Photo Express Service

Future World

Getting In and Around

TRANSPORTATION TO EPCOT CENTER:
These two WDW entertainment worlds are
very easy to get to.

By car: Take Exit 26B off I-4 and follow the
signs along Epcot Center Drive through Epcot
Center's main gate. Epcot Center has a
9,000-space parking lot; daily parking costs
$4. Parking is free for Walt Disney World
resort guests with proper identification. Trams
carry visitors from their parking space right to
the ticket booths.

By WDW monorail and bus: In general,
allow about 30 minutes to get from one point
to another, whether you go by bus or by
monorail. Contact WDW Information (824-
4321) before leaving your room to confirm the
following routes and to check on the latest
operating schedules. (Schedules coordinate
with Epcot Center operating hours, so there's
little chance of being stranded.)

• From the *Contemporary* resort, *Grand
Floridian* resort, or *Polynesian* resort, take the
local hotel monorail to the TTC, walk down
the ramp and across the platform, and board
the TTC-Epcot Center monorail.

• From the *Disney Inn*, take the bus to the
TTC, then change to the TTC-Epcot Center
monorail.

• From the Magic Kingdom, take the
express monorail to the TTC, then walk down
the ramp and up the adjacent ramp to board
the TTC-Epcot Center monorail.

• From the Disney-MGM Studios Theme
Park, take the bus directly to Epcot Center.

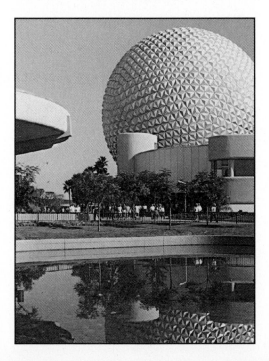

• From *Fort Wilderness*, take the bus to
the TTC, then change to the TTC-Epcot Center monorail.

• From *Wilderness Lodge*, take the bus to
the TTC, then change to the TTC-Epcot Center monorail.

• From the villas, take the bus directly to
Epcot Center.

• From the Disney Village Marketplace,
take the bus directly to Epcot Center.

• From Disney Village Hotel Plaza, take the
bus directly to Epcot Center.

• From the *Caribbean Beach* resort, take
the bus directly to Epcot Center.

• From the *Swan* and *Dolphin* hotels, take
the tram or walk directly to the World Showcase entrance.

• From the *Yacht Club* and *Beach Club*
resorts, take the tram or walk to the World
Showcase entrance.

• From *Port Orleans* and *Dixie Landings*,
take the bus directly to Epcot Center.

• From the *Disney Vacation Club*, take the
bus directly to Epcot Center.

• From *All-Star Sports* and *All-Star Music*
resorts, take the bus directly to Epcot Center.

HOURS: Epcot Center is usually open from
9 A.M. to 9 P.M.; hours are extended during
Presidents' week, spring school breaks, summer months, and certain holidays. Occasionally, during busy periods, the park may open
earlier or close later. Call 824-4321 for up-to-
the-minute schedules.

GETTING ORIENTED: Epcot Center is
shaped something like a giant hourglass.
Future World fills the northern bulb, while
World Showcase occupies the southern half.
In Future World, which is anchored on the
north by the imposing "geosphere" known as
Spaceship Earth, most pavilions are arranged
around the bulb's perimeter. The exceptions
are the two CommuniCore buildings (East and
West), which occupy the area at the center of
the bulb. In World Showcase, pavilions are
arranged around the edge of World Showcase
Lagoon, with the American Adventure directly
south of Spaceship Earth on the southern-
most shore of the lake.

BABY CARE: Changing tables and facilities
for nursing mothers can be found at Baby
Services, near the *Odyssey* restaurant
between World of Motion (in Future World)
and Mexico (in World Showcase). Check at
Earth Station for operating hours. Disposable
diapers also are kept behind the counter at
many merchandise locations in both worlds;
just ask.

CAMERA NEEDS: A large Camera Center is located on the west side of the Entrance Plaza. A good variety of film is available, and several different types of cameras can be rented or purchased. There is a satellite camera shop in Journey Into Imagination. Film is available at many World Showcase locations.

ENTERTAINMENT: There are many shows and musical performances throughout the day. Most of the larger shows are performed at the America Gardens Theatre in World Showcase. The Disney characters wear costumes appropriate to the pavilion they are visiting and will pose for pictures. IllumiNations, a spectacular after-dark laser, light, and music show, is a highlight of any Epcot Center visit. (Details are on page 250.) Pick up an entertainment schedule when you arrive at Guest Services or at any merchandise location.

FIRST AID: Minor medical problems can be handled at First Aid, which is near the *Odyssey* restaurant, between the World of Motion (in Future World) and Mexico (in World Showcase).

GETTING AROUND: Five 66-foot water taxis, the *FriendShip* launches, shuttle guests back and forth across World Showcase Lagoon. Docks are located at both sides of World Showcase Plaza, in front of Germany, and near Morocco. Several double-decker buses, in styles once found all over New York City, London, and Berlin, can be boarded for a ride around the World Showcase Promenade, stopping at several points along the way.

VISITORS WITH DISABILITIES: Nearly all the attractions, shops, and restaurants in Epcot Center are completely barrier-free. Parking for guests with disabilities is available; inquire at the Auto Plaza. The monorail platform is accessible via elevator. Wheelchairs can be rented at the Stroller and Wheelchair Rentals shop on the east side of the Entrance Plaza, at the Gift Stop on the west side, and at the International Gateway. The Walt Disney World

Guide for Guests With Disabilities is available at Earth Station. Assistive Listening Devices, which amplify the audio in selected attractions, are available at Earth Station. They cost $4 for the day and guests must leave a $40 refundable deposit. Written descriptions of most Epcot Center attractions also are available for hearing-impaired guests at Earth Station. Special complimentary tour cassettes are available at Earth Station for sight-impaired guests. A refundable $25 deposit is required for the cassette player.

INFORMATION: Once inside Future World, visit Earth Station, beside Spaceship Earth, to use the computer terminals of the WorldKey Information Service there. Hosts and hostesses also are on hand. Visit the WorldKey satellite in World Showcase outside Germany.

LOCKERS: These can be found at the Bus Information Center in the bus parking lot, just outside the Entrance Plaza, and in a small area on the west side of the plaza, underneath Spaceship Earth.

LOST AND FOUND: Located on the west side of the Entrance Plaza.

MEMORABILIA: Gateway Gifts, located alongside Spaceship Earth in the Entrance Plaza, Centorium in Future World's Communi-Core East, and Disney Traders in World Showcase Plaza are the three main sources for Epcot Center souvenirs. The Gift Stop and the Stroller and Wheelchair Rentals shop near the Entrance Plaza are good shopping spots, too. Souvenirs of the participating nations are found in each World Showcase pavilion and at Disney Traders in World Showcase Plaza.

MONEY MATTERS: Currency exchange and other banking services are available at the Sun Bank on the east side of the Entrance Plaza, just beyond the ticket booths. Currency exchange also is available at the American Express Travel Office on the west side of the Entrance Plaza. Both credit cards (American Express, Visa, and MasterCard) and traveler's checks are accepted in shops—(with the exception of fast-food locations, where you must pay with cash or traveler's checks only) in restaurants as well.

PACKAGE PICKUP: Cumbersome or heavy purchases can be transported free of charge (by Disney hosts or hostesses) to this small office on the west side of the Entrance Plaza for later pickup. Ask your salesperson to arrange this service.

THE GIFT STOP: Rental wheelchairs and strollers are available, and film, gift items, sundries, and tobacco are sold. Located near the parking lot for guests with disabilities at the entrance to the park.

PETS: No pets are permitted in Epcot Center, but there is the Pet Care Kennel just east of the Entrance Plaza. *Do not leave pets in the car.* It is against the law in Florida. The cost for boarding pets is $4 per day per pet; pets may not be boarded overnight at the Epcot Center kennel.

STROLLER AND WHEELCHAIR RENTALS: Available in the shop of that name on the east side of the Entrance Plaza, and at the International Gateway. Wheelchairs also are available at the Gift Stop. Replacement strollers and wheelchairs are available in Germany and at the International Gateway. Remember to keep your rental receipt; it can be used on the same day in the Magic Kingdom, at the Disney-MGM Studios Theme Park, or again in Epcot Center should you leave and return at a later hour.

ADMISSION: Tickets and Passports are available for one, four, and five days. The Disney organization defines a ticket as admission for one day only; other forms of admission media (for longer periods) are called Passports. One-day tickets may be used at the Magic Kingdom, Epcot Center, or the Disney-MGM Studios Theme Park, but not at more than one site on the same day. Four-day Super Passes and Five-day Super Duper Passes can be used at the Magic Kingdom, Epcot Center, and the Disney-MGM Studios Theme Park on the same day; unlike one-day tickets, they also include unlimited use of the transportation system inside Walt Disney World. The Five-day Super Duper Pass also allows admission to River Country, Typhoon Lagoon, Discovery Island, and Pleasure Island for a seven-day period beginning with the first use of the pass. Guests staying at Walt Disney World resorts can purchase a Be Our Guest Pass valid for the length of their stay. The Be Our Guest Pass offers savings over the Four-Day Super Passes and Five-Day Super Duper Passes, and includes unlimited admission to the Magic Kingdom, Epcot Center, the Disney-MGM Studios Theme Park, Pleasure Island, Typhoon Lagoon, River Country, and Discovery Island for the duration of your stay. Cash, traveler's checks,

personal checks (with proper ID), American Express, Visa, and MasterCard can be used to pay for all admission media. Multi-day Passports do not have to be used on consecutive days. Note that old multi-day World Passports are not accepted for admission to Disney-MGM Studios Theme Park.

ADMISSION PRICES*

ONE-DAY TICKET
(Restricted to use in Epcot Center only.)

Adult	$ 35.90
Child**	$ 28.50

FOUR-DAY SUPER PASS
(Valid in all three parks for four days and includes use of WDW transportation system.)

Adult	$126.70
Child**	$ 99.25

FIVE-DAY SUPER DUPER PASS
(Valid in all three parks for five days, includes use of WDW transportation system, and allows admission to Typhoon Lagoon, River Country, Discovery Island, and Pleasure Island for up to seven days from the first use of the Super Pass.)

Adult	$174.30
Child**	$138.40

BE OUR GUEST PASS
(Available to WDW resort guests only. Valid in all three parks, Typhoon Lagoon, Pleasure Island, Discovery Island, and River Country for the duration of stay and includes unlimited use of WDW transportation system.)

Length of Stay	Adult	Child**
3 nights/4 days	$139.44	$109.87
4 nights/5 days	$162.67	$128.84
5 nights/6 days	$183.80	$145.76
6 nights/7 days	$201.76	$160.57
7 nights/8 days	$213.37	$170.09
8 nights/9 days	$223.87	$178.51
9 nights/10 days	$234.42	$186.96
10 nights/11days	$244.98	$195.41

The cost of an **ANNUAL PASSPORT** is $200.60 for adults and $174.25 for children; renewals are $179.40 for adults and $153.05 for children.

Note: Multi-day Passports need not be used on consecutive days.

These prices were correct at press time, but may change during 1994.

*The prices quoted include sales tax.
**3 through 9 years of age

Future World

A mere listing of the basic themes covered by the Future World pavilions—agriculture, communications, the ocean, energy, health, imagination, and transportation—tends to sound a tad academic, and perhaps even a little forbidding. But when these serious topics are presented with that special Disney flair, they become part of an experience that ranks among Walt Disney World's most exciting. Some of these subjects are explored in the course of lively and unusual Disney "adventures," involving a whole arsenal of remarkable motion pictures, special effects, and Audio-Animatronics figures so lifelike that it is hard to remain unmoved. Other themes come into play at hands-on exhibits full of touch-sensitive video screens, two-way television sets, computers that play special games, and other high-tech equipment. The basic elements of Future World are warm, attractive, and appealing in their own right, from the palm-dotted Entrance Plaza and the massive (but airy) glass-walled buildings of CommuniCore East and West to the stupendous fountain just past Spaceship Earth and the many-faceted "geosphere" that has rapidly become the universal symbol of Epcot Center.

There is so much to see and enjoy that it's hard to know just what to do first. Many guests simply stop at Spaceship Earth on their way into Epcot Center and proceed to wander at random from one pavilion to the next through the morning. As a result, many of the pavilions are frustratingly crowded in the morning—especially Spaceship Earth, which has its largest crowds before lunch.

A wise alternative is to choose one pavilion from those described below—or perhaps two, if you've arrived early enough to be there when the gates to Epcot Center open—and then to head for World Showcase, moving clockwise around the lagoon on one day of your visit and counterclockwise on the next. Then in the afternoon, when the majority of guests are lining up at World Showcase pavilions, return to Future World. World of Motion, Horizons, Universe of Energy, and The Living Seas have relatively few visitors during the late afternoon hours; CommuniCore East and World of Motion's TransCenter are not only fascinating spots to pass the exceptionally busy hours after lunch, but also very cool refuges when high temperatures prevail outdoors. And although queues can be found during peak seasons at Journey Into Imagination, The Land, and Wonders of Life throughout most of the late morning and afternoon—not only for the several attractions that each one houses, but also at the pavilion entrances—the period from late afternoon through closing is usually less hectic.

Getting Oriented

As a guest crosses the enormous Entrance Plaza, the gleaming silver ball straight ahead (and facing south) is Spaceship Earth (not to be confused with Earth Station, which is at its base). CommuniCore East (at left) and West (to the right) are the two large crescent-shaped buildings that flank the large fountain just past Spaceship Earth. Universe of Energy, Wonders of Life, Horizons, and World of Motion lie to the left (east) of CommuniCore East; Journey Into Imagination, The Land, and The Living Seas are located to the right (west) of CommuniCore West. The World Showcase section of Epcot Center surrounds the shoreline of the large World Showcase Lagoon.

Future World pavilions are described here as a visitor encounters them while moving counterclockwise (from right around to the left, that's west to east around the area).

1. Spaceship Earth
2. CommuniCore West
3. The Living Seas
4. The Land
5. Journey Into Imagination
6. World of Motion
7. Horizons
8. Wonders of Life
9. Universe of Energy
10. CommuniCore East

Spaceship Earth

As it looms impressively just above the earth, this great faceted silver geosphere—visible on a clear day from an airplane flying along either Florida coast—looks a little bit like the gigantic spaceship in *Close Encounters of the Third Kind* ready to blast off. It looks large from a distance, and seems even more immense when viewed from directly underneath. It's no surprise that most visitors simply stop beneath it and gawk. The show inside, which explores the continuing search by human beings for ever more efficient means of communication, remains one of Epcot Center's most visually compelling.

Weighing 16 million pounds, measuring 165 feet in diameter and 180 feet in height, and encompassing 2,200,000 cubic feet of space, this geosphere is held aloft by six legs supported by pylons sunk 100 feet into the ground. The distinctive sheen of its covering derives from a sort of quarter-inch-thick sandwich made of two anodized aluminum faces and a polyethylene core. This sheath is made up of 954 triangular panels, not all of equal size or shape.

A common misconception about Spaceship Earth is that it is a geodesic dome. Not so. The designers had to make up the word *geosphere* because the structure is unlike any other pre-existing building. A geodesic dome is composed of only half a sphere, while Spaceship Earth is completely round. Nor can it be compared to the similarly faceted cre-ation that housed the U.S. Pavilion at Montreal's Expo 67, which actually was only three-quarters of a sphere. In fact, this extraordinarily large Disney creation is not even a perfect sphere; the steelworkers' requirements dictated its slightly uneven dimensions. Presented by AT&T.

SPACESHIP EARTH RIDE: The noted science fiction writer Ray Bradbury, together with a number of consultants and advisers from the Smithsonian Institution, the Los Angeles area's prestigious Huntington Library, University of Southern California, and the University of Chicago (among others), collaborated with Disney designers in developing this memorable journey. It begins in an inky black time tunnel complete with a musty smell that suggests the ages, and continues through history from the days of Cro-Magnon man (30 or 40 thousand years ago) to the present.

En route, an Egyptian temple shows off the pictorial representations of words and sounds known as hieroglyphics, which were first used around 3000 B.C., and hieratic writing, a form of script used to write on papyrus. A Phoenician scene set in the ninth century B.C. acknowledges civilization's debt to those tireless traders who introduced a 22-character alphabet (based on sounds) that put written communication, once the province of the intelligentsia alone, within the grasp of the masses. The Roman systems of roads, the Islamic empire, the efforts of 11th- and 12th-century Benedictine monks to handcopy

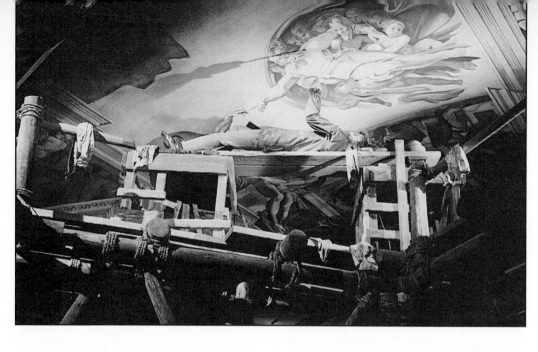

religious and classical manuscripts, the Gutenberg press, the Renaissance in Italy, and a number of the 20th century's inventions are all represented, and in most cases it's not necessary to be a history scholar to understand why. The Greek theater scene, whose meaning here may not be as widely understood as it should be, reminds viewers that it was the Greeks who refined the alphabet (by the addition of vowels) and then went on to use the language so expressively. Then, as now, theater was an important means of examining and transmitting the moral and social questions of the time.

The attraction features some remarkable special effects: the flickering candles in the scene where a monk (himself crafted with such precision and authenticity as to appear to be breathing) has nodded off; the smell of smoke coming from the fall of Rome, to name only a couple.

And every scene is executed in exquisite detail. The symbols on the wall of that Egyptian temple really are hieroglyphics, and the content of the letter being dictated by the Pharaoh was excerpted from a missive actually received by an agent of a ruler of the period. The actor in the Greek theater scene is delivering lines from Sophocles' *Oedipus Rex*. In the scene depicting the fall of Rome, the graffiti reproduces markings from the walls of Pompeii. In the Islamic scene, the quadrant—an instrument used in astronomy and navigation—is a copy of one from the tenth century. The type on Johannes Gutenberg's press actually moves, and the page that the celebrated 15th-century printer is examining is a replica of one from a Bible in the collection of the above-mentioned Huntington Library. In the Renaissance scene, the book being read is Virgil's *Aeneid*; the musical instruments in that scene are a lute and a *lyra da braccio*, both replicas of real period

pieces. During the 20th-century scenes, the steam-powered press is a reproduction of one that had been developed by William Bullock around 1863, notable because it used paper in continuous rolls rather than individual sheets.

Some visitors wonder as to the identity of the excerpts from the radio and television shows broadcast in this area. Take note: The former include *The Lone Ranger*, *The Shadow*, a commentary by Walter Winchell, and the Joe Louis–Max Schmeling 1938 rematch. It's the first round, and Schmeling, who had inflicted Joe Louis' first loss in a 1936 12th-round K.O., is on the mat. The referee is counting—and the crowds are going wild. Among the television programs are Walter Cronkite's reports from the March 10, 1964, New Hampshire Republican primary, Walt Disney introducing *The Wonderful World of Color*, Ed Sullivan and the Harlem Globetrotters, the Colts versus Browns NFL championship game (1964), and *Ozzie and Harriet*, featuring David and Ricky Nelson. Film buffs may recognize clips from the movies *Girl Shy* with Harold Lloyd (1924), *Top Hat* with Fred Astaire and Ginger Rogers (1935), and *20,000 Leagues Under the Sea* (1954).

All these sights are enough to keep necks craning and heads turning as the "time machines" wend their way upward. The most dazzling scene is the ride's finale, when the vehicles arrive at the topmost point in the geosphere, and visitors gaze in awe into a vast inky dome full of what seem like thousands of tiny stars. These are projected by a "star ball," created by the Disney special effects department when it was discovered that the ceiling of the geosphere was too large for conventional planetarium equipment.

Note: The lines for this attraction are usually longest during the morning hours, and at their shortest just before park closing time.

GATEWAY GIFTS AND CAMERA CENTER:
These two shops are located quite near the entrance to Spaceship Earth. The former sells Epcot Center souvenirs—T-shirts, mugs, toys, etc.—as well as suntan lotion, tissues, and the like. Film and various other Kodak products are sold at the Camera Center. Cameras, including RCA Video Camcorders, are sold or rented here and same-day film processing is available.

EARTH STATION: The similarity of names between this area (just south of Spaceship Earth) and that of the attraction itself can be confusing to first-time visitors, and that's unfortunate because this area is one of the most vital parts of Epcot Center.

Not only is it the principal source of Epcot Center information, but it also is the spot to make dinner reservations via the easy-to-use touch-sensitive TV screens. For more specific details on making these reservations, see page 222. When the terminals are not being utilized to arrange tables for dinner, they can be used to get an overall picture of Epcot Center, to learn about each pavilion in considerable detail, and to discover nearly everything else that a guest could conceivably want to know about Epcot Center. If the system's electronic A-to-Z index to shops, restaurants, attractions, and services does not answer a question, it's possible to communicate with a specially trained human host or hostess, who will be able to hear and see the querying guest with the aid of a microphone and video camera unobtrusively placed adjacent to the screen. These hosts and hostesses also manage the message service for Epcot Center guests. (Many WorldKey Information Service hosts and hostesses speak Spanish; some speak other languages.) Resort reservations can be made at the Reservations Desk.

Meanwhile, overhead, huge multifaceted screens provide an overview (albeit a somewhat cubistic one) of everything Epcot Center offers, while hosts and hostesses are on duty in person at the counter. They also keep records of any lost children who may be at Baby Services at any given time.

CommuniCore West

This pavilion, the large crescent-shaped building located just west of the three-tiered fountain south of Earth Station (to your right while facing World Showcase Plaza), is the setting not only for one of Future World's most attractive fast-food eateries, but also for an exhibit known as FutureCom that is similar to the lively Epcot Computer Central in CommuniCore East.

FUTURECOM: How people gather information—via signs and satellites, newspapers and traffic lights, ticker tape and telephones—is the topic here. Dominating the area is a sculpture known as the Fountain of Information, made up of just about all the forms of communication with which 20th-century denizens are bombarded: books and records, magazines, maps, TV screens, laser discs, signs, labels, seed catalogs, stock certificates, movie films, neon lights, and more.

Equally compelling are a couple of hands-on exhibits that show new technology. At one bank of touch-sensitive TV screens, a visitor merely touches the machine to find out what's happening in his or her home state. Another exhibit demonstrates video teleconferencing; increasingly, businesses are using this device in lieu of flying their employees all over the country for meetings. At Epcot Center it gives guests the chance to see themselves on TV.

Don't miss the Phraser. It actually speaks, in a curious monotone, the words that guests peck out on a typewriter keyboard, and it does so with remarkable accuracy—as long as the words follow standard rules of pronunciation.

Also amusing is an adjacent Network Control game, which, by giving visitors a chance to try it for themselves, demonstrates how network controllers at the telephone companies manage the flow of long-distance telephone calls. The idea of the nearby Chip Cruiser game is to use "laser beams" to blast computer-control-room contaminants before they affect the service. Presented by AT&T.

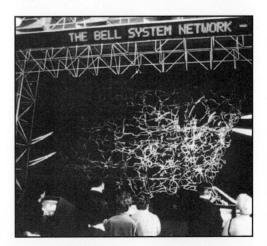

EPCOT OUTREACH: No single Epcot Center pavilion pretends to tell the whole story of the subject it covers, but with this information and resource center (to the northern half of CommuniCore West, the section closest to Spaceship Earth), no visitor can complain about the lack of fact-finding sources at Epcot Center. That's because Epcot Outreach provides access to information from encyclopedias, periodicals, and wire services via a computerized data service. A research librarian and a group of assistants can extract appropriate printed materials from the files at hand to answer any lingering questions that might remain. The topics covered? Anything and everything that's presented in either Future World or World Showcase.

Teacher's Center: Educators can preview films, videos, filmstrips, multimedia kits, and computer software. Bonuses are the complimentary lesson plans on Future World themes, geared to students from elementary through high school levels.

The Living Seas

A trip four fathoms deep into the Caribbean Sea awaits visitors here. The Living Seas is the largest facility ever dedicated to mankind's relationship with the ocean and was designed by the Disney Imagineers, the company's creative design organization, in cooperation with a board of some of the world's most distinguished oceanographic experts and scientists.

At the entrance to The Living Seas is a styl-ized rockwork marquee that suggests a natural coastline with waves cascading into tidal pools. Upon entering, there's a 125-foot-long sea mural that leads to a display depicting the technological advances in undersea exploration, from Leonardo da Vinci's sketches of underwater breathing devices and submersibles to photos of John Lethbridge's diving barrel and Frederic de Drieberg's 1809 breathing device. Also featured is the diving suit from Walt Disney's classic film *20,000 Leagues Under the Sea*, and the actual 11-foot-long model *Nautilus* used in the movie. Next, as part of the introduction to The Living Seas, is a 2½-minute multimedia presentation that salutes the pioneers of ocean research, beginning with early ships, diving bells, submarines, and aqualungs. The show also features a seven-minute special effects film that attempts to demonstrate the critical role of the ocean as a source of energy, minerals, and protein. Some scenes were filmed in very remote parts of the world.

There's a ride through a Caribbean coral reef, housed in a huge tank 200 feet in diameter and 27 feet deep, plus Sea Base Alpha,

where hands-on activities, underwater movies, video monitors, and the opportunity to communicate with the divers in the tank are sure to prolong visitors' stays. The *Coral Reef* restaurant offers fresh seafood in a setting where diners can look out at the coral reef through acrylic windows 18 feet high and 8 inches thick. Tables are arranged on tiers so that all patrons have an unobstructed view. Presented by United Technologies.

CARIBBEAN CORAL REEF RIDE: To reach the two-passenger sea cabs that make the trip to the coral reef, visitors enter "hydrolators," elevatorlike capsules that actually descend about an inch while creating the illusion of diving deep under the sea. The manmade reef exists in a 5.7 million-gallon tank where more than 200 varieties of sea-life, ranging from tiny crustaceans to large predators, live in a simulated environment that accurately re-creates the chemistry and life-support ecosystems of the Caribbean Sea. Among the 5,000 inhabitants are sea bass, parrot fish, puffers, barracuda, butterfly fish, angelfish, sharks, croakers, hog snappers, dolphins, and diamond rays.

In addition to the vast array of sealife and vegetation, guests also get to see scuba divers testing and demonstrating the newest diving gear and underwater monitoring equipment, as they carry on training experiments with dolphins. Wireless radios allow the divers to talk to onlookers and explain their work. Other undersea attractions include a diver in a "JIM" suit, the latest in atmospheric diving-wear technology (at Sea Base Alpha, guests have the chance to try one on personally), two one-person submarines, and two mini-robotic submersibles.

Scientists had to develop foods to simulate the taste, chemistry, and nutritional value of natural coral. The resulting meal for parrot fish, for example, consists of dry dog food, chickens' laying pellets, a complete amino-acid solution, and a vitamin B-complex solution, all held together by dental plaster. Yum! Following the ride, guests are conveniently deposited at the Visitors Center of Sea Base Alpha.

SEA BASE ALPHA: This prototype undersea research facility, set up on two levels connected by escalators, includes a visitors center and six modules, each dedicated to a specific subject. One module focuses on ocean ecosystems and shows various forms of adaptation, including camouflage, symbiosis, and bioluminescence. A 6,000-gallon tank displays another coral reef where Bermuda morays, barracuda, and bonnethead sharks swim about. Another module is dedicated to the study of porpoises and manatees. A large holding tank features a step-in port, where guests can see the mammals up close. At another Sea Base Alpha station, a delightful

show stars an Audio-Animatronics submersible named Jason who describes the history of robotics and their use in underwater exploration to visitors. In the same area, guests can try on a cut-away "JIM" suit, and test its maneuverability by doing a series of tasks as part of a game. There also are video screens around the Sea Base where visitors can test and expand their knowledge of oceanography.

SEA BASE CONCOURSE: Adjacent to the six modules, the concourse features three displays. The floor-to-ceiling diver lock-out chamber is where the crew enters and exits the ocean environment. Visitors can see the divers enter the chamber, ascend, and disappear through the ceiling of the concourse. A full-size mock-up of the latest one-person submersible vehicle, the Deep Rover, is suspended from the mezzanine of the concourse. The Deep Rover is capable of descending more than 3,000 feet below the ocean's surface.

WHERE TO EAT IN EPCOT CENTER

For all the details on all the restaurants in Epcot Center—including both those in Future World and World Showcase—plus information about how to obtain restaurant reservations, see the *Good Meals, Great Times* chapter that begins on page 209.

The Land

Occupying six acres, this enormous sky-lighted pavilion examines the nature of one of everybody's favorite topics—food. A film, *Symbiosis*, dramatically explores the creative partnerships between mankind and the land we inhabit. A boat ride takes a look at farming in the past and future. Guided tours give interested visitors the chance to learn more about the experimental agricultural techniques actually being practiced in the pavilion and nearby greenhouses, and to get ideas about applications in the garden. In addition, the subject of nutrition is touched upon in one of Future World's wackiest attractions, an Audio-Animatronics musical show (called the Kitchen Kabaret Revue) which was inspired by the Country Bear Jamboree in the Magic Kingdom.

Since this also is the home of two of Epcot Center's most interesting eating spots, The Land is understandably popular. During peak seasons, lengthy queues do build up, not only for the boat ride but also for entry to the pavilion itself, especially around 11 A.M. (Those with reservations for the guided tour or for a meal in *The Land Grille Room* restaurant are permitted to bypass the queue within 15 minutes of the time of their appointment.) The best plan is to visit the pavilion first thing in the morning, have a quick breakfast here, and perhaps make reservations for lunch in *The Land Grille Room*. Or wait until afternoon, when—though there may be a wait for the boat ride—it probably won't be necessary to line up just to get inside. Count on spending a total of two hours at The Land, longer if plans include eating here. Presented by Nestlé USA.

LISTEN TO THE LAND: This 13½-minute boat ride ventures into three ecological communities (rain forest, desert, and prairie) that covered much of the world before humans arrived on the scene. It then cruises through a turn-of-the-century American farm and, finally, moves among growing areas full of live plants for a mind-expanding sample of innovative agricultural techniques. In an Aquacell area, fish and shrimp are raised in a controlled environment, and in the Desert Farm area, plants receive nutrients through a drip irrigation system that delivers just the right amount of water, and no more—important in an arid climate.

As fantastic and unreal as they appear, the plants on view in the experimental greenhouses are all living. In contrast, those in the biomes (ecological communities) were manufactured in Disney studios out of flexible, lightweight plastic that simulates the cellulose found in real trees. The trunks and branches were molded from live specimens; the majestic sycamore in the farmhouse's front yard, for example, duplicates one that stands outside a Burbank, California, car wash. Hundreds of thousands of polyethylene leaves, made in Hong Kong, were then snapped on. These are fire retardant, as are the blades of grass, which are made of glass fibers implanted into rubber mats. In the South American rain forest scene, the water on the leaves and trunks is supplied by a special drip system that provides a constant flow of moisture.

KITCHEN KABARET REVUE: Bonnie Appetit is the star of this zany show about good nutrition. Each of the four acts focuses on one of the main food groups—dairy products, fruits and vegetables, meats and proteins, and grains and cereals. But that is almost peripheral to the entertainment, presented by the Kitchen Krackpots band, Mr. Dairy Goods and the Stars of the Milky Way, the Boogie Woogie Bak'ry Boy, the Cereal Sisters (Mairzy Oats, Rennie Rice, and Connie Corn), the Colander Combo, the Fiesta Fruit, and Mr. Hamm and that incurable punster Mr. Eggz, who joke up a corny storm. ("Cheese! I cheddar to think about it," says one. And: "Why was Chicken Little so upset when his mom fell asleep in a hot tub? His brother was born hard-boiled.") The characters are endearing, especially Mr. Broccoli, with his punk-rocker hairdo and pink-rimmed glasses. Note that this show may be different when you visit since Nestlé recently took over as the pavilion's sponsor from Kraft General Foods.

HARVEST TOUR: Guided tours take place daily every half hour between 9:30 A.M. and 4:30 P.M. They cover basically the same topics as the boat ride, but because they last at least 45 minutes, they can go into far more detail. And participants do have an opportunity to ask questions—and listen to what the home gardeners and farmers who commonly make up at least part of the tour groups have to say. Guides are all members of the agricultural operations staff, and all have degrees in some area of agriculture. Reservations, which are required, must be made in person early on the day of the tour near the Broccoli & Co. shop at the entrance to the Kitchen Kabaret Revue on the pavilion's lower level. The Listen to the Land boat ride is a suggested prerequisite.

SYMBIOSIS: Presented in the Harvest Theater (near The Land's entrance) on a 23-by-60-foot screen, this 19-minute 70mm motion picture examines the delicate balance between technology's progress and environmental integrity, reinforcing the sound ideas behind some of the techniques seen in The Land's growing areas. There are some horror stories about the misuse of land, including tales of the pollution of lakes and streams throughout the world. But there also are some tremendously reassuring tales—the timely rescue of the Thames, Europe's Lake Constance, and Oregon's Willamette River from death-by-pollution, and sound forest management practices in Sweden, in Germany's Black Forest, and in the United States' Pacific Northwest. Filming took place in about 30 nations, and there is some terrific scenery. The breathtaking opening scene shows the magnificent rice terraces located near Banaue in the Philippines. Don't let the ominous-sounding name of the film put you off: This is a highlight of any Epcot Center visit.

BROCCOLI & CO.: This little shop between the Farmers Market and the Kitchen Kabaret Revue stocks merchandise such as hydroponic plants, seeds, books, topiaries, and kitchen accessories, including magnetized plastic stick-ons to embellish the front of a refrigerator, place mats, and more.

Journey Into Imagination

The oddly shaped glass pyramids that house Journey Into Imagination (as you face World Showcase Lagoon and then straight ahead to your right) are striking, but they pale by comparison with the experiences inside—which are among the most exciting at Epcot Center. Dreamfinder, a jolly, red-headed, professorial figure, who sports a carrot-colored beard and is accompanied by a purple baby dragon called Figment, is only one of the pavilion's delights. He appears in person outside and again when he escorts guests through the imagination world during a 14-minute ride inside.

There's also a dazzling 3-D movie, starring Michael Jackson, called *Captain EO*. Not to mention the electronic fun house known as the Image Works. Or the quirky fountains outside—the Jellyfish Fountains that spurt streams of water that spread out at the top, look like their namesake sea creature for an instant, and then fall back to earth; or the Serpentine Fountains, which send out smooth streams of water that arc from one garden plot to another in the most astonishing fashion.

Plant lovers will recognize the sculpted trees in this garden as *podocarpus*—the same type that are planted in many other locations (but pruned to many different shapes) throughout Epcot Center.

Count on spending an hour and 15 minutes at the very least at this pavilion—two hours wouldn't be too long at all. During peak seasons, the queue outside seems to be longest between around 10 A.M. and noon and remains fairly lengthy throughout most of the day. Early mornings and late evenings are the least congested times to visit. Presented by Kodak.

JOURNEY INTO IMAGINATION RIDE: It is here that Dreamfinder creates Figment out of a lizard's body, a crocodile's nose, a steer's horns, two big yellow eyes, two small wings, and a pinch of childish delight—and commences the visitor's journey into the world of imagination.

First timers may not realize that the 14-minute ride doesn't present a random assortment of scenes that are handsome and scary by turns, but rather an organized exploration of how imagination works and the areas of life in which it functions.

First there is a visit to the Dreamport, the area of the mind to which the senses are constantly sending data to be stored for later use by the imagination. Subsequent scenes depict the way imagination suffuses the worlds of the visual arts, of literature, of the performing arts, and of science and technology. In the course of all this, laser beams dance, lightning crackles, and letters pour out of a giant typewriter like notes from an organ. The images are as fanciful as imagination itself.

It's interesting to note that the iridescent painting-in-progress on the wall in the visual arts scene—a so-called "polage" produced by refracting light through polarized filters—is the largest of its kind anywhere. The artist who executed the mural had previously done paintings no larger than four feet in height. Also, when you see flashing lights (about three-quarters of the way through the ride), be sure to sit up straight and smile—your picture is being taken. You'll see your photo at the end of the ride.

IMAGE WORKS: It's a rare Image Works visitor who doesn't experience at least some of the emotion felt by one four-year-old girl who cried every time her parents tried to take her home. That's not surprising, because Image Works is literally crammed with activities that give every visitor the chance to use his or her imagination.

For instance, at Dreamfinder's School of Drama, near the entrance to the Image Works, visitors have the opportunity to be in a TV show. Guests step onto a small stage and, thanks to a Chroma-Key video effects technique that involves foreground and background matting, perform in short video stories. Spectators and performers alike see the results as they happen via strategically placed video screens. It's *always* fun to watch the groups of senior citizens, teenagers, or families jumping crazily around on stage following on-screen instructions from Dreamfinder (and, in fact, having the time to spend more than just a few seconds watching these goings-on is sufficient reason to allot more time to your overall Epcot Center visit).

A new exhibit at Image Works is Figment's Coloring Book, where guests use state-of-the-art computer technology to electronically paint giant, dimensional coloring-book images of Figment and Dreamfinder. The Sensor is a sort of electronic maze whose various elements react to a visitor's presence by producing lights and sounds. Upon entering the Rainbow Corridor, you'll find a tunnel full of neon tubes in all the hues of the rainbow. Image Warp's pneumatically powered Mylar mirrors produce moving versions of old-style fun house reflections in a room wackily illuminated by strobe lights. Then there's the Lumia—a plastic ball seven feet in diameter, inside which swirling patterns of light and color appear in response to the sounds of voices of different frequencies and intensities. Another new feature is Making Faces, a set of screens that allow you to electronically capture your own image and then apply different noses, hairstyles, ears, eyes, and even accessories. At Stepping Tones, hexagonal splotches of colored light on the floor correspond to sounds—a drumroll, a flourish on the harp, a couple of chords sung by a men's chorus, a snippet of hoedown fiddling, and

such—that are emitted when the area is trodden upon; the last red hexagon in the room, located in the farthest corner from the entrance, sends out the sound of a beautiful chord played on a harp. In fact, the first tones re-create the music heard in *Close Encounters of the Third Kind*. The floor was "orchestrated" by an avant-garde San Francisco Bay Area composer so that all possible combinations sound interesting at the very least—and the more the merrier. In the new Mirage Room, Figment stars in a series of animated sequences using a unique holographic process. At Optical Illusion you'll see an animated hot-air balloon race between Figment and Dreamfinder.

Other activities include Light Writer, which involves drawing geometric patterns with laser beams, and the Magic Palette, where a special stylus and a touch-sensitive control surface can be used to create all kinds of images, mostly in Day-Glo colors. People often queue up to try these, while huge kaleidoscopes nearby and the very unusual pin screens are practically overlooked. Manufacturing the latter involved putting thousands of straight pins through a screen illuminated with colored lights from below (visitors run their hands across the bottom, thereby creating sweeping patterns of color).

The Electronic Philharmonic, one of the most amusing sections of the Image Works, allows guests to take turns conducting an orchestra. It's been renovated so now the feeling of conducting is even more realistic. Here's how this works: Each patch of light on the console represents a group of instruments (strings, woodwinds, brass, percussion). Raising and lowering one's hand above that patch of light increases and decreases the volume of the sound produced by that section of the "orchestra"; by covering three out of four patches of light, it is theoretically possible to bring up only the strings or only the brass.

CAPTAIN EO: This dazzling, 3-D musical fantasy stars Michael Jackson as the captain of a spaceship. The band of characters includes Hooter, Fuzzball, and Geex. Their mission: to transform the dismal planet ruled by the evil Supreme Leader (played by Academy Award-winner Angelica Huston) into a happy place through the magic of music and dance. Jackson wrote and performs two songs: "We Are Here to Change the World" and "Another Part of Me." The theater is outfitted with state-of-the-art audio and video equipment, as well as devices that help create the spectacular series of special three-dimensional effects.

CAMERAS AND FILM: A good selection of film is for sale here, along with a small selection of cameras, filters, cable releases, and other necessities of life for the traveling photographer. Some souvenir items also are available.

World of Motion

This wheel-shaped, stainless-steel-clad structure, 318 feet in diameter and about 60 feet high, presents the story of transportation past, present, and future through a whimsical show full of Audio-Animatronics figures (the most colorful since the hairy-legged Pirates of the Caribbean in the Magic Kingdom) and exhibits that look far into the future of transportation.

The tall trees on the plaza in front of the pavilion are sycamores: They were grown from seeds planted more than a dozen years ago. The tops are being pruned flat and the branches trimmed so that in a few years passengers on the monorail will look across a flat plane of treetops, while guests on the ground will be shaded by a spreading canopy of green. Presented by General Motors.

WORLD OF MOTION RIDE: Chronicling our passion for always getting somewhere just a little bit faster, this appealing, if rather unsophisticated, show reflects the eccentric humor of one of its chief designers—longtime Disney art director Ward Kimball, who also shares the credit for creating Jiminy Cricket. The 14 1/2-minute ride-through attraction begins with a look back to the sometimes painful days when foot power was the only means of transportation. It then moves wackily forward through time as mankind tries out ostriches and zebras, dreams of magic carpets, invents the wheel, rides in chariots, and tinkers with flying machines, balloons, steam carriages, riverboats, stagecoaches, buckboards, airplanes, automobiles, and assorted other vehicles.

In the show's 22 scenes, about 150 Audio-Animatronics figures make their debut. (Actually, some of the faces of the "people" in the group are used several times, but since they

wear different expressions, only the exceptionally keen of eye recognize the duplication.)

In order to lend verisimilitude to each scene, bicycles, streetlights, cars, carts, wagons, and trains were added as props—some of them genuine antiques and some of them line-by-line reproductions. The Wells Fargo Stagecoach in the Western wagons scene is a 150-year-old item imported from Phoenix, Arizona, and then restored, along with several others unearthed in northern California. In the city scene, the telephone wire is the real thing (made around 1920), and all of the early automobiles are authentic. Especially amusing is the final scene, which shows Americans enjoying the good life on the road in a trio of spiffy vintage cars that looked modern not too long ago.

The journey through the history of transportation is followed by trips through special "speed rooms" that provide a dizzying you-are-there feeling. The film was shot in 70mm, and includes a visit to a breathtaking city of the future, where trainlike vehicles shoot through the air from skyscraper to skyscraper.

It's worth noting that this attraction is almost empty during the first half-hour after park opening; it usually is at its busiest from midmorning until around 5 P.M.

TRANSCENTER: Far from being just a showroom for the latest model GM cars, this area situated at the ride's exit contains entertaining exhibits about the 20th century's most important means of transportation. One section, called the Bird and the Robot, stars a cigar-puffing, Groucho Marx-like toucan bird originally built for Tokyo Disneyland's Enchanted Tiki Room, and a General Motors assembly-line robot whose dexterity and flexibility make it easy to understand how similar devices can be used for painting and welding a new car on an assembly line.

Then there's *The Water Engine*, an amusing animated film that explores possible alternatives to the internal-combustion engine (including "Equus Cheapus"), and the

"Dreamer's Workshop," an exhibit that shows off sleek prototype cars of the future like the Aero 2000, an experimental four-seat subcompact designed specifically for display at Epcot Center. Other areas demonstrate the torture test that GM vehicles must pass—locks flicking up and down, windows and visor mirrors and door handles opening and closing, keys turning, and more so as to make the TransCenter a fine place to spend time when you don't feel like queuing up at another attraction.

Horizons

For generations, visionaries have been making predictions about life in the future. Jules Verne forecast rockets that would fly like bullets. The 19th-century French artist Albert Robida envisioned subways and dirigible taxis and sketched what life in Paris would be like in 1950. And in the 1930s, pulp science-fiction magazines circulated ideas about automatic barber chairs that would give their owners shoeshines and haircuts, about air conditioners that would pipe in alpine chills, about robots that would do housework, and about suntan lamps and televisions.

The three-acre Horizons show, which draws on the wisdom of countless scientists, adds its own predictions in a pavilion located between Universe of Energy and World of Motion, just beyond CommuniCore East. After a nod to the visions of earlier centuries in a Looking Back at Tomorrow sequence, the pavilion's continuously moving, suspended, four-passenger vehicles convey guests into the OmniSphere Theatre. Here, on a pair of spectacular hemispherical screens (80 feet in diameter), projectors with special lenses show filmed scenes of a Space Shuttle launch and of growing crystals, together with animated sequences of life in a space colony, a DNA chain, computer chips, and more. All this is a prelude to a voyage through a series of sets demonstrating aspects of life in the future.

In Nova Cite, the first destination, advanced

transportation and communication systems, such as holographic telephones and trains that work by magnetic levitation, keep members of far-flung families in touch with one another. In the Mesa Verde sequence, voice-controlled robot harvesters and genetically engineered fruits and vegetables populate a once-arid desert. Overhead, "hoverlifts" with spinning blades function as automatic shade controls, and "helium lifters" drop their hooks, collect baskets of the harvest from the robots, and fly the produce off to market. In the future farmer's home, shown nearby, there's an electronic pantry that delivers food to the inhabitants at the push of a button and a home communications center where youngsters can study math (or other subjects) by computer.

In the Sea Castle sequence, depicting a movable—but otherwise islandlike—floating city in the Pacific, schoolchildren take underwater field trips to nearby mining and kelp-farming operations operated by robot devices. And in Omega Centauri, a free-floating colony in space, crystals are grown for use by computers back on Earth and colony inhabitants keep in shape in a health-and-recreation center that features games like zero-gravity basketball (seen in shadow along the rear wall), and rowing and bicycling in simulators that allow space folk the opportunity to pursue their favorite sport in any environment they choose. Boaters, for instance, may shoot the Colorado River's rapids in the Grand Canyon, or paddle a Louisiana bayou, or float through the canals of Venice. Home life is just like that on Earth, but with a couple of twists: When a boy newly arrived at the colony doesn't put on his shoes in the morning, he floats away. (They're magnetic shoes, designed for this zero-gravity environment.) And when the family gets together to celebrate a birthday, those who can't attend in person put in an appearance via a holographic telephone.

There's another fine experience at the ride's conclusion: Visitors pick the journey's ending. Just push a button, and a special audience-polling device inside your vehicle delivers the 30-second experience that the majority of your fellow riders have requested. The car tilts back and vibrates, and the sound effects enhance the sensation of great speed created by fast-moving, close-up filmed visuals of travel on land, in the sea, and in space, not unlike those found in the speed rooms in the nearby World of Motion.

Trivia buffs will be curious about the sources of the science-fiction clips presented in the Looking Back at Tomorrow sequence. These include the films *Metropolis* (1926) and *Woman in the Moon* (1928) by the director Fritz Lang; *Mars and Beyond* and *Magic Highways U.S.A.*, shown on the *Disneyland* programs of the 1950s; and Woody Allen's *Sleeper* (1973).

Wonders of Life

The 72-foot-tall steel DNA molecule at the entrance to this pavilion beckons guests to a humorous, informative, and healthful experience. Housed in a 100,000-square-foot geodesic dome and two attached buildings, this $100 million attraction allows guests to enjoy both a serious and amusing look at health, fitness, and modern lifestyles. Wonders also boasts Epcot Center's first authentic thrill ride called Body Wars—a fast and furious ride through the human body.

From outside the gold-topped dome, the Wonders of Life sign seems to rest on the flumes of water shot up by two fountains.

Once inside the building, guests find themselves at the Fitness Fairgrounds. A mobile measuring 50 feet in diameter is suspended from the 65-foot ceiling and it swings gently in the air currents of the building.

At the Fairgrounds, a variety of shows and activities for both children and adults are offered. "Goofy About Health," is an eight-minute multi-screen montage that sees Goofy go from a sloppy-living guy to a health-conscious fellow. Using old Goofy cartoons that haven't been seen for many years, the show traces Goofy's ups and downs, and winds up with new footage of Goofy at his doctor's office. The film is shown in a 100-seat open theater where visitors can come and go as they wish.

At the Anacomical Players Theater, a corny (but nonetheless informative) show is presented by an improvisational theater group. Audience members are asked to participate, and it's all a lot of fun. This theater seats 100 people. The third theater at the Fitness Fairgrounds is enclosed. The film shown here, *The Making of Me*, is a 14-minute story starring Martin Short. It is about a man who wonders how he came into existence. To find out, he travels back in time to the birth of his parents, their first few years together, and their decision to have a child—him. Footage from an actual delivery is part of the film, and it is very sensitively done and provides a very tangible and touching view of childbirth. It was written and directed by Glenn Gordon Caron, who directed the TV show "Moonlighting" and the film *Clean and Sober*. Parents should be aware, however, that the film is quite graphic and so may not be suitable for some children.

There are plenty of hands-on activities in areas surrounding the theaters. Guests can ride Wonder Cycles, computerized stationary bicycles that enable guests to pedal through a variety of locales including Disneyland and the Rose Parade. At Coach's Corner, golf, tennis, or baseball swings are analyzed, and a professional knowledgeable in each sport offers free, albeit taped, advice to help you on your way. The Sensory Funhouse offers hands-on activities for kids. It's the Disney version of a children's museum, where education and entertainment go hand in hand.

At the Met Lifestyle Revue, guests punch in such information as age, weight, height, exercise habits, whether they smoke, and perceived stress levels at an interactive computer terminal. The computer then processes the information and offers some advice on how to lead a healthier and less stressful existence.

Frontiers of Medicine, located toward the rear of the Fitness Fairgrounds, features the only completely serious segment of Wonders of Life. Here guests can see some scientific and educational exhibits of leading-edge developments in medicine and health sciences. The exhibits change regularly.

Pure & Simple offers a variety of healthy snacks, including oat bran waffles and smoothies (made with frozen yogurt). There is a pleasant seating area, and nearby Well & Goods, Ltd. features men's, women's, and children's athletic wear, most of which features Disney characters participating in a variety of sports, and some educational materials. Presented by Metropolitan Life.

BODY WARS: The state-of-the-art technology that sends guests on a rollicking ride through space at the Star Tours attraction at the Disney-MGM Studios is also at Wonders of Life in the form of the thrill ride called Body Wars. After boarding the vehicles, which are actually the same type of flight simulators employed by military and commercial airlines in pilot training, guests are whisked away on a bumpy, rocky, and exciting ride through the human body. (Note that when instructed to

fasten your seatbelt, do so. This is a rough ride.) Movie buffs immediately will think of the film *Fantastic Voyage* and the more recent *Inner Space*. The queue area features exhibits from a fictional company specializing in the latest technology in the miniaturization of people. Guests pass through two special effects portals and are declared ready to do a routine medical probe of the human body—from the inside.

Signs posted outside Body Wars warn that in order to ride passengers must be free of back problems, heart conditions, motion sickness, and other such physical limitations. Pregnant women and children under three are not permitted to board. Children under seven must be accompanied by an adult.

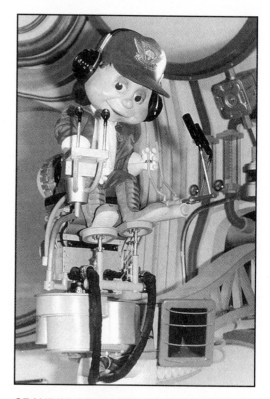

CRANIUM COMMAND: The third major area of Wonders of Life welcomes guests into the mind of a 12-year-old boy. Inside a 200-seat theater, the enormously exaggerated head of our 12-year-old subject is piloted by Buzzy, a delightfully corny Audio-Animatronic figure. The two large eyes are actually rear-projection video screens, and it is through them that the audience gets an idea of how a 12-year-old thinks and reacts. The other animated participant, General Knowledge, helps Buzzy learn which portion of the mind is required for a particular situation. The right and left brain, the stomach, the heart, and the adrenal gland are all represented by familiar celebrities. Our personal favorite is George Wendt ("Norm" from "Cheers") operating the stomach. It's an altogether whimsical and very entertaining show—one of the best at Epcot Center.

Universe of Energy

When strolling through Future World toward World Showcase Plaza, it's easy to spot this pavilion's mirrored, asymmetrical pyramid off to the left. But the facade doesn't provide any clue at all to the 38 minutes of surprises in store for those who venture inside. One of the most technologically complex experiences at Epcot Center, the Energy show consists of three motion pictures and a ride-through attraction. Not one of these is exactly what you might expect.

The first film, seen when you enter the pavilion, examines types of energy used today. Its vivid images of falling water, leaping fire, burning coal, enormous piles of logs, jet engines, and beautiful yellow flowers are the makings of a fine photo essay—but there's a twist: The 14-by-90-foot projection surface is not at all a conventional flat motion picture screen, but is made up of 100 solid triangular elements. These actually rotate on cue from a computer, in synchronization with the changing images, to produce what its creator (Czech filmmaker Emil Radok) described as a "kinetic mosaic."

The second film, shown in an adjoining area, is a 4½-minute animated feature depicting the eras in which today's fossil fuels were created. This film was photographed with the multiplane camera developed by the Disney organization over 50 years ago, and the feeling of depth it gave to the forest scenes in famous films like *Bambi* and *Snow White* also enhances the cinemascape here.

But contrary to the expectations of some visitors, there's not an adorably Disneyesque creature in the show. The animals lumbering across the giant screen (which measures 32 feet by 155 feet, over half the length of a football field) are gigantic prehistoric beasts, and the landscape is an eerie one, full of volcanoes, exotic plants, and bizarre insects. Even more astonishing is the moment at the conclusion of the movie when the whole seating area suddenly begins to rotate, and then breaks up into six smaller sections that slowly move forward—usually to the accompaniment of a chorus of oohs and aahs from startled members of the audience.

Before very many people have even begun to grasp the transformation, the vehicles have embarked upon an odyssey through a three-dimensional re-creation of the primeval world suggested in the film, an otherworldly region of sulfur-scented air, eerie blue moonlight, unearthly fogs, and lava so ominously authentic that few visitors dare reach out and touch it—even when told that one of its main ingredients is a type of commercial styling gel.

Huge trees crowd the forest. Millipedes duel on a log to the left of the vehicles. Brontosauruses wallow in the lagoon out front. A lofty allosaurus battles dramatically with an armored stegosaurus a bit farther along, and an elasmosaurus bursts out of a tidal pool with frightening suddenness—all under the vulturelike gaze of winged creatures known as pteranodons. All of these were created only after months of research, including interviews with countless well-known paleobotanists and paleontologists. The Audio-Animatronics animals are the largest of their type ever to be fabricated, and the 250 prehistoric trees are the first ever to come off any production line. There are so many sounds, smells, and sights here that the time passes in a flash, and before you know it the vehicles have entered another theater.

Here a 12½-minute motion picture, shown on a 220° screen whose breadth intensifies the impact of every image, dramatizes sources of energy for the future. During the filming of the North Sea segment, temperatures dropped so low that the three 65mm cameras used in the filming—specially

mounted to generate the almost seamless image projected on the curved screen—had to be taken indoors and defrosted before work could continue. Footage depicting the Space Shuttle's thunderous blastoff, so unusual that even NASA wanted a copy, serves as the film's grand finale and provides images that stay with you as you travel into another Energy adventure, a splendid computer-animated light show of what looks like dancing laser beams.

Fully as intriguing as the whole Energy experience is the advanced technology behind it. The traveling vehicles measure 29 feet long and 18 feet wide, and weigh about 30,000 pounds when fully loaded with their complement of 96 passengers. Yet they are guided along the concrete floor by a guide wire only ⅛-inch thick. And some of the pavilion's required energy is generated by two acres of photovoltaic cells mounted on the roof. These cells generate enough energy to run six average homes.

On leaving the pavilion, home gardeners should note that the Southern live oaks immediately to the east of the Universe of Energy (to your right as you face the entrance) are pruned to follow the slanted roofline of the pavilion. These trees were among a handful started from acorns for Hotel Plaza Boulevard (the broad street that runs down the center of Hotel Plaza) for Walt Disney World's opening more than 20 years ago; a quartet of their siblings, in an unpruned state, can still be seen in front of The American Adventure, in World Showcase. Presented by Exxon.

CommuniCore East

Officially, CommuniCore—short for Community Core—is the central area of Future World, just beyond (south of) Earth Station. It comprises the two large crescent-shaped buildings to the left and right (east and west) and the fountain in the center. The entire complex, which explores the subject of present-day technology, ranks as one of the most interesting areas at Epcot Center.

EPCOT COMPUTER CENTRAL: Computers that talk and play games are the focus of this area located to the left of the fountain plaza entrance to the building. Within the area, there are several activity islands (described below).

SMRT-1: He looks like a little purple space man; he talks in a sweet little-boy voice; he has a great time playing simple guessing games with guests, of whom he asks questions like "Is Lincoln buried in Grant's Tomb?" and plays games like "Guess Your Birthday." He also chortles with considerable glee when someone flubs an answer.

None of this would be very remarkable if not for the fact that the questioner, SMRT-1, is a computer. To judge from the rapt faces

that surround him throughout most of Epcot Center's operating hours, guests enjoy the games as much as he does. It's amusing just to watch, even if the time spent waiting for a turn to talk back isn't in the day's program.

Compute-A-Coaster: Via a bank of touch-sensitive video screens, this area makes the point that designing rollercoaster-type thrill rides is the job of a computer. Players get the chance to build their own coaster using the parts that the computerized program provides—long and short rises, a loop-the-loop, a semi-spiral, and a big drop. The reward for a job well done: a simulated (and rather remarkably scary) ride on the finished product.

Backstage Magic: Accessible via a ramp along the north wall of Epcot Computer Central, this short show is designed to explain the evolution of computers, how they work, and how they are used at Walt Disney World, and to provide a glimpse of the role computers will be playing in the 21st century. It features an array of special effects that help bring computers to life, plus I/O (for input/output), a mime who adds a little life to computers.

Great America Census Quiz: It's difficult to say which aspect of this attraction is more compelling: the chance to use those amazing touch-sensitive TV screens, or the facts that are revealed about this nation in the course of the computers' guessing games. A list of topics appears on the screen at the start of the quiz, and guests choose the ones on which they'd most like to be questioned: The Fifty States, School Days, On the Farm, Communication Line, Home Sweet Home, Population Clock, and many more. The answers reveal—among other interesting facts—that there are approximately 12,000 centenarians alive in the United States today, that women in the 1800s had an average of seven children, that

the citizens of Alaska have a higher average income than those of any other state, that Florida will be the fastest-growing state during the rest of the century, and that more motorbikes are registered in Michigan than in any other state. Every time someone answers a question incorrectly, a bleep is heard, provoking an embarrassed titter from the erring player—and a good deal of warmhearted sympathy from lookers-on.

Get Set Jet Game: The idea of this game, which aims to demonstrate the use of computers in some passenger-related sections of the aviation business, is to load the greatest possible number of passengers and luggage and to complete a required checklist of safety and maintenance precautions within 60 seconds. To accomplish this successfully requires considerable hand-eye coordination, but the game is amusing even for members of the all-thumbs crowd. The touch-sensitive video screens on which the game is played are located practically alongside those of the Great America Census Quiz.

Incidentally, the mysterious-looking 14-foot sphere near the entrance to the Communi-Core East was designed by the same artist who created the massive lucite sculpture at the entrance to Future World.

ENERGY EXCHANGE: Biomass, synthetic fuels, and solar, wind, nuclear, and mechanical energy are among the subjects explored here. But although the overall subject matter is serious, the exhibits are so diverting that it's entirely possible to spend an hour or more in the area without being aware of the passage of time. One display gives guests the opportunity to compare the amount of energy that they personally can generate by pedaling a stationary bicycle with the power contained in a gallon of gasoline. (Even pedaling at top speed, human beings come in a poor second.) In a nearby related exhibit, turning a crank lights a bulb, and a monitor tells how long it would take to produce $1 worth of electricity.

Elsewhere, there are buttons to push to activate taped programs discussing hydropower, geothermal power, and wind power (and windmills). One bank of touch-sensitive video screens provides information about conserving energy in the home—about radiators and registers, the proper use of a fireplace and a wood-burning stove, air conditioning, and other such stuff. Another set of screens answers queries on energy sources, energy conservation, and the energy outlook; it also solicits guest opinions about thought-provoking and sometimes controversial energy-related issues. A coal-mining display informs guests about different kinds of coal and shows samples; it also compares reserves of U.S. coal with the nation's other recoverable energy resources and with oil from the Middle East. There is a model of an offshore drilling platform and an exhibit that explains what a "guyed" platform is about. How wells are drilled—from hole-making to processing drilling fluid and oil-shale rock—is one of the many other topics. Presented by Exxon.

EPCOT QUIZ: Test your knowledge of Epcot Center at these computer trivia games.

ELECTRONIC FORUM: Located in CommuniCore East (close to the lagoon), this attraction contains Future Choice Theater, Epcot Center's ongoing poll of guest opinions. It works this way: Visitors enter a small theater whose seats are equipped with a number of push buttons. A moderator at the front of the room gives a brief account of an issue (often accompanied by videotapes or film clips that feature people who are authorities on the subject). The moderator then solicits individual opinions, and participants push a button for the right answer. The feelings of the audience are immediately flashed on a screen at the front of the room; often the responses are broken down by age group or sex.

Most people really enjoy themselves here, and better still, few ever have to wait more than the 20 minutes that each session takes

to gain admission. The theater is open seasonally from 11 A.M. to 7 P.M. In any event, that time speeds by thanks to the exhibits outside the theater—a veritable armada of television sets showing regional news, national news, Disney news, sports news, and weather. While one channel broadcasts live from the House of Representatives, others bring the news from French Canada, news from the Caribbean and South and Central America (in Spanish), and from Japan (in Japanese). As a backdrop, there's an exhibit that explains how the satellites responsible for these stations work.

CENTORIUM: This large, sleek shop, the most spacious in all of Epcot Center, stocks a vast selection of Epcot Center and Disney character memorabilia and souvenirs— bumper stickers, watches, books, key chains, pennants, T-shirts, license plates, pencils, hats, visors, memo pads, and much more. In addition, there are all kinds of items related to other areas of Future World, such as dolls that look like the little dragon Figment (one of the Disney creations found exclusively at Epcot Center). Upstairs there is a large selection of Disney-themed sports apparel. Youngsters will particularly enjoy the glassed-in elevator.

ILLUMINATIONS: A spectacular display of lasers, fireworks, and dancing fountains to the accompaniment of symphonic music is one of the highlights of any Epcot Center visit. The extravaganza is scheduled nightly at closing time throughout the year. Check for exact times upon arriving at the park.

World Showcase

Noble sentiments about humanity and the fellowship of nations, which have motivated so many world's fairs in the past, also inhabit World Showcase. But make no mistake about it: This half of Epcot Center, located to the south of Future World, is unlike any previous international exposition.

It is instead a group of pavilions that encircle World Showcase Lagoon (a body of water that, incidentally, is the size of 85 football fields) to demonstrate Disney conceptions about participating countries in remarkably realistic, consistently entertaining styles. You won't find the real Germany here; rather, the country's essence, much as a traveler returning from a visit might remember what he or she saw. Shops, restaurants, and an occasional special attraction are all housed in a group of structures that is an artful pastiche of all the elements that give that nation's countryside and towns their distinctive flavor. Although occasional liberties have been taken when scale and proportion required, careful research governed the design of every nook and cranny.

In the shops, all wares on display represent the country in whose pavilion they are offered for sale. The food focuses on native cuisine, and the entertainment is as authentic as the Disney casting directors can make it, with native performers consistently featured. And craftspeople are occasionally on hand to demonstrate their art in the appropriate shops. Thanks to special Epcot Center cultural exchange programs and the personnel department's energetic efforts to recruit nationals from around Central Florida, nearly all the World Showcase staff members in restaurants, shops, and attractions were born in the countries the pavilions represent (or at least spent many years living there), and that contributes still more atmosphere. The ongoing efforts of the entertainment department mean that festivities are always in the works, and that new performers are continually making Epcot Center debuts.

Home gardeners should be sure to note the World Showcase landscaping: Each pavilion's plantings closely approximate what would be found in the featured nation. The 1.3-mile World Showcase Promenade, which links pavilions on the shores of the World Showcase Lagoon, has its own interesting vegetation, beginning in World Showcase Plaza with 75-foot Washingtonia fan palms, Arizona-California natives that were imported to Central Florida. Underneath them is a garden full of rosebushes, numbering among the more than 10,000 tree roses, teas, grandifloras, and miniatures planted throughout World Showcase. The Y-shaped trees nearby are callery pears, which can be seen in several other spots in World Showcase. Those encircling the lagoon on the Promenade are camphor trees, which should eventually grow to a height of 60 or 80 feet and about the same dimensions in breadth, to provide the walkway with abundant and welcome shade.

Note that World Showcase pavilions are at their least crowded from the time the park opens until about 11 A.M., and then again from 6 P.M. or 7 P.M. until park closing. So while most of the crowds are standing in line at Future World attractions, shows at World Showcase often are almost empty.

Pavilions are described here in the order that they would be encountered while moving counterclockwise (west to east) around the lagoon after crossing the bridge from Future World.

Canada

Celebrating the beauties of America's neighbor to the north, the area devoted to the western hemisphere's largest nation is complete with its own mountain, waterfall, rushing stream, rocky canyon, mine, and splendid garden massed with colorful flowers. There's even a totem pole, a trading post, and an elaborate, mansard-roofed hotel similar to ones built by the Canadian railroads as they pushed west around the turn of the century. All this is imaginatively arranged somewhat like a split-level house, with the section representing French Canada on top, and another devoted to the mountains alongside it and below. From a distance, the Hôtel du Canada, the main building here, looks like little more than a bump on the landscape—as does Epcot Center's single Canadian Rocky Mountain. But up close they both seem to tower as high as the real thing, thanks to a motion picture designers' technique known as forced perspective, which involves exaggerating the relative smallness of distant parts of a structure to make the totality appear taller than it really is.

The gardens were inspired by the Butchart Gardens in Victoria, British Columbia, a famous park created on the site of a limestone quarry. The hotel is modeled after Ottawa's Victorian-style *Château Laurier*.

Willow, birch, sweet gum, plum, and maple trees can all be found in the Victoria Gardens; Canada's hemlocks are represented here by deodar cedars, a Himalaya native that can withstand torrid Florida summers with aplomb.

Entertainment is provided by the Caledonia Bagpipe Band, featuring two pipers and a drummer.

O CANADA!: This motion picture, presented in CircleVision 360 inside Canada's mountain, portrays the Canadian confederation in all its coast-to-coast splendor—the prairies and the plains, the sparkling shorelines and rivers, and the untouched snowfields and rocky mountainsides. The Royal Canadian Mounted Police also put in an appearance. The maritime provinces are all pictured, with their covered bridges and sailing ships, as is Montreal, with its Old World cafés and imposing churches; the scene in the Cathédral de Notre Dame, with its organ booming and choirboys in attendance, is particularly stirring. The great outdoors gets equal play. In one scene, Canada snow geese take off all around the screen, and the beating of their wings is positively thunderous. Eagles, possums, mallards, bobcats, wolves, bears, deer, bison, and herds of reindeer were all filmed. Filmed too were steers being roped at a rodeo and the chuck wagon race that takes place every year at that great provincial fair known as the Calgary Stampede. Skiers in the vast and empty Bugaboos, dogsledders, and ice skaters are featured in the winter scenes; in a hockey game, the sound system almost perfectly conveys the scratch of skates on ice and the sharp whack of sticks against a puck. And throughout, the motion picture conveys a sense of the vast size of Canada, providing a you-are-there feeling that makes all of this spectacular scenery still more memorable.

This is partly due to the filming technique, CircleVision 360. Also used in the Magic Kingdom's *American Journeys*, it involves a special five-foot-tall, 600-pound camera rig composed of nine individual 35mm cameras evenly arranged around a tubular shaft containing the motor that drives the mechanisms for all the cameras. In some scenes the rig was suspended from a helicopter; when depicting the precision-flying Canadian Snowbirds, Canada's answer to the U.S. Air Force's Thunderbirds, it was mounted on a B-25 bomber; in the Calgary sequence, it was placed in one of the racing buckboards; and in the reindeer roundup scene, which took place on the edge of the Arctic Ocean, it was concealed by burlap. Note that there are no seats in this theater.

NORTHWEST MERCANTILE: The first shop to the left upon entering the pavilion's plaza on the way to the Hôtel du Canada, this emporium does a booming business in Cana-

dian sheepskins, which are piled high just inside the entrance. Heavy lumberjack shirts, maple syrup, and other wares that trappers might have purchased back in pioneering days round out the stock. Skeins of rope, tin scoops, lanterns, and a pair of antique ice skates hanging from the long beams overhead set the mood, together with the structure itself. That, like the adjacent Trading Post, is built of adze-hewn logs and ornamented by stone statues, masks, and paintings done in the style of the Ojibwa Indians. Located to the rear of the shop are Indian artifacts and assorted souvenirs—items like toy tomahawks, fur vests and moccasins, and sleek-lined sculptures (some made of imitation marble and some carved in soapstone by the Inuit). The small tepees are made from the bark of deciduous trees, which can be gathered up only once a year when the tree goes dormant. These are among several handcrafted Canadian items that are seldom seen elsewhere in the American market.

LA BOUTIQUE DES PROVINCES: This shop offers Canadian merchandise with a French flavor.

United Kingdom

In the space of only a few hundred feet, visitors to this pavilion stroll from an elegant London square to the edge of a canal in the rural countryside—via a bustling urban English street framed by buildings that constitute a veritable rhapsody of historic architectural styles. But one scene leads to the next so smoothly that nothing ever seems amiss. Here again, note the attention to detail: the half-timbered High Street structure that actually leans a bit, the hand-painted "smoke" stains that make the chimneys look as if they had been there for centuries. When a thatched roof is required, it's right where it should be—though the roof may be made of plastic broom bristles because fire regulations prohibit the real thing. London plane trees, so common in British cities, are represented, and a sundial punctuates the Promenade. Off to the side is a pair of scarlet phone booths identical to those that used to be found all around the U.K. And there are eight different architectural styles characteristic of the streetscapes, from English Tudor and Georgian to English Victorian.

There is no single major special attraction in this pavilion; instead, it features a half-dozen fine shops and a pub that serves a selection of British-brewed beers and ales that would be the toast of any first class "local" in London itself. There's also plenty of good entertainment including a group of comedians called the Old Globe Players, who, when not engaged in general clowning on the World Showcase Promenade, coax audience members into participating in their farcical and altogether entertaining (if unsophisticated) playlets.

Sharp-eyed visitors with an interest in horticultural matters will have a field day

examining the landscaping here. The geometrically trimmed bush in front of The Toy Soldier shop is not an Irish yew, so common to the British Isles, but instead a *podocarpus*; Irish yews don't grow well in Florida. A *podocarpus*, left in its natural shape, also flanks the shop door just to the rear. A similar substitution had to be made for the London plane tree, also not suited to the Epcot Center climate; its replacement, crowding the half-timbered walls of The Magic of Wales, is a Western sycamore, which looks nearly identical and belongs to the same genus. Don't miss the perennial-and-herb garden next to Anne Hathaway's cottage (to the left of the entrance to The Tea Caddy as you face it), and the small path that leads to the garden courtyard. A traditional English hedge maze surrounds the cottage.

THE TOY SOLDIER: All the necessities are here for such beloved youthful pastimes as sailing (wooden boats), creating works of art ("colouring" books), and just having a good time (Corgi toys).

No toy shop is complete without temptations for adults, and this one is no exception: There are elegant dolls designed expressly for collectors.

Be sure to notice the display at the shop's Promenade entrance—a miniature, glitter-strewn medieval banquet hall peopled by royalty and nobles, musicians, jesters, and a host of other court figures. On the windows downstairs are the heraldic crests for eight of the U.K.'s principal cities, plus those for the three nations that make up the U.K. (Scotland, England, and Northern Ireland—but not Wales, which is a principality). In addition, there are the three crosses that, combined, make up the Union Jack—the crosses of St. Andrew, St. George, and St. Patrick.

Outside, the shop resembles a stone manor built during the last half of the 16th century; the Scottish-stepped gable parapet and the round turrets are inspired by Scotland's Abbotsford Manor, where the novelist Sir Walter Scott lived for a period, wrote his most famous romances, and died in 1832.

LORDS AND LADIES: This shop looks like a backdrop for a child's fantasy of the days of King Arthur, with its high rafters decked out with bright banners, its vast fireplace (and crossed swords above), and its immense wrought-iron chandelier. Pottery replicas of British cottages, dart boards, fragrance products, "pub mugs," limited-edition chess sets, coin and stamp sets, and tapes and records are the stock in trade at this emporium adjoining The Toy Soldier.

PRINGLE OF SCOTLAND: On a sweltering summer day in Central Florida, trying on lamb's wool and cashmere may not hold terrific appeal. But the huge selection of styles and colors in men's and women's sweaters, knitted by Scotland's most famous maker, may well prove enticing despite the temperature outside. Tam-o'-shanters, socks, hats, ties, scarves, mittens, and kilts are only some of the items offered. Don't fail to look at the fascinating tartan map on the wall across from Lords and Ladies; this identifies plaids from Glen Burn and Gordon to Langtree and St. Lawrence.

THE QUEEN'S TABLE: Sponsored by the Royal Doulton china makers, this shop (opposite Pringle of Scotland) may be one of the loveliest in Epcot Center. That's particularly true of the elegant Adams Room, embellished with elaborate moldings, hung with a chandelier made of crystal, and painted in cream and robin's egg blue in a geometric pattern designed to match the carpet. The setting is a perfect background for the selection of superbly crafted collector's statuettes. The detail is almost photographically perfect, and the prices range from $5 to $12,500.

Among the Royal Doulton shop's more affordable delights are the company's famous Bunnykins cup-and-bowl sets for youngsters. Also intriguing are the small and large Toby mugs—cups that are shaped and painted to represent the visages of famous historical figures. A small selection of attractive Royal Doulton china dinnerware also is available.

Don't fail to inspect small, serene Britannia Square just outside the shop entrance furthest from World Showcase Promenade. But for its somewhat reduced scale and the distinctively Floridian climate, it almost feels like London itself. The crests on the shop's upstairs windows are those of three major U.K. schools—Oxford, Cambridge, and Eton.

THE MAGIC OF WALES: This small emporium offers pottery, slate, jewelry, souvenirs, and hand-crafted gifts from Wales. Despite its modest size, it does the highest volume of business (per square foot of size) among the United Kingdom shops.

THE TEA CADDY: Fitted out with heavy wooden beams and a broad fireplace to resemble the Stratford-upon-Avon cottage of Shakespeare's Anne Hathaway, this shop, sponsored by Twinings Tea, stocks various types of English teas, both loose and in bags in a variety of flavors. Other items include teapots, biscuits, and candies.

France

The buildings here have mansard roofs and casement windows so Gallic in appearance that you expect to see some sad, bohemian poet looking down from above. A canallike offshoot of the World Showcase Lagoon seems like the Seine itself; the footbridge that spans it recalls the old Pont des Arts. There's a kiosk nearby like those that punctuate the streets of Paris, a sidewalk café at which to sip a glass of wine and watch the crowds go by, an elegant bookstore, and a bakery whose absolutely heavenly rich aromas announce its presence long before it's visible. Shops sell perfumes, fine leather wares, jewelry, crystal, and other luxury items. Their roofs are real copper or slate, and the cabinetry is crafted finely enough to dazzle even the most skilled woodworker. Galerie des Halles—the iron-and-glass-ceilinged market that Paris counted as one of its most beloved institutions (until its demolition many years ago)—lives again (near the Palais du Cinéma exit).

But perhaps most special of all are the people. On the Promenade in front of the pavilion, a strolling trio is on hand to entertain. The music is evocative, the repertoire familiar— "Frère Jacques" and "Sur le Pont d'Avignon" are standards. Similarly, hosts and hostesses who hail from Paris and the French provinces answer questions in lyrically French-accented English.

Some interesting background notes: The dusty rose-colored, lace-trimmed costumes that the hostesses wear were inspired by the dresses in the Impressionist painter Edouard Manet's *Le Bar aux Folies-Bergère*, and the park to the west of the pavilion, with its tall Lombardy poplars, was inspired by neo-Impressionist Georges Seurat's painting *A Sunday Afternoon on the Island of La Grande Jatte*. The main entrance to the pavilion recalls the architecture of Paris, most of which was built during the Belle Epoque ("beautiful age") years of the last decades of the 19th century when, following the designs of city planner Baron Georges Eugène Haussman, thoroughfares were widened and seven stories became the standard height for city buildings. The lane known as La Petite Rue ("the little street") is inspired by small provincial byways. The sinuously curved, art nouveau–style facade of the entrance to the arcade between La Signature and Plume et Palette ("pen and palette") recalls the entrances to Paris's great underground transportation system, the Métro. Don't miss the quiet garden on the opposite side of this arcade—one of the most peaceful spots in World Showcase.

Horticulturally, France offers still other delights, beginning on the World Showcase Promenade. Here a row of western sycamores that normally grow to 60 or 80 feet—planted in lieu of London plane trees—is being pruned French-style to a height of about 18 feet to develop knots on the end of each branch. These make a distinctive abstract pattern in winter, and in spring send out spiky leaf-bearing shoots that provide bountiful shade in summer. To the west, on the opposite side of the Promenade, a small square edged with miniature rose bushes has been planted to outline the shape of a *fleur de lis*.

PALAIS DU CINEMA: This intimate, elegant little "palace of cinema," a theater not unlike the one at Fontainebleau, is the setting for showings of *Impressions de France*, a lyrical and enchanting 18-minute-long travel film that takes viewers from one end of France to the other. The film shows off a beautiful tree-dotted estate; fertile fields and vineyards at

harvest time; a village flower market and a luscious pastry shop; the ribbed tongue of a glacier and a harbor full of squawking gulls; black-clad Breton women with headdresses made of starched lace shaped into unique styles that reveal the wearer's origin; Paris on Bastille Day—in all some four dozen locations (out of 140 originally shot). Several scenes take place in world-famous landmarks like the Eiffel Tower; Versailles and its gilt Hall of Mirrors (just outside Paris); Mont St. Michel, close to the Brittany-Normandy border in the northwest corner of the country; the French Alps near Mont Blanc, in the southeast; and Cannes, the star-studded resort city on the Mediterranean coast. The automobile competition is Cannes's Bugatti Race; the chateau—which Francophiles will immediately recognize as one of those in the Loire River valley—is fabulous Chambord. (This scene, incidentally, was shot from a helicopter which could fly within three feet of any object being photographed.)

All this is even more appealing thanks to a superbly melodic sound track almost entirely made up of the music of French classical composers such as Jacques Offenbach (1819-1880), known for his operettas; Charles-Camille Saint-Saëns (1835-1921), a conductor, pianist, organist, and composer celebrated for his lush melodies; Claude Debussy (1862-1918), who did with sound what the Impressionist painters did with light; and Erik Satie (1866-1925), known for his piano works. Selections include Debussy's *Syrinx*, the haunting piece for solo flute, and his *Afternoon of a Faun*, which accompany an aerial shot of fertile fields. Listen for Offenbach's *Gaieté Parisienne* in the biking sequence and Satie's *Trois Gymnopédies* in the Alps scene. The Aquarium section from Saint-Saën's *Carnival of the Animals* accompanies the swamp scene, and the same composer's *Organ Symphony* is heard during the Eiffel Tower ascent. The whole is woven together with transitional segments written and arranged by long-time Disney musician Buddy Baker.

The exceptionally wide screen adds yet another dimension. This is not a CircleVision 360 film; it was not shot with the nine cameras needed for the motion pictures at China and Canada. Instead, the France film used only five cameras, but it is shown on a screen made up of five projection surfaces, each measuring 21 feet in height and 27½ feet in width—200 degrees around. It's one of Epcot Center's best films.

There is generally not a long wait here except during peak seasons, but it's still best to see the film first thing in the morning or in the early evening.

PLUME ET PALETTE: One of the loveliest of the World Showcase shops, this one is devoted to art and crystal. The best of the art nouveau style is reflected in the sinuous curves

embellishing the wrought-iron balustrade edging the mezzanine and the moldings that decorate the shining cherry-wood cabinets and shelves. The woodworking is superb, and one case seems more beautiful than the next. Stained glass in purple, yellow, and lavender ornaments the top of one of them. Stylized tulips painted in a delicate antique rose color and pale green embellish still others. The curtains are a beautiful dusty pink with white lace.

All this makes a fine backdrop for an array of merchandise that includes collectible miniatures, small china boxes, and tapestries. On the mezzanine level, a handful of fine oil paintings (by well-known French landscape artists) are for sale from $300 to $3,000 each, along with attractive prints of French countryside scenes.

LA SIGNATURE: Another beautiful spot, with wallpaper that resembles watered silk, a fine chandelier, brass-and-crystal sconces, and velvet curtains, this shop stocks lovely French fragrances and bath products, as well as French apparel.

GALERIE DES HALLES: French cookies and chocolate bars—plus souvenirs—are the stock in trade at this area located at the exit from the Palais du Cinéma. The area is modeled on France's now-demolished Les Halles, originally designed by the architect Victor Baltard (1805-1874).

LA MODE FRANCAIS: This shop presents a selection of sophisticated casual clothing with a French accent. Men's and women's fashions are available.

LA MAISON DU VIN: Selections in this lovely shop range from the inexpensive to the pricey, from a few dollars for *vin ordinaire* to upwards of $290 for a relatively rare vintage. Wine tastings are held here to sample the offerings (a small charge is levied, but you get to keep the glass). Those who don't want to carry their purchases all over World Showcase may have them dispatched to Package Pick-up for retrieval at the end of the day.

Morocco

Nine tons of tile were handmade, handcut, and shipped to Epcot Center to create this World Showcase pavilion. To capture the unique quality of this North African country's architecture, 19 Moroccan artisans were brought to Epcot Center to practice the mosaic art that has been a part of their homeland for thousands of years. Koutoubia Minaret, a detailed replica of the famous prayer tower in Marrakesh, stands guard at the entrance. A courtyard with a fountain in the center—and flowers everywhere—leads to the Medina (Old City). Between the traditional alleyways and the more modern sections are the pointed arches and swirling blue patterns of the Bab Boujouloud gate, a replica of the one that stands in the city of Fez. An ancient working waterwheel irrigates the gardens of the pavilion and the motifs repeated throughout the buildings include carved plaster and wood, ceramic tile, and brass.

GALLERY OF ARTS AND HISTORY: This museum houses ever-changing exhibits of Moroccan art, artifacts, and costumes.

MOROCCAN NATIONAL TOURIST OFFICE: An information center offers literature useful in planning a visit to Morocco, and the Royal Air Maroc desk makes it easy to book a trip if the mood strikes. There is a three-screen projection area where a continuous slide show depicts the lifestyles and landscapes of the country.

CASABLANCA CARPETS: Hand-knotted Berber carpets, Rabat carpets with brightly colored geometric designs, prayer rugs, wall hangings of lifelike scenes, and handloomed bedspreads and throw pillows are among the offerings here.

JEWELS OF THE SAHARA: Silver and gold Berber jewelry and beaded pieces with glass, onyx, amber, and other natural stones are the big sellers.

TANGIER TRADERS: Here's the perfect place to buy a fez, plus woven belts, leather sandals, leather purses, and other traditional Moroccan clothing.

MARKETPLACE IN THE MEDINA: Hand-woven baskets, sheepskin wallets and handbags, assorted strawhats, and split bamboo furniture and lampshades are available.

THE BRASS BAZAAR: Brass, brass, and more brass—and it's all shiny. Pitchers, planters, pots, and serving sets.

FASHIONS FROM FES: Features contemporary women's clothing and accessories from Morocco.

BERBER OASIS: This shop on the promenade spills over with a craftsman's brasswork. Baskets and leathergoods abound.

MEDINA ARTS: A representative selection of crafts from all parts of Morocco makes this an interesting and colorful stop.

Japan

Occasionally, when the group known as the "Atsuko Koga" is performing in this pavilion, the surrounding area resounds with the most amazing drumming that most visitors will ever hear. The staccato rhythm is as rapid as the fire of a machine gun, and the booms are deeply resonant and loud.

But for the most part, serenity rules in Japan. The principal entertainment, aside from Atsuko Koga, is a young man known as Nasaji Teresawa, who pursues the 2,400-year-old art of snipping and swirling blobs of brown rice toffee into the shapes of swans, unicorns, crabs, and a score of other remarkable creatures.

The landscaping, designed in accordance with traditional symbolic and aesthetic values, also contributes to the peaceful mood. Rocks, which in Japan represent the enduring nature of the earth, were brought from North Carolina and Georgia (since boulders are scarce in the Sunshine State). Water, symbolizing the sea (which the Japanese consider a life source), is abundant; the Japan Pavilion garden has a little stream and a couple of pools inhabited (in good weather) by koi. A small bamboo device at the edge of one of these rivulets regularly fills up with water falling from above, and then, weighted by its contents, empties out and makes regular, but somehow soothing, clacking noises in the process. Evergreen trees, which in Japan are symbols of eternal life, are here in force.

Disney horticulturalists created this very Japanese landscape without using very many plants or trees native to that country, where the climate is so different from that in Florida. The evergreens near the brilliant vermilion *torii* gate are native Florida slash pines. The curly leaved trees alongside the stream are corkscrew willows. Among the few trees actually native to Japan are the sago near the courtyard entrance to the Yakitori House, the two Japanese maple trees (identifiable by their small leaves) not far away (near the first stairway from the promenade on the left side

of the courtyard as you face it), and the prickly branched, prickly leaved monkey puzzle trees near the walkway to the promenade, on The American Adventure side of the pagoda; needle-sharp thorns make this the only species of tree that monkeys cannot climb.

Visitors who have actually been to Japan will be interested to observe that most of the structures inside the pavilion have their Japanese antecedents. The pagoda that occupies such a prominent place along World Showcase Promenade was modeled after an eighth-century structure located in the Horyuji Temple in Nara. The brilliant vermilion *torii* gate on the shores of World Showcase Lagoon derives from the design of the one at the Itsukushima shrine in Hiroshima Bay, one of the most beautiful sites on the inland sea.

BIJUTSU-KAN GALLERY: A changing cultural display, this small museum has offered, among other shows, "Echos Through Time—Japanese Women and the Arts," an exhibit of traditional and contemporary Japanese art forms.

MITSUKOSHI DEPARTMENT STORE: There are kimonos in silk, cotton, and polyester; attractive all-cotton T-shirts bearing Japanese characters; expensive, almost sculptural traditional headdresses that seem fabricated of lacquer-stiffened netting; and an excellent selection of bowls and vases meant for flower arranging. But on the whole, no one would ever apply the term "quaint" to this spacious store set up by Mitsukoshi—an immense,

The American Adventure

When it came to creating The American Adventure, the centerpiece of World Showcase, the Disney Imagineers were given virtually a free hand. So the 110,000 bricks of the imposing colonial-style structure that houses the show, a counter-service restaurant, and a shop are real brick—made *by hand* from soft, pinkish-orange Georgia clay. The show inside stands out because of its wonderfully evocative settings, its innovatively detailed sets, and the 35 superb Audio-Animatronics players, some of the most lifelike ever created by the Disney organization: The American Adventure's Ben Franklin even walks up stairs. The digital sound system also is the most advanced that the Disney organization has ever used, and the show is the most technically complex, involving the world's largest

three-century-old retail firm that was once dubbed "Japan's Sears." Some of the china dinnerware is too often seen elsewhere in the U.S. in department stores or inexpensive chain import stores to arouse more than passing interest. It's unfortunate that this familiarity also makes it easy to dismiss some of the other merchandise that, though it appears to be of the same trinket quality, has considerable meaning in Japanese culture. One example is the dolls, of which there are literally rows and rows, priced from $3.50 to $3,000, and clad in elaborate kimonos sashed with wide, stiff *obis*. These are traditionally given to female children on Girls' Day, a popular Japanese national holiday. The blank-eyed, egg-shaped pâpier-maché scarlet masks, which come in a wide range of sizes from small to very large, are part of the traditional New Year celebration. The Japanese color in one eye when making a New Year's resolution, keep the one-eyed "face" in plain view throughout the next 364 days as a reminder of the holiday vow, and celebrate success when the year draws to its close by completing the face.

The structure housing the merchandise was inspired by a section of the Gosho Imperial Palace, which was constructed in Kyoto in the year 794 A.D., and is widely recognized as a fine example of early Japanese architecture.

rear-projection screen (72 feet in width) and a number of very sophisticated sets that rise up from below the stage to the delight and awe of the audience. A superb vocal group called The Voices of Liberty entertains inside the building.

Be sure to note the four luxuriant trees out front. They were originally planted in 1969 on Hotel Plaza Boulevard, the main thoroughfare of Disney Village Hotel Plaza, and along with a handful of their contemporaries (which can be seen in their pruned and unpruned states throughout Epcot Center, most notably trimmed diagonally alongside Future World's Universe of Energy) have been moved four times in the intervening years. Presented by Coca-Cola and American Express.

THE AMERICAN ADVENTURE SHOW: One of the truly outstanding Epcot Center attractions, this 29-minute presentation celebrates the American spirit from our nation's earliest years right up to the present. A recent renova-

tion means that the show is very current. Beginning with the arrival of the Pilgrims at Plymouth Rock and their hard first winter on the western shore of the Atlantic, the Audio-Animatronics narrators—a brand-new Ben Franklin and a brand-new, cigar-puffing Mark Twain—recall certain key people and events in American history—the Boston Tea Party, George Washington and the grueling winter at Valley Forge, the influential black abolitionist Frederick Douglass, the celebrated 19th-century Nez Percé Chief Joseph, and many more. The Philadelphia Centennial Exposition is remembered, along with women's rights campaigner Susan B. Anthony (also a new figure), telephone inventor Alexander Graham Bell, and the steel giant and philanthropist Andrew Carnegie. Naturalist John Muir converses on stage with Teddy Roosevelt. Charles Lindbergh, Rosie the Riveter, Jackie Robinson, Marilyn Monroe, and Walt Disney are all represented. So are John Wayne, Lucille Ball, Margaret Mead, John F. Kennedy, Martin Luther King, Jr., Muhammed Ali, and Billie Jean King. The idea is to recall episodes in history, both negative and positive, which most contributed to the growth of the spirit of America, either by engendering "a new burst of creativity" (in the designers' words) "or a better understanding of ourselves as partners in the American experience." The presentation is hardly comprehensive; instead, it's "a hundred-yard dash capturing the spirit of the country at specific moments in time."

Throughout the show, the attention to historical detail is meticulous. Every one of the rear-projected illustrations was executed in the painting style of the era being described.

The Chief Joseph and Susan B. Anthony figures are speaking their originals' very own words. The exact dimensions of the cannonballs in another scene were carefully investigated—then reproduced. In the Philadelphia Centennial Exposition scene, Pittsburgh's name is spelled without the *h* that subsequent years have added.

For information about how each of the various historical figures actually spoke during their lifetimes, researchers contacted about half a dozen historians and cultural institutions—the Philadelphia Historical Commission, Harvard's Carpenter Center of Visual Arts, the State Historical Society of Missouri, the Department of the Navy's Ships Historical Branch, and others. When recordings were not available, educated guesses were made: Bell's voice was created on the basis of contemporary comments about his voice's clarity, expressiveness, and crisp articulation, coupled with the fact that his father taught elocution. To select Will Rogers's speeches for the Depression scene, whole pages of quotes were collected, reviewed, edited, and re-edited; the voice is the humorist's own, from an actual broadcast, as is that of FDR, here heard over the radio in the roadside gasoline stand scene. That particular scene was suggested by a *Life* magazine photograph; details were based upon research in architectural magazines from the 1930s. Even the type of radio and the style of microphone, and the price (18¢) and the color (red) of gasoline in the tanks were the result of researchers' long hours and close scrutiny.

One of the most interesting aspects of the show is its inner workings, however. Under-

neath the entire theater is a movable carriage device that designers have dubbed "the war wagon," measuring 65-by-35-by-14 feet and weighing 175 tons. The basement that supports "the war wagon" is itself supported by pilings driven approximately 300 feet into the ground; it carries ten different sets and during the presentation rolls forward or backward to position the appropriate set underneath the stage at the appropriate time. Also, because the height of the space underneath the theater is relatively limited, the sets themselves were specially designed to allow certain sections to contract telescopically as proved necessary. These operations are computer controlled.

The 12 life-size statues on either side of the stage represent the "Spirits of America." These are, on the left, from front to rear, Individualism, Innovation, Tomorrow, Independence, Compassion, and Discovery; and, on the right, from front to back, Freedom, Heritage, Pioneering, Knowledge, Self-Reliance, and Adventure. The 44 flags flanking the Hall of Flags corridor in the escalator area are those that have flown over the United States. Revolutionary War flags, Colonial flags, and even flags representing the countries that had claims to American soil before Independence, can all be seen. A special highlight of the show is the majestic music played throughout by the Philadelphia Symphony Orchestra. The "Golden Dreams" sequence was also updated to include scenes from the last 12 years. Notable additions are Muppet creator Jim Henson, Ryan White—the young hemophiliac who succumbed to AIDS after a courageous battle with the disease—and basketball star Earvin "Magic" Johnson.

As one of the most compelling of all the World Showcase attractions, The American Adventure is occasionally quite busy. Perhaps the best time to schedule a visit to the show is first thing in the morning or in the early evening. Seats in the front of the house give the optimal view of the Audio-Animatronics characters (although all seats provide an acceptable view). While waiting for the show to begin, be sure to read the quotes on the walls—Wendell Wilkie, Jane Addams, Charles Lindbergh, Ayn Rand, Archibald MacLeish, Herman Melville, Thomas Wolfe, and George Magar Mardikau are all represented.

HERITAGE MANOR GIFTS: Visit this shop for pre-1940s Americana. Decorative gifts include glassware, hand-made wooden and cloth items, hand-painted porcelain, toys, and food products.

AMERICA GARDENS THEATRE: A variety of entertainment, including an exceptionally lively show of international folk dances and songs, is presented periodically in this lakeside amphitheater in front of The American Adventure Pavilion. The folk show is particularly worth a detour; get performance times from the information desks at Earth Station (on your way into the park), or check at any WorldKey Information System kiosk. Show times also are posted on the promenade at the east and west entrances to the amphitheater.

Be sure to note the pruning of the western sycamores overhead; the old-fashioned pollarding method used, which involves trimming the treetops flat and allowing the lower branches to fill out and interlock, eventually produces a thick canopy. The flower beds outside are planted in red, white, and blue; the bushes are East Palatka holly.

Italy

The arches and cut-out motifs that adorn the World Showcase reproduction of the Doge's Palace in Venice are just the more obvious examples of the attention to detail lavished on the individual structures in this relatively small pavilion. The angel atop the scaled down Campanile was sculpted on the model of the original right down to the curls on the back of its head—then covered with real gold leaf, despite the fact that it was destined to be set almost 100 feet in the air. The other statues in the complex, including the sea god Neptune presiding over the fountain in the rear of the piazza, are similarly exact. Even the marblelike material used in the facade resembles that used in the real Doge's Palace. And the pavilion even has an island like Venice's own, its seawall appropriately stained with age, plus moorings that look like barber poles, with several distinctively Venetian gondolas tied to them. St. Mark the Evangelist also is remembered, together with the lion that is the saint's companion and Venice's guardian; these can be seen atop the two massive columns flanking the small arched footbridge that connects the landfall to the mainland. The only deviation from Venetian fact is the alteration of the site of the Doge's Palace in reference to the real St. Mark's Square.

The pavilion is equally interesting from a horticultural point of view. The island boasts a brace of kumquat trees, citrus plants typical of the Mediterranean, and a couple of olive trees that can be seen on both side walls of the Delizie Italiane; originally located in a Sacramento, California, grove, they were moved to Anaheim and then were piled onto a flatbed truck, their branches spreading wide,

for the trip to Florida. But they got only as far as the Arizona border. As Disney gardeners tell the story, that state's regulation prohibiting loads beyond a given width is so erratically enforced that no problems had been anticipated. So it came as quite a surprise when the inspector on duty decreed that the trees be trimmed to ten feet. A chain saw soon materialized, and within minutes the ancient olives were shorn. Despite horticulturalists' fears, the trees survived, leaving only their scars to remind visitors of the ordeal; the darker bark is what remains of the original, while the lighter areas are the new growth. The tall trees that stand like dark columns at various points in the pavilion are Italian

cypress, which are very common in Italy; Florida slash pines replace that nation's abundant Italian stone pines, which would not grow here.

Entertainment is another highlight of the pavilion. A very lively group known as Il Commedia di Bologna puts on 15-minute shows such as "The Great Impasta," in which selected members of the audience have the chance to play heroes, heroines, and the vilest of villains in a style reminiscent of the renaissance *commedia dell' arte*. Il Commedia di Bologna players are very funny (if very broad) and shouldn't be missed.

DELIZIE ITALIANE: This open-air market on the western edge of the piazza is a good spot for a sweet snack with its selection of tasty Italian chocolates and other goodies for sale.

LA BOTTEGA ITALIANA: A selection of items from Benetton, the Italian casual wear manufacturer, is featured here. Colorful sweaters, shirts, slacks, jeans, and accessories are all available.

LA GEMMA ELEGANTE: Located to the rear of the piazza on its eastern edge, this small shop focuses on jewelry. There are gold and silver chains galore, and some are expensive, but it's also possible to find handsome—and affordable—beads, earrings, and pendants made of Venetian glass; intricate glass-mosaic brooches and pillboxes bearing images of tiny bouquets; cameos; and coral necklaces.

IL BEL CRISTALLO: The production of fine glassware has been a tradition in Italy for centuries, and so a shop like this one just off the promenade on the Germany side of the piazza was a must for the pavilion. Typical Venetian glass paperweights and other items, their bright colors trapped in smooth spheres or teardrops of clear or milky glass, small porcelain figurines and flower bouquets so finely crafted that they look almost real, pastel flowers made of beads, and lead crystal bowls and candlesticks are all on display. The name of the shop means "the beautiful crystal."

Germany

There are no villages in Germany quite like this one. Inspired in part by towns in the Rhine region and Bavaria, and in part by communities in the German north, it boasts structures reminiscent of those found in such diverse urban enclaves as Frankfurt, Freiburg, and Rothenburg. There are stair-stepped roof lines and towers, balconies and arcaded walkways, and so much overall charm that the scene seems to come straight out of a fairy tale. The beer hall to the rear is almost as lively as the one at Munich's famed Oktoberfest, especially during the later shows, and the shops, which offer a range of merchan-

dise from wine and sweets to ceramics and cuckoo clocks, toys and books, and even art, are so tempting that it's hard to leave the area empty-handed. The various elements that make up the Germany Pavilion are described here as they would be encountered while walking from west to east (counterclockwise) around the cobblestone-paved central plaza, which is known as the St. Georgsplatz, after the statue at its center. St. George, the patron saint of soldiers, is depicted with the dragon that legend says he slew during a pilgrimage to the Middle East.

Try to time your World Showcase peregrinations to bring you to Germany on the hour, when the handsome, specially designed glockenspiel at the plaza's rear can be heard to chime in a melody composed specifically for the pavilion.

DER BÜCHERWURM: This two-story structure, whose exterior is patterned after a merchants' hall known as the *Kaufhaus* (located in the southern German town of Freiburg in Breisgau), stocks prints and English books about Germany; handsome prints of German cities full of gabled old houses and gloriously spired cathedrals; and an assortment of souvenir items like ashtrays and vases and spoons bearing images of German cities. The building itself is worth noting. In order to correctly reproduce the statues of the German emperors on the facade, designers hired a photographer who, shooting from a "cherry picker," submitted closeups from a number of angles. Observant travelers may remember that the Freiburg building has one additional statue—that of Emperor Maximillian—omitted here in the interests of maintaining the proper proportions. (Film and sundries also are available.)

VOLKSKUNST: This small, exceptionally appealing establishment is full of a burgher's bounty of German timekeepers, plus a smattering of other items made by hand in the rural corners of the nation. The latter include

est and largest vintners. Wine tastings are held here daily. The selection includes not only those meant for everyday consumption, but also fine estate wines whose prices run into the hundreds of dollars per bottle. These are white (with a few exceptions), because white wine constitutes the bulk of Germany's vinicultural output. (In fact, only 20 percent of all German bottlings are red.) Long, tall beer mugs and glasses, wine glasses in traditional German colors of greens and ambers, fragile crystal goblets, decanters, and other accessories also are available. The setting itself is quite attractive—low-ceilinged and cozy and full of fir cabinets that have been embellished with carvings of vines and bunches of grapes. The original designs, which decreed that all those grapes be painted purple, were altered to include plenty of green fruit, the main ingredient in white wine.

beer steins in all sizes, from the petite to the enormous and expensive ($2,800); wood carvings made in the southern German town of Oberammergau; bright, fringed Tyrolean scarves; nutcrackers; and a whole collection of "smokers," carved wooden dolls with a receptacle for incense and a hollow pipe for the smoke to escape. As for cuckoo clocks, some are small and unprepossessing, and some are so immense that they'd look appropriate only in some cathedral-ceilinged hunting lodge. The largest measures about five feet in height and is embellished not only with carvings of birds and rabbits and a hunting horn and crossed rifles, but also with a genuine pair of antlers. A must.

DER TEDDYBÄR: Located alongside Volkskunst, this toy shop would be a delight if only for the lively mechanized displays high up on either side of the entrance and against the rear wall: Some of the stuffed lambs and the dolls in the full-skirted folk dresses (known as *dirndls*) have been animated so that tails wag and skirts swirl in time to German folk tunes. The shop also is home to one of WDW's very best selections of toys. There are wonderfully detailed LGB-brand miniature trains and the expected assortment of expensive stuffed keepsakes from Steiff. Colorful wooden toys are tempting as well, along with all kinds of building blocks. Last but not least, the collection of dolls is simply wonderful.

WEINKELLER: The Germany Pavilion's wine shop, situated between the cookie shop and the *Biergarten* toward the rear of St. Georgsplatz, offers approximately 250 varieties of German wines produced and bottled by H. Schmitt Söhne, one of Germany's old-

SÜSSIGKEITEN: It is a mistake to visit this tiny, tile-floored confectionery shop on an empty stomach: Chocolate cookies, butter cookies, and almond biscuits mix with caramels, nuts, and pretzels are on the crowded shelves; and there are boxes upon boxes of *Lebkuchen*, the spicy crisp cookies traditionally baked in Germany at Christmas, not to mention Gummi Bears (which the packages announce as *Gummibaeren*). Children enjoy the special alphabet cookies and animal crackers, both of which are different from those made in U.S. bakeries. Don't miss the attractive display of old Bahlsen cookie tins by the door. Incidentally, Bahlsen, the shop's sponsor, was among the first companies in the world to pack baked goods in airtight wrappers to preserve freshness; the firm's logo is an Egyptian hieroglyph that signifies *long life.*

DIE WEIHNACTS ECKE: This is a shop that can set a visitor's mind to thoughts of Christmas—even in the dog days of summer. Ornaments, decorations, and gifts manufactured by various German companies line the shelves of this store.

GLAS UND PORZELLAN: Featuring glass and porcelain items made by the German firm of Goebel, this is an attractive establishment with rope-turned columns, curved moldings, delicate scrollwork, and tiny carved rosettes. But no matter how attractive the backgrounds, the stars of the show are the M. I. Hummel figurines, which Goebel manufactures. Cherubic, rosy-cheeked children, shown carrying baskets, trays, umbrellas, and other items, as in the drawings of a young German nun named Berta Hummel, are favorites of collectors around the world. One group features redheads, while others have youngsters perched on the edges of ashtrays. There is always an elaborate showpiece at the center of the shop, and a Goebel artist is here to demonstrate the process by which Hummel creations are painted and finished. An excellent display (which includes figurines in all stages of completeness) tells the story.

China

Dominated by a Disney equivalent of Beijing's Temple of Heaven, and announced by a pair of banners which offer good wishes to passersby (the Chinese characters translate: *May good fortune follow you on your path through life* and *May virtue be your neighbor*), this pavilion offers a level of serenity that makes an appealing contrast to the hearty merriment of nearby Germany and the Latin gaiety of Mexico. Part of this quiet environment is the byproduct of the soothing traditional Chinese music that plays over the sound system. The attractive gardens also make a major contribution. They are full of rosebushes (because roses are native to China), and there is a century-old mulberry tree (to the left of the main walkway into the pavilion), with a pomegranate tree and a wiggly looking Florida native known as a water oak nearby. In addition, a spacious emporium devoted to Chinese wares has opened, and two Chinese restaurants add to the overall atmosphere. However, all this is secondary to the fabulous motion picture shown inside the Temple of Heaven—a CircleVision 360 film that is one of the best World Showcase attractions.

WONDERS OF CHINA: LAND OF BEAUTY, LAND OF TIME: This 19-minute presentation shows the beauties of a land that few Epcot Center visitors will ever see firsthand—and does it so vividly that it's possible to see the film over and over and still not fully absorb all the wonderful sights. The Disney crew was the first Western film group to film certain sites, and their remarkable effort includes such marvels as Beijing's Forbidden City; vast, wide-open Mongolia and its stern-faced tribespeople; the 2,400-year-old Great Wall; the Great Buddha of Leshan, eight centuries old and dramatically imposing; the muddy Yangtze River and the 3,000-year-old city of Suzhou, whose location on the Grand Canal, which is generally believed to be the largest manmade waterway in the world, encouraged Marco Polo to call it the Venice of the East. There are shots of the very European city of Shanghai, as well as Hangzhou, where a handful of Chinese are shown doing their morning exercises along the river's edge. Also shown are Huangshan Mountain, wreathed in fog; the Shilin Stone Forest of jagged rock outcroppings in Yunnan Province; Urumqi, whose distance from the sea in Xinjiang Province earned it the title of the most inland city on earth; Lahsa, in Tibet, and its Potala Palace, boasting a thousand rooms and ten times that many altars. Just as fantastic are the Reed Flute Cave and the bizarrely shaped hills of Kweilin above. To complete the picture, there are fields of snow and of wheat, high meadows and beaches dotted with tropical palms, harbors and rice terraces, calligraphers, checkers and Ping-Pong players, lightning-fast acrobats, championship horseback riders, camels and a panda bear, glittering ice sculptures, and millions of bicycles.

Almost every step of the way, the film

crews were besieged by curious Chinese, even in empty Mongolia. For the Huangshan Mountain sequence, which lasts only seconds, the crew and about three dozen hired laborers had to carry the 600-pound camera uphill for nearly a mile. The Chinese government would not permit Disney cameramen to shoot aerial footage in some areas, so Chinese crews were sent aloft to record the required scenes, first on videotape and later—after approval from the Disney director in charge of the project—on film. You can see for yourself just how well this collaboration worked.

Be sure to spend some time before viewing the film examining the details that embellish the building that houses the theater. The design is based on that of the Hall of Prayer for Good Harvest, the major section of Beijing's Temple of Heaven complex, which was built in the year 1420 (during the Ming Dynasty) and reconstructed after being damaged by lightning in 1896. The name of the World Showcase structure is represented by the characters above the entrance. The number of stones in the floor was chosen for auspicious associations; the center stone is surrounded by nine stones because nine is a lucky number in China. Around the edge of the room rise 12 columns—because 12 is both the number of months in the year and the number of years in a full cycle of the Chinese calendar. Closer to the room's center, there are four columns—one for each of the seasons; the japonicus vines entwining each column symbolize long life, while the square beam that they all support alludes to earth, and the round beam above signifies heaven. The dragons on the beams allude to imperial strength, while the phoenixes are reminders of peace and prosperity. The measurements and proportions are all similarly symbolic. Be sure to stand on the round stone in the absolute center of the anteroom: Every whisper is amplified.

When exiting, pass by the House of the Whispering Willows, an exhibit of ancient Chinese art and artifacts. Changed about every six months, it invariably includes fine pieces from well-known collections. Note that the best time to see the film is during the first couple of hours that Epcot Center is open and again just before closing.

YONG FENG SHANGDIAN SHOPPING GALLERY: This vast Chinese emporium, located off the narrow, charming Street of Good Fortune at the exit to the film, offers a huge assortment of Chinese merchandise—silk robes, prints, paper umbrellas and fans, embroidered items, change purses and glasses cases, and more. Trinkets, medium-priced items, and expensive antiques are all available in an array that may be matched in few other places in the U.S. The calligraphy on the curtains wishes passersby *good fortune, long life, prosperity, health, and happiness.*

Norway

Set between the Mexico and China pavilions is Norway, Walt Disney World's 11th World Showcase attraction. Built in conjunction with many Norwegian companies, the pavilion celebrates the history, folklore, and culture of one of the world's oldest countries.

Most appropriately, visitors tour Norway by boat—16-passenger, dragon-headed longboats like those Eric the Red and his fellow Vikings used a thousand years ago—to begin a voyage through time. The journey begins in a tenth-century Viking village where a ship is being readied to head out to sea. Seafarers then find themselves in a mythical Norwegian forest, populated by trolls who cause the boats to plummet backwards downriver, through a maelstrom to the majestic grandeur of the Geiranger fjord, where the vessel narrowly avoids spilling over a waterfall. Ultimately, after a harrowing plunge through a rocky passage, the boats wind up in the North Sea, caught in the fury of a full-blown storm. Lightning flashes reveal an enormous oil rig; as the boat passes the concrete platform legs, the storm calms and a friendly coastal village appears on the horizon.

Survivors disembark there and enter the village. Moments later, guests are invited to a theater where the journey continues on-screen, giving visitors a very tangible sense of the natural scenic spectacles and unique personalities that make up modern Norway. Outside the theater, visitors find they have returned to a cobblestone town square, an architectural showcase in the styles of such Norwegian towns as Bergen, Alesund, Oslo, and Setesdal.

There's also a Norwegian castle fashioned after Akershus, a 14th-century fortress still standing in Oslo's harbor. Shops in the castle stock authentic Norwegian handicrafts and folk items: hand-knit woolens, wood carvings, and glass and metal artworks.

THE PUFFIN'S ROOST: A collection of Norwegian gifts, sweaters, activewear, hand-crafted jewelry, fine leather goods, pewter, candy, toys, and trolls are the wares for sale at this shop.

Mexico

The tangle of tropical vegetation surrounding the great pyramid that encloses this pavilion and the *Cantina*, the Mexican restaurant at the lagoon's edge on the promenade, provide only the barest suggestion of the charming area inside. Dominated by a reconstruction of a quaint plaza at dusk, this area is rimmed by balconied, tile-roofed, colonial-style structures. Crowding a pretty fountain area is a quartet of stands selling Mexican handicrafts, and off to the left is an attractive shop stocked with other handsome wares. Mariachi bands keep things lively. To the rear, the *San Angel Inn*, a corporate cousin of the famous Mexico City restaurant, serves authentic Mexican fare. Behind it, the pavilion's main show chronicles Mexican culture from earliest times right up to the present.

Queues for the boat ride often extend into the promenade in the morning—but if you just want to visit the shops and see the cultural exhibit inside the pyramid entrance, it's perfectly fine to walk straight in, bypassing the line. Note that the pyramid itself was inspired by Meso-American structures dating from the third century A.D. The serpent heads on either side of the stairway evoke the Aztec god Quetzalcoatl.

EL RIO DEL TIEMPO: THE RIVER OF TIME: In the course of this six-minute boat trip, sprinkled with vignettes of pre-Columbian, Spanish-Colonial, and modern Mexican life, visitors greet a Mayan high priest, watch stylized dances by performers in vivid costumes, and are assailed by vendors at a lively market. A band costumed to look like skeletons entertains at one juncture (in a reference to the Day of the Dead, a holiday celebrated in Mexico with candies and sweets shaped like skulls or skeletons). In addition, there are a handful of film clips depicting present-day Acapulco (with its cliff divers and flying dancers), Tulum, Manzanillo (and its speed boats), and Isla Mujeres (with its gorgeous sea life). The assemblage of film, Audio-Animatronics figures, and props is reminiscent of the Magic Kingdom's It's A Small World. During peak seasons, long lines, which prevail from mid-morning on, usually thin out in the afternoon as the crowds drift into the more distant parts of World Showcase. If you are in the area, skip the boat ride the first time around and return in the evening or late in the afternoon when the crowds are likely to be far smaller.

PLAZA DE LOS AMIGOS: Brightly colored paper flowers, sombreros, wooden trays and bowls, peasant blouses, baskets, and pottery make this shopping area (*mercado* in Spanish) at the plaza's center as bright and almost as lively as one in Mexico itself. The colorful pâpier-maché piñatas that figure so strongly in the scenery here are so popular that Epcot Center has to buy them from suppliers by the truckload. Irresistible.

ARTESANIAS MEXICANAS: This shop stocks more expensive versions of some of the merchandise sold in the Mercado—onyx ashtrays, bookends, plaques, chess sets, malachite, and unique Mexican decorative gifts.

LA FAMILIA FASHIONS: Mexican ready-to-wear and fashion accessories for women and children, plus examples of silver and turquoise jewelry are available here.

EL RANCHITO DEL NORTE: Gifts and souvenirs from northern Mexico are the featured items.

World Showcase Plaza

PORT OF ENTRY: Features unique gifts, clothing, and accessories from around the world including countries not featured in World Showcase. Sunglasses, film, and cigarettes are available.

DISNEY TRADERS: Merchandise combining the charms of Disney characters and World Showcase themes are the stock in trade. Sunglasses, film, cigarettes, and sundries also are available.

International Gateway

SHOWCASE GIFTS: Disney memorabilia, convenience items, and a package pickup depot are located at this spot near the France entrance.

WORLD TRAVELER: Disney fashions and character merchandise, plus film, 35mm and video camera rentals, and a drop-off for two-hour film processing are conveniently located here.

STROLLER AND WHEELCHAIR RENTAL: Strollers and wheelchairs are available for rent at this location. Remember to keep your rental receipt; it can be used on the same day in the Magic Kingdom, at the Disney-MGM Studios Theme Park, or again in Epcot Center should you leave and return at a later hour.

HOT TIPS

- Stop by Earth Station for an entertainment schedule in order to be sure you won't miss any of the special shows scheduled for the day or evening.
- Visit World Showcase in the morning—it's normally uncongested until about 11 A.M. See Future World in the evening. Remember that lines throughout Epcot Center are longest during midday, and shortest (sometimes nonexistent) during the early evening.
- Go to the Wonders of Life Pavilion early in the day since lines can get unmanageable later on.
- During peak seasons, preferred reservation times at Epcot Center's full-service restaurants are usually fully booked by 10 A.M. So be sure to arrive at Epcot Center early to get a jump on the day and help assure that you get the restaurant and seating time of your choice. Remember, too, that non-prime dining hours are often available to those making late reservations, so adjustment of your eating schedule may well help you to try the restaurant of your choice. Walt Disney World resort guests can make reservations in advance. Check with the Guest Services desk in your hotel.
- Save the shops, CommuniCore East and West, and the World of Motion's TransCenter for the afternoon when just about everything else is very crowded.
- Don't queue for the World Showcase Promenade buses. You'll get where you're going faster by walking.
- Don't see all the World Showcase films in one day, especially if you're traveling with children.
- Be sure to allow extra time for Image Works at the Journey Into Imagination and Sea Base Alpha at The Living Seas.
- The jumping fountains outside the Journey Into Imagination are a favorite with children of all ages.

Disney-MGM Studios Theme Park

Welcome to "the Hollywood that never was and always will be." So said Walt Disney Company Chairman Michael Eisner when he officially opened the Disney-MGM Studios Theme Park. A bit corny? Sure. But also true.

In the solid Disney tradition, a dream Hollywood set in some indeterminate time in the 1930s and 1940s has been lovingly created. A rose-colored view of the movie-making capital has been combined with a backstage tour that breaks new ground, a variety of entertaining attractions, and a delightful selection of eateries to create this Walt Disney World enclave.

The Studios are situated on a 110-acre site southwest of Epcot Center. The watertower, known to punsters (for obvious reasons) as the "Earffel Tower," is reminiscent of the types of towers looming over most Hollywood studios of the era. Here, however, it gets that special Disney touch and is capped by a mousketeer-style hat.

What makes this area of Walt Disney World different from other Disney creations is the extent to which guests can participate in the attractions. Our best advice is to volunteer, wherever and whenever possible. It's fun, and it adds enormously to the experience.

The Studios will be expanding during the next few years. Twilight Zone Tower of Terror debuts this year. During the mid-1990s, Sunset Boulevard will be paved with Roger Rabbit's Hollywood, featuring the Toontown Trolley and the Benny the Cab Ride.

Disney-MGM Studios Theme Park

CATASTROPHE CANYON

RESIDENTIAL STREET

EARFFEL TOWER

JIM HENSON'S MUPPETS ON LOCATION

JIM HENSON'S MUPPET★VISION 3D

TEENAGE MUTANT NINJA TURTLES®

INSIDE THE MAGIC

SOUNDSTAGE I

SOUNDSTAGE II

SOUNDSTAGE III

HONEY I SHRUNK THE KIDS

NEW YORK STREET

MICKEY AVENUE

VOYAGE OF THE LITTLE MERMAID

BACKSTAGE STUDIO TOUR

THE STUDIO SHOWCASE

STAR TOURS

THE GREAT MOVIE RIDE

THE MAGIC OF DISNEY ANIMATION

SUPERSTAR TELEVISION

MONSTER SOUND SHOW

"DINOSAURS" LIVE!

INDIANA JONES™ EPIC STUNT SPECTACULAR

HOLLYWOOD BOULEVARD

CROSSROADS OF THE WORLD

TWILIGHT ZONE TOWER OF TERROR OPENING JUNE 1994

THEATER OF THE STARS

KENNEL

ENTRANCE PLAZA

AUTOMATIC TELLER

BUS PARKING

MEDICAL PARKING

LEGEND

🚻 **Rest Rooms** *All & accessible*

📞 **Telephones**
(All 3 Services listed below are available at each site)
   📞 Telephones
   📞 Touch ✳88 Smart Phones
   📞 Amplified Telephones

⊙ **Kennel Club**

📷 **Two-Hour Photo Express Service**

✉ **Mail Drop Location**

➕ **First Aid**

🅂 Banking

♿ Wheelchair Rentals

● Strollers

■ Lockers

🛈 Guest Information Board

◻ Kodak "Photo Spot" - Symbols indicate prime photo-taking locations

▲ Hospitality Building
   Baby Services
   Lost and Found
   Lost Children
   Guest Relations

DINING

1. The Hollywood Brown Derby
2. Starring Rolls
3. 50's Prime Time Cafe
4. Tune In Lounge
5. Mama Melrose's Ristorante Italiano
6. Sci-Fi Drive-In Diner
7. Hollywood & Vine Cafeteria
8. Soundstage Restaurant featuring "Beauty and the Beast"
9. The Catwalk Bar
10. Min and Bill's Dockside Diner
11. Disney-MGM Studios Commissary
12. Backlot Express
13. Studio Catering Co.
14. Dinosaur Gertie's Ice Cream of Extinction

SHOPS

15. Oscar's Super Service
    Oscar's Classic Car Souvenirs
    Movieland Memorabilia
    Sid Cahuenga's One-of-a-Kind
    Crossroads of the World
16. The Darkroom
    Cover Story
    Celebrity 5 & 10
    Sweet Success
    L.A. Prop and Storage
17. Mickey's of Hollywood
18. Keystone Clothiers
    Lakeside Newsstand
19. Golden Age Souvenirs
20. Endor Vendors
21. The Disney Studio Store
22. Animation Gallery
23. The Loony Bin
24. Fototoons
25. The Villains Shop
26. Stage One Company Store
27. Under The Sea
28. Indiana Jones™ Adventure Outpost

Getting In and Around

TRANSPORTATION TO THE DISNEY-MGM STUDIOS THEME PARK: It's very simple to get to this Disney theme park.

By car: Take exit 26B or exit 27 off I-4 and follow the signs for the Disney-MGM Studios Theme Park. The entrance to the Studios is about half a mile from I-4. There is a 7,500-space parking lot. Parking is $4; free for Walt Disney World resort guests. Trams carry visitors from their parking space to the ticket booths.

By WDW bus: Buses make the trip to the Studios from a variety of locations: from the Magic Kingdom and its surrounding resorts (*Contemporary*, *Grand Floridian*, *Polynesian*, and *Disney Inn*), from the villas, from the Disney Village Marketplace, from Disney Village Hotel Plaza, from the *Caribbean Beach* resort, from *Port Orleans*, from *Dixie Landings*, from the *Disney Vacation Club*, from *Wilderness Lodge*, from the *All-Star Sports* and *All-Star Music* resorts, and from Epcot Center. Call 824-4321 to confirm all the available transportation options.

By launch: Guests staying at the *Swan*, *Dolphin*, *Yacht Club*, and *Beach Club* can take a boat to the Studios.

HOURS: The Disney-MGM Studios Theme Park is usually open from 9 A.M. to 7 P.M.; hours are extended during holiday weekends and the summer months. Call 824-4321 for up-to-the-minute schedules.

BABY CARE: Changing tables and facilities for nursing mothers can be found at the Guest Services building at the main entrance.

CAMERA NEEDS: The Darkroom is located to the right as you enter the park. Kodak Disc Cameras, camcorders, and 35mm cameras are available for rent (with a deposit) or for purchase, and two-hour film processing is offered. A wide assortment of film and accessories is sold, and film also is available in most of the shops.

ENTERTAINMENT: The Sorcery in the Sky fireworks show, presented during busy seasons, is among WDW's most spectacular nighttime displays. Also during busy seasons, the Star Today program features a prominent celebrity who makes several appearances around the premises. For information about the star of the day, stop by the Guest Services building. "Streetmosphere Characters" are the entertaining troupe of performers along Hollywood Boulevard. Watch for autograph hounds, budding starlets, gossip columnists, and others who are out doing their thing all day and evening. Check at Guest Services for exact showtimes.

STUDIOS TIP BOARD: Located at the end of Hollywood Boulevard, this information center is staffed by hosts and hostesses who can tell guests which attractions are about to begin a new show and which have the shortest lines. It is updated constantly via a system of two-way radios, so the suggestions offered on the big blackboard are well worth following. The hosts also can provide general information. Restaurant reservations for several of the Studios' eateries can be made here as well.

FIRST AID: Minor medical problems can be handled at First Aid, in the Guest Services building at the main entrance.

VISITORS WITH DISABILITIES: Most of the attractions, shops, and restaurants are accessible to guests in wheelchairs. Special parking for guests with disabilities is available; inquire at the Auto Plaza. Wheelchairs can be rented at Oscar's Super Service Station, just inside the main entrance. Quantities are limited. A guidebook for guests with disabilities is available at Guest Services. For hearing-impaired guests, an Assistive Listening Device is available at Guest Services. A $25 deposit is required. Tape cassettes (with a $25 refundable deposit) and portable tape players are available at Guest Services for guests who are blind or sight-impaired.

LOCKERS: Public facilities, which cost 50¢
per locker, are located next to Oscar's Super
Service Station at the main entrance.

LOST CHILDREN: Report lost children to the
Guest Services building at the main entrance,
call 560-4668, or tell an employee.

LOST AND FOUND: Claim or report lost articles at the Guest Services building on the day
of your visit. To claim or report lost articles
after your visit, call 560-4245.

MONEY MATTERS: An automated bank teller
is located next to the ticket sales window at
the main entrance. Credit cards (American
Express, Visa, and MasterCard) and traveler's
checks are accepted for merchandise and
tickets and at full-service restaurants. Cash
only is accepted at food carts and counter-
service establishments. Disney Dollars, available in colorful $1, $5, and $10 denomina-
tions, are good for dining and merchandise
and can be exchanged at any time for U.S.
currency, though many guests take a few
home as inexpensive souvenirs.

STROLLER AND WHEELCHAIR RENTAL:
Both are available for rent at Oscar's Super
Service Station inside the main entrance, but
quantities are limited. Remember to keep your
rental receipt; it can be used on the same day
in the Magic Kingdom, Epcot Center, or again
at the Studios.

ADMISSION: Tickets and Passports are
available for one, four, and five days. The Disney organization defines a ticket as admission for one day only; other forms of admission media (for longer periods) are called
Passports. One-day tickets may be used at
the Magic Kingdom, Epcot Center, or the Disney-MGM Studios Theme Park, but not at
more than one site on the same day. Four-
day Super Passes and Five-day Super Duper
Passes can be used at the Magic Kingdom,
Epcot Center, and the Disney-MGM Studios
Theme Park on the same day; unlike one-day
tickets, they also include unlimited use of the
transportation system inside Walt Disney
World. The Five-day Super Duper Pass also
allows admission to River Country, Typhoon
Lagoon, Discovery Island, and Pleasure
Island for a seven-day period beginning with
the first use of the pass. Guests staying at
Walt Disney World resorts can purchase a Be
Our Guest Pass valid for the length of their
stay. The Be Our Guest Pass offers savings
over the Four-Day Super Passes and Five-
Day Super Duper Passes, and includes unlim-
ited admission to the Magic Kingdom, Epcot
Center, the Disney-MGM Studios Theme
Park, Pleasure Island, Typhoon Lagoon, River
Country, and Discovery Island for the dura-
tion of your stay. Cash, traveler's checks,
personal checks (with proper ID), American

Express, Visa, and MasterCard can be used
to pay for all admission media. Multi-day
Passports do not have to be used on consec-
utive days. Note that old multi-day World
Passports are not accepted for admission to
Disney-MGM Studios Theme Park.

ADMISSION PRICES*

ONE-DAY TICKET
(Restricted to use in the Studios only.)

Adult	$ 35.90
Child**	$ 28.50

FOUR-DAY SUPER PASS
(Valid in all three parks for four days and
includes use of WDW transportation system.)

Adult	$126.70
Child**	$ 99.25

FIVE-DAY SUPER DUPER PASS
(Valid in all three parks for five days, includes
use of WDW transportation system, and
allows admission to Typhoon Lagoon, River
Country, Discovery Island, and Pleasure Island
for up to seven days from the first use of the
Super Pass.)

Adult	$174.30
Child**	$138.40

BE OUR GUEST PASS
(Available to WDW resort guests only. Valid in
all three parks, Typhoon Lagoon, Pleasure
Island, Discovery Island, and River Country for
the duration of stay and includes unlimited use
of WDW transportation system.)

Length of Stay	Adult	Child**
3 nights/4 days	$139.44	$109.87
4 nights/5 days	$162.67	$128.84
5 nights/6 days	$183.80	$145.76
6 nights/7 days	$201.76	$160.57
7 nights/8 days	$213.37	$170.09
8 nights/9 days	$223.87	$178.51
9 nights/10 days	$234.42	$186.96
10 nights/11days	$244.98	$195.41

The cost of an **ANNUAL PASSPORT** is
$200.60 for adults and $174.25 for children;
renewals are $179.40 for adults and $153.05
for children.

**Note: Multi-day Passports need not be used
on consecutive days.**

These prices were correct at press time, but
may change during 1994.

*The prices quoted include sales tax.
**3 through 9 years of age

Hollywood Boulevard

Enter the gates of the Disney-MGM Studios Theme Park and the mosaic of flashy neon, chromed art deco and streamlined moderne architecture, and star-gazing street characters immediately plunge guests into the Hollywood of the 1930s and 1940s. Palm-lined Hollywood Boulevard conveys the spirit of a city that never existed, but one we all wish had. Assorted characters ask guests for autographs, while would-be starlets search for their big break. There's a guy selling maps to the stars' Beverly Hills homes and roving television reporters, all of whom populate this rosy image of Hollywood's heyday.

Great movie music is piped in when small strolling bands aren't entertaining; the streets are spotless; and as is the case in the Magic Kingdom and Epcot Center, guests are transported to another time and place.

The shops of Hollywood Boulevard are described here. For details about the restaurants at the Studios, see the *Good Meals, Great Times* chapter.

East Side of the Street

MOVIELAND MEMORABILIA: Located just to the left of the main entrance, this kiosk stocks stuffed toys, hats, books, sunglasses, film, key chains, and other souvenirs. It's a good place to pick up that one last item forgotten during your travels through other parts of WDW.

CROSSROADS OF THE WORLD: In the middle of the entrance plaza, Mickey Mouse keeps watch from atop this Hollywood Boulevard landmark. The circular shop offers souvenirs, sunglasses, film, raingear, sundries, and information.

SID CAHUENGA'S ONE-OF-A-KIND: Authentic antiques and curios are the stock-in-trade here. Autographed photos, old movie magazines and posters, and assorted Hollywood memorabilia are among the collectibles with which old Sid is willing to part—for a price.

MICKEY'S OF HOLLYWOOD, PLUTO'S TOY PALACE, DISNEY & CO.: These three shops are connected, similar to the set-up at the Magic Kingdom's Emporium and Epcot Center's Centorium. This is the place to find T-shirts, sweatshirts, hats, plush toys, watches, jackets, socks, wallets, tote bags, books, and sunglasses, all emblazoned with the Studios logo.

KEYSTONE CLOTHIERS: Jackets complete with flashing electric bulbs (selling for about $200), women's fashions, and jewelry are the specialties of this flashy shop. There's a wonderful pair of earrings—one Mickey and one Minnie—that will set you back $290. A favorite item sold here is a Mickey Mouse umbrella that sprouts two ears when opened.

LAKESIDE NEWSTAND: A terrific selection of comic books is found here, along with a wide variety of movie magazines. Souvenirs also are available.

West Side of the Street

OSCAR'S CLASSIC CAR SOUVENIRS & SUPER SERVICE: The 1947 Buick parked out front gets plenty of attention. Automotive memorabilia, mugs, models, and key chains are for sale. The car, by the way, is not. The gas being pumped from the tanks out front is from the Mohave Oil Co., the same company whose oil tanks explode at Catastrophe Canyon on the Backstage Tour. Services offered here include stroller and wheelchair rental, lockers, and products for infants.

THE DARKROOM: The art deco facade of this shop allows guests to enter through an aperture-like doorway. Rental cameras are available: Kodak Explorer 35mm cameras cost $5 per day to rent, with a $100 refundable deposit; and Kodak VHS video cameras rent for $40 per day, with a refundable deposit of $600 and a driver's license or $800 without a license. Video cameras also are available on a discounted multiple-day rental program. Deposits can be charged on American Express, MasterCard, or Visa. Film is not included in the rental price. Cameras also are available for purchase, as is a wide variety of film and accessories.

COVER STORY: Just through The Darkroom, this is where guests can have their images put on the front cover of a large choice of favorite popular magazines, including *Life*, *Cosmopolitan*, *Sports Illustrated*, *Muscle*, *Time*, and—for the younger set—*Muppet*. Costumes and appropriate accessories are provided by the shop.

CELEBRITY 5 & 10: Modeled after a 1940s Woolworth's, this large shop carries trinkets, costume jewelry, picture frames, shirts, jackets, aprons, teddy bears, magnets, and memorabilia associated with old Hollywood. This is the place to pick up a director's clapboard and other non-Disney, film-related merchandise.

SWEET SUCCESS: Specialty candies and more mundane treats are available at this sweet-smelling shop—plus plush M & M toys.

L.A. PROP AND STORAGE: A wide variety of children's clothing featuring characters from *Beauty and the Beast*, *Pinocchio*, and *Aladdin* are among the offerings at this shop.

Shopping Beyond the Boulevard

GOLDEN AGE SOUVENIRS: Located between the Monster Sound Show and SuperStar Television, there are gifts from television and radio programs, plus Disney Channel merchandise.

ENDOR VENDORS: Just outside Star Tours, this shop offers intergalactic souvenirs associated with the Star Wars films and the Star Tours attraction.

THE DISNEY STUDIO STORE: Just outside the Walt Disney Theater, this is the place for T-shirts, sweatshirts, hats, and accessories emblazoned with Disney Studios designs.

THE LOONY BIN: A perfect stop between the Backstage Studio Tour and the Special Effects and Production Tour. Lots of Roger

Rabbit merchandise and some gag gifts are on sale. There's a host of hands-on fun in the form of props from the movie *Who Framed Roger Rabbit?*

FOTOTOONS: Visitors have a chance to have their photograph taken and combined with their favorite cartoon character.

ANIMATION GALLERY: Located in the Animation Building, this is the place to find original Disney animation cels, exclusive limited edition reproductions, figurines, and other collectibles. It's a pleasant place to browse, even if buying isn't on your mind.

STAGE ONE COMPANY STORE: This is the shop where guests can find merchandise featuring the likenesses of Miss Piggy, Kermit the Frog, Fozzie Bear, and other Muppets in addition to a variety of Disney-character items.

THE VILLAIN'S SHOP: From Cruella DeVille to Queen Malificent, this shop stocks merchandise featuring the meanest and nastiest of Disney's villainous characters.

TEENAGE MUTANT NINJA TURTLES CART: Coloring books, plastic cups, shoelaces, stickers, T-shirts, and other merchandise featuring the Ninja Turtles is on sale at this shop on wheels on New York Avenue.

UNDER THE SEA: Located near the Voyage of The Little Mermaid, this shop offers a variety of merchandise featuring Ariel, Sebastian, Flounder, and friends. T-shirts, sweatshirts, bathing suits, towels, and much more are available.

INDIANA JONES ADVENTURE OUTPOST: Located next to the attraction, this shop features an exclusive assortment of adventure clothing and memorabilia, all with the Indiana Jones insignia.

The Great Movie Ride

Housed in a full-scale reproduction of historic Mann's Chinese Theatre, this attraction captivates the imagination of guests from the start. The queue area winds through the precisely reproduced lobby and into the heart of filmmaking, where guests will see some famous movie scenes on a large screen. (Note that if the queue extends outside the building, you're in for a long wait. It takes about 25 minutes to reach the ride vehicles once you've entered the theater.)

Visitors board ride vehicles in an area where a giant cyclorama of Hollywood Hills hangs just below a soundstage lighting grid. Several tiers of sets picturing hillside homes, Griffith Park Observatory, and the original vintage "Hollywoodland" sign blend with a California sunset. The vehicles then pass under an old-fashioned theater marquee and on into a Hollywood set.

More than 60 Audio-Animatronics dancers atop a large-tiered revolving cake greet guests, in a replay of the "By a Waterfall" scene from the Busby Berkeley musical *Footlight Parade*. These dancing girls are not among Disney's finest Audio-Animatronic creations. Gene Kelly's most memorable performance from *Singin' in the Rain* is the next scene on the tour. Rain seems to drench the soundstage, but doesn't dampen the spirits of the Audio-Animatronic Kelly, who sings his heart out. Then Mary Poppins and Bert the chimney sweep entertain as Mary floats from above via her magical umbrella and Bert dances on a rooftop to the tune of "Chim Chim Cher-ee."

From the world of musical entertainment, guests move on to adventure. James Cagney re-creates his role from *Public Enemy* as the ride proceeds along Gangster Alley. A Prohibition-style mob shootout begins and guests find themselves in the midst of an ambush. An alternate route leads to a trip to a western town, where John Wayne can be seen on horseback eyeing some would-be bank robbers. The thieves blow the safe and flames pour from the building. The heat can be felt from the trams, so don't be too surprised.

The ride vehicles whisk guests past danger and into the spaceship *Nostromo* from the film *Alien*. Officer Ripley guards the corridor while a convincing monster threatens riders with its slimy body from an overhead compartment. (Note that this scene and the gangster and western scenes are presented in a darkened setting and may be upsetting to younger children.) Next stop is the Well of Souls from *Raiders of the Lost Ark*, where Harrison Ford and John Rhys-Davies struggle to remove the ancient ark from its sepulcher.

In the jungle, Tarzan's familiar cry fills the air as he swings in on a vine. Jane is there, too, atop an elephant, and Cheetah screeches and jumps around appropriately. As nightfall approaches, a legendary film scene is replayed. Rick and Ilsa say their goodbyes as the plane's engines sputter in the timeless *Casablanca* finale. The plane, by the way, may actually be the same one used in the movie. When Disney Imagineers set out to find an Electra 12A (built by Lockheed during the 1930s), they found it on an airfield in Hondo, Texas. Number 1204, according to the oral history offered by its owner, not only appeared in *Casablanca*, but in several other movies as well. It was most recently used in a made-for-television movie about the disappearance of Amelia Earhart.

Guests are taken from the airfield in *Casablanca* to the swirling winds of Munchkinland, where a house has just fallen upon the Wicked Witch of the East. Her sister, as portrayed by Margaret Hamilton, appears to keep the tension peaked. This Audio-Animatronic figure represents the third generation of this technology, and she is quite impressively lifelike. But happy endings prevail and guests follow Dorothy, the Tin Man, the Cowardly Lion, the Scarecrow, and Toto along the Yellow Brick Road to the Emerald City of Oz.

As the ride draws to a close, a film montage of memorable moments from Academy Award-winning films is shown.

The 50 Audio-Animatronic figures created for this ride were done by many of the same artists who created the characters in the Hall of Presidents in the Magic Kingdom. Attention to detail is very precise. John Wayne's horse and rifle, for example, match those he used in his westerns. The costumes worn by the Julie Andrews and Dick Van Dyke Audio-Animatronics figures are modeled after the originals from *Mary Poppins*. And Gene Kelly personally inspected his likeness before it was shipped from California to Florida.

Backstage Studio Tour

On this 25-minute tram tour, guests go backstage to see work in progress on television shows and movies. The tour begins in the queue area with a presentation of the history of The Walt Disney Studios shown on overhead television monitors and narrated by Tom Selleck and Carol Burnett. There are some funny comments from such luminaries as Mel Brooks, Clint Eastwood, Richard Dreyfus, Robert Zemeckis, Francis Ford Coppola, and Eddie Murphy.

In typical Disney fashion, the line weaves up and back through a gallery of milestones and memories from the early days of the Disney Studios. There is a sign as guests enter the gate for the backstage tour that announces a 45-minute wait from that point. It takes about 30 minutes to wind through the main queue area when full, so be prepared. The crowds seem to thin out during the late afternoon hours, so if the line is beyond the 45-minute mark, your time will be better spent at one of the other attractions.

The Backstage Shuttles are comfortable and roomy trams and tours are hosted by enthusiastic guides. (Note that when boarding the trams, those on the left side will get wet at Catastrophe Canyon, while those on the right will stay dry. Choose accordingly.) The trams pull out and guests have a view of bungalows housing production departments where actual work is being done on several television shows, such as the Disney Channel's "Mickey Mouse Club" and Ed MacMahon's "Star Search." Guests pass through the "greens" department, where trees, plants, and shrubs are kept until they are needed on the set. The tram then winds through a tunnel where guests can see the wardrobe department at work on the left through large windows. Original costumes worn by Julia Roberts in *Pretty Woman*, Warren Beatty in *Dick Tracy*, Bill Campbell in *The Rocketeer*, Whoopi Goldberg in *Sister Act*, and the stars of "The Golden Girls" can be glimpsed through the windows. More than 100 artists produce the costumes for all of Disney's motion picture, television, and entertainment projects, and with 2.25 million garments, Walt Disney World has the world's largest working wardrobe.

Next guests see a 65-foot portion of a Delta L-1011 fuselage from the nose to the wings. The section was actually removed from an airplane which was flown by Lockheed for many years. The mock-up was designed and built by Delta Air Lines and located at the Studios for use in filming commercials, motion pictures, promotional shots, and in-flight demonstration videos.

The tram then passes through the camera, props, and lighting departments, where equipment is stored until it is needed both on

and off the studio's sets. Disney's camera equipment is so advanced that many visiting network television crews often borrow it when covering Space Shuttle launches at the Kennedy Space Center, about 70 miles to the east. A look into the scenic shop reveals carpenters at work on sets which are finished later on the soundstages.

The tram turns into the backlot residential street where empty, hollow facades give the outward appearance of a lovely neighborhood. Used mainly for exterior shots, the houses on the street include Vern's home from *Ernest Saves Christmas*. There's also the facade of "The Golden Girls" home and the house from "Empty Nest." Exterior shots for the shows have been filmed here. A backlot church can play two parts: one side looks like a small-town church, while the front has the big-city look.

With a bit of flourish, the tour guide explains how landscapes can be created by set designers to fill certain needs and then asks "where, in Central Florida, can you find an active oil field in the middle of a dry, rocky, barren desert canyon prone to flash floods?" The answer is Catastrophe Canyon, which produces some of the best special effects most visitors will ever experience. As the story goes, the crews are filming a movie in which a backstage tram gets stuck in the canyon during a flash flood. But the guide will tell you that it's safe to go in because they're not filming today. Astute guests will notice that the oil company, Mohave, is the same one represented at Oscar's Super Service on Hollywood Boulevard.

In a spectacular series of special effects, a rain storm begins; then there's an explosion, complete with flames that are so hot even riders on the right side of the tram feel them; followed by a flash flood that is so convincing it forces everyone to lean the other way. The road along which the tram rides shifts and dips hydraulically, lending even more reality to the scary adventure. A later behind-the-scenes look reveals the tanks that release enough water to fill ten Olympic-size swimming pools. Some of the water is blown out by air cannons, which can shoot 25,000 gallons of water over 100 feet. To put that in better perspective, if a basketball was stuck into one of the cannons, it could be shot over the top of the Empire State Building.

From Catastrophe Canyon, the tram rides by New York City where meticulously reproduced facades line the urban streets. Though the brickwork looks authentic, these backless facades are constructed mostly of fiberglass and styrofoam. Production designers spent a year and a half designing and constructing the New York lot. The skyscrapers, including the Empire State Building and the Chrysler Building, are actually painted flats. Forced perspective (the same technique that makes Cinderella Castle appear much taller than it is) is employed here to make the 4-story Empire State Building appear as if it's the real

104-story structure. Tour groups often encounter film crews setting up or taking down equipment from shoots done on the lot. Be sure to take careful note of the storefronts, as you'll encounter them again later during a short film starring Bette Midler. Though clearly a New York reproduction, the streets can be altered to fit the role for any city USA. Both the Empire State Building and the Chrysler Building can be removed and facades changed to serve any purpose. If crews are not filming, guests can explore the New York street on foot.

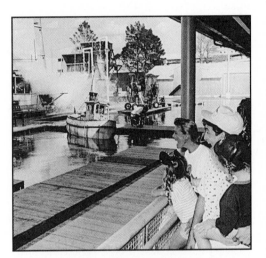

Inside the Magic Special Effects & Production Tour

This is a walking tour and guests begin by following Roger Rabbit's big pink footprints to the Loony Bin shop and the *Studio Catering Company* where sodas and snacks are sold. The Loony Bin stocks Roger Rabbit souvenirs and offers a chance to play with some of the props used in the movie. Children especially love the boxes that emit animal sounds, street sounds, and laughter when opened. A hole in one wall is in the shape of Roger Rabbit, and kids can climb through, something they tend to do over and over again. Following the footprints leads to another queue area, where a Goldie Hawn/Rick Moranis video is presented to entertain tourers while they're waiting. The wait here averages 15 minutes.

First stop on the walking tour is the Studio Showcase where props and costumes from the latest movie releases and popular television shows are on display. Next, at an outdoor special effects area, a guest plays the role of submarine commander "Captain Duck." This show demonstrates effects used to produce battle scenes at sea. Pyrotechnics, simulated depth charges, torpedo blasts, and strafing runs all combine in an

action-packed adventure. Then it's on to the prop room where guests get to see a variety of familiar creatures, including members of the cast of *Captain EO*. Be sure not to miss the sketches on the walls showing the genesis of several of the props displayed.

Two children are chosen from the crowd in the prop room to participate in the next portion of the tour. A giant bee, used in *Honey, I Shrunk the Kids*, is suspended from the ceiling. One of the children is put atop the bee and one on the wing. In this part of the tour, guests are shown how film shot against a blue screen can then be superimposed onto any background chosen by the producers. The kids are filmed, and the footage is cut in with real scenes from the movie.

Then it's on to the soundstages where specially designed, soundproof catwalks allow visitors to gawk and talk all they want. The tour takes in three soundstages, where at any given time filming may be in progress for movies or television shows. It also is possible, however, that nothing will be happening on the set. Overhead monitors show explanations of the use of soundstages, and the art of filming a television series is explained by an assortment of stars, including Warren Beatty.

From this area, guests are led into a walkway where a Bette Midler short film is presented on overhead monitors. The film was shot entirely at the Studios, exclusively for the Disney-MGM Studios Theme Park. Guests will recognize the sets from the New York City street set. It's a cute tale in which Midler discovers she's holding a winning lottery ticket, and it graphically records her trials and tribulations as she tries to retrieve it after it falls out of her window. At the film's conclusion, guests are escorted into a large soundstage in which the interior sets for the movie are displayed. On the soundstage a hostess explains some of the special effects used to create certain highlights of the film.

The final stop on the tour is the Post Group, where George Lucas, C3PO, and R2D2 narrate a presentation about editing techniques, and Mel Gibson explains sound effects.

WHERE TO EAT AT THE DISNEY–MGM STUDIOS THEME PARK

A complete list of all Disney-MGM Studios Theme Park eateries—full-service restaurants, fast-food emporiums, snack shops, and food vendors—can be found together with all other WDW eating spots in the *Good Meals, Great Times* chapter.

Superstar Television

Roles in famous television shows are up for grabs at this remarkable attraction. In the outdoor pre-show area, with scores of TV sets strung overhead, a host or hostess chooses members of the audience to star in a variety of famous television scenes. **Note:** Although a few guests are chosen from the rear of the area, most would-be stars are picked from nearer the front. While just being in the audience will provide a lot of laughs, if there's even a little ham in you, move up front and volunteer loudly.

Audience members are led into a 1,000-seat theater reminiscent of the days of live television broadcasting. At the same time, would-be stars head backstage for costuming, makeup, and meetings with the directors.

The stage has several sets, and as the camera operators shoot the actors in action, the audience watches on one of eight six-foot-wide projection screens suspended from the ceiling. But the pictures on the screens vary significantly from the live goings-on on stage because the use of "blue-screen" electronic techniques allows backstage editors to merge the live action with historic clips from the classic shows.

The first scene features a gentleman guest in the news reporter's seat on the "Today" show on July 17, 1955, the day Disneyland opened. Applause signs flash when appropriate, and audience members respond enthusiastically for their fellow tourists. Next, a woman guest gets to play the Ethel Mertz part opposite Lucille Ball's Lucy Ricardo in what is perhaps the single most famous scene from "I Love Lucy." Complete with white smock and tall white hat, the guest star tries to wrap chocolates as they quickly come along a conveyor belt, and though seen dozens of times, the scene is still funny, even with an amateur in the role of Lucy's second banana.

Soap opera fans will get an especially big kick out of a scene from "General Hospital," in which chosen members of the audience play two of the three leading roles in a love triangle. Another guest plays the part of Tim "the Tool Man" Taylor in a scene from "Home Improvement."

Several youngsters are chosen to star in the opening theme song from "Gilligan's Island," while three guests dress up as the "Vonzells" and sing "Da Doo Run Run" on the "Ed Sullivan Show." Other scenes include a classic from "Cheers," in which Woody the bartender, Norm, and Cliff star with four guests. One lucky youngster has the opportunity to hit a grand slam homerun at New York's Shea Stadium and then be interviewed by Howard Cosell. Scenes from "The Tonight Show," with Johnny Carson, "The Three Stooges," and "The Golden Girls" round out the fun.

There are no bad seats in the house since the eight monitors can be seen easily by the entire audience. This attraction tends to be less crowded during the morning hours, so try it then, and if time permits go again as each new cast brings a fresh flavor to the presentation. The entire attraction takes about 45 minutes, from the choosing of stars to the end. Presented by Sony.

The Magic of Disney Animation

This is one the finest, funniest, and most entertaining of all the attractions at the Studios. Try to time your visit for around 11 A.M. when the exhibit usually opens. The animators who work in the building normally quit for the day between 5 P.M. and 6 P.M.

In the lobby, 13 of the many Oscars won by the Disney Animation Team and a collection of drawings of characters and original cels from *Snow White*, *Aladdin*, and other Disney cartoon classics are on display. From the lobby, guests move into the Disney Animation Theater, where an uproariously funny film starring Robin Williams and Walter Cronkite offers a lesson in the basics of animation. It even allows guests a look at what it's like to be a cartoon character through the eyes of Williams.

The producers of this film will tell you that each scene was a struggle to complete, because Walter Cronkite had trouble keeping a straight face. Williams is at his best as one of the lost boys from *Peter Pan*. His nonstop banter is so funny that a second trip may be necessary to take it all in. In one segment, he's turned into a variety of recognizable characters, including Mickey Mouse. "I can even be a corporate symbol," he proclaims in his best Mickey Mouse voice. All in all it's great fun, and Cronkite is an absolutely perfect straight man.

The eight-minute film is followed by a walk through the working animation studios, where the tour continues to be narrated by Williams and Cronkite, who appear on overhead monitors. First stop is the story room, where animators develop story lines. Onward to the drawing boards where Mickey, Minnie, and other characters undergo the metamorphosis from pencil sketch to moving picture. Working at their desks in full view of visitors, animators are seen creating the drawings that will later appear in real films.

Guests also view the cleanup room, the special effects area, and the special camera that was designed to transfer drawings to cels. Then artists can be seen hand painting up to 25 different colors onto these transparent sheets.

The 135-member animation team at the Disney-MGM Studios Theme Park works in shifts, to cover seven days a week. To produce one 24-minute film, the team must complete 34,650 drawings, and add scenes from at least 300 background paintings before finishing the work with musical scores and special effects.

Be sure to stop in at the Animation Gallery, where original Disney animation cels, exclusive limited-edition reproductions, books, figurines, and other collectibles are for sale.

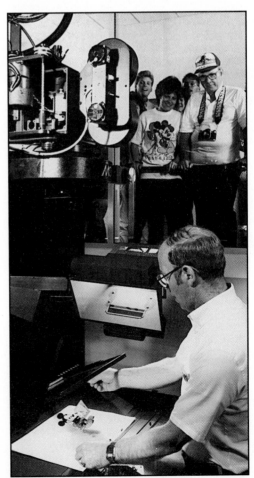

Monster Sound Show

Parents, don't be fooled by the name. There is nothing scary about this attraction, where guests have the opportunity to create the sound effects for a short film, with predictably funny results.

The pre-show begins outside the theater with a short video presentation starring David Letterman in a very funny introduction to what's inside. His comments close with an atypical (for a Disney attraction) warning that, "If you break anything, security guards in mouse suits will beat you senseless."

Upon entering the 270-seat theater, the host chooses several "Foley" artists from the audience. (Foley is the Hollywood sound-effects system named for its creator, Jack Foley.) The audience is then treated to a cute Martin Short/Chevy Chase comedy-mystery film that includes the sounds of thunder, rain, creaking doors, and falling chandeliers. The amateur sound crew watches the film a second time as they try to match the proper sound effects to the action on-screen. The third viewing of the film features the new soundtrack created by the studio's newest Foley artists. The thunder never seems to match the storm and the crash of the chandelier seems most often to take place as the creaking door opens, but that's the whole point and it's all a lot of fun.

The show features many original gadgets created by sound master Jimmy Macdonald. Macdonald, who became the voice of Mickey Mouse during the 1940s, was responsible for more than 20,000 sound gadgets during his 45 years with Walt Disney Studios in California. There are some special artifacts, including Tinkerbell's chimes, a door used in *Alice in Wonderland*, and the coconut shells used to produce the hoofbeats in the *Legend of Sleepy Hollow*. But most of the sounds are created by the ingenious use of barrels, nails, sandpaper, and other gadgets that go bonk, buzz, zip, or bump.

The post-show area, SoundWorks, offers some hands-on fun for the rest of the audience. Earie Encounters allows visitors to reproduce the flying-saucer sounds from the 1956 film *Forbidden Planet*. At Movie Mimics, guests can dub in the voice of Roger Rabbit and other stars; and at Soundsations, our personal favorite, an adventure in "3-D audio" puts guests in an enclosed room filled with sound so realistic that the wind from a hair dryer can almost be felt. Presented by Sony.

Jim Henson's Muppet*Vision 3-D

One of the most entertaining attractions at the Disney-MGM Studios Theme Park, this spectacular 3-D movie, which is shown in a theater specifically constructed for it, is quite remarkable. As with so many Disney attractions, a lot of the appeal is in the details. The 12-minute pre-show is very entertaining and gives some clues of what's to come. The comedy comes directly from the Muppet Labs, presided over by Dr. Bunson Honeydew—and his long-suffering assistant, Beaker—and introduces a new character, Waldo, the "Spirit of 3-D."

But the 3-D effects, spectacular as they are, are only part of the show: There are appearances by live Muppet characters, a clutch of fiber-optic effects, fireworks, and lots of very funny details built into the walls that surround the seating area of the huge theater. There are carryings-on for most of the senses—sight, smell, and touch, among them—and it's hard to know where to look first. It is more like a "4-D" experience. We're glad that they've put the show in such a large theater, to allow the crowds to enjoy it without too long a wait.

Indiana Jones Stunt Spectacular

Earthquakes, fiery explosions, and assorted other dramatic stunts give guests some insight into the science of movie stunts and special effects at this impressive 2,000-seat amphitheater. Stuntmen and women recreate scenes from Indiana Jones films to demonstrate the skill required to keep audiences on the edge of their seats. Show director Glenn Randall, who served as stunt coordinator of such well-known adventure films as *Raiders of the Lost Ark*, *Indiana Jones and the Temple of Doom*, *Poltergeist*, *Never Say Never Again*, *E.T.*, *Firestarter*, and *Jewel of the Nile*, calls the show "big, visual excitement."

But the 30-minute show isn't all flying leaps. Guests also see how the elaborate stunts are pulled off—safely—while the crew and an assistant director explain what goes on both in front of and behind the camera.

In one segment, a scene from *Raiders of*

the Lost Ark is staged. A 12-foot tall rolling ball chases a Harrison Ford lookalike out of the temple. There is steam and flame so intense that the audience can feel the heat. The crew dismantles the set, revealing the remarkable lightness of movie props, as two assistants roll it uphill for the next show.

In a scene on a busy Cairo street market, "extras" chosen from the audience participate. The famous scene in which Indiana Jones pulls a gun while others are fighting with swords is played out. The death-defying action continues, and leads to the sensational desert finale, where the hero and his sweetheart must escape on a flying wing.

There are moments during this presentation when the audience might wonder if, just for a minute, something has gone wrong. But by revealing the tricks of the trade, the directors and stars show that what appears to be very dangerous is actually a perfectly safe, controlled bit of movie magic. It's a great show.

Voyage of the Little Mermaid

A live musical production adapted from this instant animated classic is presented in a theater with an underwater feel to it. Live characters such as Flounder, sea horses, snails, an octopus, and Sebastian are artfully created by puppeteers dressed completely in black so that only the characters are visible. Ariel is the star of the show and performs a selection of songs from the film. Prince Eric also plays a part. Some of the special effects inside the theater, including cascading water, lasers, and a lightning storm, may be a bit intense for younger children. But, of course, there is a happy ending and Max the dog, Ariel, and Prince Eric live happily ever after.

Star Tours

Having witnessed the unyielding popularity of this attraction at Disneyland in Anaheim, California, the decision was made to open a counterpart here. The attraction, which was inspired by George Lucas's Star Wars film trilogy, offers guests the chance to board Star-Speeders which are actually the same type of flight simulators that are regularly employed by the military and commercial airlines to train pilots. Synchronizing a stunning film with the virtually limitless motion of the simulator allows guests to truly feel what they see. (Note that when instructed to put on your seatbelt, do so. This is a very rough ride.)

Visitors enter an area where the famed Star Wars characters R2D2 and C3PO are working for a galactic travel agency. They spend their time in a bustling hangar area servicing the Star Tours fleet of spacecraft. Riders board the 40-passenger craft for what is intended to be a leisurely trip to the Moon of Endor, but the ride quickly develops into a harrowing flight into deep space, including encounters with giant ice crystals and laser blasting fighters. The flight is out of control from the start, as the rookie pilot proves that Murphy's Law applies to the entire universe.

The sensations are extraordinary and the technology quite advanced. (By the way, this same technology is used at Body Wars in the Wonders of Life Pavilion in Future World at Epcot Center. There guests take a rollicking ride through the human body, not unlike scenes from the film Fantastic Voyage.)

Signs outside Star Tours warn that passengers must be free of back problems, heart conditions, motion sickness, and other physical limitations to ride. Pregnant women and children under three are not permitted to board. Children under seven must be accompanied by an adult.

Honey, I Shrunk the Kids Movie Set Adventure

The set for the backyard scenes of the popular Disney movie has been re-created as an oversize playground for kids (and adults, too). Stalks of grass soar 20 and 30 feet high and enormous tree stumps and extra-large Lego toys provide unusual climbing opportunities. Kids especially love to climb into the discarded film canister and slide back out along an oversize reel of film. A hose with a small leak also provides entertainment as it squirts in a slightly different location each time. It's all great fun, and all these props serve to make the kids look and feel very tiny indeed.

Jim Henson's Muppets on Location

Kermit, Miss Piggy, Fozzie Bear, Gonzo, and Bean Bunny take a break from filming their latest musical epic to sign autographs and pose for photos. The background music is provided by Dr. Teeth and the Electric Mayhem Band. Check your entertainment schedule for showtimes.

Twilight Zone Tower of Terror

The Hollywood Tower Hotel, slated to open in June of this year, is the decrepit home of the Studios' newest thrill ride. Rod Serling's voice greets you as you enter a sitting room. The room was clearly beautiful at one time but has fallen into a state of disrepair. There is a television set on which Rod Serling does a typical monologue inviting you to enter into another part of the building—and The Twilight Zone. During his spiel, he informs you that the only working elevator in the hotel is the freight elevator. Guests are led through an old hallway past a passenger elevator and on toward the boiler room where they enter a cage elevator. Once inside, passengers are seated on benches and a safety bar comes down. The doors close and the elevator begins its ascent. At the first stop the elevator doors open and guests have a view down an endless hallway. The doors close again and you continue your trip skyward. On the second stop, another hallway appears and then a strike of lightning causes it to disappear. A new technology turns the view into a starfield. Strange, eerie music begins. When the elevator stops for the third time, it moves horizontally forward. You've actually moved into the so-called "drop elevator." Once inside, the elevator travels very quickly up to the 13th floor. The doors open and passengers have a view of the Studios. Guests walking around on the streets below can see into the elevator and hear the screams of the terrified riders. At that point, by the way, you are 157 feet in the air. Now the elevator drops a bit very fast. The flash of light you see is a camera capturing your look of horror. The doors shut and the real freefall begins. It's over in two seconds but it sure seems a lot longer. On exiting the hotel, Rod Serling reminds you that next time you enter an old hotel, be sure to use the stairs. One bit of interesting trivia: The motors running the elevators are twice as powerful as those that propel the elevators at New York City's 110-story World Trade Center.

Beauty and the Beast Stage Show

Belle, Gaston, Mrs. Potts, Lumiere, and the cast of the Disney film *Beauty and the Beast* come to life on stage at the Backlot Theater five times each day. The 25-minute show is as entertaining as they come. The staging is just right and the music very addictive. The tale is traced from Belle's dissatisfaction with her provincial life in a small French town to the battle between the staff of the Beast's castle and Gaston and the townspeople. Lumiere and his group perform "Be Our Guest" with a delightful display of giant dancing spoons and Jello molds. The happy-ending finale is an absolute delight.

Teenage Mutant Ninja Turtles

Leonardo, Raphael, Michelangelo, and Donatello, those famous turtles from the sewers of New York City, make daily appearances on the New York Street backlot. The Ninja Turtles perform their theme song and then take time to sign autographs and shake hands. Cowabunga, dudes!

Aladdin's Royal Caravan

Inspired by the animated film *Aladdin*, this daily procession at the Disney-MGM Studios Theme Park depicts Prince Ali's grand entrance into the city of Agrabah. Moviegoers will remember that Aladdin is transformed into Prince Ali using one of his wishes granted by the genie. A brass band leads the way down Hollywood Boulevard, followed by the genie who has transformed himself into a 32-foot giant. The genie appears several more times during the caravan: He is bathing in a tub on the back of an inflatable camel, he wears formal white tails in honor of the prince, and then he transforms himself into two parts—top half and bottom half—each trying to find the other as they run around Abu, Aladdin's faithful monkey companion. Parade times vary. Check your entertainment schedule.

HOT TIPS

- Arrive at the Disney-MGM Studios Theme Park before the posted opening time. The gates usually open about 8:30 A.M.
- Check the Studios Tip Board to get an idea of showtimes and crowds.
- See Muppet*Vision 3-D, Voyage of the Little Mermaid, and Star Tours early in the day before the crowds build up.
- If you'd like to have a sit-down lunch and/or dinner, make reservations when you arrive at the park for the *50's Prime Time Café*, the *Brown Derby*, the *Sci-Fi Dine-In*, or *Mama Melrose's Ristorante Italiano*.
- Snag a good spot along Hollywood Boulevard to see Aladdin's Royal Caravan.
- Once Twilight Zone Tower of Terror opens, it's likely to have very long lines. See it early in the day and *never* right after a meal.

Everything Else in the World

The Magic Kingdom, Epcot Center, and the Disney-MGM Studios Theme Park take up only about 460 acres of the total Walt Disney World terrain, while the total turf of the entire World comprises 43 square miles! Quite a lot of this domain is crammed with all sorts of diverse and irresistible activities of a quantity and quality seldom found anywhere else on the globe.

There are superb golf and tennis; there are beaches for sunbathing; lakes for speedboating and sailing; canoes for rent and winding streams to paddle along; bicycles for hire; campfire sites; nature trails; and picnic grounds. And that list still doesn't include River Country, Disney's own old-fashioned swimming hole; Typhoon Lagoon, a state-of-the-art water park; Disney Village Marketplace, a wide assortment of shops; and the botanical garden and bird sanctuary that's called Discovery Island.

Add to all that Pleasure Island, an after-dark entertainment complex with nightclubs and restaurants. Among the other activities worth mentioning is the program known as Wonders of Walt Disney World, in which youngsters attending grades five through ten are offered the opportunity to go behind the scenes—to meet the Disney entertainers and receive instructions from Disney animators or to visit the World's extraordinary 7,500-acre conservation area (among other unique on-site ecological activities).

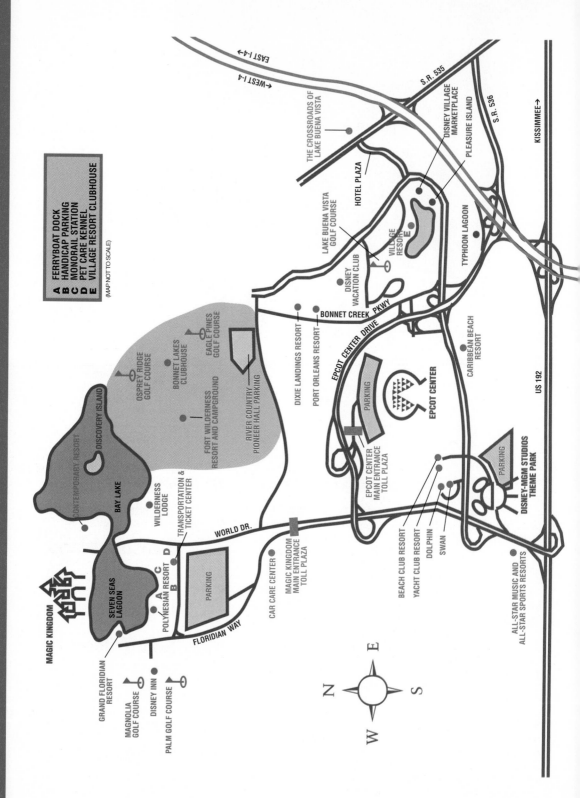

A FERRYBOAT DOCK
B HANDICAP PARKING
C MONORAIL STATION
D PET CARE KENNEL
E VILLAGE RESORT CLUBHOUSE

(MAP NOT TO SCALE)

MAGIC KINGDOM

GRAND FLORIDIAN RESORT

MAGNOLIA GOLF COURSE

DISNEY INN

PALM GOLF COURSE

SEVEN SEAS LAGOON

POLYNESIAN RESORT

FLORIDIAN WAY

WORLD DR.

CAR CARE CENTER

MAGIC KINGDOM MAIN ENTRANCE TOLL PLAZA

PARKING

CONTEMPORARY RESORT

BAY LAKE

DISCOVERY ISLAND

WILDERNESS LODGE

TRANSPORTATION & TICKET CENTER

FORT WILDERNESS RESORT AND CAMPGROUND

RIVER COUNTRY PIONEER HALL PARKING

OSPREY RIDGE GOLF COURSE

BONNET LAKES CLUBHOUSE

EAGLE PINES GOLF COURSE

DIXIE LANDINGS RESORT

PORT ORLEANS RESORT

BONNET CREEK PKWY

EPCOT CENTER DRIVE

EPCOT CENTER

PARKING

EPCOT CENTER MAIN ENTRANCE TOLL PLAZA

BEACH CLUB RESORT

YACHT CLUB RESORT

DOLPHIN

SWAN

PARKING

DISNEY-MGM STUDIOS THEME PARK

ALL-STAR MUSIC AND ALL-STAR SPORTS RESORTS

CARIBBEAN BEACH RESORT

US 192

DISNEY VACATION CLUB

LAKE BUENA VISTA GOLF COURSE

VILLAGE RESORT

TYPHOON LAGOON

HOTEL PLAZA

THE CROSSROADS OF LAKE BUENA VISTA

DISNEY VILLAGE MARKETPLACE

PLEASURE ISLAND

S.R. 535

S.R. 536

KISSIMMEE →

EAST I-4 →

← WEST I-4

N
E
S
W

WDW Village

Shops

A visit to Disney Village Marketplace can involve eating in a restaurant, meeting a film star, or just sitting on a bench by the water looking at the boats zipping back and forth across Buena Vista Lagoon. But for most people, those are the extra added attractions of a complex whose real raison d'être is shopping.

Located on the shores of Buena Vista Lagoon, in eight low-lying, shingle-sided buildings, the Disney Village Marketplace boutiques stock everything from toys and books to fashions and accessories for the whole family. There are several stores that carry the staggering range of merchandise related to the family of Disney characters. The shops are open daily from 9:30 A.M. to 10 P.M.

The best way to take it all in is simply to wander at will. Stop for lunch or a snack after a couple of hours, then go out and stroll some more. The descriptions below suggest the types of merchandise that each store offers. Particular items may not be there when you are, but comparable goods should be available. Note that weekends are fairly busy, but even then the pace tends to be leisurely. Kids who get bored by their elders' browsing can be turned loose at the marina, or at an innovative playground near the Village Stage (where the annual Christmas pageants are presented).

MICKEY'S CHARACTER SHOP: This is the largest Disney merchandise shop in all the World. As you enter, be sure to take a look up at Mickey, Minnie, and Donald flying high in a 20-foot-tall hot-air balloon. Dumbo, Jiminy Cricket, Minnie and Mickey, Chip and Dale, Tigger and Eeyore, and Tramp and his Lady are all here too—stuffed, in porcelain, and emblazoned on everything from T-shirts and back scratchers to pencils and carry-all bags. Be sure to check out the larger-than-life stuffed Mickey.

Located about five miles from the Magic Kingdom and only two-and-a-half miles from Epcot Center, Walt Disney World Village comprises a number of hotel and villa-type accommodations (with and without kitchen facilities), the Lake Buena Vista Club, the Walt Disney World Conference Center, the Disney Village Marketplace, several lakes, and a number of sports facilities—among other things. It is relatively quiet, and the pace is far more leisurely than that which exists around the theme parks. In the Buena Vista Lagoon, along whose shores the shopping area was constructed, there are even a few alligators.

But the Village is still convenient to the main activities of the World and is easily accessible from either exit 25 or exit 26B from I-4. The best route is the exit off the Epcot Center interchange. But it's also possible to take the exit from S.R. 535 (although this route usually is more congested and far less scenic). Buses also make the trip to and from Epcot Center, the Magic Kingdom, the Disney Village Marketplace, and the Disney-MGM Studios Theme Park on a regular basis; holders of ID cards issued by WDW resorts and Disney Village Hotel Plaza establishments, as well as bearers of certain Passports, can ride them at no extra charge.

YOU & ME KID: By coincidence, this shop bears the same name as one of the Disney Channel's most popular shows. And in the same way the Disney Channel tries to offer something for every member of the family, so too does this store. There's plenty of room for merchandise for infants, boys, girls, and pre-teens. There are toys, clothing, gift items, stuffed animals, and lots of other things for each age group.

TOYS FANTASTIC: Located in the You & Me Kid building, this shop stocks a wide variety of Mattel toys and games including the full line of Mattel-Disney merchandise.

CHRISTMAS CHALET: If anything can set a mind to dreaming of white Christmases when the mercury is hitting 95° outside (and the humidity is just about the same), this lovely shop, also in the You & Me Kid building, is it. Arranged at the edges of the rooms are small treasures in traditional reds and greens—ornaments covered with feathers, others made of wood, metal, glass, felt, and calico. The selection is one of the best of its type anywhere. In addition, there are character collectibles, and other unique Christmas trinkets.

CRISTAL ARTS: This shop sells roughly the same sort of cut-glass merchandise available at Main Street's Crystal Arts in the Magic Kingdom. Large green, blue, or red cut-glass bowls and vases are available, along with clear-glass mugs, glass sculptures, and other items engraved to customers' specifications with initials, messages, or pictures. If you bring a favorite photograph to this shop, the engraver can have it reproduced on a plate or other item.

GREAT SOUTHERN COUNTRY CRAFT CO.: There is fine hand-made pottery, plus a boutique featuring country and folk crafts. It's a showplace of Americana gift items.

LILLIE LANGTRY'S OLD-FASHIONED PHOTO STUDIO: This is where guests can pose for sepia-toned prints in Edwardian suits or flounced-and-furbelowed gowns of a degree of frilliness rarely found outside a film studio's wardrobe department.

HARRINGTON BAY CLOTHIERS: This shop is designed like a Bermuda plantation home and offers traditional and casual men's clothing from designers including Polo by Ralph Lauren, Tommy Hilfiger, and Nautica. The store is located near the Captain's Tower, close to the parking lot.

GOURMET PANTRY: Not long ago, one vacationer searching for coffee and orange juice for the next day's breakfast passed up this store on the assumption that he'd find only escargots and smoked oysters. Wrong! These foods can be found here, but there also are breads and pastries, meats and cheeses, cereals, yogurt, beer and soft drinks, and many more items—both mundane and exotic. Unusual teas and specially blended, freshly ground coffees also are available, and, occasionally, free tastes are offered to passersby. Assorted chocolates, jellybeans, cookies, and fudge are sold both prepackaged and in an area where shoppers can select their own favorites. Godiva chocolates, specialty sandwiches, and salads also are available. The line of Gourmet Mickey cookware and utensils is

fully represented. Villa guests take note: Purchases will be delivered to your villa at no extra charge; if you aren't going to be home, the delivery person will even stash perishables in your refrigerator. To order by phone, touch "31" on your room telephone, or, when calling from outside, dial 828-3886.

DISCOVER: Concerns for Mother Nature are fully demonstrated in the relaxed atmosphere of this environmentally correct merchandise shop. Among the offerings are birdhouses, wind chimes, educational toys for children, environmentally oriented music, and other unique gift items.

THE CITY: Trend-setting fashions and accessories for men and women can be found at this shop. Perry Ellis, Nicole Miller, Diesel, Stussy, Quick Silver, and Cross Color collections are represented.

COUNTRY ADDRESS: Sophisticated fashions are offered at this location. Adrienne Vittidini, Karen Kane, Platinum, and Liz Claiborne are among the designers showcased. Accessories, Lancôme cosmetics, and perfume also are available.

RESORTWEAR UNLIMITED: This shop features lightweight, bright, and trendy fashions. An assortment of sportswear, playwear, and swimwear is enhanced by bold jewelry, hats, and handbags.

24KT PRECIOUS ADORNMENTS: An elegant shop featuring a wide selection of gold fashion jewelry, ranging from unique designer items to Disney character charms and watches. Located next to *Chef Mickey's Village* restaurant.

CROSSROADS OF LAKE BUENA VISTA

Constructed by the WDW folks, the shopping center located just across the road from Disney Village Hotel Plaza is a convenient dining and shopping area for both visitors and Walt Disney World employees. The 137,000-square-foot retail center is anchored by a Gooding's supermarket, which is open 24 hours a day. There is a full-service pharmacy inside Gooding's. (*Fort Wilderness*, villa, and treehouse guests will find this an especially convenient stop.) Other shops include Camp Beverly Hills, for California sportswear; Chico's, for casual clothing; Sunworks, which stocks women's sportswear and swimwear; O.K. Kiddo for children's clothing; Foot Locker, for athletic shoes; Character Connection, the Disney merchandise shop; Beyond Electronics, which stocks stereos, tape recorders, and gadgets; White's Books; and Mitzi's Hallmark. There also is a dry cleaner, an eyeglass store, a branch of Sun Bank, and a post office. Dining options include *T.G.I. Fridays, McDonalds, Taco Bell, Perkins, Pizzeria Uno, Red Lobster, Pebbles, Jungle Jim's*, an ice cream shop, and a pizza parlor.

In addition to the shops and services, there's the Pirate's Cove Adventure Golf, an innovative miniature golf course.

TEAM MICKEY'S ATHLETIC CLUB: The locker room decor is the perfect setting for sports clothing, activewear, and sports equipment for the whole family. This is the place to find T-shirts, sweatshirts, and other items with Disney University logos, as well as Mickey and Goofy emblazoned on shirts. There also is a large selection of Reebok and Nike athletic shoes.

THE CAPTAIN'S TOWER: At the center of the Disney Village Marketplace, this open-air shop is the focal point for major promotions. The merchandise changes three to four times a year depending on special events and the latest fashion trends.

VILLAGE SPIRITS: Located next to Country Address, this shop can expand your wine cellar with selections from a wide choice of American and imported wines. Popularly priced wines keep company with some very rare vintages bought at auction. Spirits, liqueurs, cognacs, ales, and other alcoholic

DISNEY INSTITUTE

Innovative, participatory programs focusing on subjects such as show business, animation, interior and landscape design, sports and fitness, public affairs, and the arts will be among the options available to Disney Institute guests. This brand-new vacation resort, to be situated in the Disney Village Resort area, is slated to open in July 1995. A typical Institute vacation will last three, four, or seven days. Guest speakers and performances will play a major role in each program.

The idea behind the Institute is to offer guests a real-life active vacation and one that enriches both the mind and the body. In the animation workshop, for example, participants will learn the art of animation and create a cartoon of their own with a Disney filmmaker.

The Institute will be a self-contained resort including a state-of-the-art fitness center where personal trainers help guests design their own ongoing fitness program. There also will be a large recital hall where ballet companies and orchestras will perform.

Families and couples traveling together do not have to sign up for the same program. It's possible for a family of four to participate in four different workshops and still spend evenings together.

For additional information about the Disney Institute, call 827-4230.

potables are available, including one of the state's largest collections of miniatures. Glassware, corkscrews, ice buckets, and an abundance of other bar accessories also are featured. Wine tastings are held daily. So much for the myth that no wine or liquor is allowed at Walt Disney World.

EUROSPAIN: An array of hand-crafted gifts and decorative items from prestigious Spanish artisans and designers. Presented by Arribas Brothers.

WINDJAMMER DOCK SHOP: You go through this shop on the way to *Cap'n Jack's Oyster* Bar. The shop stocks glassware and clothing featuring the Cap'n Jack logo.

RESTAURANTS

For a complete listing of all Walt Disney World Village restaurants, bars, and snack shops, see *Good Meals, Great Times*.

Lakeside Activities

The 35-acre Buena Vista Lagoon that borders this village of cedar-shingled shops also gives it much of its atmosphere: When the sidewalks radiate heat, the water looks cool and inviting; in the slanting rays of the late afternoon sun, it glistens like a sheet of silver.

There's always something going on. Little Water Sprites zip to and fro, speeding to the dock from feeder canals to the west, while more laid-back folks float gently along in pedal boats or V-hulled tent-topped metal-canopy boats.

It's pleasant to sit and watch all this activity from the benches at the Buena Vista Lagoon marina, centrally located in Disney Village Marketplace; over ice cream sundaes at *Donald's Dairy Dip* on the lake's west shore; or over frozen fresh strawberry margaritas at *Cap'n Jack's Oyster Bar*. Those who would rather participate need walk only a few steps to the marina, where several types of boats can be rented from morning until dusk. Opening and closing hours change from season to season; call 828-2204 for details. No swimming is allowed. (Prices are subject to state tax.)

WATER SPRITES: These tiny craft are very popular. Though they don't really move very fast, they feel as if they do; and, in any event, they get up enough speed to cover quite a lot of territory on Buena Vista Lagoon. Half-hour rentals cost $11. There are usually lines of people waiting for boats between 11 A.M. and 4 P.M.; plan accordingly. The minimum age to rent or drive one of these boats (even accompanied by an adult) is 12.

CANOPY BOATS: These metal, V-hulled, 16-foot craft can accommodate up to ten adults; some people stock up on picnic supplies at the Gourmet Pantry and turn an afternoon sail into a party. Cost is $17.50 per-half hour.

FISHING EXCURSION: A two-hour guided catch-and-release fishing trip, aboard a pontoon boat with room for six passengers, leaves the Disney Village Marketplace Marina daily at 7 A.M. and 6 P.M. The fee for one to six people is $110 which includes the guide and driver, rods, reel, tackle, and soft drinks. Reservations are required 24 hours in advance. Call 828-2461.

Celebrations and Special Events

France, makes its annual debut. In all, there are appearances by some three dozen characters garbed in period costumes made from brocades, satins, silks, velvets, wool, rough homespun, and monk's cloth—a baker, butcher, candlemaker, flower seller, fruit and vegetable peddler, weaver, and others. A concert of carols precedes each evening's tableau.

There's nearly always something going on under the Captain's Tower at the Disney Village Marketplace. Some weeks the place might be stacked high with shiny new hardcover books; on another day, it might feature cruisewear and resort fashions. Crafts demonstrations and art shows are staged now and again, along with manufacturers' promotions. In the past, these have included a barnyard festival with animals from the petting farm at *Fort Wilderness* and birds from Discovery Island; a citrus promotion; a Trivial Pursuit promotion; and the dollmaker Madame Alexander, who was introducing a new line that had collectors lining up in the wee hours of the morning.

In addition, there are a number of annual events—some in celebration of holidays.

KIDS NIGHT OUT (JUNE–AUGUST): A special program for kids of all ages features music, comedians, face painters, jugglers, balloon artists, magicians, environmental and animal programs, and a wide variety of shows.

BOAT SHOW (OCTOBER): Because this Central Florida region has no ocean beaches, most events of this type are staged in shopping malls and exhibition halls. Here, however, boats are displayed not only throughout the Marketplace, but also in the water; and with over 200 boats from all manufacturers, this is the area's biggest in-the-water boat show.

FESTIVAL OF THE MASTERS (NOVEMBER): This art show, which takes place in November each year, is generally considered one of the South's best because only artists who have won an award in the past three years are invited to enter.

CHRISTMASTIME: Thanksgiving marks the beginning of the Christmas season here when a Christmas tree is set up in the village. Then the "Glory and Pageantry of Christmas," a nativity play fashioned after a 13th-century pageant whose origins are in southern

USEFUL STOPS

A Guest Services facility is located at You & Me Kid facing *Goofy's Grill.* Services include reservation assistance, lost and found, film and stamp sales, photo processing, an Automated Teller Machine, wheelchair and stroller rental, gift wrapping, and general information.

BUS TRANSPORTATION: The Disney Village Marketplace bus stop and shelter is located next to Harrington Bay Clothiers. There is bus service to the Lake Buena Vista Club, the villas, the *Caribbean Beach* resort, the *Swan* and *Dolphin* hotels, the *Yacht Club* and *Beach Club, Port Orleans, Dixie Landings,* the *Disney Vacation Club, Wilderness Lodge,* Disney Village Hotel Plaza, *All-Star Sports* and *All-Star Music* resorts, the Disney-MGM Studios Theme Park, Epcot Center, and the Magic Kingdom. From the Magic Kingdom, monorails and ferries go to the *Contemporary* resort and *Grand Floridian* resort, buses to the *Disney Inn,* the *Polynesian* resort, and *Fort Wilderness.* For more information on transportation within the rest of the World, see *Transportation and Accommodations.*

FOREIGN CURRENCY EXCHANGE: This can be done at the Sun Bank during regular banking hours. See *Getting Ready To Go.*

TRAVELER'S CHECKS: These can be purchased at the Sun Bank; outside the bank, there is an American Express Cardmembers Cheque Dispenser, which cardholders (who have previously obtained a special number) may use to purchase traveler's checks.

Pleasure Island

A six-acre island entertainment complex with nightclubs, restaurants, shops, and movie theaters fills the need for evening and late-night entertainment options for Walt Disney World guests. Pleasure Island is connected to the Disney Village Marketplace by three footbridges. There are seven nightclubs, several restaurants (described in detail in *Good Meals, Great Times*), an unusual variety of shops, and the AMC multiplex cinemas, featuring current films. The nightclubs open at about 7 P.M. and don't close until after 2 A.M. The Pleasure Island shops are open from 10 A.M. to 1 A.M., and the restaurants are open from about 11:30 A.M. to midnight.

There is no fee to enter the Pleasure Island premises, its shops, or restaurants until 7 P.M. After 7 P.M., a single admission of $13.95 allows access to all clubs and the nightly street party spectacular. Be Our Guest Passes and Super Duper Passes include Pleasure Island admission. Guests under age 18 must be accompanied by a parent. (Tickets are not required for *Portobello Yacht Club* or the *Fireworks Factory*.)

Remember, the drinking age in Florida is 21. Guests over 18 will be admitted to the clubs (except *Mannequins*), but will not be served alcohol. A valid U.S., foreign, or international driver's license with a photo, an active U.S. military identification card, or a passport are the only forms of proof accepted.

LATE-NIGHT STREET PARTY: Every night at Pleasure Island is like New Year's Eve. There is a fireworks show with special-effects lighting and confetti, and a talented troupe of dancers entertain along the streets.

MANNEQUINS DANCE PALACE: If a day of walking around Walt Disney World hasn't left your feet too weary, this is the place to head to dance the night away. Guests enter through an elevator that rises to the third floor. Lights, contemporary dance music, and an overall exuberant atmosphere dominate the scene. The name of the club is derived from the many mannequins strategically placed all around the establishment. Each of the figures is tied to dance in some way. There are several "cats" from the musical of the same name, and wonderful recreations of Deborah Kerr and Yul Brynner dressed as Anna and the King of Siam from the "Shall We Dance" scene in the film version of *The King and I*.

The main dance floor is actually a turntable, and the music is provided by a D.J. whose audio booth is about as high tech as they come. The lighting is a major attraction at *Mannequins*. There are 58 robotically con-

trolled lighting instruments, and a matrix of lights behind the stage has been dubbed the "toaster oven" by Disney Imagineers (because it warms the entire room when lit). There also are machines that can cause bubbles to float in the air, hurl confetti, or even make it snow in the club.

Specialty drinks, beer, and wine are available at a number of locations within the club, which is restricted to guests 21 and older.

NEON ARMADILLO MUSIC SALOON: Live country & western music is performed nightly and the dance floor is usually full. The Southwestern decor is highlighted by a wonderful brass chandelier in the shape of a spur and inlaid wood tabletops decorated in Navajo blanket patterns. Specialty drinks, beer, and wine are served.

ADVENTURERS CLUB: "Explore the unknown, discover the impossible," states the credo posted at the entrance. Just about all of the items on display were collected at garage sales and antiques shows and shops all around the world by Disney Imagineers. The place is modeled on the paneled libraries and elegant salons of similar clubs of the 19th century, and is jam-packed with photos, furniture, trinkets, books, letters, statuettes, and other memorabilia. The cozy recesses hide rooms where the masks on the walls come to life, and there are cast members portraying members of the house staff, including the maid and the curator, and several club members, prime among them an inept pilot named Hathaway Brown, the club chairperson, and a world-renowned bug expert. These players interact with guests with very amusing results.

Down the flight of stairs there is more "stuff" than anyone could ever hope to see in one visit, so just stroll around, read the cap-

tions on some of the photos, and enjoy the cool, air conditioned atmosphere. Drinks are served at the bar. If you have a seat on one of the stools, and ask the bartender to work his or her magic, your stool (or the one of an unsuspecting friend) may very slowly sink toward the floor leaving you, or your friend, significantly shorter. Then it's on to the library, where a haunted organ sets the scene for the outrageous storytellers. The show is a little corny, but nonetheless entertaining.

COMEDY WAREHOUSE: A comedy troupe performs five times each evening from 7 P.M. to 1 A.M. There are five comedians and one musician. It's a very funny, entertaining show that features improvisational comedy based on audience suggestions. E! Entertainment Television is taping its "Stand Up Sit Down Comedy Show" here. The show is hosted by Robert Klein and features name performers including Gilbert Gottfried, Larry Miller, and Richard Belzer. The tapings are open and free to the public. The comics often return in the evening for extra performances. When a

headliner is appearing there is an extra $5 fee to enter the shows. Guests perch on stools in a tiered arena so every seat offers a good view, even if the stools are a little tough on bad backs. Popcorn is the snack of choice, and specialty drinks, beer, wine, and soft drinks are all available.

PLEASURE ISLAND JAZZ COMPANY: The newest club on the island is reminiscent of jazz clubs from the 1930s. It's situated in a building that looks like an old warehouse and once inside there is a wide assortment of amusement park and carnival memorabilia. There is live entertainment nightly featuring jazz tunes from the 1930s to the present. Guests sit at small cocktail tables on comfortable padded chairs. The music is not too loud so conversation is possible. Tapas-style appetizers and wine by the glass are available as are mixed drinks, beer, and soft drinks.

ROCK & ROLL BEACH CLUB: A novel combination of dancing, dining, and the beach awaits guests at this establishment. The dance floor is located on the lowest level of the building, and there are billiard tables and games on the second and third floors.

Live bands perform hits from the 1950s to the present. The band plays 45 to 50 minutes of each hour, and a D.J. takes over during the breaks to offer uninterrupted musical entertainment. The atmosphere is a little frenetic, but nonetheless exciting. Alcoholic beverages and soft drinks also are available on the first level at the Orbiter Lounge.

8TRAX: The seventies are back. Rock and roll music from the early 1970s and sounds from the disco era fill this dance spot. To keep things in the 1970s mode, the staff dresses in polyester bell-bottom suits.

WEST END STAGE: Live bands, including some top-name groups, perform at this new, covered stage nightly. The Island Explosion, Pleasure Island's own dance troupe, also performs here.

Shopping at Pleasure Island

The variety of merchandise found at Pleasure Island's shops is a little more eclectic than that found at the other Walt Disney World emporia. Some items may not, however, be available at all times.

MUSIC LEGENDS: Compact discs, T-shirts, and memorabilia from the early days of rock and roll to heavy metal and hip-hop are available at this spot. There are three sections highlighting different types of music. If a name band is being featured at the West End Stage, you'll be able to find their merchandise here.

AVIGATOR'S SUPPLY: A brand label designed exclusively for Pleasure Island, the whimsical winged alligator is emblazoned on a wide variety of merchandise, including T-shirts, sweatshirts, magnets, and tote bags. There also is a broad selection of aviation-related gifts, clothing, and accessories. Leather bomber jackets, heavy-duty duffle bags, airplane clocks and sculptures, and a variety of collectibles round out the offerings. There also are shirts with the Adventurers Club logo available.

CHANGING ATTITUDES: A "new age" shop with an assortment of merchandise in only black and white. T-shirts, unique electronic gadgets, and other personal items are among the goods on sale.

DOODLES: Hats, horns, and other party items are available here. Logo merchandise from the various clubs also is on sale.

FRONT PAGE: The desire to have your picture on the cover of a national magazine can be satisfied here. A wide variety of magazine titles is sold, and costumes and appropriate accessories are available at the shop.

HAMMER & FIRE: A unique outlet offering jewelry, accessories, and decorative gifts. Titanium is used in some unusual jewelry, and colorful stoneware, platters, and wall hangings round out the selections. This shop has become a favorite of local residents in search of a special gift.

THE MOUSE HOUSE: Pleasure Island's character shop stocks the usual selection of

EATING AT PLEASURE ISLAND

For a complete list of Pleasure Island restaurants, fast-food emporiums, and snack spots, see *Good Meals, Great Times.*

T-shirts, sweatshirts, plush toys, gift items, hats, books, and other such merchandise.

SUSPENDED ANIMATION: Posters, prints, lithographs, cels, and original Disney animation art are sold here. It's a pleasant place to browse, even if you don't plan to buy.

DTV: The enormous surge in popularity of Disneyana collecting inspired the Walt Disney Company to reissue the line of old-time Disney merchandise found here. Dolls, puppets, posters, clothing, and figurines of Mickey, Minnie, and Donald in their earlier incarnations are on sale. Worth a stop if only for the nostalgic feelings the goods inspire.

SUPERSTAR STUDIOS: Star in your own music video. Guests lip sync favorite songs for either audio or video recordings. A particular favorite with teens.

PROPELLER HEADS: Pleasure Island's arcade features the usual array of blipping and bleeping video games, and is enormously popular with younger guests. It's open from 11 A.M. to 2 A.M.

Typhoon Lagoon

A furious storm once roared 'cross the sea;
Catching ships in its path, helpless to flee;
Instead of a certain and watery doom;
The winds swept them here to Typhoon
Lagoon!

So reads the legend guests see (looking a bit like old Burma-Shave roadside signs) as they drive into Typhoon Lagoon, a 56-acre, state-of-the-art aquatic theme park. The watery playground has been inspired by an imagined legend: A typhoon hit a small resort village years and years ago, and the storm—plus a resultant earthquake and volcanic eruption—left the village in ruins. The "local" residents, however, were very resourceful, and rebuilt their town as best they could. Trees toppled onto and into buildings, a ship was marooned atop a strangely magical mountain, and debris was strewn all around. Still they persevered, and while some structures in their resort community continue to lean, some are held up by ropes, and others have trees growing through their roofs, this is an oasis of damp fun.

Whether the typhoon, earthquake, and eruption actually ever took place doesn't really matter, because Typhoon Lagoon is a delightful place to spend a day. The assortment of visual treats is sizable, and since Typhoon Lagoon is four times the size of River Country, there's a full day's worth of activities to sample. The surf lagoon is larger than two football

fields and normally kicks up four-and-a-half-foot waves; two speed slides whisk guests through a cave at 30 miles per hour; a couple of winding storm slides offer a twisting journey; whitewater routes give groups and families a chance to ride the rapids together; and a special area just for young kids duplicates the slides in miniature.

The centerpiece of Typhoon Lagoon is the world's largest manmade watershed mountain, Mt. Mayday. Atop its peak, the *Miss Tilly*, a shrimp boat out of Safen Sound, Florida, is precariously perched. The smokestack atop *Miss Tilly* erupts every 30 minutes, shooting a 50-foot flume of water into the air. The cool water cascades down the mountain and helps to keep guests comfortable while they wait in line for the assorted slides. Guests who make the 85-foot climb up Mt. Mayday will be rewarded with a great view over the action.

There are a number of thatched coverings that can provide shade or protection from an unexpected thunderstorm. Lifeguards are on duty all over this park. There are six at the lagoon and several more at each of the slide areas. Streams and waterfalls are found throughout the area, and geysers set into the walkways keep the ground wet and cool.

What follows is a description of all the specific activities available at Typhoon Lagoon. What we'll leave to your imagination is the pure pleasure of pulling up a lounge chair, opening a book, and watching the people.

TYPHOON LAGOON: The main swimming area spreads out over two-and-a-half acres and contains 2.75-million gallons of water. The Caribbean blue lagoon is surrounded by a white-sand beach, and its main attraction is the four-plus-foot waves that come crashing to the shore every 90 seconds. Guests are welcome to bodysurf—just ride the waves with their bodies. Water collects in 12 huge chambers above the lagoon and falls through trap doors creating the waves which are sufficiently large so that amateur and professional surfing championships are planned for the park. There also are two smaller tidal pools, Whitecap Cove and Blustery Bay, where less adventurous guests can loll about in water made for bobbing, not riding.

CASTAWAY CREEK: A 2,100-foot circular river that winds through the park offers a lazy, relaxing orientation to Typhoon Lagoon. Tubes are free and are the most enjoyable way to make the trip along the 15-foot-wide, 3-foot-deep waterway that courses through a rain forest where guests are cooled by mists and spray; past caves and grottoes that provide welcome shade on hot summer days; and an area known as Water Works, where "broken" pipes from a water tower dump buckets of water on passersby. The 2½ feet per second current is calm and restful, and aside from a few floating props, the journey is unimpeded. There are exits along the way where guests can hop out for a while and do something else, or just dry off a bit and then jump right back in. In the way that the Walt Disney World Railroad offers an overall perspective of the Magic Kingdom, so does Castaway Creek reveal the breadth of Typhoon Lagoon. It takes 25 to 35 minutes to ride around the park without taking a break.

HUMUNGA KOWABUNGA: These two speed slides, reported to have been carved into the landscape by the historic earthquake, will send guests zooming through caves at speeds of 30 miles per hour. The 214-foot slides offer a 51-foot drop, and the view from the top is a little scary. But it's over before

you know it, and once-wary guests hurry back for another try. Disney Imagineers, when doing their research for the park, discovered that large crowds tend to gather where speed slides exist at other parks, in order to watch women wearing bikinis lose their bathing suit tops on the way down. Ever considerate, the Imagineers built a grandstand so that the voyeurs in the crowd have a place to sit. Modest maidens beware! A one-piece suit is far safer than a skimpy two-piece. Guests also are warned that they should be free of back trouble, heart conditions, and other physical limitations to take the trip. Pregnant women are not permitted to ride.

SHARK REEF: For those Walt Disney World guests who have longed to jump into the tank at Epcot Center's The Living Seas, here's your chance. Guests obtain free snorkel equipment for a swim through an artificial coral reef where they come face to face with lots of fish. The reef is constructed around a sunken, upsidedown tanker (where guests who don't care to swim among the fish can get a close look from the portholes). There are 362,000 gallons of seawater around the reef. The sharks, by the way, are small nurse sharks and bonnethead sharks, both passive members of the species. They don't eat anything bigger than they are, and though the bonnetheads look like small hammerhead sharks, don't fret, you're safe. At any given time, there will be about 4,000 critters in the water. The colors are vibrant, and though the trip takes only about 10 to 15 minutes, it's a great introduction to the world of snorkeling. Guests must shower before entering the reef's deeps. Open during busy seasons only.

JIB JAMMER, RUDDER BUSTER, STERN BURNER: These three body slides send guests off at about 20 miles per hour down winding fiberglass slides, in and out of rock formations and caves, and through waterfalls. It's a somewhat tamer ride than Humunga Kowabunga, but still offers a speedy descent. The three slides are about 300 feet long, and each offers a different view and experience. It's altogether a cooling and enjoyable trip.

WHITEWATER RIDES: Three whitewater raft rides offer guests a variety of trips, all taken aboard oversize inner tubes. All the slides course through caves, waterfalls, and intricate rock work, making the scenery an attraction in itself. At **Mayday Falls**, guests ride down a 460-foot slide. The ride starts out fast, then slows down in a catch pool. But don't relax, because you'll soon be sent on a quick trip to the bottom. **Keelhall Falls** is a vortex, or spiral, ride which sends guests on a roundabout trip down a 400-foot slide. The winding nature of this trip makes it seem a little faster than Mayday Falls, but actually the speed is the same, about ten miles per hour. At **Gangplank Falls**, groups or families have the chance to take a ride together in six-and-a-half-foot wide tubes that hold four people. The 300-foot-long slide offers a similar ride, but with the added enjoyment of sharing the experience.

KETCHAKIDDIE CREEK: Only open to those four feet tall or under (unless accompanied by a small child), this kiddie area offers the same

rides scaled down for pint-size visitors. Children *must*, however, be accompanied by an adult. There are slides, floating boats, fountains, waterfalls, squirting whales and seals, a mini-rapid ride, a grotto with a thin veil of water that kids just love to run back and forth through, and assorted floating toys to keep youngsters busy all day. There are even kid-size restrooms marked "boys" and "girls."

WHEN TO ARRIVE: Typhoon Lagoon gets very crowded early in the day and the parking lot often closes by 10 A.M. or 11 A.M. Once the lot is full, only guests staying at Walt Disney World resorts using WDW transportation will be admitted to the park, so plan accordingly.

WHERE TO EAT: There are two restaurants at Typhoon Lagoon, both offering similar fare and outdoor seating at tables with colorful umbrellas. *Leaning Palms*, which was known as *Placid Palms* before the typhoon hit, was renamed to fit its somewhat unorthodox architecture. Burgers, hot dogs, chef's salads, and assorted snacks are sold here. *Typhoon Tilly's Galley & Grog* offers a similar, but somewhat more limited, menu, and also features a separate area just for ice cream and frozen yogurt. There are several food carts around the park selling beer, wine, soda, ice cream, popcorn, and nachos. A couple of picnic areas also are on hand, where guests can bring their own food or enjoy a sampling from one of the restaurants. Getaway Glen is located to the left of the main entrance, past *Leaning Palms*, and Cascade Cove is near Shark Reef.

RESTROOMS AND CHANGING ROOMS: Restrooms with showers are located near the main entrance. Other restrooms and dressing rooms are available farther into the park near *Typhoon Tilly's*. These are labeled "Buoys" and "Gulls." Coin lockers are available at most restroom and dressing room locations.

SHOPPING: Singapore Sal's, located just to the right of the main entrance, is set in a ramshackle building that was left a bit worn after the typhoon. There is an assortment of props used to lend flavor, including an old boat set upright that serves as a closet. The old wheelhouse hides four dressing rooms, and oars and other boating paraphernalia are strung from the walls and the ceiling, lending an overall cluttered look to the shop. It's a little dark, but that's because the line of Typhoon Lagoon merchandise features bright neon colors. Women's, men's, and children's clothing, sunglasses, hats, bathing suits, towels, suntan lotion, souvenirs, thongs, beach chairs, and sweatshirts are among the wares available here.

FIRST AID: A first aid station capable of handling minor medical problems is located just to the left of the main entrance.

ADMISSION PRICES*

ONE-DAY TICKET

Adult	$21.73
Child**	$17.49

ONE-DAY TICKET (after 4 P.M. in summer)

Adult	$16.17
Child**	$12.72

The cost of a **ONE-YEAR PASS** is $83.48 for all guests.

Note: Admission is included with a Be Our Guest Pass or a Super Duper Pass. The park is typically closed for refurbishment during January and February.

These prices were correct at press time, but may change during 1994.

*The prices quoted here include sales tax.

**3 through 9 years of age

Fort Wilderness

In a part of the state where campgrounds tend to look like pastures—barren and very hot—the *Fort Wilderness* campground, located almost due east of the *Contemporary* resort, is an anomaly—a forested 650-acre wonder of tall slash pines, white-flowering bay trees, and ancient cypress hung with streamers of gray-green Spanish moss. Seminole Indians once hunted and fished here.

In all, there are some 1,190 woodsy campsites arranged in several campground loops; along some of them, Fleetwood trailers are available for rent, completely furnished and fitted out with all the comforts of home. For information about these campsites and trailers, see *Transportation and Accommodations*.

Scattered throughout the campground loops, there are a number of sporting facilities including two tennis courts and tetherball and volleyball courts. *Fort Wilderness* has riding stables, two swimming pools, a marina full of boats, a canoe livery, a beach, electric carts and bikes for rent, and a nature trail. Some of these facilities are available for the use of campground guests only; some are open to guests at WDW-owned resort hotels and villas as well; some also can be enjoyed by guests lodging at the establishments at the Disney Village Hotel Plaza as well as off the property.

There's also a petting farm where goats and ducks and other farm animals run free inside a white-rail fence, and it's fun to walk through the barn that houses the large, sleek horses that pull the Magic Kingdom's Main Street trolleys.

Two stores, the Settlement and Meadow Trading Posts, stock campers' necessities and some Disney souvenirs. And then there's Pioneer Hall, widely known as the home of the Hoop-Dee-Doo Musical Revue (described in *Good Meals, Great Times*). This rustic structure (made of Western white pine shipped all the way from Montana) also has a cafeteria and lounge.

Last but not least in the *Fort Wilderness* catalog, there's River Country. This eight-acre expanse of water-oriented recreational facilities embodies everyone's idea of what the perfect old-fashioned swimming hole should be like. It's a separate attraction, with its own hours and admission fees.

How to Get to Fort Wilderness

BY CAR: From outside the World, take the Magic Kingdom exit off I-4 (number 27) onto U.S.-192, go through the Magic Kingdom Auto Plaza, and, bearing to your right, follow the *Fort Wilderness* or River Country signs. This is the most expeditious way to go, even for WDW resort guests.

BY BUS: Take the monorail from the *Contemporary* resort and the *Grand Floridian* resort; the bus from the *Polynesian* resort, the *Disney Inn*, the Disney Village Marketplace, the *Caribbean Beach* resort, Epcot Center, the Disney-MGM Studios, the *Swan*, the *Dolphin*, the *Yacht Club*, the *Beach Club*, *Port Orleans*, *Dixie Landings*, *Disney Vacation Club*, *All-Star Sports* and *All-Star Music* resorts, and from Disney Village Hotel Plaza establishments to the Transportation and Ticket Center. Change there to the bus to *Fort Wilderness*. Count on 30 to 45 minutes in transit. To ride many of these buses, you must show an ID card from one of the WDW-owned properties or a Hotel Plaza establishment; certain Passports will also do.

BY BOAT: Guests at WDW-owned properties, and those with admission tickets to River Country or Discovery Island, also can go by boat from Magic Kingdom marinas (about 30 minutes' ride), from the *Contemporary* resort (about 25 minutes' ride), and from *Wilderness Lodge* (about 15 minutes).

SOUVENIRS AND SUPPLIES: Staple food items and all sorts of other necessities of the camping life are available, along with souvenirs, at *Fort Wilderness's* two stores—the Settlement Trading Post, located not far from the beach at the north end of the campground; and the Meadow Trading Post, located near the center of *Fort Wilderness*.

For a complete list of places to eat in *Fort Wilderness*, see *Good Meals, Great Times*.

BEACHES: The clear waters of Bay Lake, which lap the 315-foot-long, 175-foot-wide, white-sand beach at the north end of the campground, are delightful. And swimming is allowed inside the roped-off areas. Open to guests at *Fort Wilderness* only.

BIKE RENTALS: Tandems, dirt bikes, surreys, and assorted other two-wheelers can be hired at the Bike Barn for trips along *Fort*

Wilderness's bike paths and roadways—or just for getting around. Cost is $3 per hour, or $8 per day.

BLACKSMITH SHOP: The pleasant fellow who shoes the draft horses that pull the trolleys down Main Street in the Magic Kingdom is on hand at some time every day to answer questions and talk about what he does; occasionally guests can watch him at work, fitting the big animals with the special polyurethane-covered, steel-cored horseshoes that are used here to protect the horses' hooves.

BOAT RENTALS ON BAY LAKE: Zippy little Water Sprites, sailboats, pontoon boats, and pedal boats (described in *Sports*) are available for rent at the marina, at the north end of the campground.

CAMPFIRE PROGRAM: Held nightly near the Meadow Trading Post near the center of the campground, it features Disney movies, a sing-along, and cartoons. It's free for WDW resort guests only. Chip and Dale usually put in an appearance.

CANOE RENTALS: *Fort Wilderness* is ribboned with tranquil canals, sometimes in full sun and sometimes canopied by tall trees, which make for delightful canoe trips of one to three hours—or longer if you take fishing gear and elect to wet your line. Rentals are available at the Bike Barn ($4 per hour, $10 per day).

ELECTRIC CART RENTALS: Available at the Bike Barn ($21 per day) for sightseeing or transportation.

ELECTRICAL WATER PAGEANT: This twinkling cavalcade of lights (described in more detail in *Good Meals, Great Times*) can be seen from the beach here nightly at 9:45 P.M.

FISHING EXCURSIONS ON BAY LAKE: WDW's restrictive fishing policy means plenty of angling action—largemouth bass weighing two or three pounds, mainly—for those who sign up for the special 8 A.M., 12 P.M., and 3 P.M. fishing excursions. The fee is $110 for a two-hour excursion (each additional hour is $25) and includes gear, driver/guide, and refreshments; no license is required. Guests whose accommodations have kitchens may keep their catch. WDW also has made arrangements with a local taxidermist for guests who prefer to take their catches home as souvenirs. Call 824-2757 for reservations.

FISHING IN THE CANALS: Largemouth bass can be caught here as well. Those without their own gear will find cane poles and lures for sale at the trading posts; equipment also is available for rent at the Bike Barn. Poles are $2.10 per hour and $7.35 for the whole day. No license is required.

HAYRIDES: The hay wagon departs from Pioneer Hall and carries guests on a trip through wooded areas near Bay Lake. A ride lasts about an hour, and concludes back at Pioneer Hall. Tickets can be purchased from the hayride host. The price is $5 for adults; $3 for children 3 to 11. Children under 12 must be accompanied by an adult.

THE HORSE BARN: The world-champion Percherons and all the draft horses that pull trolleys down Main Street in the Magic Kingdom call this corner of *Fort Wilderness* home. You can watch them chomping placidly on their food, and occasionally see young colts and fillies as well. The Tri Circle D insignia above the barn door also is the WDW brand; two small circles, Mouse ears style, atop a large one with the letter *D* inside.

LAWN MOWER TREE: The tree that somehow, mysteriously, grew around a lawn mower is a *Fort Wilderness* point of interest worth hunting down. It's just off the sidewalk leading to the marina.

PETTING FARM: This fenced-in enclave just behind Pioneer Hall is home to some extra-friendly goats, a miniature Brahma bull, some sheep, a few rabbits, chickens, and assorted barnyard critters. (A colony of prairie dogs didn't work out because its members persisted in burrowing out of their compound; no sooner would their Disney caretakers try to thwart them—by digging a bigger hole and installing a below-ground-level wire fence—than the little creatures would gnaw right through it.) Pony rides are available for $2 between 9 A.M. and noon and 1 P.M. and 5 P.M. Though mainly designed for youngsters, the Petting Farm also is a lot of fun for the adult crowd, and it's a good place to pass the time while waiting for seating at the Hoop-Dee-Doo Musical Revue in nearby Pioneer Hall.

SWIMMING: *Fort Wilderness* has two pools.

TENNIS: Two tennis courts are available; play is on a first-come, first-served basis.

TRAIL RIDES: Offered from the middle of the campground, these horseback trips depart four times daily between 8:30 A.M. and 4 P.M. and take riders meandering into the Florida wilderness at a walking pace, where it is not uncommon to see deer, wild birds, and even an occasional alligator. Galloping is not part of the game, so you don't need riding know-how to sign up. Cost is $16 per person for both day visitors and for guests at WDW-owned properties. No children under nine are allowed to ride. There is a weight limit of 250 pounds. Reservations are recommended; phone 824-2803 up to five days in advance.

VOLLEYBALL, TETHERBALL, AND BASKETBALL COURTS: Open only to guests at WDW-owned properties, these are scattered throughout the camping loops. No charge.

WATERSKI TRIPS: Ski boats with drivers and equipment can be hired for $70 an hour at the marina, including instruction. Reservations should be made two to three days (but no more than seven days) in advance. Call 824-2757.

WILDERNESS SWAMP TRAIL: A mile-and-a-half long, this smooth footpath into the woods skirts the marshes along the shore of Bay Lake, then plunges into a forest full of tall, straight-standing cypress trees. It is near Marshmallow Marsh, at the northern end of the campground.

HOOP-DEE-DOO MUSICAL REVUE

Sturdy, porch-rimmed Pioneer Hall is best-known Worldwide as the home of the Pioneer Hall Players, an energetic troupe of singing-and-dancing-and-wisecracking entertainers who keep audiences chuckling and grinning and whooping it up for two hours, during a procession of barbecued ribs, fried chicken, corn-on-the-cob, strawberry shortcake, and other stomach-stretching viands. If you have time for only one of the Disney dinner shows, make it this one (for more details see *Good Meals, Great Times*). Reservations are hard to come by. Reservation policies are detailed on page 21.

River Country

The Perfect Swimming Hole

It's next to impossible to go through childhood reading such classics as *The Adventures of Huckleberry Finn* and *The Adventures of Tom Sawyer* (and other great tales of growing up) without developing a few fantasies about what it would be like to swim in a perfect swimming hole. A group of Disney Imagineers (who actually knew a commercial re-creation of such a place as kids) have concocted a Disney version on a somewhat larger scale at River Country, a water-oriented playground that occupies a corner of Bay Lake at *Fort Wilderness* campground.

Fred Joerger—the same Disney rock builder who created Big Thunder Mountain, Schweitzer Falls at the Jungle Cruise, and the caves of Tom Sawyer Island in the Magic Kingdom—has helped design rocks used to landscape one of the largest swimming pools in the state The rocks, scattered with pebbles acquired from stream beds in Georgia and the Carolinas, look so real that it's hard to believe they aren't.

More to the point, the place is great fun. Slipping and sliding down the curvy water chutes at top speed; getting tangled up, all arms and legs, in the whirlpools of Raft Rider Ridge; and whamming into the water from the swimming pool's high slides makes even careworn grown-ups smile, grin, giggle, chortle, and roar with delight. People who climb to the top with trepidation embark on the lightning-fast journey to the bottom only because it seems too late to back out; at the bottom they rush back for more. Line-haters queue up—over and over again. Those who associate lakes with muck and weeds go into ecstasies over the way the soft sand on the River Country bottom squiggles between their toes.

WHAT TO DO: There are several basic sections of River Country—the 330,000-gallon swimming pool; Bay Cove (aka the "Ol' Swimmin' Hole"), the big walled-off section of Bay Lake that most people consider the main (and best) part of River Country; and an adjoining junior version of the above for small children, with its own beach; and the grassy grounds, with picnic tables and a squirting fountain in which to play. On the edge of the lake, there's also a boardwalk nature trail through a lovely cypress swamp, and a wide (if not terribly long) white-sand beach.

Heated in winter, the oversize swimming pool has a pair of water slides that begin high enough above the water to make an acrophobe climb right down again. They plunge at such an angle that it's impossible to see the bottom of the slide from the top. Daredevils who don't chicken out are shot into the water from a height of about seven feet—hard enough, as one commentator observed, to "slap your stomach up against the roof of your mouth." Gutsy kids adore the experience; those who like their thrills a bit tamer might prefer to watch.

The heart of River Country, Bay Cove—actually a part of Bay Lake—is fitted out with rope swings, a ship's boom for swooping and plunging, and assorted other constructions designed to put hearts into throats as swimmers plunge from air to water. The big deals, however, are the two flume rides—one 260 feet long (accessible by a boardwalk and stairway to the far right of the swimming hole as you face it) and a smaller one, 100 feet shorter (accessible by a stairway to the left of that)—and the white-water raft ride.

The flumes, which are like overgrown, steep-sided waterslides, corkscrew through the greenery at the top of the ridge known as Whoop-'N-Holler Hollow, sending even the most stalwart shooting into the water, usually

---

ADMISSION PRICES*

ONE-DAY TICKET
Adult	$14.05
Child**	$11.13

ONE-DAY TICKET (after 3 P.M. in summer)
Adult	$10.07
Child**	$ 7.95

COMBINATION RIVER COUNTRY/ DISCOVERY ISLAND TICKET
Adult	$17.76
Child**	$12.99

NOTE: Admission to River Country and Discovery Island is included in a Be Our Guest Pass and a Super Duper Pass.

These prices were correct at press time, but may change during 1994.

*The prices quoted include sales tax.
**3 through 9 years of age

like greased lightning. White Water Rapids, as the white-water raft ride mentioned above is known, involves a more leisurely trip through a series of chutes and pools in an inner tube, from the crest of Raft Rider Ridge (adjoining Whoop-'N-Holler Hollow) into Bay Cove. It's not a high-speed affair like the flumes, but some people like it better. The pools are contoured so that the water swirls through them in whirlpool fashion. You tend to get caught in the slow circling water, and when other tubers come sliding down the chutes at you, bare arms and legs get all tangled up.

ADMISSION: River Country is an attraction in its own right, with a separate admission charge that includes transportation to the site and use of all the facilities. A River Country and Discovery Island combination ticket, which includes transportation and admission to both, also is available, and the Be Our Guest Pass and the five-day Super Duper Pass includes admission to River Country and Discovery Island. Note that children under ten must be accompanied by an adult. Some of the River Country adventures require swimming ability.

WHEN TO GO: Daytime temperatures in Orlando are such that it's possible to enjoy River Country almost all year-round, though it is perhaps most pleasant in spring when the weather is getting hot but the water is still cool. In summer, the place can be very busy indeed. Ticket windows close as the crowd approaches capacity. During WDW's busiest times of year, that may happen as early as 11 A.M. It's worth noting, however, that those who already have tickets will be admitted anyway. Consequently, if you plan to visit River Country in the afternoon of a summer day, it's smart to buy your combination River Country/Discovery Island ticket at the ticket booth at the entrance to the Magic Kingdom on your way into the park. River Country is usually closed for refurbishing during January.

One of the World's best-kept secrets is the joy of River Country after 3 P.M. in the summer. Crowds begin to thin out dramatically then, but usually not so much that the place is empty; and a special reduced admission ticket is offered after 3 P.M. River Country closes at 7 P.M. during the summer.

HOW TO GET THERE: From the Transportation and Ticket Center, buses drop passengers off within walking distance of River Country. It's also possible to go by boat. Launches leave regularly from the dock near the gates of the Magic Kingdom. For guests arriving at River Country by car, a bus picks up at the *Fort Wilderness* parking lot and takes them to the entrance.

TOWELS, DRESSING ROOMS, SUPPLIES: Men's and women's dressing rooms, and coin-operated lockers are available. Quarters for these can be obtained at the concession window, but to avoid waiting in line for change, it's best to bring your own.

Towels are available for rent at $1 each at the concession window, but they're small, so you'll probably want to bring at least one beach towel.

FOOD: *Pop's Place*, the main snack spot features quarter-pound burgers, hot dogs, salads, beer and soda, and the like. During peak season the *Waterin' Hole*, a smaller stand nearby, offers a more limited selection. Picnicking is permitted. You can eat on the beach or seek out a table on the shady lawns.

Discovery Island

This 11½-acre landfall (a member of the American Association of Parks and Aquariums) on the southeast shore of Bay Lake—which is itself a natural marvel full of exotic birds and a whole United Nations of plants—is a delightful place to go for a change of pace from the Magic Kingdom. Here you're in the domain of the animals; human beings are just visitors. The mood is different from anywhere else in the World, and the scenery is remarkably lush.

Before the World began, this island was flat and scrubby, just a tangle of vines. But Disney planners, thinking of Robert Louis Stevenson's classic *Treasure Island*, decided to turn it into a horticultural and zoological paradise. They cleared the vegetation, brought in 15,000 cubic yards of sandy soil, and added 500 tons each of boulders and trees. They built hills, carved out lagoons, sowed grass seed, and planted 20 types of palm trees, ten species of bamboo, and dozens upon dozens of other plants from Argentina, Bolivia, the Canary Islands, China, Costa Rica, Formosa, the Himalayas, India, Japan, Peru, South Africa, Trinidad, and other nations around the world. Then they added winding paths, built aviaries and filled them with birds, and added a few props to carry through the *Treasure Island* theme. A wrecked ship salvaged from off the coast of Florida was installed on the beach, and a Jolly Roger hung from the lookout post. The creation was dubbed Treasure Island.

Since then, that theme has been abandoned and the island's name changed. But the ship is still there, as is the vegetation (lusher than ever). And the avian population is flourishing so well that the droning of the motors of the Water Sprites on Bay Lake almost is drowned out by chirps and tweets, crows and hoarse caws, cries and squeaks, and the lonely sounding squawks of peacocks.

Now nobody makes any bones about the fact that the birds and the extraordinary vegetation constitute the island's chief attraction. Far from taking a backseat to the manmade, nature is the big deal on Discovery Island. The sweet-smelling flowers in pinks and reds and yellows that polka-dot the billowing greenery, the ferns that hang in the forests, the trees that canopy the footpaths, the butterflies, the dense thickets of bamboo, and the graceful palms—not to mention the birds themselves—are all very real; during Discovery Island hours—that is, from 10 A.M. to 5 P.M. (to 7 P.M. during the summer) every day—visitors provide a good show for the birds and animals. The last boat to the island leaves one hour and 15 minutes before closing.

WHAT TO SEE: It's possible to walk the length of the paths and boardwalks that wind through the island in 45 minutes or so. But spending a good part of a day—or at least several hours—is a far better idea, since there is so much to see that it warrants more than just a rushed look. This is especially true in spring, when the birds are in breeding condition—looking their best, putting on courting displays, and sometimes collecting material for nests. Even during other seasons, however, each stop yields rewards. An ibis might be spotted building its nest. A sleeping tortoise—dinosaur-like, with the papery, wrinkled skin of an old person's neck—suddenly awakes and creeps forward to join a clump of rocks that turns out to be other tortoises.

Many animals run free. Peacocks trail their spotted trains of iridescent green, blue, and gold around the grounds. They lose their tail feathers every September, and spend the winter growing new plumage in preparation for their springtime mating dance—a slow turning to and fro, sometimes punctuated by a quiver and a shudder of their graceful fans. The large rabbitlike animals are Patagonian cavies, members of the guinea pig family, who in the wild live in burrows to escape predators. Keeping quite calm, you can approach them slowly to examine them at close range.

In addition, there are special points of interest, which are marked on maps available on the island:

Trumpeter Springs: The trumpeter swans who live here, the largest members of the waterfowl family, belong to a species that once was nearly extinct—as a result of hunting in the early part of this century.

Parrots Perch: The macaws, cockatoos, and other trained birds that comprise the Discovery Island Bird Show make their home here. The show combines the bird's antics with a message about the efforts taking place on the island to save them through captive breeding.

Bamboo Hollow: This is where you'll find lemurs, primitive monkeys from Madagascar. Lemurs are endangered in the wild.

Crane's Roost: Small Demoiselle cranes, Asian muntjac deer, and white crested hornbill can be seen at this spot on the island.

Avian Way: One of the largest walk-through aviaries in the world, this enclosure, occupying close to an acre, is the home of the United States' most extensive breeding colony of scarlet ibis. Their incredible color, even richer than that of ibis in the wild, derives from a diet that is especially rich in carotenes. Even those in the forest are striking. The early South American explorers who first saw them thought that the trees were covered with blood.

Pelican Bay: Brown pelicans became almost extinct because the chemical DDT washed into rivers and absorbed by fish that the birds subsequently ate caused their eggs to have such thin shells that even the weight of the mother pelican nesting on them broke them before hatching. It is only since Florida's 1965 ban on the chemical that the population has begun to grow again. The Discovery Island birds, though now healthy, have suffered injuries that have left them crippled in ways that would make it impossible for them to survive in the wild.

Flamingo Lagoon: Native flamingos—which nested in colonies some 20,000 strong when John James Audubon visited Florida in the early part of the 19th century—have not lived in the wild here since around 1920. The Discovery Island birds are Caribbean flamingos. They have grown accustomed to human presence, as the early Florida flamingos could not, and are breeding.

Tortoise Beach: Early explorers used to lead Galapagos tortoises, now rare and endangered, onto their ships; because the animals can live for some time without food or water, they provided the crews with fresh meat for the duration of a trip. There are five here; the largest weighs some 500 pounds.

HOW TO GET THERE: Watercraft from the Magic Kingdom, the *Polynesian* resort, the *Contemporary* resort, the *Grand Floridian* resort, *Fort Wilderness*, and River Country all call regularly at Discovery Island. To ride these, you must show a Discovery Island admission ticket or a WDW resort ID.

ADMISSION: Cost is $9.01 ($5.04 for children three through nine); combination tickets that include River Country admission as well also are available (described in this chapter's River Country section). Discovery Island admission is included with a Be Our Guest Pass or a Super Duper Pass.

PHOTOS: The birds on Discovery Island offer wonderful photographic possibilities. Don't forget your camera. Film is available on the island.

BEACH: Swimming isn't allowed, but the peaceful strand flanking the shipwreck is great for sunbathing and sand castle building—or just for sitting and watching the brightly colored sails of the Hobie Cats (from the *Fort Wilderness* marina) go by.

FOOD: It's fun to pack a picnic, with supplies from the Gourmet Pantry at the Disney Village Marketplace or one of *Fort Wilderness* campground's trading posts, for lunch on the beach near the handsome old wreck (which is still aging gracefully along the Bay Lake shore). Sandwiches, hot dogs, ice cream sandwiches and bars, frozen-juice bars, and beer and soft drinks are available at the snack bar, the *Thirsty Perch*.

DISCOVERY ISLAND KIDVENTURE: Children 8 to 14 can explore Discovery Island and *Fort Wilderness* on four-hour guided tours. Cost is $26.50 per person and includes lunch, transportation, craft materials, and a souvenir photo. Reservations are required. Call 824-3784.

Wonders of the World

Walt Disney World Seminar Productions, a division of Disney University, offers a unique behind-the-scenes look at the Walt Disney World Resort through a variety of education programs for guests of all ages. Young people (ages 10 through 15) can step backstage for a look at art, entertainment, and nature, while adults can study the culture and landscapes of Epcot Center or participate in a series of multi-day business and educational programs.

Wonders of Walt Disney World education programs spark imaginations and fuel ambitions for students interested in learning about the environment, art, or entertainment. Each six-hour learning adventure was developed in cooperation with leading educators and are recognized as authentic learning experiences. In many cases, students can earn school credit, special recognition, or an excused absence for completing the program. The cost is $75 and participants receive a colorful program book with follow-up activities, access to the theme parks and backstage areas during the program, lunch, and a personalized certificate of completion. Choose from three unique programs:

Wildlife Adventure: Exploring the Environment (Tuesdays and Thursdays) takes students on a safari through the pristine Walt Disney World conservation area. Discussions on wildlife identification, ecosystems, and environmental issues come to life as participants observe alligators, vultures, snakes, and other creatures in their natural habitat. The day include a visit to Discovery Island or The Living Seas for an up-close look at caring for captive animals and a lesson in mankind's responsibility to protect wildlife environments.

Art Magic: Bringing Illusion to Life (Mondays through Fridays) shows how artists at WDW create the illusion of reality in movies and the theme parks. This adventure includes a behind-the-scenes look at the animation process. Following a discussion on the artists and steps involved in developing an animated film, participants get to visit the Animation Production Floor and paint a keepsake Mickey Mouse cel. The students then step back "on stage" to study the use of theme, color, and forced perspective. The day concludes with a special hands-on experience where the participants learn tips on drawing Disney characters.

Show Biz Magic: The Walt Disney World of Entertainment (Mondays through Thursdays) introduces young people to the diversity of entertainment at WDW. Discussions on nonverbal communication, show preparation, auditions, being a good audience, and star qualities are reinforced through talks with performers from a variety of entertainment areas. Highlights of this adventure include a visit to a rehearsal area, the chance to watch a live stage show, and a trip into the tunnel system beneath the Magic Kingdom for a look at show preparation areas.

Program content and prices are subject to change without notice. For individual reservations, call 354-1855. There are special rates for groups of 11 or more; phone 824-4730.

Adults can get in on the fun, too. The **Disney Learning Adventures for Adults** take guests 16 and older on a guided behind-the-scenes tour of Epcot Center. In **Hidden Treasures of World Showcase**, participants discover the often overlooked art, architecture, costumes, landscape, and entertainment of the international pavilions at World Showcase. In **Gardens of the World**, a Disney horticulturist guides guests through a study of the plants, flowers, and trees of World Showcase. Each program is a four-hour walking tour and costs $20 per person in addition to theme park admission. Class size is limited to 20 people. For reservations phone 354-1855.

Walt Disney World Seminar Productions also offers a variety of programs designed specifically for business and education professionals. **The Disney Approach to Business & Management Seminars** and the **Disney Educator Programs** are multiday courses held exclusively at WDW.

The Disney Approach to People Management, **The Disney Approach to Quality Service**, **The Disney Approach to Creative Leadership**, and **The Disney Approach to Orientation** are packaged seminars offering business professionals insight into management techniques, philosophies, and operational procedures practiced at WDW. A unique combination of classroom activities and behind-the-scenes field experiences help participants see how the Disney methods can be adapted to their organizations.

Communicating Disney Style, **Marketing Positive Images**, and **Creating Motivational Learning Environments** are professional development programs designed specifically for educators. Participants learn practical ways to adapt Disney communication and marketing and motivation techniques to classrooms and schools.

Each three-day business and educator seminar is offered as a presentation or workshop to convention groups of 15 or more staying on the Disney property.

For additional information about these programs write to Walt Disney World Seminar Productions; Box 10,000; Lake Buena Vista, FL 32830-1000; 824-7997 or fax 824-4866.

Sports

Many first-time visitors don't realize that Walt Disney World is much more than just the Magic Kingdom, Epcot Center, and the Disney-MGM Studios Theme Park. Within WDW's 27,000-odd acres there are more tennis courts than at most tennis resorts, more holes of championship-caliber golf than at most golf centers, and so many acres of other diversions—from fishing and bicycling to boating and swimming—that the quantity and variety are matched by very few other vacation destinations.

So while the golfers in the family are earnestly pursuing a perfect swing on one of the six first class layouts, tennis buffs can be wearing themselves out on the courts, sailors can be sailing, waterskiers can be skimming back and forth across powerboat wakes, and anglers can be dangling a cane pole in a canal—in the hopes of bringing in a big bream for dinner.

Instruction (formal or impromptu), as well as guides, drivers, and assorted leaders and supervisors (as required), make each sports offering as much fun for rank beginners as for hard-core aficionados. Moreover, the ready accessibility of all these WDW sporting activities—via an excellent system of public transportation (see *Transportation and Accommodations*)—means that no member of a visiting family or group need give up play time to chauffeur others around.

(Prices noted below are subject to change, and do not include applicable state tax.)

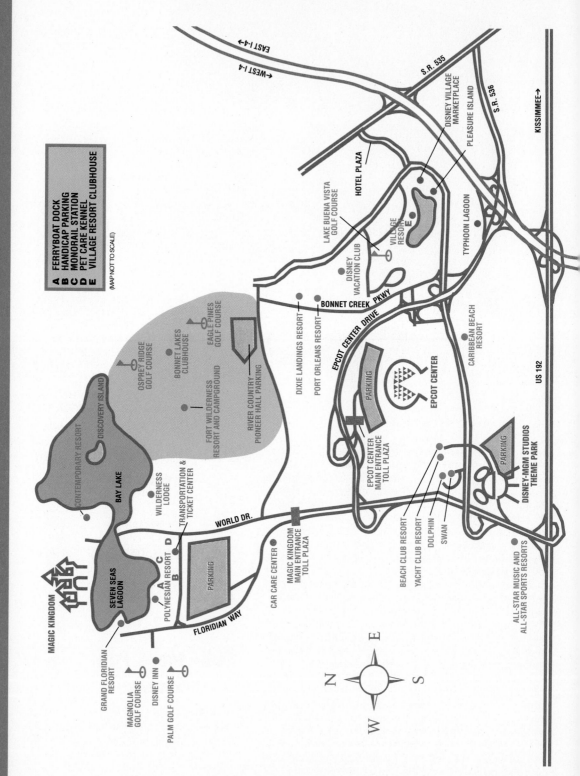

A FERRYBOAT DOCK
B HANDICAP PARKING
C MONORAIL STATION
D PET CARE KENNEL
E VILLAGE RESORT CLUBHOUSE

(MAP NOT TO SCALE)

EAST I-4
WEST I-4
S.R. 535
S.R. 536
KISSIMMEE

DISNEY VILLAGE MARKETPLACE
PLEASURE ISLAND
HOTEL PLAZA
TYPHOON LAGOON
LAKE BUENA VISTA GOLF COURSE
VILLAGE RESORT
DISNEY VACATION CLUB
CARIBBEAN BEACH RESORT
US 192

BONNET CREEK PKWY
DIXIE LANDINGS RESORT
PORT ORLEANS RESORT
EPCOT CENTER DRIVE
PARKING
EPCOT CENTER
EPCOT CENTER MAIN ENTRANCE TOLL PLAZA
PARKING
DISNEY-MGM STUDIOS THEME PARK

OSPREY RIDGE GOLF COURSE
BONNET LAKES CLUBHOUSE
EAGLE PINES GOLF COURSE
FORT WILDERNESS RESORT AND CAMPGROUND
RIVER COUNTRY PIONEER HALL PARKING
DISCOVERY ISLAND

MAGIC KINGDOM
SEVEN SEAS LAGOON
BAY LAKE
CONTEMPORARY RESORT
WILDERNESS LODGE
TRANSPORTATION & TICKET CENTER
WORLD DR.
CAR CARE CENTER
MAGIC KINGDOM MAIN ENTRANCE TOLL PLAZA
PARKING

GRAND FLORIDIAN RESORT
MAGNOLIA GOLF COURSE
DISNEY INN
PALM GOLF COURSE
POLYNESIAN RESORT
FLORIDIAN WAY

BEACH CLUB RESORT
YACHT CLUB RESORT
DOLPHIN
SWAN
ALL-STAR MUSIC AND ALL-STAR SPORTS RESORTS

N
E
S
W

Tennis Everyone

No one comes to Walt Disney World just for a tennis vacation; there just isn't the country-club ambience of a tennis resort where everyone is totally immersed in the game. But the facilities and instruction program at WDW are extensive enough that such holidays are certainly within the realm of possibility. And at the very least, a couple of sets of tennis on one of the World's 27 courts is a good way to unwind after a mad morning in the parks.

In February, March, April, June, and July the courts at the tennis locations endure fairly heavy use, but there is usually a lull between noon and 3 P.M., and again from dinnertime until 10 P.M. Even during these months, however, it's often possible to get a reservation.

WHERE TO FIND THE COURTS: There are six tennis courts at the *Contemporary* resort, just beyond the garden wing to the north of the Tower. This is WDW's major tennis facility. It boasts three backboards, and an automatic ball machine to work on groundstrokes and volleys. There are two additional courts tucked away behind the *Disney Inn*, and three cradled by adjacent woods and a section of the golf course at the Lake Buena Vista Club. There also are two courts at the *Fort Wilderness* resort. There are two clay courts at the *Grand Floridian*. There are two courts at the *Disney Vacation Club*. The *Swan* and *Dolphin* hotels share eight courts, and there are two additional courts at the *Yacht Club* and *Beach Club* resorts. All WDW tennis is played on hard courts (except at the *Grand Floridian*) that are open from 8 A.M. to 10 P.M. daily (hours may vary during winter months).

COURT RESERVATIONS: Courts may be reserved 24 hours in advance. Call 824-3578 to play at the *Contemporary* resort; 824-1469 for the *Disney Inn*; 824-2438 for the *Grand Floridian*; 824-2433 for the Lake Buena Vista Club; and 934-4000, ext. 6000 for both the *Swan* and *Dolphin*. The *Fort Wilderness*, *Disney Inn*, and *Disney Vacation Club*, and the

Lake Buena Vista Club courts are available on a first-come, first-served basis. The limit on the number of hours a day any single group of players can occupy a court—a restriction in effect only during very busy periods—is two hours on any morning, afternoon, or evening. That means that you can spend six hours a day on a court even at the busiest times.

For players without partners, the "Tennis Anyone?" program will help find an opponent. Just call the Pro Shop at the *Contemporary* resort to get your name posted.

FEES: It costs $10 per hour to play at the *Contemporary* resort ($25 per family for an entire stay); $12 at the *Grand Floridian*, *Swan*, and *Dolphin*; no charge at the *Disney Inn*, the Lake Buena Vista Club, *Fort Wilderness*, *Yacht Club*, *Beach Club*, or *Disney Vacation Club*.

INSTRUCTION: The tennis program at the *Contemporary* resort offers clinics ($35; free for resort guests from 2 P.M. to 3 P.M. Mondays through Saturdays). Video cameras are used to record players' on-court efforts for subsequent review; children as young as 3 and adults as old as 80 have participated. Nobody will try to change your game radically; the idea is to help you play better with what you have.

Private lessons also are available, by appointment, at the *Contemporary* resort. The cost is $37 per hour and $20 per half hour with a staff professional, all of whom are certified by the United States Tennis Association; $45 per hour and $25 per half hour with a head pro who supervises the entire WDW tennis program. Videotape reviews are included as part of hour-long lessons at the *Contemporary* resort for an additional $10. For more information about private lessons and group development sessions, call 824-3578.

Lessons also are available at the *Grand Floridian* for $35 per hour. For reservations call 824-2433.

TOURNAMENTS: Individual tournaments may be arranged by calling the Pro Shop at the *Contemporary* resort. The fee for running a tournament is $40 per hour.

RACQUET RENTAL: Good-quality racquets are available for rent at $4 an hour for adults. New balls may be purchased (for $4.25 per can of three) or used balls rented by the basket for $3.

LOCKERS: Locker facilities, which are free of charge, are available at all tennis court areas with the exception of the *Grand Floridian*.

A Matter of Courses

Most people probably don't think of Walt Disney World immediately when they contemplate a golf vacation. Yet there are six superb courses right in the Vacation Kingdom: The Magnolia, the Palm, and Oak Trail flank the *Disney Inn*, and extend practically to the borders of the Magic Kingdom. Just a short drive away is the Lake Buena Vista Golf Course, whose borders are framed by the *Disney Village* resort and the *Disney Vacation Club*. Osprey Ridge and Eagle Pines play from a clubhouse located near *Fort Wilderness*.

None of the original three Joe Lee-designed courses will set anyone's knees to knocking in terror from the regular men's or women's tees, though both the Palm and Magnolia are demanding enough to serve as the site of an annual stop on the PGA Tour tournament trail. Depending on the tee from which a golfer chooses to play, the Disney courses are challenging and/or fun, and they are constructed to be especially forgiving for the mid-handicap player. What's more, they're remarkably interesting topographically, considering that the land on which Lee started was about as hilly as a tabletop.

Osprey Ridge was designed by Tom Fazio and was created to be a reasonable challenge for beginners as well as more advanced players. Eagle Pines, designed by Pete Dye, is a "low profile" layout where the course is built on the same level as, or lower than, the surrounding land.

At the three Joe Lee courses, the greens fees (including the required cart) are about $75; twilight rates, in effect beginning at 3 P.M., are $35. Fees at Osprey Ridge and

Eagle Pines are slightly higher: $85 for daytime play; twilight rates are $45. The fee to play Oak Trail is $22 for adults for 9 holes, $27 for 18 holes; juniors (under 17) pay $10 for 9 holes and $15 for 18 holes. This is a walking course only. Proper golf attire is required. Shirts must have collars and if shorts are worn they must be Bermuda length.

For tee-off times on any of the six courses, just phone 824-2270. Especially from February through April, it's a good idea to reserve starting times well in advance for play in the morning and early afternoon (though starting times after 3 P.M. are almost always available at the last minute). Those with confirmed reservations at the WDW resorts (which include guests at any of the seven hotels at Disney Village Hotel Plaza) can reserve tee times 30 days in advance. Day visitors can reserve only seven days ahead.

The Golf Courses

AT THE DISNEY INN: The wide-open, tree-dotted Magnolia, which flanks the hotel to the north, plays from 5,414 (women's) to 7,190 (championship) yards at par 72. The par-72 Palm to the south—shorter and tighter, with more wooded fairways and nine water hazards—plays from 5,398 to 6,957 yards. The Palm was ranked among the nation's top 100 courses by *Golf Digest* magazine. Together, this pair (and the Lake Buena Vista course) hosts the big Walt Disney World/Oldsmobile Golf Classic every year, a good indication of the quality of the play to be found. Driving ranges are located near the Magnolia and Palm courses. (There's also one at the Lake Buena Vista course.)

Oak Trail: This nine-hole, par-36, 2,913-yard layout—a championship course nestled on a 45-acre corner of the Magnolia—was designed especially with the beginner in mind. The design incorporates sand and water traps.

skills they already possess. Instruction is provided via small classes with a high teacher-student ratio. Part of each lesson is recorded on videotape and then given a thorough viewing and critique. Then, to hammer in what has just been learned, the instructor repeats his or her suggestions and admonitions on an audio-cassette tape that students can take home.

The studios, which last about one-and-a-half hours each, are offered at 9 A.M., 11:30 A.M., and 2:30 P.M. Mondays through Saturdays at the Magnolia driving range. Call 824-2270 for reservations; the studio fee is $50, $90 for a playing lesson.

Private lessons: These are available at two locations for $30 per half hour with an assistant ($60 with the *Disney Inn* head pro Kevin Weikel or Lake Buena Vista Club head pro Dave Bolton).

Call 824-2270 to book private lessons at the *Disney Inn*; 828-3741 to arrange instruction at the Lake Buena Vista Club.

EQUIPMENT RENTAL: Titleist D.T.R. rental clubs ($20), buckets of range balls ($4 each), and shoes ($6) are all available at the Pro Shop—what you rent here may be better than your own gear.

AT BONNET CREEK GOLF CLUB: The Tom Fazio-designed Osprey Ridge is a par-72 layout that plays from 5,402 yards from the women's tees to 6,680 yards from the men's tees. The pro yardage measures 7,101. This is a circular 18-hole course, which means that the ninth hole does not play back to the club-house. This unique course allows guests a look at some of the more remote areas of the WDW property, as it winds through the wooded landscape near *Fort Wilderness*. There are some tees and greens that are 20 feet to 25 feet above the basic grade.

In contrast, the Pete Dye-designed Eagle Pines is a low-profile layout. It also is a par-72 course and plays to 4,838 yards from the women's tees, 6,309 from the men's tees, and 6,772 from the pro tees. Many of the fairways are dished rather than crowned, as in conventional designs. The course also plays directly out from the clubhouse, but golfers can return at the ninth hole.

AT THE LAKE BUENA VISTA CLUB: Located to the south of the clubhouse and the Buena Vista Lagoon, this narrow, par-72 layout plays from 5,315 to 6,829 yards. The shortest of the 18-hole courses, with the narrowest fairways, it offers a fun round of golf to everyone regardless of skill level.

INSTRUCTION: The Walt Disney World Golf Studio is the most compelling aspect of the golf instruction available at WDW. Each Golf Studio instructor works to help golfers develop their own styles by building on what

TOURNAMENTS

The Walt Disney World/Oldsmobile Golf Classic, a popular spectator event that ranks as the most important on WDW's sports calendar, takes place in the fall, usually in October, and features most of the pro tour's top players. So guests who plan to play golf during their WDW vacation are advised *not* to schedule a visit during tournament week.

You can, however, play alongside the pros if you are willing to pay for it: The price of a one-year membership in the Classic Club is about $4,800. As a tourney sponsor, each member plays with a competing pro daily, for three of the four days of the tourney. While the pros are competing for cash prizes, the amateurs vie for trophies and plaques in a separate but simultaneous competition. The fee also includes lodging during the tournament, free greens fees for a year, and admission to the Magic Kingdom, Epcot Center, and the Disney-MGM Studios Theme Park for a week. For details, phone 828-2250.

At other times of the year, smaller private competitions are held for civic, corporate, and social groups; to arrange a tournament (at no charge beyond the normal greens and cart fees), contact the Tournament Coordinator at 824-2275.

Waters of the World

Boating

Walt Disney World is the home of the country's largest fleet of pleasure boats. Cruising on Bay Lake and the Seven Seas Lagoon can be excellent sport, and a variety of boats are available for rent at the marinas at the *Contemporary* resort, on the western shore of Bay Lake; at *Fort Wilderness*, to the southeast beyond Discovery Island; at the *Polynesian* resort, which occupies the southern edge of the Seven Seas Lagoon; at the *Grand Floridian* resort; at the *Caribbean Beach* resort, *Yacht Club*, *Beach Club*, and the *Disney Vacation Club*. In addition, boaters can explore the lakes of Disney Village Marketplace, including 35-acre Buena Vista Lagoon.

To rent, day visitors and resort guests alike must show a resort ID, a driver's license, or a valid passport. Rental of certain craft may carry other special requirements (described below).

Note that no privately owned boats are permitted on any of the WDW waters.

SPEEDBOATS: Particularly when the weather is warm, there are always dozens of small boats zipping back and forth across the surfaces of Bay Lake, the Seven Seas Lagoon, and the lakes at Disney Village Marketplace. These are called Water Sprites, and they are just as much fun as they look. Though they don't go very fast, they're so small that a rider feels every bit of speed, and they zip around quickly enough so that a lot of watery terrain can be covered in a half-hour rental period ($11). You can rent them at the *Contemporary* resort, *Polynesian* resort, the *Grand Floridian* resort, *Fort Wilderness*, and Disney Village Marketplace marinas. During warm weather, lines of people waiting to rent these swift little craft usually form at about 11 A.M. and remain fairly constant until about 4 P.M. The minimum rental age is 12. Even with an accompanying parent or adult, children under 12 are not allowed to drive.

SAILBOATS: The size of Bay Lake and the Seven Seas Lagoon—and their usually reliable winds—makes for good sailing, and the *Contemporary* resort, *Polynesian* resort, *Grand Floridian*, *Fort Wilderness*, *Yacht Club* and *Beach Club*, and the *Caribbean Beach* resort marinas rent a variety of sail craft. Sunfish, which can hold two, go for $10 an hour. Capris, accommodating from one to six—more stable because of their leaded keel, wider beam, and greater weight, and consequently better for beginners—cost $12 an hour. Hobie Cat 14s and 16s cost $12 and $15 an hour respectively; catamaran experience is required. The Hobie 16, which has a mainsail and a jib, requires two to sail it, but cannot accommodate more than three. Sailing conditions are usually best in March and April, and before the inevitable late-afternoon thundershowers in the summer—and that's when demand is greatest. So don't tarry. Head for the marina as soon as the urge to sail strikes.

PONTOON BOATS: Flotebotes—motor-powered, canopied platforms-on-pontoons, really—are perfect for families, for inexperienced sailors, and for older visitors more interested in serenity than thrills. They're available at the resort marinas ($35 an hour).

CANOPY BOATS: These 16-foot, V-hulled motorized boats with canopies also are good for slow cruises, and can accommodate up to six adults. They can be rented for $17.50 per half hour at the Disney Village Marketplace Marina, the *Polynesian*, the *Contemporary*, the *Grand Floridian*, the *Yacht Club* and *Beach Club*, the *Disney Vacation Club*, *Port Orleans*, and *Caribbean Beach*.

PEDAL BOATS: These craft are for rent for $8 per hour or $5.50 per half-hour at most WDW lakeside marinas for excursions on the WDW lakes. They're also available, for resort guests only, at *Fort Wilderness's* Bike Barn, at the *Swan* and *Dolphin* hotels, at the *Yacht Club* and *Beach Club*, at the *Caribbean Beach*, and at *Port Orleans*.

CANOEING: A long paddle down the glass-smooth, wooded *Fort Wilderness* canals is such a tranquil way to pass a misty morning that it's hard to remember that the bustle of the Magic Kingdom is just a launch ride away. Canoes are for rent at *Fort Wilderness's* Bike Barn ($4 per hour, $10 per day). Most trips last from one to three hours; those who take fishing gear can easily stay out longer. Canoes are restricted to the Walt Disney World canals.

WATERSKIING: Ski boats with driver and full equipment ($70 an hour) are available at the *Fort Wilderness*, *Polynesian*, *Grand Floridian*, and *Contemporary* resort marinas. Anyone is allowed to waterski, but there is no reduction of the posted price even if you bring along your own skis and other equipment.

Fishing

The 70,000 bass with which Bay Lake was stocked in the mid-1960s have grown and multiplied as a result of WDW's restrictive fishing policy. No angling is permitted on Bay Lake or the Seven Seas Lagoon, except on the guided two-hour *Fort Wilderness* fishing expeditions. There's one leaving the campground marina each morning at around 8 A.M., one at noon, and one each afternoon at around 4 P.M.; a maximum of five fishing persons can be accommodated on each. The fee is $110 for two hours ($25 for each additional hour) and includes gear, driver/guide, and coffee and pastries (in the morning) or soft drinks (in the afternoon). No license is required. Largemouth bass weighing two to three pounds each are the most common catch, though someone occasionally will reel in a bream or a bigger largemouth. Bass up to 12 pounds have been recorded.

A catch-and-release guided fishing excursion leaves Cap'n Jack's Marina at the Disney Village Marketplace twice a day at 7 A.M. and 6 P.M. for a two-hour excursion. Reservations are required: 828-2461.

Fishing on your own is permitted in the canals in the *Disney Village* resort area and at *Fort Wilderness*. *Fort Wilderness* campers can toss in their lines from any shore. (The waters around the treehouses are reputed to be particularly productive.) Licenses are not required. Rods and reels are available for rent at the Bike Barn, and cane poles and lures are for sale at the *Fort Wilderness* trading posts. At *Dixie Landings* there is a stocked fishing hole. Gear is available.

Swimming

Between Bay Lake and the Seven Seas Lagoon, Walt Disney World resort guests have five miles of powdery white sand beach at their disposal. And that doesn't include the many swimming pools that come in all shapes and sizes. River Country and Typhoon Lagoon (see *Everything Else in the World*) only add to the fun.

BEACHES: When Walt Disney World was under construction during the mid-1960s, Bay Lake, with an eight-foot layer of muck on its bottom, was found to be unpolluted. It was drained and cleaned, and below the

muck, engineers unearthed the pure, white sand that now edges parts of the shore, most notably at the *Contemporary* resort, the *Grand Floridian* resort, the *Caribbean Beach* resort, and on the lake's *Fort Wilderness* shore. These four sections of beach, plus the ones at the *Polynesian* and the *Yacht Club* and *Beach Club*, make up WDW's sandy areas. They aren't the walk-forever strands found on Florida's coasts, but they are long enough that most people don't bother to go to the end.

POOLS: There are two each at the *Contemporary* resort, the *Polynesian* resort, the *Disney Inn*, *Fort Wilderness* resort, and *All-Star Sports* and *All-Star Music* resorts; seven at the *Caribbean Beach* resort; four at the villas; one at the *Swan*; a huge lap pool and a themed grotto pool with slide at the *Dolphin*; two quiet pools at the *Yacht Club* and *Beach Club* and Stormalong Bay, a themed pool area between the resorts featuring a sunken ship and snorkeling; Doubloon Lagoon at *Port Orleans*; five at *Dixie Landings,* plus Ol' Man Island, a themed pool and recreation area; and one each at the Lake Buena Vista Club, the *Grand Floridian* resort, *Wilderness Lodge*, the *Disney Vacation Club*, Typhoon Lagoon, and at River Country. The pools at the *Yacht Club* and *Beach Club*, *Port Orleans*, and *Dixie Landings* are open to guests of those hotels only. There's no charge for admission, towels, or chairs anywhere, except at River Country and Typhoon Lagoon. For lap swimming, the best are at the *Contemporary* resort, the *Swan*, and the *Dolphin*. There are no diving boards at any of the pools; to practice cannonballs, head for River Country or Typhoon Lagoon. Lifeguards are on duty during most daylight hours. There is no formal swimming instruction at WDW. In addition, each of the seven hotels that make up Disney Village Hotel Plaza has its own pool.

DAY VISITORS: Pools and beaches at the resort hotels are not open to day guests (or to guests staying at the hotels at Disney Village Hotel Plaza). If you're just at WDW for the day and want to take a cooling break from the heat, head for River Country or Typhoon Lagoon. (See *Everything Else in the World*.)

More Fun Stuff

VOLLEYBALL AND BASKETBALL:
Courts are scattered throughout the *Fort Wilderness* camping loops, but are open to WDW resort guests only. There also is a court at the *Yacht Club* and *Beach Club*.

JOGGING: Except in winter, late fall, and very early spring, the weather is usually too steamy in Central Florida to provide the exhilarating jogging found in cooler climes. If you run early in the morning in warm seasons, the heat is somewhat less daunting. (The scenery also is good enough to take your mind off the excess perspiration.) Guests staying at villa accommodations can just head out the door and run along a 32-station, 3.4-mile winding drive where everything is green and blessedly quiet. The 1.4-mile promenade around the *Caribbean Beach* resort's lake also is perfect for jogging. *Fort Wilderness* offers a partially paved, 2.3-mile course that's punctuated by exercise stations. The walkways around *Dixie Landings* also are perfect for jogging. Maps are available at Guest Services desks in hotels and villa check-in areas; mileages range from 3.4 to 4.2 miles.

BIKING: Pedaling along the eight miles of bike paths that weave through the *Disney Village* resort and the lightly trafficked roads there and at *Fort Wilderness* can be a pleasant way to spend a couple of hours—especially in the winter, or in the mornings and late afternoons during the rest of the year, when it's not too hot. Both areas are sufficiently spread out that bicycles are a practical means of getting around. If you don't bring your own bike, you can rent one at *Fort Wilderness's* Bike Barn or at the Reception Center for $4 an hour or $8 per day. Tandems are available at the Bike Barn ($4 an hour or $9 a day). Bikes also can be rented at the *Caribbean Beach* resort and the *Disney Vacation Club*, and *Wilderness Lodge*. Anyone is allowed to ride bikes on the property.

FITNESS: The *Contemporary* resort's Olympiad Health Club (located on the hotel's third floor) has Nautilus gym equipment—perfect for a good workout. Afterward, it's almost not necessary—though it's decidedly pleasant—to relax in the sauna. For use of the facil-

ities, the cost is $5. The hours at the health club are 7 A.M. to 8 P.M. daily. Call 824-3410 for appointments and further information on hours. There also is a health club at the Lake Buena Vista Club with Universal equipment. It is a coed facility. The club is open from 7 A.M. to 6 P.M. daily. The key (complimentary for resort guests) is available at the Pro Shop. The St. John's Health Spa at the *Grand Floridian* resort is open to hotel guests only ($5 per visit or $15 for entire stay) and offers a sauna, nutrition and exercise counselors, and Nautilus equipment. The Magic Mirror health club at the *Disney Inn* has free weights, an exercise bike, and other equipment. It's open from 8:30 A.M. to 6 P.M. daily and cost is $4 per visit or $10 for your entire stay. The Ship Shape Health Club at the *Yacht Club* and *Beach Club* resorts offers exercise machines, aerobics classes, steamroom, sauna, and spa. It's open from 6:30 A.M. to 9:30 P.M. A one-day visit costs $5, or $10 for your entire stay. At the *Disney Vacation Club*, Slappy Joe's features Nautilus equipment and a sauna. It's open from 7 A.M. to 10 P.M. At the *Dolphin*, the Body by Jake health club (operated by TV workout pro Jake Steinfeld) features state-of-the-art Polaris equipment, aerobics, free weights, and personal trainers. The club is open from 8 A.M. to 10 P.M. Cost is based on the equipment and classes chosen. There also is a small health club at the *Swan*, with exercise equipment and aerobics classes.

HORSEBACK RIDING: Trail rides into the pine woods and scrubby palmetto country leave from the middle of *Fort Wilderness* campground four to six times daily depending on the season. This is not for gallopers—you can't ride off on your own—and the horses have been culled for gentleness, so that the trips are suitable even for nonriders. Cost is $16 a person for both day visitors and resort guests (no children under nine are permitted to ride). There is a weight limit of 250 pounds. For reservations, which are recommended, phone 824-2832 up to five days in advance.

Good Meals, Great Times

Although fast food is in great supply, it is by no means all of the Walt Disney World food story. Epcot Center adds international flavors to the WDW palate. The numerous restaurants at the Disney Village Marketplace, the unique options at the Disney-MGM Studios Theme Park, and the first other-than-Disney-run eateries at Pleasure Island make deciding where to dine a confusing dilemma.

Because the number of eateries around the World is so large and so varied, this chapter presents meal information in three different ways. To find a specific restaurant, we've provided an alphabetized directory to all restaurants on the property with their exact locations. If you are getting hungry in a particular part of the World, the second section of this chapter offers an area-by-area rundown of all operative eateries. Finally, this chapter also contains a meal-by-meal selection of eating places. These restaurants are organized by breakfast, lunch, and dinner specialties, and we've indicated certain entries for which we think it's worth going a bit out of your way. Menus and prices vary during the year. **Note:** All Walt Disney World restaurants are now nonsmoking only. Smoking is prohibited in lines for fast-food counters as well. The letters that conclude each entry are a key to the meals served there: breakfast (B), lunch (L), dinner (D), or snacks (S).

Restaurants of WDW

The list below includes all the restaurants, lounges, and snack spots currently operating in Walt Disney World—at the hotels, at *Fort Wilderness* resort, at the Disney Village Marketplace, at Pleasure Island, and at the Magic Kingdom, Epcot Center, and the Disney-MGM Studios Theme Park.

In the sections following this listing, all the restaurants are described in detail. As an indication of what you should expect to spend for a meal, we've classified restaurants as very expensive (dinners $50 and up); expensive (lunches over $25, dinners $30 and up); moderate (lunches $10 to $25, dinners $20 to $30); inexpensive (lunches under $15, dinners under $20). These prices are for an average meal for two, not including drinks, tax, or tips.

Acadian Pizza 'n' Pasta: *Dixie Landings*; in Colonel's Cotton Mill

Adventureland Veranda: Magic Kingdom; at the east edge of Adventureland

Akershus: Epcot Center; in the Norway Pavilion, in World Showcase

Ale and Compass: *Yacht Club* resort; in the lobby

All-Star Music Resort Food Court: *All-Star Music* resort, in the Commercial Center

All-Star Sports Resort Food Court: *All-Star Sports* resort, in the Commercial Center

Aloha Isle: Magic Kingdom; in Adventureland, adjoining the *Adventureland Veranda* on the west

Ariel's: *Beach Club* resort; on the first floor

Artist Point: *Wilderness Lodge*, in the main lodge building

Aunt Polly's Landing: Magic Kingdom; in Frontierland, on Tom Sawyer Island

Au Petit Café: Epcot Center; on the World Showcase Promenade in the France Pavilion, in World Showcase

Backlot Express: Disney-MGM Studios Theme Park; near the Epic Stunt Theater

Back Porch Lounge: *Disney Inn*; in the *Disney Inn* restaurant

Banana Cabana: *Caribbean Beach* resort; near the pool

Barefoot Bar: *Polynesian* resort; near the pool

Basin Street Burgers and Chicken: *Port Orleans*, at the Sassagoula Floatworks and Food Factory

Baton Rouge Lounge: Disney Village Marketplace; on the main deck of the *Empress Lilly*

Beaches and Cream Soda Shop: *Yacht Club* and *Beach Club* resorts; in the central area between the two hotels

Beach Shack: *Fort Wilderness* resort; near the beach

Beverage Base: Epcot Center; in CommuniCore East, in the *Stargate* restaurant

Biergarten: Epcot Center; to the rear of the St. Georgsplatz in the Germany Pavilion, in World Showcase

Bistro de Paris: Epcot Center; upstairs at the France Pavilion, in World Showcase

Bleu Bayou Burgers and Chicken: *Dixie Landings*; in Colonel's Cotton Mill

Boatwright's Dining Hall: *Dixie Landings*; adjacent to the Cotton Co-Op Lounge

Bonfamille's Café: *Port Orleans*; off the main lobby, across from the front desk

Bonnet Creek Golf Club: Bonnet Creek Golf Clubhouse

Boulangerie Pâtisserie: Epcot Center; France Pavilion, around the corner from *Chefs de France*, in World Showcase

Bridgetown Broiler: *Caribbean Beach* resort; at Old Port Royale

Cabana Bar & Grill: *Dolphin*; at the pool

Cajun Broiler: *Dixie Landings*; in Colonel's Cotton Mill

Cantina de San Angel: Epcot Center; on the World Showcase Promenade opposite the Mexico Pavilion's pyramid

Cape May Café: *Beach Club* resort; in the lobby

Cap'n Jack's Oyster Bar: Disney Village Marketplace; on the edge of Buena Vista Lagoon

Captain Cook's Snack and Ice Cream Company: *Polynesian* resort; on the lobby level of the Great Ceremonial House

Captain's Tavern: *Caribbean Beach* resort; at Old Port Royale

Carnivale Bar: *Dolphin*; in the *Ristorante Carnivale*

Catwalk Bar: Disney-MGM Studios Theme Park; above the *Soundstage* restaurant

Chef Mickey's Village Restaurant: Disney Village Marketplace; on Buena Vista Lagoon

Chefs de France: Epcot Center; France Pavilion, in World Showcase

Churro Wagon: Magic Kingdom; at the entrance to Frontierland

Cinnamon Bay Bakery: *Caribbean Beach* resort; at Old Port Royale

Columbia Harbour House: Magic Kingdom; in Liberty Square near the entrance to Fantasyland

Concourse Grille: *Contemporary* resort; Grand Canyon Concourse (fourth floor)

Contemporary Café: *Contemporary* resort; on the fourth floor

Copa Banana: *Dolphin*; on the lobby level

Coral Café: *Dolphin*; on the lower level

Coral Isle Café: *Polynesian* resort; on the second floor of the Great Ceremonial House, around the corner from *Papeete Bay Verandah*

Coral Reef: Epcot Center; in Future World's The Living Seas

Cotton Co-Op: *Dixie Landings*; in Colonel's Cotton Mill

Crew's Cup Lounge: *Yacht Club* resort; next to the *Yachtsman's Steakhouse*

Crockett's Tavern: *Fort Wilderness* resort; in Pioneer Hall

Crystal Palace: Magic Kingdom; near the Adventureland Bridge, at the north end of Main Street

Diamond Horseshoe: Magic Kingdom; in Frontierland at the edge of Liberty Square

Diamond Mine: *Disney Inn*; in Happy's Hollow

Dinosaur Gertie's: Disney-MGM Studios Theme Park; on Echo Lake

Disney-MGM Studios Commissary: Disney-MGM Studios Theme Park; near the Great Movie Ride

Dolphin Fountain: *Dolphin*; on the lower level

Donald's Dairy Dip: Disney Village Marketplace

D-Zertz: Pleasure Island; near Propeller Heads

Egg Roll Wagon: Magic Kingdom; in Adventureland, outside the *Adventureland Veranda*

El Pirata y El Perico: Magic Kingdom; in Adventureland, opposite Pirates of the Caribbean

Empress Lounge: Disney Village Marketplace; aboard the *Empress Lilly*

Empress Room: Disney Village Marketplace; aboard the *Empress Lilly*

Enchanted Grove: Magic Kingdom; east side of Fantasyland, opposite *Tomorrowland Terrace*

Fantasyland Pretzel Wagon: Magic Kingdom; between Pinocchio Village Haus and Cinderella's Golden Carrousel

Farmers Market: Epcot Center; on the first floor of Future World's The Land

Fiesta Fun Center Snack Bar: *Contemporary* resort; first floor

50's Prime Time Café/Tune In Lounge: Disney-MGM Studios Theme Park; on the south side of Echo Lake

Fireworks Factory: Pleasure Island; near the *Empress Lilly*

Fisherman's Deck: Disney Village Marketplace; aboard the *Empress Lilly*

Flagler's: *Grand Floridian*; on the second floor of the main building

Disney Inn Restaurant: *Disney Inn*; off the lobby

Garden Grove Café: *Swan*; on the first floor

Garden View Lounge: *Grand Floridian*; on the Windsor level

Gasparilla Grill and Games: *Grand Floridian*; on the first floor of the main building

Good's Food To Go: *Disney Vacation Club*; on the boardwalk

Goofy's Grill: Disney Village Marketplace; near Crystal Arts

Grand Floridian Café: *Grand Floridian*; on the first floor of the main building

Handwich Wagon: Disney-MGM Studios Theme Park; near Echo Lake

Harry's Safari Bar & Grille: *Dolphin*; on the third floor

Hill Street Diner: Pleasure Island; near Avigators Supply Company

Hollywood & Vine Cafeteria: Disney-MGM Studios Theme Park; on Hollywood Boulevard

Hollywood Brown Derby: Disney-MGM Studios Theme Park; on Hollywood Boulevard

Hot Dog Wagon: Disney-MGM Studios Theme Park; near the Chinese Theater

Hot Dog Wagon: Epcot Center; near the American Adventure, in World Showcase

Hurricane Hanna's Grill: *Yacht Club* and *Beach Club* resorts; near Stormalong Bay

Jacques Beignet's Bakery: *Port Orleans*; at the Sassagoula Floatworks and Food Factory

Kimonos: *Swan*; on the first floor

King Creole Broiler: *Port Orleans*; at the Sassagoula Floatworks and Food Factory

King Stefan's Banquet Hall: Magic Kingdom; in Cinderella Castle

Kringla Bakeri og Kafe: Epcot Center; in the Norway Pavilion, in World Showcase

Lake Buena Vista Club: Near the villas

Lake Buena Vista Club Snack Bar: In the clubhouse near the villas

The Land Grille Room: Epcot Center; on the second floor of Future World's The Land

Leaning Palms: Typhoon Lagoon; near the main entrance

Le Cellier: Epcot Center; near Victoria Gardens and the *O Canada!* film's exit in the Canada Pavilion, in World Showcase

Liberty Inn: Epcot Center; alongside The American Adventure

Liberty Square Market: Magic Kingdom, in Liberty Square

Liberty Tree Tavern: Magic Kingdom; in Liberty Square

Lobby Court Lounge: *Swan*; in the lobby

L'Originale Alfredo di Roma Ristorante: Epcot Center; on the east side of the piazza in the Italy Pavilion, in World Showcase

Lotus Blossom Café: Epcot Center; China Pavilion, in World Showcase

Lumiere's Kitchen: Magic Kingdom; in Fantasyland, near 20,000 Leagues Under the Sea and Dumbo, the Flying Elephant

Lunching Pad: Magic Kingdom; near Mickey's Star Traders, in Tomorrowland

Main Street Bake Shop: Magic Kingdom; on the east side of Main Street, halfway between the Hub and Town Square

Mama Melrose's Ristorante Italiano: Disney-MGM Studios Theme Park; on New York Street

Mardi Grogs: *Port Orleans*; near the pool

Marrakesh: Epcot Center; Morocco Pavilion, in World Showcase

Martha's Vineyard Lounge: *Beach Club* resort; near *Ariel's*

Matsu No Ma Lounge: Epcot Center; in the Japan Pavilion, in World Showcase

Meadow Trading Post: *Fort Wilderness* resort; near the playing fields

Mickey's Tropical Revue: *Polynesian* resort; Luau Cove

Min & Bill's Dockside Diner: Disney-MGM Studios Theme Park; on Echo Lake

Minnie Mia's Italian Eatery: Disney Village Marketplace; near the Gourmet Pantry

Mitsukoshi: Epcot Center; on the second floor of the large building on the west side of the plaza in the Japan Pavilion

Mizner's Lounge: *Grand Floridian*; on the Alcazar level

Montego's Deli: *Caribbean Beach* resort; at Old Port Royale

Muddy Rivers: *Dixie Landings*; near Ol' Man Island

Narcoossee's: *Grand Floridian*; at the end of the dock near the marina

Nine Dragons: Epcot Center; China Pavilion, in World Showcase

1900 Park Fare: *Grand Floridian*; on the first floor of the main building

Oasis: Magic Kingdom; in Adventureland, near the Jungle Cruise

Odyssey: Epcot Center; astraddle the Future World/World Showcase boundary

Olivia's: *Disney Vacation Club*; on the boardwalk

Orbiter Lounge: Pleasure Island; in the *Rock & Roll Beach Club*

Palio: *Swan*; on the first floor

Papeete Bay Verandah: *Polynesian* resort; second floor of the Great Ceremonial House

Pecos Bill Café: Magic Kingdom; near the Walt Disney World Railroad's Frontierland depot

Pinocchio Village Haus: Magic Kingdom; in Fantasyland, adjoining It's A Small World on the east

Plaza: Magic Kingdom; on Main Street around the corner from *Plaza Ice Cream Parlor*

Plaza Ice Cream Parlor: Magic Kingdom; on the east side of Main Street

Plaza Pavilion: Magic Kingdom; east of the *Plaza Restaurant*, on the edge of Tomorrowland

Polynesian Revue: *Polynesian* resort; Luau Cove

Pop's Place: *Fort Wilderness* resort; inside River Country

Portobello Yacht Club: Pleasure Island; near the *Empress Lilly*

Port Royale Hamburger Shop: *Caribbean Beach* resort; at Old Port Royale

Potato Wagon: Magic Kingdom; in Liberty Square, next to *Columbia Harbour House*

Potato Wagon: Epcot Center; in the United Kingdom Pavilion in World Showcase

Preservation Pizza Company: *Port Orleans*, at the Sassagoula Floatworks and Food Factory

Pretzel Wagon: Epcot Center; in the Germany Pavilion, in World Showcase

Pure & Simple: Epcot Center; in Future World's Wonders of Life

Refreshment Corner: Magic Kingdom; on the west side of Main Street

Refreshment Outpost: Epcot Center; between the China and Germany pavilions, in World Showcase

Refreshment Port: Epcot Center; next to the Canada Pavilion, in World Showcase

Rip Tide Lounge: *Beach Club* resort; in the lobby

Ristorante Carnivale: *Dolphin*; on the lower level

Riverside Market and Deli: *Dixie Landings*; in Colonel's Cotton Mill

Roaring Fork Snack Bar: *Wilderness Lodge*, in the main lodge building

Rose & Crown Pub & Dining Room: Epcot Center; in the United Kingdom Pavilion

Round Table: Magic Kingdom; in Fantasyland near Cinderella's Golden Carrousel

Royale Pizza & Pasta Shop: *Caribbean Beach* resort; at Old Port Royale

San Angel Inn: Epcot Center; inside the Mexico Pavilion's pyramid, in World Showcase

Sand Bar: *Contemporary* resort; in the Marina Pavilion near the beach

Sand Trap Grill: Bonnet Creek Golf Club

Sand Trap Food Cart: *Disney Inn*; downstairs next to the Pro Shop

Scat Cat's Club: *Port Orleans*; at the Sassagoula Floatworks and Food Factory

Sci-Fi Dine-In Theater: Disney-MGM Studios Theme Park; near Star Tours

Settlement Trading Post: *Fort Wilderness* campground; near the marina

Sleepy Hollow: Magic Kingdom; in Liberty Square, opposite Olde World Antiques

Snack Isle: *Polynesian* resort; in a separate building near the east swimming pool

Sommerfest: Epcot Center; in the Germany Pavilion, in World Showcase

Soundstage: Disney-MGM Studios Theme Park; near the Animation Building

Southern Trace Bakery: *Dixie Landings*; in Colonel's Cotton Mill

Space Bar: Magic Kingdom; at the base of the StarJets in the center of Tomorrowland

Splash Grill: *Swan*; near the pool

Stargate: Epcot Center; in Future World's CommuniCore East

Starring Rolls Bakery: Disney-MGM Studios Theme Park; on Hollywood Boulevard

Station Break: Magic Kingdom; beneath the Main Street train station

Steerman's Quarters: Disney Village Marketplace; aboard the *Empress Lilly*

Studio Catering Company: Disney-MGM Studios Theme Park; near the Loony Bin

Sum Chows: *Dolphin*; on the lower level

Sunrise Terrace Restaurant: Epcot Center; in Future World's CommuniCore West

Sunshine Tree Terrace: Magic Kingdom; in Adventureland, adjoining the *Enchanted Tiki Room*

Tambu Lounge: *Polynesian* resort; on the second floor of the Great Ceremonial House

Tempura Kiku: Epcot Center; on the second floor of the Japan Pavilion

Teppanyaki Dining Rooms: Epcot Center; on the second floor of the Japan Pavilion

Territory Lounge: *Wilderness Lodge*, in the main lodge building

Thirsty Perch: Discovery Island

Tomorrowland Terrace: Magic Kingdom; at the Fantasyland edge of Tomorrowland

Tony's Town Square: Magic Kingdom; east side of Town Square

Tournament Tent: Magic Kingdom; in Fantasyland, near the Fantasy Faire Theater

Trail's End Buffeteria: *Fort Wilderness* resort; in Pioneer Hall

Troubadour Tavern: Magic Kingdom; in Fantasyland, next to Peter Pan's Flight

Tubbi Checkers Buffeteria: *Dolphin*; on the lower level

Tune-In Lounge: Disney-MGM Studios Theme Park; adjacent to the *50's Prime Time Café*

Turkey Leg Wagon: Magic Kingdom; in Frontierland, near *Pecos Bill Café*

Typhoon Tilly's: Typhoon Lagoon; near Shark Reef

Victoria & Albert's: *Grand Floridian*; on the second floor of the main building

Villa Centers: At the villa pool areas

Village Lounge: Disney Village Marketplace; next to *Chef Mickey's Village Restaurant*

Westward Ho: Magic Kingdom; in Frontierland, near *Pecos Bill Café*

Whispering Canyon Café: *Wilderness Lodge*, in the main lodge building

Wok Shop: *Caribbean Beach* resort; at Old Port Royale

Yacht Club Galley: *Yacht Club* resort; off the lobby

Yachtsman Steakhouse: *Yacht Club* resort; overlooking Stormalong Bay

Yakitori House: Epcot Center; on the east side of the Japan Pavilion's plaza, in World Showcase

Main Street

FULL SERVICE

Tony's Town Square: One of the best bets for Magic Kingdom meals. The menu offers Italian specialties, steaks, and seafood. Pizza and burgers with selected toppings are perennial favorites. Other lunch specialties include fresh pasta salads, a deli platter, and a fresh-fruit plate. At dinner there are grilled fresh fish, New York strip steaks, lasagna primavera, chicken with basil, and spaghetti with meatballs. For dessert: Italian pastries and spumoni complement a cup of freshly brewed espresso or cappuccino. Children's menus and menus for guests with special dietary needs are available. The decor comes straight out of Walt Disney's film, *Lady and the Tramp*. It is genteelly Victorian, with plenty of polished brass and curlicued, beautifully painted woodwork. The terrazzo-floored patio gives diners a fine view over the action in Town Square. Full breakfasts also are served: eggs, pancakes, *Lady and the Tramp* character waffles, cold cereals (with skim milk on request), cinnamon biscuits, and Danish pastry. Moderate. B, L, D.

Plaza: This airy, many-windowed establishment, around the corner from the *Plaza Ice Cream Parlor*, is done in mirrors with sinuously curved art nouveau frames. The menu offers hot dishes, along with fresh salads, hamburgers, turkey burgers, and cold sandwiches—plus milk shakes, floats, and the biggest sundaes in the Magic Kingdom. Café mocha, which combines chocolate and coffee, is another specialty. Moderate. L, D, S.

CAFETERIA SERVICE

Crystal Palace: One of the Magic Kingdom's landmarks, and its only cafeteria. Modeled after a similar structure that once stood in New York State and after another that still graces San Francisco's Golden Gate Park, it

serves standard cafeteria fare. Menu offerings include prime ribs, spit-roasted chicken, baked fresh fish, pasta dishes, and healthy salads. A wide assortment of tempting desserts also is available.

This is civilized fare, and the fact that it's here at all is just more proof—as if any were needed—that the Magic Kingdom is not just for kids. The place is huge but not overwhelming, because the tables are well-spaced throughout a variety of nooks and crannies. Tables in the front look out onto flower beds and the passing throng beyond, while those at the east end have views into a secluded courtyard.

The *Crystal Palace* also is one of the few spots in the Magic Kingdom to serve full breakfasts—scrambled eggs and hashed brown potatoes, biscuits, sausage, bacon, ham, hotcakes, French toast, Danish pastry, and cold cereal. Moderate. B, L, D, S.

VENDORS

Throughout the Magic Kingdom, there are ice cream wagons that sell Cookies 'n' Cream ice cream sandwiches, Mouseketeer Bars, and two especially wonderful frozen treats—lowfat strawberry yogurt and strawberry bars.

Popcorn wagons all over the park contribute their lovely aromas all day long. The Center Street Wagons near the intersection of Main Street, U.S.A. and Center Street sell hot dogs, pastries, and soft drinks.

At Epcot Center and the Disney-MGM Studios Theme Park, vendors purvey soft drinks, strawberry bars, popcorn, and ice cream galore.

FAST FOOD AND SNACK SPOTS

Refreshment Corner: The small, round tables at this spacious, old-fashioned, red-and-white stop on the west side of Main Street (located near the *Crystal Palace*) spill out onto the sidewalk. Except when the weather is terrifically hot, it's a delightful spot for fast food—hot dogs (plain or cheese, regular and jumbo sizes), brownies, soft drinks, and coffee. During busy periods a pianist is on hand to plink away on the restaurant's white upright. Inexpensive. L, D, S.

Main Street Bake Shop: This genteel little tearoom, with its small, round tables and cane chairs, is a good place for a light breakfast, a mid-morning coffee break, or a mid-afternoon rest stop. Assorted pastries, cakes, and pies are the main temptations. Also offered are delicious chocolate chunk, oatmeal raisin, Snickerdoodle, sugar, fudge, and peanut butter cookies, and cinnamon rolls baked fresh on the premises. Inexpensive. B, S.

Plaza Ice Cream Parlor: Ice cream lovers from all over the country converge on this corner of the Kingdom, which boasts the Magic Kingdom's best variety of ice cream flavors. Inexpensive. S.

Adventureland

FAST FOOD AND SNACK SPOTS

Adventureland Veranda: Bougainvillea cascades over the edges of a red-tile roof that looks as if it came straight out of the tropics. Tables are clustered outside on a small patio and inside under slowly rotating fans hung from mahogany ceilings. Off to the east end of this pretty, sprawling restaurant are a couple of open-air patios with views of Cinderella Castle. Screened from the gazes of passersby, these are among the most delightful meal sites in all the Magic Kingdom. Special *Adventureland Veranda* hamburgers and chicken with teriyaki sauce are among the offerings. Other Americanized versions of Oriental specialties also have their fans. For dessert: fresh fruit and assorted pies.

Note that waiting lines here usually take a few minutes longer than those of similar lengths in other fast-food establishments because of the greater number of choices. Inexpensive. L, D, S.

Aloha Isle: Adjoining the *Adventureland Veranda* (on the west), this refreshment stand often sells pineapple spears and juice along with other tropical offerings including Dole Whip soft serve. Inexpensive. S.

Egg Roll Wagon: Located just outside the *Adventureland Veranda*, this wagon features an assortment of egg rolls. Inexpensive. S.

El Pirata y el Perico: In English, the Spanish name of this snack stand, directly across from Pirates of the Caribbean means "The Pirate and The Parrot." The offerings: hot dogs with assorted toppings, including chili and cheese, tacos, taco salads, nachos, and a good selection of Disney Handwiches. Open during busy seasons. Inexpensive. L, S.

MAGIC KINGDOM MEALTIME TIPS

- The hours from 11 A.M. to 2 P.M., and again from about 6 P.M. to 8 P.M., are the mealtime rush hours in Magic Kingdom restaurants. Eat earlier or later whenever possible.
- When a restaurant has more than one food-service window, don't just amble into the nearest queue. Instead, inspect them all, because the one farthest from a doorway occasionally will be almost wait-free.
- Lines at the *Adventureland Veranda* don't move as quickly as those at most other fast-food eateries.
- Sit-down restaurants offering full-scale meals are usually less crowded at lunch than they are at dinner.
- To avoid queues, eat at a restaurant that offers reservations—*Tony's Town Square* restaurant, *Liberty Tree Tavern* in Liberty Square, and *King Stefan's* at both lunch and dinner, and the *Diamond Horseshoe*, a western-style saloon in Frontierland that presents an amusing show at lunchtime. Reservations for the *Liberty Tree Tavern*, *Tony's Town Square,* and *King Stefan's* can be made at the restaurants; *Diamond Horseshoe* reservations should be made at the podium outside Disneyana Collectibles on Main Street; book them as soon as you arrive in the Magic Kingdom.

Oasis: Tucked away near the Jungle Cruise. The perfect spot for a soft drink. Inexpensive. S.

Sunshine Tree Terrace: So close to the Enchanted Tiki Birds that you can hear the Audio-Animatronics parrot José squawking his spiel. Offerings here are some of the tastiest in the Kingdom: orange slush, nonfat frozen yogurt shakes, frozen yogurt, soft drinks, and the excellent citrus swirl—soft-serve nonfat frozen yogurt swirled through with a not-too-sweet frozen-orange-juice concentrate. Inexpensive. B, S.

Frontierland

FULL SERVICE

Diamond Horseshoe Jamboree: Several times daily, from about noon until early evening, a troupe of singers and dancers presents a sometimes corny, occasionally sidesplitting, always entertaining show in this Wild West dancehall saloon. Waitresses serve potato chips, cookies, sandwiches, before the show begins. Reservations are required, and they're hard to come by. They must be made in person, at the reservation podium outside Disneyana Collectibles on Main Street, and you can't count on getting them if you arrive much more than an hour after the Magic Kingdom opens. Those who miss the deadline can line up for possible cancellations, but with little hope of success except on days when the weather is so bad that some visitors depart early. Inexpensive. L, S.

FAST FOOD AND SNACK SPOTS

Pecos Bill Café: This is not one of those Magic Kingdom eateries that is tucked away so that only those who look will find it. Sooner or later, almost every guest passing from Adventureland into Frontierland—ambling by the Frontierland depot of the Walt Disney World Railroad on the way to Splash Mountain—walks by *Pecos Bill*. And as a sidewalk café, this establishment—fitted out with leather-seated chairs, ceilings made of twigs, and red-tile floors—has few peers. There are tables indoors (in air conditioned rooms) and outdoors, under umbrellas and in an open-air courtyard. Lean hamburgers, cheeseburgers,

barbecued chicken sandwiches, and hot dogs are the staples. Inside three shaggy animal heads hang on the walls in keeping with the Wild West theme. Guests who stand around long enough will see one animal turn to another and wink, for these are Audio-Animatronics figures, just like the ones on the walls at the Country Bear Jamboree. Inexpensive. L, D, S.

Turkey Leg Wagon: Located just outside *Pecos Bill Café*, this stand features extra-large smoked turkey legs. Inexpensive. L, D, S.

Aunt Polly's Landing: The much-trumpeted sense of getting away from it all that islands always convey comes home once again out on Frontierland's Tom Sawyer Island. Though only a couple of minutes' ride across the Rivers of America via the Tom Sawyer Island rafts, this landfall manages to seem remote even when there are dozens of youngsters clamoring through its caves, over its hills, and across its rickety barrel bridges. Therein lies the charm of *Aunt Polly's*. While the adults in a party get some well-needed R&R sipping lemonade in the shade of the old-fashioned porch and watching the gleaming white riverboats docking or chugging by, the kids can go out exploring. And, at nearby Fort Sam Clemens, kids can ping the toy rifles perched on the gunholes as if there were no tomorrow—an activity as delightful for youngsters as it is dispensable for grown-ups. It doesn't even matter that *Aunt Polly's* offers a selection barely wider than the fare that that lady might have served her youthful nephew—peanut-butter-and-jelly and ham and cheese sandwiches, cold fried chicken, apple pie, soft-serve ice cream, cookies, iced tea, lemonade, and soda. An excellent choice for lunch. Inexpensive. L, S.

Westward Ho: Soft drinks, cookies, pretzels, and potato chips are available at this stand across from *Pecos Bill Café*. Inexpensive. S.

Liberty Square

FULL SERVICE

Liberty Tree Tavern: At this pillared and porticoed eatery opposite the riverboat landing, the floors are made of wide oak planks, the wallpaper looks as if it might have come from Williamsburg, the curtains hang from cloth loops, and the venetian blinds are made of wood. Pieces of pewter and Windsor and ladder-backed chairs are scattered throughout the premises; there's a spinning wheel and a hope chest in the waiting room; and an old-fashioned writing desk and a cradle, copper bowls, and tea kettles arranged near the wide fireplace. The window glass was made using 18th-century casting methods, and most of the tables and chairs were mass-produced (for sturdiness' sake). So the *Liberty Tree Tavern's* charm is not of a random type.

At lunch, the staples are oversize salads and assorted sandwiches. Dinner offerings include fresh fish, shrimp, prime ribs, chicken, and lobster. Oysters and New England clam chowder are served at both meals. Same-day reservations are accepted and must be made in person at the restaurant. Expensive. L, D.

FAST FOOD AND SNACK SPOTS

Columbia Harbour House: A fast-food shrimp house with some class. Clam chowder, salads, assorted sandwiches, and fish

HEALTHIER OPTIONS

Dieters need not abandon all restraint for want of suitable foodstuffs at WDW. Most restaurants offer foods that are suitable for a variety of diets, including lowfat, low-cholesterol, and low-salt entrées. Most restaurants, including fast-food stands, are now featuring fresh salads, grilled chicken sandwiches, fresh fruit, turkey burgers, and non-fat frozen yogurt.

also are available. There are enough antiques and other knickknacks decking the halls to raise this place, located near the Liberty Square entrance to Fantasyland, above the ordinary. Model ships, copper measures, harpoons, and nautical instruments, and little tie-back curtains, small-print wallpaper, and low-beamed ceilings give the place a cozy air—despite its size. Inexpensive. L, D, S.

Sleepy Hollow: Soft drinks, cookies, hot dogs, Disney Handwiches, and a special Legendary Punch (fruity and not half bad) are for sale at this snack stand located opposite Olde World Antiques, near the Liberty Square bridge. Eat on the secluded brick patio outside. Inexpensive. B, L, D, S.

Liberty Square Market: Fresh fruit including bananas, apples, and sliced melon on ice are among the offerings at this refreshing spot. Inexpensive. S.

Fantasyland

FULL SERVICE

King Stefan's Banquet Hall: The hostesses at this establishment (named for Sleeping Beauty's father) wear 13th-century-style French headdresses and long medieval gowns with overskirts. The hall itself is high-ceilinged and as majestic as the old mead

hall it is supposed to represent. The delightful fruit or seafood salads or roast beef sandwiches on the noontime menu make lunch here pleasant indeed. At dinner, there are prime ribs, seafood, and chicken. There's also a children's menu and Cinderella is usually on hand to entertain children and grownups alike.

Reservations are required for both lunch and dinner. To make them, present yourself at the Castle door as soon after arriving in the Magic Kingdom as possible. Expensive. L, D.

FAST FOOD AND SNACK SPOTS

Pinocchio Village Haus: This is another of those Magic Kingdom restaurants that seems a lot smaller from the outside than it really is, thanks to a labyrinthine arrangement of a half-dozen rooms decorated with antique

cuckoo clocks, European tile-fronted ovens, oak peasant chairs, and murals depicting characters from Pinocchio's story—Figaro the Cat, Cleo the Goldfish, Monstro the Whale, and Geppetto, the puppet's creator. The menu offers hot dogs, hamburgers, turkey burgers, cold sandwiches, and pasta salad. Inexpensive. L, D, S.

Enchanted Grove: A small stand that's the perfect spot for lemonade, lemonade slush, or a soft-serve swirl. Inexpensive. S.

Troubadour Tavern: Soft drinks and chips are available at this small refreshment stand west of Cinderella's Golden Carrousel. Inexpensive. S.

Round Table: Ice cream gets top billing here—soft-serve cones in chocolate, vanilla, and chocolate-vanilla swirl; hot-fudge sundaes; and root-beer floats. Inexpensive. S.

Tournament Tent: Soft drinks, milk shakes, chips, brownies, and cookies are on the menu. (Open seasonally.) Inexpensive. S.

Lumiere's Kitchen: Located near Dumbo, the Flying Elephant, catering to kids with a variety of selections to please even finicky eaters. Inexpensive. L, D, S.

Tomorrowland

FAST FOOD AND SNACK STOPS

Tomorrowland Terrace: The largest fast-food spot in the Magic Kingdom, where the menu features hot and cold sandwiches and soups and salads. Inexpensive. L, D, S.

Lunching Pad: This small spot between the Space Port and Mickey's Star Traders serves natural foods, frozen yogurt, and fresh fruit. Inexpensive. S.

Plaza Pavilion: Just east of the *Plaza*, this sleek pink-and-purple-and-orange spot on the edge of Tomorrowland serves pan pizzas, pasta salad, and Italian specialty sandwiches. Some particularly pleasant tables look past the graceful willow trees nearby, toward the Hub Waterways and an impressive topiary sea serpent. Inexpensive. L, D, S.

Space Bar: Located at the base of the StarJets in the center of Tomorrowland's vast concrete plaza, this small spot offers Disney Handwiches, which are bread cones with a variety of fillings that can be easily consumed using only one hand, and chips, plus assorted desserts and a variety of soft drinks. Inexpensive. L, S.

A WORD TO THE WISE

Ride Space Mountain *before* eating, not afterward. The trip can uncomfortably jostle even the strongest stomach.

In Epcot Center

Restaurants within each area of Epcot Center are described as they would be encountered in Future World while moving counterclockwise from Spaceship Earth, and in World Showcase while walking counterclockwise around World Showcase Lagoon. **Note:** Reservations are an absolute must at certain Epcot Center restaurants, and they may not be easy to come by without following the instructions in the box on page 222.

Future World

FULL SERVICE

The Land Grille Room: Sleek wood-trimmed booths, upholstered in garnet-red velvet and illuminated with handsome brass lamps, make this an exceptionally attractive restaurant. Dinners feature Maine lobster, stir-fried shrimp with vegetables and pasta, prime ribs, steak, and Oriental-spiced chicken. At lunch, the dinner entrées are available along with a variety of sandwiches, including a club sandwich of roasted turkey, Smithfield ham, lettuce, and tomato on toasted cheese bread. There also is a small children's menu available. Breakfast is served here, as well.

An added bonus is that the restaurant revolves, and as it does so it provides a fine view over the thunderstorm, sandstorm, prairie, and rain forest scenes of the Listen to the Land boat ride down below. The scenes were designed with diners in mind, and provide them with a peek into a farmhouse window out of viewing range of the waterborne passengers below. Reservations are suggested for lunch and dinner; those holding reservation confirmation tickets for either meal may bypass any queue that might exist at the pavilion's front entrance within 15 minutes of the scheduled meal seating time. Moderate to expensive. B, L, D.

Coral Reef: Decorated in cool greens and blues to complement its Living Seas surroundings, this restaurant offers diners a panoramic view of the living coral reef through large, clear, viewing windows. The acrylic windows are eight feet high and more than eight inches thick. The dining room is constructed on several tiers, so all 264 guests have an unobstructed view. The menu features fresh fish and shellfish, including baked clams, oysters on the half shell, pan-fried swordfish served with a Thai curry lobster sauce, Mediterranean shrimp baked with tomatoes, leeks, and onions, and Maine lobster with crabmeat stuffing. Landlubber selections also are available. The menu varies seasonally, and reservations are necessary. Expensive. L, D.

FAST FOOD AND SNACK SPOTS

Sunrise Terrace: Pizza, pasta, and antipasto salad are the specialties at this eatery located in CommuniCore West, opposite the *Stargate* restaurant. The decor is traditional Italian, accented by some unusual neon lights. Inexpensive. L, D, S.

Farmers Market: One of the most interesting of the Epcot Center eateries, and a wrinkle on the Walt Disney World fast-food scene, this handful of very special counter-service stands is located on the lower level of The Land Pavilion. Each of these stands boasts a unique menu. The soup-and-salad stand offers New England fish chowder, seafood salad, impressive fruit salad, breast of chicken salad, and rottini pasta salad. The *Bakery's* morning offerings include bagels and cream cheese, jumbo cinnamon rolls, Danish pastries, and bran, corn, and blueberry muffins. After 11 A.M., apple pies appear, along with cheesecake and chocolate cake, rich-looking brownies, hermit cookies with cinnamon, and loaves of date-nut bread and cheese bread (the same cheese bread served upstairs in *The Land Grille Room*)—plus chocolate-chip cookies baked on the premises. (These are so delicious that some Disney employees make special trips to The Land just to nibble on them.)

The *Barbecue Store* sells barbecued beef sandwiches, barbecued chicken-breast sandwiches, half chickens, beans, and cornbread muffins. The *Cheese Shoppe* offers cheese, fruit platters, quiche, fettuccine with chicken, and vegetable lasagna. The *Picnic Fare* selections include assorted cheeses, smoked sausage, and fresh fruit. A sandwich stand regales the hungry with several types of hefty combinations, including the Disney Handwich, while an ice cream stand tempts guests with cooling cones and cups. The *Potato Store* serves steaming baked potatoes stuffed with beef-in-wine sauce, cheddar cheese with bacon, or other fillings. Even the *Beverage House* here offers something special—not only chocolate, strawberry, or vanilla milk shakes, chocolate milk, buttermilk, hot chocolate, and an array of soft drinks, but also vegetable juice, peach nectar, papaya juice, and orange juice.

Each stand has a farm-style facade done in bright colors, not unlike those that might be found in agricultural exhibit buildings at a midwestern state fair. With bright, umbrella-topped tables nearby, the effect is cheery. Because of the wide variety of foods available here, this is one of the best bets in Epcot Center for a family that can't agree on what to eat. It's also a good spot for weight watchers. Inexpensive. B, L, D, S.

Odyssey: Located practically astride the Future World/World Showcase border, near the Mexico Pavilion, the *Odyssey* is accessible via three walkways—near the Mexico Pavilion, the World of Motion, or the World Showcase Plaza's WorldKey Information System kiosk. This handsome, hexagonally shaped establishment looks less like a fast-food eatery than a moderately fancy sit-down restaurant. That's partly because of the decor, a subtle amalgam of rusts and ochres, with a carpeted floor and walls and a profusion of green plants. It's also partly because the food-service lines are tucked away from the main dining area. The fact that tables are spread over several levels enhances the already-pleasant ambience by making the whole place feel smaller than it really is. There's never the feeling of having arrived in a cavernous mess hall.

As for the menu, it's absolutely all-American: burgers, hot dogs, plus platters of chicken, tuna, and ambrosia salads. Freshly baked pies are a special treat. There are character shows featured here four times each day. Check at Earth Station for exact times. Inexpensive. L, D, S.

Pure & Simple: Located in the Wonders of Life Pavilion, this snack spot offers a variety of healthy treats including waffles with fruit toppings, sandwiches, salads, frozen yogurt, yogurt shakes, muffins, fruit juices, and more. Inexpensive. S.

Stargate: This large fast-food establishment, located in CommuniCore East, is handsomely decorated in shades of blue, mauve, and magenta. It's a particularly good bet when the weather is temperate enough to allow dining at the tables on the terrace outside—or when bound for World Showcase with finicky eaters in tow. It's also one of the few Epcot Center restaurants open for breakfast. The Disney characters make appearances during breakfast hours. Cold cereals, Danish pastries, fruit cups, blueberry muffins, and cheese omelets served with creditable home-fried potatoes are available then. But the real specialty is the extremely satisfying, if extravagantly named, Stellar Scramble. Made of scrambled eggs, cheese, ham, onions, and green pepper, this "breakfast pizza" might not win any prizes among connoisseurs of haute cuisine, but it's unquestionably tasty. At lunch and dinner, offerings include chicken sandwiches, hot dogs, hamburgers, fruit salads, and chef's salads. The Beverage Base is located inside and features soft drinks and frozen yogurt. The restaurant stays open until the park closes. Inexpensive. B, L, D, S.

World Showcase

FULL SERVICE

Rose & Crown Pub & Dining Room: The fare here is called "pub grub"—that is, fish and chips, steak-and-kidney pie, chicken-and-leek pie, and roast lamb. For lunch, however, it's possible to order hot roast beef with gravy and mashed potatoes, and a really delicious fresh vegetable platter served with a Stilton cheese and walnut dressing. At dinner the standard offerings are supplemented with roast prime ribs and horseradish sauce and, as appetizers, a dish known as Scotch eggs—hard-boiled, covered with sausage meat and fried, then chilled and served with mustard sauce on the side. (It's usually inedible back in Great Britain, but it's really quite tasty here in Florida.) A mixed grill of broiled pork loin, beef tenderloin, and veal kidney also is available for dinner. For dessert there's traditional sherry trifle, a confection of layered whipped cream, custard, strawberries, and sherry; and raspberry fool, strictly whipped cream and raspberry purée. Bass India Pale ale from England, Tennent's lager beer from Scotland, and Harp lager beer and Guinness stout, both from Ireland, are on tap. They're served cold, in the American fashion, not at room temperature, as Britons prefer.

The decor is really beautiful, mainly polished woods, etched glass, and brass accents. In fine weather it's pleasant to lunch under the sunny yellow umbrellas on the terrace outside and watch the sleek *FriendShip* ferries chugging across World Showcase Lagoon. On the little island just to the east, the wind ruffles the leaves of the Lombardy poplars, a species of tree that is found along roadsides all over Europe.

Horticulturally speaking, it's also interesting to note the vines on the pub's northwest wall. These Virginia creepers grow amazingly fast and, when Epcot Center opened, showed only a few tentative tendrils close to the ground. The spreading tree nearby is a laurel oak, distinguished from the southern live oaks more widely seen at Epcot Center by its upright growth and its leaves, which are shiny on both sides instead of just one.

As for the pub's architecture, it incorporates three separate styles. The wall facing the World Showcase Promenade is reminiscent of urban establishments popular in Britain since the 1890s, while that on the south evokes London's *Cheshire Cheese* pub, with its brick-walled flagstone terrace, slate roof, and half-timbered exterior. The canal facade, with its stone wall and clay-tile roof, reminds visitors of the charming pubs so common in the British countryside.

The pub section of the *Rose & Crown* serves such snacks as Stilton cheese and fresh-fruit platters, miniature steak-and-kidney or chicken-and-leek pies, and the above-mentioned Scotch eggs—along with all the brews noted above and traditional British mixed drinks like shandies (Bass ale and ginger beer), lager beer with lime juice, black velvets (Guinness stout and champagne), and black and tans (Bass ale and Guinness stout). This drinking-and-snacking spot is quite popular, so it's often necessary to queue up at the door. But the wait is seldom very long since few guests linger over their drinks. Reservations are not accepted in the pub area but are suggested for the adjacent dining room. Expensive. L, D, S.

Chefs de France: Multiple-star restaurants are rare even in France, so it's a notable coup that WDW has somehow managed to lure three of France's finest cuisiniers to run this rather remarkable restaurant. Paul Bocuse and Roger Vergé operate three- and two-star restaurants respectively in France (Bocuse's is outside Lyon, Vergé's just north of the French Riviera), and together with Gaston LeNôtre (widely recognized as France's premier preparer of pastries and other delicious dessert delicacies), they form a most unusual, absolutely formidable gastronomic trio. Bocuse, Vergé, and LeNôtre operate this unique World Showcase restaurant, and they have designed a menu that features fresh ingredients readily available from Florida purveyors. One or more of the French chefs

EVERYTHING YOU NEED TO KNOW ABOUT EPCOT CENTER RESTAURANT RESERVATIONS

Because restaurant reservation procedures have changed more than once since Epcot Center opened, it's important to confirm that the procedures described below are still in effect at the time you arrive. To check, call 824-4321. Also, try to arrive five minutes before your reserved seating time.

For dinner reservations: Guests staying at WDW hotels and Disney Village Hotel Plaza establishments can make advance reservations by telephone up to three days in advance. Consult your hotel's information kit for precise details. Otherwise, reservations must be made *on the day of the meal* at the WorldKey Information System screens in Earth Station— the building immediately past the waiting area for Spaceship Earth as one walks through Future World from the Entrance Plaza. Shortly after Epcot Center opens for the day, a line of would-be reservation-makers usually develops, and those at the end have less chance of booking a table at a popular restaurant at a popular time. For this reason, and because nobody really wants to wait on an unproductive line, it's helpful to arrive at the Epcot Center turnstiles about half an hour before the published park opening. Preferred seating times (5:30 P.M. to 7:30 P.M.) are usually booked by 10 A.M., so plan your evening meal with that in mind. Decide in advance where you want to eat and when (and choose a couple of possible alternate dining times and locales), and then send a member of your party on ahead to Earth Station to make reservations. (It will help if you've familiarized yourself with the location of Earth Station and the WorldKey Information System stations.) Each of the restaurants

has something special about it, and there's always a good menu selection even for unadventurous eaters—even in the more exotic restaurants of World Showcase. By the same token, don't arbitrarily dismiss the idea of an early seating if you can get it: If you lunch at 11 A.M., a 5 P.M. dinner will not only be welcome, but more importantly, it will provide the opportunity to spend the most pleasant and uncrowded evening hours enjoying the Epcot Center attractions. And don't abandon an Epcot Center restaurant experience altogether.

For lunch reservations: This meal provides guests with another chance to enjoy the most popular Epcot Center restaurants. It also has another important appeal: With a reservation for 1 P.M., it's possible to spend some of the most crowded hours in the park consuming a pleasant meal while less fortunate visitors are waiting in some of the longest lines of the day. Reservations for lunch also can be made at the WorldKey Information System or in person at the restaurant of your choice on the day you wish to dine. Complete this chore as early in the day as possible. Also note that you may be able to walk right in— say, if the time you have in mind is not too popular (like 10:45 A.M.). Most restaurants open for lunch between 10:30 A.M. and 11 A.M.

If all else fails: It sometimes happens that someone holding a reservation does not show up at the appointed seating time (reservations are held for only 15 minutes), so it certainly doesn't hurt to stop and inquire when passing a restaurant for which you have a sudden appetite.

makes regular visits to WDW to supervise and adjust certain items on the menu, though there has been very little need to tinker.

As you might expect, the fare here is fiercely French, but the foundation of the menu is nouvelle cuisine, which involves lighter sauces, using much less cream and butter than the classic style of French cooking. At dinner, appetizers include chilled potato, leek, and Lyon-style onion soup; salmon soufflé seasoned with tarragon and served with a white-butter sauce; oysters baked with spinach and champagne sauce; and ramekins of snails in garlicky herbed butter and hazelnuts. Diners choose among entrées from grouper doused with a rich lobster sauce, roast duck with wine sauce and prunes, fillet of grouper with salmon mousse, veal with a mushroom sauce, and chicken fricassee in a mild vinegar brown sauce. At lunch the menu offers various quiches, platters of French cheeses, country-style pâtés, and a croissant stuffed with braised ham and cheese. Hot dishes are offered, such as Lyon-style sausage baked in pastry (and doused with a beef-and-wine-flavored Bordelaise sauce), and a shrimp, crab, and fish casserole in a rich lobster sauce. A beef stew redolent of wine and a rich onion soup are available at lunch and dinner, as are an array of absolutely fabulous pastries and desserts (some wonderful LeNôtre specialties) and the thick, strong coffee known as café filtre (it's the French equivalent of Italian espresso). The atmosphere is as much a delight as the food. Tablecloths are crisp linen, and decorative touches of brass and etched glass abound. A modest wine list accompanies both lunch and dinner menus. Note that this can be one of the most expensive of all World Showcase restaurants. Reservations necessary. Expensive. L, D.

Bistro de Paris: One flight above *Chefs de France*, this restaurant evokes early 20th-century Paris. Peach and green curlicues decorate the ceiling above brass light fixtures and sconces, large mirrors, leaded colored glass, and simple wood chairs. A traditional bistro menu (created by the same trio of French chefs responsible for the fare at *Chefs de France*) features steamed fillet of grouper, chicken breast in puff pastry, and braised beef. The heartiness of the fare makes it an especially good dining choice in cool weather. (There's a separate menu "for the little gourmet"—kids under 12—at reduced prices.) Reservations accepted. Expensive. L, D.

Au Petit Café: Located prominently in front of the France Pavilion, along the World Showcase Promenade, this sidewalk café is a delightful place to stop for a snack or light meal. Under a large canopy with small round tables and black-jacketed waiters, it's as pleasant as it can be, and it can't be beat as a people-watching headquarters. No reservations are accepted, and long lines can develop. So don't stop if you're tired or ravenous. Moderate to expensive. L, D, S.

Akershus: The Norwegian castle of Akershus, which dominates Oslo's harbor, is the most impressive of Norway's medieval fortresses. It is actually half fortress and half palace, and many of its grand halls continue to be used for elaborate state banquets. At Epcot's *Akershus*, guests are treated to an authentic royal Norwegian buffet called the *koldtbord*, literally "the cold table." The diverse mix of offerings includes both hot and cold meats and seafood, and a selection of salads, cheeses, and breads. Traditional Norwegian desserts also are served, as are cocktails and Norwegian beer. Hosts and hostesses are on hand to answer any questions about the menu that guests may have. Expensive. L, D.

WHERE TO EAT IN EPCOT CENTER IF YOU DON'T HAVE RESERVATIONS

In Future World try the Farmers Market for quiche, soups, salads, sandwiches, ice cream, and pastries. The *Odyssey* restaurant, near World Showcase Plaza, is another good bet. So are *Sunrise Terrace* (in CommuniCore West) and the *Stargate* restaurant (in CommuniCore East).

In World Showcase, there's *Le Cellier* for lunch and dinner, a cafeteria in the Canada Pavilion. France offers the informal full-service eatery known as *Au Petit Café* (though there are sometimes queues), and Japan has its *Yakitori*

House, good for skewered bits of barbecued beef and chicken. Try the open-faced sandwiches at *Kringla Bakeri og Kafe* in Norway. The American Adventure offers the *Liberty Inn*, the China Pavilion has the *Lotus Blossom Café*, and outside Mexico, there's the *Cantina de San Angel*.

Marrakesh: The tastiest part of the Morocco Pavilion features a variety of examples of traditional and modern Moroccan cuisine. Waiters are dressed in *djellabah* (long robes). Moroccan menu specialties include roast lamb, chicken brochette, couscous (coarse steamed wheat served with lamb or chicken), and bastila (layers of thin pastry with chicken strips, almonds, saffron, and cinnamon). Sampler platters also are available. The beautiful tilework was done by Moroccan craftsmen. Belly dancers and Moroccan musicians entertain diners at both lunch and dinner. Be aware that this food may not be to everyone's taste, particularly children's. Reservations accepted. Expensive. L, D.

Mitsukoshi: This complex of dining and drinking spots, all operated by the Japanese firm for which it is named, occupies the second level of the large structure on the west side of the Japan Pavilion plaza. There are two options:

Tempura Kiku: This small corner of the *Mitsukoshi* restaurant is devoted to the batter-dipped, deep-fried chicken, beef, seafood, and fresh vegetables that are collectively known as tempura. The individual tidbits are crisp, tasty, and delicious. Expensive. L, D.

Teppanyaki Dining Rooms: The style of these five rooms is not unlike that popularized by the *Benihana* chain all around America: Guests sit counter-style around large flat grills, while white-hatted chefs chop vegetables, meat, and fish at lightning speed and then stir-fry it all just as quickly. Whether or not all the chopping and cooking is accompanied by a mildly comic routine depends on the sense of humor of the chef, but in any case the establishment is quite convivial. The seating arrangements make it quite natural to strike up a conversation with fellow diners; in fact, it's almost impossible to keep to yourself. Reservations necessary. Expensive. L, D.

L'Originale Alfredo di Roma Ristorante: This restaurant's *trompe l'oeil* ("trick the eye") perspective paintings make diners believe they're seeing real scenes rather than mere murals, and lend character to the decor of this popular establishment. As in the famous Roman restaurant of the same name, the specialty is fettucine Alfredo—wide, flat noodles tossed in a sauce made of butter and imported Parmesan cheese. But many other sizes and shapes of pasta, all of it made right on the premises, also are available; they are significantly enhanced by tomato, meat, pesto (basil, garlic, and Parmesan), or carbonara (egg, bacon, cream, and Pecorino cheese) sauces. There also are a number of less familiar Italian preparations involving chicken, eggplant, seafood, sausage, and veal, which are all very good. For dessert, choose from a number of specialties such as ricotta cheesecake, spumoni, tortoni, or gelati. Even if you don't eat here, it's fun to stop and just peer through the glass kitchen windows to watch the cooks cranking out the rigatoni, ziti, linguine, lasagna, fettucine, and spaghetti (which, the eminently readable menu reminds guests, were brought to America by Thomas Jefferson from Europe in 1786). Reservations necessary. Expensive. L, D.

Biergarten: Located at the rear of the St. Georgsplatz in the Germany Pavilion, this huge, tiered restaurant is set in a courtyard rimmed with geranium-studded balconies and punctuated by an old mill. It's every bit as jolly as Italy's *Alfredo's*, especially in the evenings, partly because of the long tables that encourage a certain togetherness among guests, partly because Beck's beer is served in 33-ounce steins. But equal credit for the gemütlich atmosphere must go to the restaurant's lively half-hour-long dinner shows, in which yodelers, dancers, and other traditional southern-German musicians—each appropriately clad in lederhosen or dirndls—play accordions, cowbells, a musical saw, and a harplike stringed instrument known as the "wooden laughter." The performances are exceptional, and the *Biergarten* offers an extremely entertaining evening. Diners are usually invited to join in the fun on stage. The food is hearty and very German: smoked pork loin, roast chicken, the spicy marinated beef known as sauerbraten, grilled bratwurst, bauernwurst, bierwurst, and jaegerwurst, potato salad, "wine"-kraut, and potato dumplings make up the offerings. Although there's no big show at lunchtime, a few "street" entertainers are usually on hand—and the setting is pleasant nonetheless, with the big mill waterwheel slowly turning and the sound of water splashing into the millstream blending with the rousing oompah music. Reservations suggested, particularly during peak seasons. Moderate to expensive. L, D.

Nine Dragons: One more item on Epcot Center's varied international restaurant list offers provincial Chinese cooking styles, including Mandarin, Cantonese, Hunan, Szechuan, and Kiangche. Entrées include braised duck (served Cantonese style), Kang Bao chicken (stir-fried chicken, peanuts, and hot dried peppers), and beef and jade tree (sliced steak and Chinese broccoli). Appetizers range from Chinese pickled cabbage to pan-fried dumplings and hot-and-sour soup. A selection of Chinese teas, beers, and wines also is available. The dessert menu features red-bean ice cream, toffee apples, and assorted Chinese pastries. Reservations necessary. Expensive. L, D.

San Angel Inn: A corporate cousin of the famous Mexico City restaurant of the same name, the food at this establishment, located to the rear of the plaza inside the Mexico pyramid, may come as a surprise to most visitors. Although the tacos and tortillas and other specialties that usually fall under the broad umbrella of Mexican food are available, the menu also offers a wide variety of more subtly flavored fish, poultry, and meat dishes. To start, there's queso fundido for two (melted cheese and Mexican pork sausage with corn or flour tortillas) as well as guacamole. A compote made of sweet Mexican turnips and oranges also is available—and delicious. As entrées, the menu offers pollo en pipian, chicken strips simmered in pumpkin seed sauce; mole poblano, chicken simmered with spices and a bit of chocolate; huachinango à la Veracruzana, fresh fillet of red snapper poached in wine with onions, tomatoes, and peppers; and much more that is good and tasty. Mexican desserts are largely unfamiliar to Americans, with the possible exceptions of the custard known as flan, and arroz con leche, best known in the United States as rice pudding. Still, such desserts as crepas de cajeta, thin pancakes filled with milk caramel; and helada con cajeta, vanilla ice cream with a milk caramel topping; are well worth trying. Dos Equis brand beer, tart lemon-flavored water, and delicious margaritas make good accompaniments. Reservations necessary. Expensive. L, D.

CAFETERIA SERVICE

Le Cellier: This low-ceilinged, stone-walled establishment tucked away on the lowest level of the Canada Pavilion, just off Victoria Gardens (not far from the exit from the *O Canada!* film), looks a little like the ancient wine cellars for which it is named. It offers a full menu of Canadian foods—which are a lot more interesting than one might initially have thought. The savory, Quebec-born pork-and-potato-filled pie known as tourtière is dished out in enormous slices, each one fully three inches high and covered with a tempting golden crust. Tangy Canadian cheddar cheese adds zip to some appetizing fruit platters, and roast prime ribs, chicken and meatball stew, and sautéed fresh salmon complete the selection of entrées. For dessert there's maple-syrup pie, a sweet cousin to pecan pie, and trifle, a traditional British treat made of layers of yellow cake, custard, strawberries, and real whipped cream—all soaked with sherry. Canada's own Labatt's beer is served in bottles. The combination of all this should make *Le Cellier* a prime destination for those who haven't been able to get a lunch reservation at one of the more publicized World Showcase restaurants but still want something more substantial than what the fast-food eateries are offering. Queue haters should be sure to avoid the lunchtime rush hour, which runs from about 11:30 A.M. to 2 P.M. The dinner menu features beef and maple dumpling stew, fresh poached salmon topped with crabmeat and a light cream sauce, and sautéed médaillons of turkey breast. (The line also is longer right after the *O Canada!* film, but don't be deceived; it moves quickly.) Moderate. L, D, S.

FAST FOOD AND SNACK SPOTS

Refreshment Port: A perfect spot for a quick thirst quencher, next to the Canada Pavilion. Fresh fruit, frozen yogurt, and cookies are available. Inexpensive. S.

Yakitori House: The nature of the food offered at this small but comfortable establishment in the Japan Pavilion is representative of the pace of life in that country. The average Japanese spends about seven minutes consuming his or her guydon, a beef-stew-like concoction flavored with soy sauce, spices, and the Japanese rice wine known as sake—all served over rice. That, together with skewered chicken known as yakitori (which is basted with soy sauce and sesame oil as it broils), teriyaki sandwiches, and Japanese sweets and beverages, makes up the offerings here. Located in the Japanese gardens to the left of the plaza, the restaurant occupies a scaled-down version of the 16th-century Katsura Imperial Summer Palace in Kyoto; sliding screens, lanterns, and kimono-clad hostesses add to the atmosphere. Inexpensive. L, D, S.

Liberty Inn: To many foreigners, American food means hamburgers, hot dogs, and French fries, and these are the staples at the *Liberty Inn*, located alongside The American Adventure on the far end of the World Showcase Lagoon. Chili, apple pastries, dessert cups, and chocolate chip cookies round out the selections. As a result, the place is a delight for small children, and also quite a pleasant spot for their parents. There's veranda seating, a pretty fountain, and a full complement of antique-looking decoys and chests. Inexpensive to moderate. B, L, D, S.

Refreshment Outpost: Another good spot for a refreshing cold drink. Fresh fruit, frozen yogurt, and cookies. Between the Germany and China pavilions. Inexpensive. S.

Lotus Blossom Café: Adjacent to Yong Feng Shangdian shopping gallery at the China Pavilion, this fast-food counter offers sweet-and-sour pork, egg rolls, and soup. There's a covered, outdoor seating area for 200 people. Inexpensive. L, D.

Boulangerie Pâtisserie: This bakery-and-pastry shop in the France Pavilion is not hard to find: Just follow the wonderful aroma and then watch the crowds line up to consume the establishment's flaky croissants and brioches, éclairs, fruit tarts, and chocolate mousse. These are served by women wearing black pinafores with ruffled white blouses, under the management of the stellar trio of chefs who run the popular *Chefs de France* restaurant not far away—Paul Bocuse, Gaston LeNôtre, and Roger Vergé. Hint for those who hate to wait: Arrive before 10 A.M. (this has become a favorite breakfast stop among Epcot Center veterans) or stop here about half an hour before park closing. Inexpensive. B, S.

Sommerfest: Bratwurst sandwiches, soft pretzels, apple strudel, Black Forest cake, Beck's beer and wine are offered at this outdoor establishment near the Germany Pavilion. Inexpensive. L, D, S.

Cantina de San Angel: Located along the World Showcase Promenade, just outside the entrance to Mexico's pyramid, this fast-food stand serves quick snacks like beef-filled soft tortillas; tostadas con pollo, tortillas topped with chicken and refried beans; and—perhaps best of all—churros, a sort of fried dough rolled in cinnamon and sugar. The *Cantina* is first rate for a tasty rest stop on a hot afternoon. Dos Equis brand Mexican beer is available, and the establishment's plant-edged terrace makes a fine grandstand for viewing the passing parade. Inexpensive. L, D.

Kringla Bakeri og Kafe: Tucked between an ancient wooden church and a cluster of Norwegian shops, this eating spot serves kringles, a sweet candied pretzel eaten on special occasions in Norway; vaflers, heart-shaped waffles topped with powdered sugar and jam; kransekake, almond-pastry rings; and smörbrods, open-faced sandwiches of smoked salmon, beef, or ham. Ringnes Beer, brewed in Norway, also is available. There is a 55-seat outdoor eating area. Inexpensive. B, L, S.

In the Disney-MGM Studios Theme Park

The restaurants in the Disney-MGM Studios Theme Park are the only places in the entire complex where a hint of the present meets the Hollywood of the 1930s and 1940s. It's true that the decor and atmosphere of the Studio eateries fiercely clings to eras gone by, but the ingredients in the food have been updated and most menus offer lowfat, low-calorie items. The meatloaf at the *50's Prime Time Café*, for example, is made with veal and shiitake mushrooms and the chili is vegetarian and served over angel hair pasta. And in a tribute to the Hollywood image, most establishments also offer a couple of "trendy" California creations.

All the Disney-MGM Studios Theme Park restaurants are described below. Reservations policies are subject to change, so be sure to call Walt Disney World Information at 824-4321 to check up-to-the-minute procedures.

FULL SERVICE

Hollywood Brown Derby: The home of the famous Cobb Salad is alive and well. This re-creation of the former Vine Street mainstay is quite faithful, right down to the caricatures (lovingly reproduced from the original *Derby* collection) that cover the walls. Even arch rivals Louella Parsons and Hedda Hopper (portrayed by convincing actresses) still reign over the restaurant from reserved tables, just as they did when the *Brown Derby* was in its heyday.

The 235-seat restaurant is predominantly decorated in teak and mahogany, and the elegant chandeliers and perimeter lamps (shaped like miniature derbies) are reminiscent of the original eatery. The china is embossed with the *Brown Derby* logo, and hosts and hostesses are all dressed in black tie. The atmosphere is just about authentic save for the theme park clientele who show up in shorts and tennis shoes.

The menu features the famed Cobb Salad, created by owner Bob Cobb in the 1930s. It's a mixture of finely (perhaps a bit too finely) chopped fresh salad greens, tomato, bacon, turkey, egg, blue cheese, and avocado. It's tossed tableside and served with old-fashioned French dressing. The modern incarnation of the salad also is available with shrimp or lobster. Other menu selections of note include Fettuccine Derby, pasta in a Parmesan cheese sauce with chicken and red and green peppers, and fillet of red snapper. The dessert tray is tempting—try another *Brown Derby* institution, grapefruit cake. A children's menu is available, although the slightly formal atmosphere is not likely to enchant most youngsters. Reservations are necessary. WDW resort guests can make them up to three days in advance touching "56" on their room phones. Disney Village Hotel Plaza guests can make reservations up to two days in advance by calling 824-8800. Other visitors must make reservations in person on the same day. Expensive. L, D.

50's Prime Time Café—Tune In Lounge: The setting is straight out of the favorite sit-coms of the 1950s. Each of the plastic laminate kitchen tables is set under a pull-down lamp, and the idea is to evoke a suburban kitchenette. Video screens set all around the room show black-and-white clips (all related to food) from favorite 1950s TV comedies, and these nostalgic bits are visible from each of the 226 seats. The placemats pose televi-

stars twinkle overhead in the night sky, and there are real drive-in theater speakers mounted next to each car. All the tables face a large screen where a 45-minute compilation of the best (and worst) of science fiction trailers and cartoons plays in a continuous loop. Popcorn is served before the meals, which include the Monster Mash—actually a Sloppy Joe made with turkey. Tossed in Space is the (huge) chef's salad and They Grow Among Us is a sampling of fruits. The Red Planet is an assortment of vegetables with linguini, and Meteoric Meatloaf is made with smoked meat. There also are hot and cold sandwiches and a variety of desserts, including Cheesecake that Ate New York; Twin Terrors, a banana split; Science Gone Mad, a mixture of fruit cobblers; and When Berries Collide, a strawberry shortcake. There also is a children's menu. Moderate to expensive. L, D.

Mama Melrose's Ristorante Italiano: A pizzeria has opened in a warehouse that has been converted into a dining room. Pizzas are prepared in a woodburning oven. Fresh fish and steaks are grilled over a hardwood charbroiler. Other menu items include lasagna, chicken, veal chops, and pasta with a variety of toppings. Reservations are recommended. WDW resort guests can make them up to three days in advance by touching "56" on their room phones. Hotel Plaza guests can call 824-8800. All other guests must make reservations in person on the same day. The restaurant is open during busy seasons only. Moderate to expensive. L, D.

CAFETERIA SERVICE

Hollywood & Vine "Cafeteria of the Stars": The distinctive art deco facade ushers guests into a contemporary version of a 1950s diner—all stainless steel with pink accents. An elaborate 42- by 8-foot wall mural depicts notable Hollywood landmarks, including the Disney Studios, Columbia Ranch, and Warner Brothers (back when they were the only studios in the San Fernando Valley). At the center

sion trivia quizzes and meals are served either on Fiesta Ware plates or TV dinner-style on three-compartment trays. The waitresses play "Mom" with considerable enthusiasm; they make recommendations and encourage guests to clean their plates (*or no dessert!*).

The menu is packed with "comfort foods." For openers there's alphabet soup, vegetarian chili, and the French Fry Feast, served either plain or with chili and cheese. Specialties of the house include Magnificent Meat Loaf, made with fresh veal and shiitake mushrooms and served with mashed potatoes and mushroom gravy; broiled chicken and spuds; chicken pot pie; and Granny's pot roast. There also are burgers with a variety of toppings, turkey burgers, hot roast beef sandwiches, club sandwiches, Aunt Selma's chicken salad, and the Apple-A-Day TV Tray (an apple served with cottage cheese and assorted fruits). Milkshakes, ice cream sodas, and root beer floats are filling accompaniments. And when you've finished everything on your plate, "Mom" will ask if you'd like dessert. Standouts include S'mores (you'll feel like you're back at summer camp), a graham cracker topped with chocolate and toasted marshmallows; sundaes; banana splits; and strawberry-rhubarb pie. Beer and wine are served. Kids love this place and a children's menu is available. Reservations are necessary. WDW resort guests can make them up to three days in advance touching "56" on their room phones. Disney Village Hotel Plaza guests can make reservations up to two days in advance by calling 824-8800. Other guests must make reservations in person on the same day. Moderate. L, D, S.

Sci-Fi Dine-In Theater: This 250-seat eatery re-creates a 1950s drive-in theater. The tables are actually flashy, 1950s-era cars, complete with fins and whitewalls. Fiber-optic

of the mural is the Fox Carthay Circle Theater, where *Snow White* premiered in 1937.

The 368-seat cafeteria presents a varied menu. At breakfast, there's the Hollywood Scramble, two eggs served with bacon or sausage and a choice of potatoes or grits and a breakfast biscuit; French toast; pancakes; omelettes; lox and bagels; assorted hot and cold cereals; and fresh fruit. Muffins, Danish, and croissants also are served. Lunch features a variety of salads, including the Seafood Serenade, a chilled salad of shrimp, grilled tuna, crab, and greens served with a Cajun remoulade sauce. Baby-back ribs, roasted chicken, and tortellini also are served midday. The dinner menu adds prime ribs, veal chops, and mesquite-grilled pork chops. Pies head the dessert list. Beer and wine are available, and a children's menu is posted. No reservations. Moderate. B, L, D.

FAST FOOD AND SNACK SPOTS

Soundstage: The setting of this 560-seat restaurant is from *Aladdin*. This is where guests can find Aladdin, Jasmin, the Genie, and Jafar, who are often available for photo opportunities. Music from the film plays all day. This is a food court and there are three distinct areas: at the pizza and pasta shop, deep-dish pizza, linguini, tortellini, and a cold pasta salad are on the menu; the sandwich shop serves three options, including a meatball sub, chicken salad, and the Soundstage Special—thinly sliced salami, pepperoni, and bierschinken, with Jarlsberg and smoked Swiss cheese; the soup and salad shop serves chef's salads, chicken salad with veg-

etables, New England-style clam chowder, and chicken broth with tortellini. Peanut butter and jelly sandwiches are available for kids at each stand, and dessert offerings are the same at all three stations: toffee cheesecake, chocolate-chip pie, and coconut cream pie. No reservations. Inexpensive. L, D.

Disney-MGM Studios Commissary: Fast food with a healthy twist is the bill of fare at this streamlined moderne eatery. The 550-seat restaurant is located between the Chinese Theater and SuperStar Television. In the open kitchen, chefs prepare chicken salad, teriyaki burgers, chicken-breast sandwiches, stir-fried vegetables, and vegetarian chili. There is a children's menu. Inexpensive. L, D.

Starring Rolls Bakery: Freshly baked rolls (not roles), pastries, muffins, and croissants are sold at this sweet-smelling shop. Coffee, tea, and soft drinks also are served, making this a good place for an eat-and-run breakfast. Inexpensive. B, S.

Dinosaur Gertie's: "Ice Cream of Extinction," claims the sign at this life-size dinosaur set on Echo Lake. Ice cream bars, fruit yogurt bars, ice cream sandwiches, and frozen bananas are the staples here. Inexpensive. S.

Backlot Express: This 600-seat counter service restaurant looks like the old crafts shops on a studio backlot. There's a paint shop, a stunt hall, a sculpture shop, and a model shop. The paint shop has paint-speckled floors, chairs, and tables; the prop shop has a delta wing kite, car engines, bumpers, and fan belts. There is outdoor seating available amidst stored streetlights, plants, and trees. Menu offerings include charbroiled chicken with flour tortillas and salsa, burgers, hot dogs, chef's salads, and chili. For dessert, there's chocolate-chip cheesecake, apple pie, carrot cake, and fresh fruit. Beer and wine are available by the glass. No reservations. Inexpensive. L, D, S.

Min & Bill's Dockside Diner: "There's good eats in our galley," proclaims the welcoming sign posted on the *S.S. Down the Hatch*, a bit of "California crazy" 1950s architecture. The little tramp steamer, complete with a cartoon-like smokestack, mast, and booms, doesn't sail. *Min & Bill's* sandwich offerings (served during busy seasons only) include sliced turkey, tuna salad, and the Santa Monica Submarine—mortadella, salami, and provolone. Specialties include the Cucamonga Cocktail, marinated gulf shrimp and fresh vegetables; San Pedro Pasta, tri-colored pasta with crab and shrimp; and fresh fruit with yogurt. Soft-serve frozen yogurt is served in cups or cones with a variety of toppings year-round. No reservations. Inexpensive. L, D, S.

Studio Catering Company: Guests on the Backstage Studio Tour come across this eatery at the end of the tram tour. Situated just behind The Loony Bin, the menu features desserts and snacks. Beer also is available. Inexpensive. S.

In the Hotels

Contemporary

Most of the hotel's restaurants are located on the Grand Canyon Concourse on the 4th floor, but there also are snack spots by the marina and in the first-floor Fiesta Fun Center.

Contemporary Café: On the Grand Canyon Concourse. Serves a bountiful, all-you-can-eat international buffet—one of the World's best buys—every evening. And each morning there's a buffet-style character breakfast hosted by Goofy and his gang. No reservations. Moderate. B, D.

Concourse Grille: On the Grand Canyon Concourse, this spot offers a variety of eggs and omelettes, pancakes, and fresh fruit for breakfast. At lunch there are soups, salads, burgers, and sandwiches. Dinner entrées include chicken, fresh fish, steaks, ribs, and chops. Moderate to expensive. B, L, D.

Outer Rim Cocktail Lounge: On the Grand Canyon Concourse, opposite the *Contemporary Café*, with a good view over Bay Lake. Specialty drinks, cocktails, and appetizers are served from 3 P.M. to 11 P.M. No reservations. Moderate. S.

Fiesta Fun Center Snack Bar: On the first floor adjacent to the gameroom, serves light fare 24 hours a day. Inexpensive. B, L, D, S.

Polynesian

Some of WDW's more interesting eating spots are located here.

Papeete Bay Verandah: Serves sit-down dinners daily, and brunch on Sundays. The prime ribs and baked stuffed flounder are the best choices for dinner, but more adventurous diners may be tempted by some of the Polynesian-style offerings. Selections include chicken with cashew nuts and teriyaki chicken. Dessert offerings include macadamia-nut pie and South Seas chocolate cake. The room itself is large and open and offers fine views across the Seven Seas Lagoon all the way to Cinderella Castle. Minnie's Menehune character breakfast is held daily from 7:30 A.M. to 10:30 A.M. Sunday brunch with Minnie is held from 10:45 A.M. to 2 P.M. After dark, Polynesian dancers and a small combo entertain quietly. Reservations are suggested for Minnie's Menehune breakfast and for dinner; phone 824-1391. Moderate. B, D, Sunday brunch.

There is no formal, printed menu. Each night there are fish, fowl, red meat, veal, and lamb selections, which depend on the best ingredients in the market, and which are described by your waiter at the table. The chef may even make a personal appearance to accommodate special requests from patrons. There also are choices of two soups, two salads, and desserts, including the specialty soufflés of fresh berries, chocolate, or Grand Marnier. There is an extensive wine list.

Once guests have selected their meal they are presented a handwritten souvenir menu. Women receive a long-stemmed rose. Jackets are required. One oddity of note: Every host and hostess here is named Victoria or Albert. Very expensive. D.

Flagler's: There are Italian influences at the hotel's largest restaurant. Pasta dishes, fresh seafood, veal, and steak, all served with an Italian flair. Dessert offerings include homemade gelato. The waiters and waitresses break into song when the mood suits, and the restaurant offers a lovely view of the hotel's marina. Expensive. B, D.

1900 Park Fare: The all-American menu takes a backseat to the decor in this 185-seat buffet restaurant. Big Bertha, a band organ built in Paris nearly a century ago, sits 15 feet above the floor in a proscenium. The bellows-powered instrument simultaneously plays pipes, drums, bells, cymbals, and xylophone. Mary Poppins joins other Disney characters here during breakfast. The dinner buffet features hot and cold seafood, salads, vegetables, breads, and roasted pork, lamb, or sirloin. Mickey Mouse and Minnie Mouse entertain at dinner. The offerings change weekly. Expensive. B, D.

Narcoossee's: The open kitchen is the focal point at this casual, airy, octagon-

Coral Isle Café: On the second floor of the Great Ceremonial House, around the corner from *Papeete Bay*. This standard coffee shop with a faintly South Seas decor serves the usual assortment of eggs every morning, plus granola and other cereals, and wonderful banana-stuffed French toast, one of the best Walt Disney World dishes. At lunch and dinner, the house does a booming business in big fruit salads, chef's salads, and a variety of sandwiches. Drinks, including the special Polynesian concoctions served at the *Tambu Lounge*, are available. A good choice when you want a no-fuss meal. Moderate. B, L, D, S.

Captain Cook's Snack and Ice Cream Company: A good spot for continental breakfasts, hamburgers, hot dogs, fruit salad, ice cream, and snacks; beer in cans also is available. Inexpensive. B, L, D, S.

Snack Isle: Most guests discover this snack bar on their way to the east pool, to which it is convenient. Breakfast items, hamburgers and hot dogs, a variety of submarine sandwiches, pizza, chef's salad and fruit salad, and light snacks like yogurt and ice cream all are available. Canned beer is sold here, as well. Inexpensive. L, D, S.

Grand Floridian

There are several good restaurants at the *Grand Floridian*, including one of the finest dining spots in the entire Orlando area.

Victoria & Albert's: The premier restaurant not only of the *Grand Floridian*, but probably of the entire Walt Disney World complex. The small dining room seats only 56, and elegant touches include Royal Doulton china, Sambonet silver, and Schott-Zweisel crystal.

Whispering Canyon Café: A traditional family-style coffee shop is open for all-day dining. The cowboy silhouette cutouts are great for picture-taking. Moderate. B, L, D, S.

Roaring Fork: Light snacks are available at the hotel's arcade. Inexpensive. L, S.

Disney Inn

Disney Inn Restaurant: One of the most relaxed spots in the World for a meal. The menu focuses on "American cuisine," featuring a variety of unique salads, sandwiches, and entreés for lunch and dinner. Seafood lovers will enjoy the all-you-can-eat rock shrimp. Traditional favorites like prime ribs, steaks, grilled chicken, and Maine lobster also are available. There's also a children's menu. Expensive. B, L, D.

Diamond Mine: A snack spot offering sandwiches, hamburgers, salads, soft drinks, coffee, and beer. Open during busy seasons only. Inexpensive. L, S.

Sand Trap Food Cart: The perfect spot for a quick snack—right at poolside. Hot dogs, soft drinks, and beer are available. Inexpensive. L, S.

Caribbean Beach

The six counter-service restaurants are located in Old Port Royale. A 500-seat common dining area serves all guests. Each counter has a variety of breakfast items as well. Moderate. B, L, D, S.

Cinnamon Bay Bakery: Freshly baked rolls, croissants, pastries, ice cream, and other treats are available.

Port Royale Hamburger Shop: Hot sandwiches, burgers, and soft drinks are on the menu.

Wok Shop: A variety of Chinese items, including egg rolls, sweet and sour chicken, soups, and lo mein are available.

Montego's Deli: Soups, salads, and cold sandwiches round out the offerings at this stand.

Bridgetown Broiler: Fajitas, prime ribs, and grilled chicken are the offerings.

shaped restaurant on the shore of the *Grand Floridian* beach. Specialties include grilled swordfish marinated in garlic, olive oil, and basil; grilled steaks; double lamb chops; veal chops; and grilled chicken. The Seven Seas, Seven Scoops Spectacular is a 48-ounce snifter filled with berries, seven scoops of ice cream, and topped with whipped cream and a touch of amaretto. Expensive. L, D.

Grand Floridian Café: Southern cooking is the specialty, and selections include a sandwich of roast turkey, smoked ham, tomatoes, bacon, cheddar cheese, and crispy onions, and honey-dipped fried chicken. There also are salads and an assortment of more traditional entrées. Moderate. B, L, D.

Gasparilla Grill and Games: Grilled chicken, hamburgers, and hot dogs are the mainstays at this take-out, self-service restaurant near the pool. Continental breakfast also is available. Inexpensive. B, L, D, S.

Wilderness Lodge

The American West theme is carried out with flair in the hotel's two restaurants.

Artist Point: Decorated with artwork representing the painters who first chronicled the Northwest landscape, this fine dining spot features wild game as well as more traditional items. Moderate. D.

BONNET CREEK GOLF CLUB

Sand Trap Bar and Grill: A variety of appetizers, sandwiches, and snacks are offered at this pleasant spot. Hamburgers, Reuben sandwiches, barbecued pork, and grilled chicken-breast sandwiches are on the menu. There is a full bar, and ice cream and milkshakes also are available. Moderate. L, D, S.

Royale Pizza & Pasta Shop: Pizza by the slice or the pie and a variety of hot pasta dishes are available.

Swan

Palio: This Italian bistro gets high marks for its homemade pasta and pizza. Other specialties include veal and fish dishes. There also is a strolling musician. Jackets are required for men. Expensive. L, D.

Garden Grove Café: Situated in a five-story greenhouse, this 24-hour dining spot offers a complete breakfast menu, and fresh fish and shellfish at lunch and dinner. The desserts baked fresh daily in the open pastry kitchen are worth special note. As you approach the restaurant take a look through the glass windows to see the chefs at work. A character breakfast is held here. Moderate. B, L, D, S.

Splash Grill: Breakfast, lunch, and snacks are available at this poolside spot. Drinks also are served. Moderate. B, L, S.

Dolphin

Harry's Safari Bar & Grille: Grilled beef, seafood, and chicken seasoned with herbs bought by "Harry" during his world travels are the specialties. Expensive. D.

Sum Chows: A broad spectrum of Asian dishes is found at this ambitious eatery. Dishes such as steamed Dungeness crab with black-bean sauce and sauteed pheasant with almonds, lime, and honey are on the menu, served in a relaxed but stylish setting. Expensive. D.

Ristorante Carnivale: Regional dishes from central Italy fill the menu here. Specialties include risotto with clams, mussels, and shrimp; grilled swordfish; and a brochette of homemade sausage, veal, and quail. A festivallike atmosphere prevails, so don't be surprised if waiters and waitresses burst into song without warning. There is a Sunday brunch with the characters here. Expensive. D, Sunday brunch.

Coral Café: This 24-hour dining spot features buffet breakfast and dinner and à la carte lunch. An à la carte menu also is available at breakfast and dinner. The Sunday brunch is quite extravagant. Moderate. B, L, D, S, Sunday brunch.

Tubbi Checkers Buffeteria: Checkerboard decor makes this cafeteria look a bit more interesting than the norm. The food is fresh and hot, and the lines are seldom very long. There also is a convenience store where snacks and baby care items are available. Moderate. B, L, D, S.

Dolphin Fountain: Homemade ice cream, including some very unusual flavors, is the highlight here. It comes in waffle cones, cups, or as part of assorted super sundaes served by an energetic young staff who break into song and dance several times during the day. Burgers, and sandwiches also are available. Moderate. L, D, S.

Cabana Bar & Grill: Burgers, grilled chicken sandwiches, fresh fruit, and yogurt are offered at this poolside eatery. Moderate. L, S.

Yacht Club

Yachtsman Steakhouse: As its name implies, aged beef is the specialty of the house. Guests can see the house butcher choosing cuts of meat in the glassed-in shop, and then see their meals prepared in the display kitchen. Fresh seafood and chicken also are available. Expensive. D.

Yacht Club Galley: Brightly colored ceramic tile tabletops help emphasize the yachting theme. Breakfast features a buffet and a full menu, lunch and dinner are à la carte only. Moderate. B, L, D.

Beaches and Cream Soda Shop: Patterned after a turn-of-the-century ice cream parlor, the menu features oversize sundaes, cones, floats, shakes, and sodas, as well as the Fenway Park Burger—which can be ordered as a single, double, triple, or a home-run. There are some breakfast items available as well. Moderate. B, L, D, S.

Hurricane Hanna's Grill: Located in the Stormalong Bay area shared by the two hotels. Hot dogs, hamburgers, sandwiches, French fries, and ice cream are on the menu. There also is a full bar. Moderate. L, S.

Beach Club

Cape May Café: A New England clambake is held every evening. A cooking pit used for steaming is in full view of diners, and menu items include lobster, clams, mussels, oysters, chicken, shrimp, corn, red-skin potatoes, stews, and chowders. There also is a character breakfast buffet each morning. Moderate to expensive. B, D.

Ariel's: The *Beach Club's* signature restaurant, named for the star of *The Little Mermaid*, features a 2,500-gallon saltwater aquarium. The menu is strong in fresh seafood (not straight from the tank, though). White linen tablecloths and seaworthy china accent the restaurant's theme. Expensive. D.

Port Orleans

Bonfamilles Café: The name of the full-service restaurant comes from the Disney movie *The Aristocats*. Steaks, seafood, and Creole cooking highlight the menu. Breakfast is also served. Moderate. B, D.

King Creole Broiler: Fresh spit-roasted chicken with red beans and rice and other traditional Creole dishes are featured here. Moderate. B, L, D, S.

Basin Street Burgers and Chicken: A variety of burgers and battered fried chicken are available. Moderate. B, L, D, S.

Jacques Beignet's Bakery: Fresh beignets, a delectable New Orleans tradition, are the attraction here. Hand-dipped ice cream and soft-serve ice cream also are on the menu. Moderate. B, L, D, S.

Preservation Pizza Company: Freshly baked pizza from traditional brick ovens, fresh pasta, and other Italian specialties are on the menu at this stand. Moderate. B, L, D, S.

Sassagoula Pizza Express: Hand-tossed pizza, salads, desserts, and soft drinks can be delivered directly to guestrooms.

Dixie Landings

Boatwright's Dining Hall: Be sure to notice the boat being built in this 200-seat, full-service eatery. The specialties of the house are Cajun dishes from the rural South. Moderate. B, D.

Acadian Pizza 'n' Pasta: Fresh pizza with a variety of toppings and pasta dishes and calzones are on the menu at this food-court location. Moderate. B, L, D, S.

Bleu Bayou Burgers and Chicken: Fried and grilled chicken and an interesting assortment of burgers are the offerings here. Moderate. B, L, D, S.

Cajun Broiler: Spit-roasted pork and chicken, and dishes native to Louisiana Cajun country, are available at this food-court stand. Moderate. B, L, D, S.

Riverside Market and Deli: This convenience store stocks sandwiches, beer, wine, snack items, and prepared salads. Moderate. B, L, D, S.

Southern Trace Bakery: Pastries, freshly baked breads, and sticky cinnamon buns are the specialties here. Moderate. B, L, D, S.

Sassagoula Pizza Express: Hand-tossed pizza, salads, desserts, and soft drinks can be delivered directly to guestrooms.

Disney Vacation Club

Olivia's: An assortment of Key West favorites plus some more traditional items are on the menu. A Winnie The Pooh character breakfast is held every Wednesday. Moderate. B, L, D.

Good's Foods to Go: Snacks, burgers, grilled chicken sandwiches, ice cream, and frozen yogurt are served. L, D, S.

All-Star Sports All-Star Music Resorts

Each of the resorts features a central food court located in the Commercial Center. Exact details of the offerings were not available at press time, but options are expected to include a hamburger stand, an Italian shop, a bakery, a barbecue spot, and a convenience store.

Pleasure Island

The six acres of Pleasure Island mostly bustle with activity during evening hours, but the restaurants are open for both lunch and dinner and offer a tempting option for WDW guests. The restaurants operate from 11:30 A.M. to midnight; most of the snack spots are open from 10 A.M. to 2 A.M. For up-to-the-minute details on opening hours call 934-7781, or check at Music Legends.

Portobello Yacht Club: The elegant Bermuda-style house combines high gables and beamed ceilings, bright Mediterranean colors and earthy terra-cotta tones. This is one of two dining spots operated by the Levy Restaurants of Chicago, and one of our favorites on the WDW property. The 326-seat establishment is divided into several informal dining rooms, each of which displays an impressive collection of maritime memorabilia: ship models, photographs, pennants, trophies, and navigational charts. An assortment of colorful mix-and-match dishes, utensils, and glasses adds a personal touch.

The bar, which is fitted with mahogany panelling and brass and chrome fixtures, recalls the classic details of pleasure boats of the 19th century, and the outdoor terrace evokes the mood of an elegant cruise ship.

The food, however, is the most special part of the *Portobello Yacht Club*. The bustling open kitchen turns out grilled meat and fish and absolutely delicious small pizzas baked in a woodburning oven. Try the quattro formaggi, a four-cheese pie that's a true taste treat, and a great appetizer or drink snack. Pasta offerings include *spaghettini alla Portobello*, pasta with shrimp, scallops, clams, mussels, crab legs, tomatoes, garlic, olive oil, wine, and herbs, and *bucatini all'amatriciana*, long pasta tubes with plum tomatoes, Italian bacon, garlic, and fresh basil. Be sure to save some room for desserts such as *crema bruccioto*, Italian custard with a caramelized sugar glaze or *cioccolato paridiso*, a rich layer cake

with chocolate ganache frosting, chocolate toffee crunch filling, and warm caramel sauce. A children's menu is available. No reservations are accepted. Expensive. L, D, S.

Fireworks Factory: The other of the duo of eateries operated by the Levy Restaurants. The 400-seat dining spot features high ceilings juxtaposed with antique brick walls, metal stairs, and a floor stained with black gunpowder. Some of the props around the restaurant are on loan from the Gruccis, the famous fireworks family of New York. There are two dining rooms and a bar.

Upon entering, guests are invited into a picniclike atmosphere where they sit at bench tables topped with black-and-yellow tablecloths. Ribs are the specialty of the house: baby backs and Texas beef. They are seasoned with a blend of spices, slowly smoked over an applewood grill, and then doused in *Fireworks Factory's* own barbecue sauce. Food is cooked to order to insure maximum flavor and freshness.

But ribs aren't the only thing on the innovative menu. If all the appetizers sound good, try the Fireworks 3 & 3 Combo of spicy hot chicken wings, sizzling catfish, and smoked barbecue shrimp served with a trio of sauces. Entrées include barbecued chicken, grilled filet mignon, pork chops, and Kansas City strip steak. Dessert selections include Atomic Chocolate Cake, topped and filled with chocolate mousse, and coated with chocolate chips; turtle pie; key lime pie; Edy's ice cream; and the Tollhouse Cookie Sundae, a large Tollhouse cookie served in a warm cast-iron skillet and topped with vanilla ice cream and hot fudge.

There also is a selection of specialty drinks including the Coconut Peach Explosion, a powerful combination of coconut, Malibu rum, and peach schnapps and the Pleasure Island Iced Tea, a mix of vodka, gin, rum, triple sec, cranberry juice, and Sprite.

A children's menu is available, as is a selection of T-shirts, sweatshirts, hats, and other items bearing the *Fireworks Factory* logo. *Fireworks'* special barbecue sauce also is available in jars to take home. Expensive. L, D.

Hill Street Diner: Located next to Avigators Supply. Individual pizzas, steak and cheese subs, chili dogs, and beer and wine are served here. Inexpensive. L, D, S.

D-Zertz: Pastries, chocolates, candy, frozen yogurt, and other such sweet treats are the mouth-watering fare available here. Coffee and cappuccino also are available, making it a pleasant spot for a quick snack. Inexpensive. S.

Disney Village Marketplace

Some of the World's best restaurants are located in this enclave on the southeastern edge of the property—at the *Lake Buena Vista Club* and among the many other eating places in the Disney Village Marketplace that are scattered among the boutiques, and nearby aboard the gleaming *Empress Lilly* riverboat restaurants. It's worth noting that while the restaurants hereabouts really hop at dinnertime, none is terribly crowded at lunch, except on Saturdays and Sundays, when Orlando and Kissimmee residents make the trip to the Disney Village Marketplace for a day of shopping. And these restaurants have the advantage of being just a couple hundred yards' dash from the marina, so kids can go hire a pedal boat or a Water Sprite (during lunchtime and in late afternoon) while parents linger over coffee or drinks.

Donald's Dairy Dip: This is a perfect spot for ice cream. Milkshakes and hot-fudge sundaes are only a couple of the many creamy creations here. Assorted Breyer's ice cream flavors, chocolate and vanilla soft-serve ice cream, frozen yogurt, and baked goods round out the menu. Inexpensive. S.

Cap'n Jack's Oyster Bar: The menu at this waterside spot is so full of good things— seafood marinara, shrimp, ceviche, crab claws, and clams and oysters on the half shell—that it's as good for a light lunch or dinner as it is for a snack, even though the place is nominally a lounge. *Cap'n Jack's* is a terrific place to be, especially in late afternoon, as the sun streams through the narrow-slatted blinds and glints on the polished tables and the copper above the bar. And the house's special frozen strawberry margaritas—made with fresh fruit, strawberry tequila, and a couple of other potent ingredients—are as tasty as they are beautiful. They're served in big balloon-shaped goblets, with a slice of lime astraddle the rim: tart, slightly fruity, and altogether delightful. Moderate. L, D, S.

Minnie Mia's Italian Eatery: Pizza, pasta, pasta salads, and sandwiches are on the menu at this restaurant. Beer and soft drinks also are available. Inexpensive. L, D, S.

Goofy's Grill: This is the shopping area's fast-food spot, serving hamburgers and French fries—to eat inside or out, plus thick milkshakes, soft drinks, and beer. Inexpensive. L, D, S.

Chef Mickey's Village Restaurant: This unassuming dining room is one of the most pleasant restaurants in Walt Disney World— and there's no waiting since reservations are accepted. There are fine views of Buena Vista Lagoon, and the sunshine that streams through the windows keeps a whole garden's

Lake Buena Vista Club: This comfortable, family-oriented restaurant serves a full breakfast. Dinner entrées include a variety of seafood, beef, and chicken dishes. A children's menu features spaghetti, chicken, and grilled cheese. The dessert specialty is an ice cream treat with hot-fudge and strawberry sauce tucked between two brownies. The cream-colored decor complements the natural wood tones. Ceiling fans and fern-filled planters add to the Southern feeling of the dining room. Reservations suggested; phone 828-3735. Moderate to expensive. B, L, D, S.

Lake Buena Vista Club Snack Bar: The only breakfast fare is coffee and pastries; otherwise hot dogs, subs, and other snacks are available. Inexpensive. B, L, S.

Villa Centers: Located at the villa's pools. Sandwiches, sodas, and beer are served. Inexpensive. L, D, S.

Aboard the Empress Lilly

Named after Walt Disney's wife, this 220-foot-long Disney version of the sternwheelers that plied the rivers of America during the 19th century rises gleaming and white at the west edge of the Buena Vista Lagoon, ornate as a Victorian ball gown, looking perpetually ready to sail off into the sunset. She really isn't, of course. Permanently moored, she's stacked from bottom to top with restaurants and lounges, and always bursting at the seams with diners and merrymakers having a very good time.

In some very interesting ways, the *Empress Lilly* is authentic, however. Like early riverboats, she has tall stacks like those that once allowed the sparks vented from the boiler's fire to cool off before hitting the all-wood deck or the often-flammable cargo. She also has "hog chains" strung between the two slanted poles that extend from the hull through the third deck. (Steamboats were flat-bottomed, with a superstructure light enough to allow them to draw only a few feet of water; the hog chains kept the boat from sagging in the middle from the weight of its cargo, and from "warping" at the stern from the weight of the heavy engine, boiler, and paddle wheel.) Since the *Empress* represents a cross between an excursion boat and a showboat, she has her share of jigsaw-cut gingerbread trimming, not only on the second story, or Promenade Deck, but also on the first level, the main deck. The railings on both decks are elaborate; the posts are turned and then bracketed to create an archway effect.

The hallways and public rooms are full of polished Honduran mahogany, Victorian-style flowered carpets, old-fashioned prints, brass fixtures, and tufted Victorian love seats with damask and velvet upholstery; the curtains

worth of house plants robust and green all year. The restaurant serves breakfast, lunch, and dinner, and offers fresh Florida seafood and a variety of pasta dishes. Chef Mickey strolls through the dining room every evening. Adjoining the restaurant is the living-roomlike *Village Lounge*. Fitted out with comfortable club chairs, it's a great spot for after-dinner drinks. Reservations are suggested and can be made by calling 828-3900. Walk-ins are welcome but there can be a wait. The hostess will provide you with a pager so that you can walk around the village and they will page you when your table is ready. Moderate. B, L, D.

Village Lounge: Located adjacent to Chef Mickey's, this relaxing spot is a good place to wait for a table at the restaurant. At Mickey's Cartoon Theater, located in the lounge, Disney classic cartoons are shown from 5 P.M. to 10 P.M. There also is a full-service bar.

CROSSROADS AT LAKE BUENA VISTA

WDW visitors also have several restaurants from which to choose at the Crossroads of Lake Buena Vista shopping center, across from Disney Village Hotel Plaza. These include *T.G.I. Friday's*, *Red Lobster*, *McDonald's*, *Taco Bell*, *Pebbles*, *Perkins*, *Jungle Jim's*, and *Pizzeria Uno*. There also is a pizza parlor and an ice cream shop.

are sheer. Each of the restaurants and lounges is a little different. Breakfast à la Disney, a character breakfast, also is featured aboard the boat. Seating times are 8:30 A.M. and 10 A.M. daily. Reservations are required; phone 828-3900.

Fisherman's Deck: This seafood spot on the forward Promenade Deck has a huge curved expanse of window—180 degrees' worth—and in the afternoon, the sunlight that washes the pale cream-colored tongue-in-groove paneled walls and the blue tufted Victorian side chairs is as remarkable as the food. At lunch, the chefs offer scallops with pasta; Caesar salad; Oriental chicken salad; hamburgers; corned beef sandwiches; fresh-fruit salads; and sandwiches made with grilled crabmeat, cheddar, tomato, and bacon. At dinner, shrimp, conch fritters, and Maine lobster are the specialties. There also are nightly specials. At both lunch and dinner, it's possible to order items from the *Steerman's Quarters*. Reservations are accepted (828-3900). Expensive. L, D.

Steerman's Quarters: This ornate main-deck salon is full of heavy red upholstery and turned mahogany spindles and paneling. It is named for the steering gear that would have occupied this area in one of the original stern-wheelers. While you're waiting for your food, you can sit by a big glass window that seems only inches away from the paddle wheel's gleaming white arms and watch it turn. Meat is the big deal—Angus steak and prime ribs—though there are a few items in the seafood category. The staff will try to accommodate

requests for items from the *Fisherman's Deck* menu as well. Reservations are accepted (828-3900). Expensive. D.

Empress Room: The most amazing thing about this restaurant (located amidship on the Promenade Deck) is not its food (though the menu is one of WDW's most ambitious), but the combination of service and atmosphere. The Louis XV decor includes painted-wood paneling, damask wallpaper, a shallow-domed ceiling with an Italian brass chandelier glittering with crystal droplets, and, between the tables-for-four along the wall, dividers fitted out with paneling and etched glass. Parts of the elaborate moldings are covered with real gold leaf (worth $8,000 when the *Empress Lilly* was constructed in 1977).

The restaurant was recently awarded a Mobil Four-Star rating, and a recent review by the *Orlando Sentinel* food critic gave it very high marks.

The culinary offerings include cream of artichoke soup with seafood, boneless frog legs with shiitake mushrooms, Caesar salad, roast loin of veal, sauteed Dover sole with macadamia nut butter and lime, roasted breast of African pheasant with natural juices, and more. The quality of the food preparation can be erratic, but this is among the most elegant eating places in the World. The restaurant seats guests from 6:30 P.M. to 9:30 P.M., and a 20 percent surcharge is added to each check for service. Jackets are required for men, and reservations are a must; they are available up to 30 days in advance (828-3900). Very expensive. D.

Fort Wilderness

Most people cook their own meals; supplies are available at the Meadow and Settlement Trading Posts (open from 8 A.M. to 10 P.M. in winter, to 11 P.M. in summer).

Trail's End Buffeteria: This informal, log-walled, beam-ceilinged cafeteria offers standard breakfasts (plus a seven-inch breakfast pizza, grits, biscuits and gravy) every morning; and during the rest of the day serves hearty lunches and dinners featuring barbecued chicken, fish, chicken pot pie, spare ribs, and more. There is a sandwich buffet and a taco bar at lunch. Specially priced children's portions are available. Saturday nights is the Hoe Down supper where an all-you-can-eat buffet of lasagna, spaghetti, and fried chicken is served from 4:30 P.M. to 9:30 P.M. Pizza is served every night from 9 P.M. until 11 P.M. (until midnight on weekends). Beer and sangría are available by the glass or by the pitcher. Moderate. B, L, D, S.

Crockett's Tavern: Appetizers, steaks, ribs, and chicken are available in this Pioneer Hall eatery. A children's menu is offered and cocktails are served. Moderate. D.

Beach Shack: Located near the Bay Lake beach. Sandwiches, soft-serve ice cream, assorted snacks, potato chips, corn chips, ice cream bars and sandwiches, and fruit bars are available. Beer also is served. Inexpensive. L, D, S.

DISNEY VILLAGE HOTEL PLAZA

At the Grosvenor: This highrise hotel features *Baskerville's*, a casual restaurant serving breakfast, lunch, and dinner in an atmosphere with a Sherlock Holmes theme. There is a Mystery Show on Saturday nights. Moderate. B, L, D. There's also *Crumpets*, a lobby café where continental breakfast, snacks, and lighter fare are available 24 hours a day. Inexpensive. B, L, S. *Barnacles* serves burgers and snacks poolside. Inexpensive. L, S.

At the Howard Johnson: The restaurant and adjacent coffee shop here offer the standard *Howard Johnson* menu in standard HoJo style—food that is reassuringly predictable, if not outstanding. The ice cream is first rate. Open 6 A.M. to midnight. Moderate. B, L, D, S.

At the Travelodge: *Traders* serves buffet and à la carte breakfast and à al carte dinner. Moderate. B, D. *Parakeet Café* offers breakfast, lunch, and snacks. Inexpensive. B, L, S.

At the Buena Vista Palace: One of the state's finest restaurants, *Arthur's 27*, is here. It boasts a wonderful view over Walt Disney World Village, and the food and service are both excellent. Very expensive. D. The *Outback*, decorated in an Australian theme, serves dinner. Expensive. D. The gardenlike *Watercress Café & Bake Shop* offers full meals and snacks. The bakery portion of the café is open 24 hours a day. There also are character breakfasts and dinners. Moderate. B, L, D, S.

At the Royal Plaza: This family-oriented resort serves a nostalgic American menu 24 hours a day at the *Plaza Diner*. Moderate. B, L, D, S. The *Giraffe* lounge features hot and cold hors d'oeuvres during its nightly happy hour from 4 P.M. to 9:30 P.M.

At the Hilton: There are four restaurants here. The *American Vineyards* offers regional American specialties, like hickory-smoked Vermont turkey, Florida stone crabs, and quail. Expensive. D. At *Benihana's Steakhouse*, chef's put on a tableside show as they cook up Japanese favorites. Moderate to expensive. D. The *County Fair* gives guests the option of serving themselves from the buffet or ordering from the menu. Moderate. B, L, D. For hot dogs and hamburgers alfresco, there's the *Rum Largo Pool Bar and Broiler*. Inexpensive. L, D, S.

At Guest Quarters: The *Parrot Patch* offers indoor and outdoor dining, with a two-story tropical bird aviary as entertainment. Moderate. B, L, D. The poolside *Bar and Ice Cream Parlor* is a good place for an afternoon snack or drink. Inexpensive. S.

Meal by Meal

When you're looking for something special in the way of a meal, and you're willing to go a bit out of your way to find it, the descriptions below should provide sufficient suggestions to sate your appetite. What follows are the highlights of WDW breakfasts, lunches, and dinners, as well as some suggestions for avoiding mealtime crowds at the eatery of your choice. This is a selective, not a comprehensive, list; for complete information see the preceding listings under "Restaurants of WDW."

Breakfast

Most people opt for eggs and bacon or something similar at their own hotel. But those who decide to go farther afield will be amazed at the choices available. For instance, the French toast served at the *Polynesian* resort's *Coral Isle Café*—made with thick slices of real sourdough bread, stuffed with bananas, deep fried, and then rolled in cinnamon and sugar—is one of the best breakfast concoctions ever.

At most breakfast spots in the hotels, there are likely to be lines between 8 A.M. and 10 A.M., the morning rush hour. So allow plenty of time at these hours, eat earlier or later, or stop at a snack shop for something light to stave off hunger until it's time for a lineless breakfast (or an early lunch). It's also possible to use the long card you'll find hanging from the doorknob of most WDW guestrooms to order breakfast from room service the night before. Villa guests will probably do

BREAKFAST WITH DISNEY CHARACTERS

At some sites, food takes second place to Mickey Mouse, Donald Duck, Minnie Mouse, Goofy, and the rest of the Disney gang, who take turns making special appearances at these especially delightful breakfast-time affairs. Breakfast à la Disney on the *Empress Lilly* riverboat restaurant at the Disney Village Marketplace takes place at 8.30 A.M. and 10 A.M. daily; the scrambled eggs-and-sausage meal is served banquet style. (To reserve, phone the *Empress Lilly* at 828-3900.) Another character breakfast, which takes place daily from 7.30 A.M. to 11 A.M. at the *Contemporary Café* in the *Contemporary* resort, features an enormous buffet, as does the one at the *Beach Club* resort's *Cape May Café*. *1900 Park Fare* at the *Grand Floridian* also offers a bountiful buffet from 7:30 A.M. to noon. Minnie's Menehune breakfast is served daily from 7:30 A.M. to 10:30 A.M. at the *Papeete Bay Verandah* at the *Polynesian* resort. Reservations are suggested. A Winnie the Pooh breakfast is held at *Olivia's* at the *Disney Vacation Club* on Wednesdays. There's also a character breakfast at the *Buena Vista Palace*, the *Hilton*, and the *Grosvenor* in Disney Village Hotel Plaza. A Sunday character brunch is served at at *Ristorante Carnivale* at the *Dolphin* hotel. At the *Swan* a character breakfast is held Wednesdays and Saturdays at the *Garden Grove*. Reservations are not necessary for most of the breakfasts. In Epcot Center, characters join guests for breakfast at the *Stargate* restaurant in Future World.

best at the *Lake Buena Vista Club*, where breakfast begins at 7 A.M.

Except during the busiest periods, restaurants in the Magic Kingdom are good choices for quick morning meals. Most fast-food spots serve coffee and pastry from park opening until about 11 A.M.

In Epcot Center, the *Stargate* restaurant in Future World's CommuniCore East offers cheese omelets, cold cereals, Danish pastries, and the Stellar Scramble (informally known as breakfast pizza). The Disney characters make appearances here. The *Farmers Market* in The Land offers bagels and cream cheese, as well as eggs and delicious pastries. The *Land Grille Room* serves a full breakfast until 10:30 A.M. France's *Boulangerie Pâtisserie*, where queues can run up to 45 minutes during most of the rest of the day, is relatively uncrowded before 10:30 A.M.—despite the fact that it offers delicious brioches and croissants and excellent coffee.

At the Disney-MGM Studios Theme Park try a home-cooked breakfast at the *Hollywood & Vine Cafeteria of the Stars* or a quick bite at *Starring Rolls Bakery*.

Lunch

Breaking up a day in the theme parks with lunch at one of the resorts can provide the energy needed to keep you going until closing time. A few of the eating spots do get crowded around midday, but the *Coral Isle Café* at the *Polynesian* resort and the *Disney Inn* restaurant at the *Disney Inn* are usually particularly peaceful. The *Disney Inn's* special dessert—french-fried ice cream, served on a peach half and drizzled with vanilla sauce—is well worth ordering.

Lunch highlights in Disney Village Marketplace are the *Minnie Mia's Italian Eatery* and *Cap'n Jack's Oyster Bar*. At Pleasure Island, there are delicious pizzas-for-one at the *Portobello Yacht Club*. Barbecued ribs, chicken, steaks, and pork chops are on the menu at the *Fireworks Factory*. Or for something lighter try some frozen yogurt from *D-Zertz*.

If you can't tear yourself away from the Magic Kingdom for even an hour to go elsewhere for lunch, there's still no lack of selection. Hamburgers and French fries are for sale at practically every turn, and then there are Italian specialties at *Tony's Town Square* restaurant; the pasta and seafood salads served at the *Columbia Harbour House*, in Liberty Square; or the vegetable and fruit salads available at the *Crystal Palace* on Main Street; the clam chowder and red velvet cake served at the *Liberty Tree Tavern* in Liberty Square; the teriyaki-sauced beef and chicken at the *Adventureland Veranda*; peanut butter and jelly sandwiches at *Aunt Polly's Landing* on Tom Sawyer Island in Frontierland; pizza at *Plaza Pavilion* in Tomorrowland; and Cinderella Salad at *King Stefan's* in Cinderella Castle.

As at breakfast, crowds can be a problem; the three hours between 11 A.M. and 2 P.M. are the busiest. To avoid the rush, eat a light breakfast and a big early lunch—or have a late breakfast and a late lunch. If necessary, snatch a mid-morning snack to tide you over until things get less hectic.

In Epcot Center, midday is a good time to sample some of the full-service restaurants offering ethnic specialties. Linger over their culinary delights, out of the heat of the midday sun, while crowds of other guests are lining up for attractions. For hamburgers and other standard fast-food fare, try the *Stargate* restaurant in CommuniCore East, *Liberty Inn* in the American Adventure, and the sleek, attractive *Odyssey* restaurant near Mexico and the World of Motion. The *Farmers Market*, in The Land, offers a huge variety, from baked potatoes and soups and salads to barbecued sandwiches and more, and is a good choice for a family that can't arrive at a consensus. The pizza quiche offered at the *Cheese Shoppe* there is a favorite, and the chocolate chip cookies from the nearby bakery make a good dessert. Ethnic fast foods are available at Japan's *Yakitori House*, China's *Lotus Blossom Café*, Norway's *Kringla Bakeri og Kafe*, and Mexico's *Cantina de San Angel*.

Among full-service eateries, *The Land Grille Room* is special for its imaginatively conceived regional American offerings, not to mention that delightful cheese bread. In World Showcase, meat pies and Epcot Center's best salad (the fresh vegetable platter) may be found at the *Rose & Crown Pub & Dining Room*; stir-fried meats and vegetables are the prime fare in the *Mitsukoshi* restaurants; Moroccan sampler platters are offered at *Marrakesh*; Chinese specialties are served at the *Nine Dragons* restaurant; hearty German food is offered in Germany's *Biergarten*; and fairly elaborate Mexican fare comprises the menu in Mexico's *San Angel Inn* restaurant. An enormous buffet is served at *Akershus* in Norway. The delightful *Au Petit Café* on the World Showcase Promenade in France is the only sit-down restaurant that doesn't require reservations, but the waiting line is often long. The most elaborate cooking is done at Italy's *Alfredo's* and at France's *Chefs de France*.

At the Disney-MGM Studios Theme Park, try the famous Cobb Salad at the *Hollywood Brown Derby*; a good home-cooked meal served by "Mom" at the *50's Prime Time Café*; soups, salads, pastas, and sandwiches at the *Soundstage* restaurant; salads, ribs, roasted chicken, and tortellini at the *Hollywood & Vine Cafeteria of the Stars*; chicken with tortillas and salsa, burgers, and chili at the *Backlot Express*; sandwiches and salads at *Min & Bill's Dockside Diner*; burgers, sandwiches, and stir-fry specials at the *Commissary*; or triple-decker sandwiches and burgers at the *Sci-Fi Dine-In Theater* restaurant.

Dinner

There's an awesome choice, from the humblest snack center to the *Empress Lilly*'s ambitious *Empress Room*. Walt Disney World is not exactly a bastion of haute cuisine, but that doesn't mean that dinner experiences are anything less than pleasant. Service is almost unfailingly good (slipping just slightly during the busiest seasons), and the best of Walt Disney World's dinners are just fine. For a night on the World, some good choices are the *Portobello Yacht Club* at Pleasure Island; *Steerman's Quarters*, *Fisherman's Deck*, and the *Empress Room*, all on the adjacent *Empress Lilly*; *Chef Mickey's Village* restaurant in Disney Village Marketplace; *Victoria & Albert's* at the *Grand Floridian*; the *Disney Inn* restaurant; the *Papeete Bay Verandah* in the *Polynesian* resort; *Ariel's* at the *Beach Club*; the *Yachtsman Steakhouse* at the *Yacht Club*; and the *Hollywood Brown Derby* at the Disney-MGM Studios Theme Park.

FOR FAMILY FARE: Children are welcome at every WDW restaurant, but the leisurely pace of service at some places can make kids fidget. But there are plenty of choices that are

GOOD MEALS, GREAT TIMES

well suited to dining en famille. Restaurants at the *Contemporary* resort especially good for families are the *Concourse Grille* and the *Contemporary Café*; *Boatwright's Dining Hall* at *Dixie Landings*, *Bonfamille's Café* at *Port Orleans*, and the food courts at the *Caribbean Beach*, *Port Orleans*, and *Dixie Landings* are other good choices. The best choices for villa guests are the *Lake Buena Vista Club* and *Chef Mickey's Village Restaurant*.

At the Disney-MGM Studios Theme Park, kids particularly enjoy the *50's Prime TIme Café* and the *Sci-Fi Dine-In*. Other options include a fine and leisurely meal at the *Hollywood Brown Derby*, or a quicker meal at one of the other eateries: the *Soundstage* restaurant, the *Hollywood & Vine Cafeteria of the Stars*, the *Commissary*, *Min & Bill's Dockside Diner*, or the *Backlot Express*.

Most of the restaurants at the Magic Kingdom cater to kids and *Pecos Bill's Café* gets high marks. At Epcot Center, the *Odyssey* is a top pick for kids.

The decision about where to dine may ultimately depend on the plan for the rest of the day. Especially in slack periods, the familiar long lines at the most popular attractions in the Magic Kingdom are practically nonexistent from about 6 P.M. onward. Even during the busiest times, the queues ease up a bit as the afternoon wanes. So it's a wise visitor who takes advantage of this phenomenon by having a late lunch—then dining after 8 P.M. This plan also allows time to catch the second, less-crowded showing of SpectroMagic.

WDW restaurants outside the Magic Kingdom are busiest in the evening between 7 P.M. and 9 P.M. Those in the Magic Kingdom are busiest between 5 P.M. and 7 P.M.

About Dinner Reservations

In most WDW restaurants, it's first-come, first-served. The lines that result can be avoided by eating early or late—or by choosing one of the handful of restaurants that accept dinner reservations. (**Note:** Reservations are held for only 15 minutes.)

GRAND FLORIDIAN RESORT: *Victoria & Albert's, Flagler's*; and *Narcoossee's* (824-2383).

POLYNESIAN RESORT: *Papeete Bay Verandah* (824-1391).

DISNEY INN: *Disney Inn* (824-1484).

YACHT CLUB: *Yachtsman Steakhouse* (934-3356).

BEACH CLUB: *Ariel's* (934-3357).

MAGIC KINGDOM: *Tony's Town Square* restaurant, *King Stefan's* in Cinderella Castle, and *Liberty Tree Tavern* in Liberty Square. Reservations can be made three days in advance for WDW resort guests (828-4000) and Hotel Plaza guests (828-8800) only. All other guests must make reservations in person on the same day.

DISNEY-MGM STUDIOS THEME PARK: Reservations are accepted at the *Hollywood Brown Derby*, *Mama Melrose's*, the *Sci-Fi Dine-In*, and the *50's Prime Time Café* three days in advance for WDW resort guests (828-4000) and Hotel Plaza guests (828-8800) only. All other guests must make reservations in person on the same day.

DISNEY VILLAGE MARKETPLACE: *Empress Room* aboard the *Empress Lilly* (828-3900); *Chef Mickey's Village Restaurant* (828-3900); *Lake Buena Vista Club* in the villa area (828-3735).

For dinner shows and supper seatings alike, you can book a table as soon as you get your confirmed reservation number, if you're staying at WDW resorts. Otherwise, you can book it 45 days ahead if you're lodging at one of the Disney Village Hotel Plaza establishments (*only* if you have made your reservation through the CRO) and 30 days if you're putting up outside Walt Disney World. *Empress Room* reservations may be made 30 days in advance, no matter where you're staying. In the case of dinner shows, if you can't get a place for an early performance, try for a later one (usually less heavily booked).

At Epcot Center it's important to remember every establishment offers unique delights. If you didn't get dinner reservations in advance, don't despair. Try a dinner of tourtière (a Canadian pork pie) and maple-syrup pie (for dessert) at Canada's atmospheric *Le Cellier*. Or sample Mexican specialties at Mexico's *Cantina de San Angel* (whose lagoon-side tables provide a fine view of the sun setting behind Epcot Center), or the skewered, grilled meats at Japan's *Yakitori House*. Cravings for more conventional fast foods will be satisfied

DINNER SHOWS

The fact that the Disney organization is the king of family entertainment is nowhere more strongly apparent than amid the whooping and hollering troupe of singers and dancers who race toward the velvet-curtained stage at *Fort Wilderness* resort's Pioneer Hall. As you plow through barbecued ribs, fried chicken, corn-on-the-cob, and strawberry shortcake, those enthusiastic performers sing, dance, and joke up a storm until your mouth is as sore from laughing as your stomach is from ingesting all the food. This is the Hoop-Dee-Doo Musical Revue, presented daily at 5 P.M., 7:15 P.M., and 9:30 P.M. Cost is $34.98 per adult, $26.50 for juniors (12 through 20), and $18.02 for children (3 through 11); reservations can be made through the CRO (W-DISNEY—934-7639) and are required well in advance, and are very hard to come by. Groups of ten or more should call 824-2885.

Mickey's Tropical Luau, presented daily at 4:30 P.M. at the *Polynesian* resort, is a Polynesian show aimed at the younger set. Disney characters, dressed in traditional costumes, dance along with the Polynesian performers. A full dinner including dessert is served. Cost is $28.62 for adults, $22.26 for juniors, and $12.72 for children.

The Polynesian Luau at the *Polynesian* resort, presented nightly at 6:45 P.M. and 9:30 P.M., also has its moments. The performers' dancing is some of the most authentic this side of Hawaii. Many of the WDW dancers have studied at the well-respected Polynesian Cultural Center in Hawaii. A full Polynesian-style meal, including frozen piña coladas and a tropical fruit dessert is served. Cost is $32.86 for adults, $25.44 for juniors, and $16.96 for children.

The *Biergarten* at Epcot Center's Germany Pavilion features a continuous show to entertain diners throughout the evening; it's complete with traditional German musicians, yodelers, and dancers. The fare here is hearty. Entrées range from $14.25 to $19.75.

Plan to arrive 15 minutes or so before starting time, and allow enough time for transportation and parking. (Prices, which include tax, are subject to change and do not include gratuity.)

at the *Stargate* restaurant in CommuniCore East, at the *Odyssey* restaurant near World of Motion and Mexico, and at the *Liberty Inn* in The American Adventure. The *Sunrise Terrace* in CommuniCore West serves Italian fare. The *Farmers Market* in The Land offers a little bit of everything.

Other restaurants require reservations (procedures are outlined on page 222). Try not to miss *The Land Grille Room*'s cheese bread, the Scotch eggs in the *Rose & Crown*, the salmon soufflé and the pastries at *Chefs de France*, and the Mexican queso fundido at Mexico's *San Angel Inn* restaurant. The *Biergarten* has lively entertainment throughout the day and evening.

Lounges

No one ever said the Magic Kingdom's no-liquor policy means that everyone in the World is a teetotaler. Actually, some of WDW's tastiest offerings are liquid (and decidedly alcoholic), and some of its most entertaining places are its bars and lounges.

CONTEMPORARY RESORT: The watering hole here is sleek and offers a great view and atmosphere aplenty.

    Outer Rim Cocktail Lounge: Overlooking Bay Lake, this lounge serves cocktails and seafood appetizers.

POLYNESIAN: The resort's Polynesian theme has inspired a whole raft of deceptively potent potables like Seven Seas (fruit juice, grenadine, orange curaçao, and rum), Chi Chis (a standard piña colada made with vodka instead of rum), and WDW piña coladas (which include orange juice in addition to rum, pineapple, and coconut cream). There's even a special Polynesian Village nonalcoholic treat—the pink Lei-Lani, an orange juice and strawberry mixture.

    Barefoot Bar: Adjoining the swimming pool lagoon, serving soda, draft beer, piña coladas, frozen daiquiris, mai tais, and various other mixed drinks. Open from 11 A.M. until 7 P.M. (summer hours are extended).

    Tambu Lounge: Cozy and clublike, this lounge adjoining the *Papeete Bay Verandah* is open daily beginning at 2 P.M., and offers a menu of Polynesian-style appetizers along with low-key entertainment nightly. A good spot for a quiet conversation. Open from 2 P.M. until 1 A.M.

GRAND FLORIDIAN: The four lounges reflect the Old Florida theme of the hotel.

    Garden View Lounge: A view of the lushly landscaped pool and garden area makes this watering hole a pleasant place to relax. Afternoon tea also is served here.

    Mizner's Lounge: Named after the eccentric architect who defined much of the flavor of southeastern Florida's Gold Coast, this lounge is on the second floor of the main building.

    Summerhouse: This bar serves guests at the pool and beach.

    Narcoossee's: Yards of Beer, an unusual manner of service allows guests to choose from a mug, a half-yard, or a yard. And they mean a yard.

SCOOPS, SUNDAES, AND SOFT SERVE

BY THE SCOOP

HOTELS: Assorted flavors and sundaes at *Captain Cook's Snack and Ice Cream Company* at the *Polynesian* resort; the *Dolphin Fountain* at the *Dolphin* hotel; *Beaches & Cream* at the *Yacht Club* and *Beach Club* resorts; *Jacques Beignet's Bakery* at *Port Orleans*; the *Southern Trace Bakery* at *Dixie Landings*; and *Cinnamon Bay Bakery* at the *Caribbean Beach*.

MAGIC KINGDOM: *Liberty Tree Tavern*, *Tony's Town Square* restaurant, *Plaza Ice Cream Parlor*, *Plaza* restaurant, *King Stefan's Banquet Hall*.

EPCOT CENTER: The ice cream stand at *Farmers Market* in *The Land*.

DISNEY-MGM STUDIOS THEME PARK: *Dinosaur Gertie's*.

DISNEY VILLAGE MARKETPLACE: *Donald's Dairy Dip*.

ASSORTED SUPER SUNDAES

HOTELS: *Narcoossee's* at the *Grand Floridian* (custard, berries, seven scoops of ice cream, whipped cream, and amaretto). Super sundaes at the *Dolphin Fountain* in the *Dolphin* hotel. *Papeete Bay Verandah*, *Snack Isle*, and *Coral Isle Café*, at the *Polynesian* resort.

MAGIC KINGDOM: *Plaza Ice Cream Parlor* and the *Plaza* restaurant on Main Street.

DISNEY VILLAGE MARKETPLACE: *Donald's Dairy Dip*, *Fisherman's Deck*, and *Steerman's Quarters*.

PLEASURE ISLAND: Tollhouse Cookie Sundae at the *Fireworks Factory*.

DISNEY-MGM STUDIOS THEME PARK: *50's Prime Time Café* (hot fudge, caramel, marshmallow, or the works), *Sci-Fi Dine-In*.

SOFT-SERVE

HOTELS: *Fiesta Fun Center* at the *Contemporary* resort, *Trail's End Buffeteria* at the *Fort Wilderness* resort, *Southern Trace Bakery* at *Dixie Landings*, *Cinnammon Bay Bakery* at the *Caribbean Beach* resort, and *Jacques Beignet's Bakery* at *Port Orleans*.

MAGIC KINGDOM: *Round Table*, *Enchanted Grove*, *Sunshine Tree Terrace*, and *Aunt Polly's*.

EPCOT CENTER: *Refreshment Port*, *Refreshment Outpost*, and *Stargate*.

DISNEY VILLAGE MARKETPLACE: *Donald's Dairy Dip*.

DISNEY-MGM STUDIOS THEME PARK: *Studio Catering Company*.

FROZEN YOGURT

MAGIC KINGDOM: *Sunshine Tree Terrace* and *Lunching Pad*.

EPCOT CENTER: *Pure & Simple*, *Refreshment Port*, *Refreshment Outpost*.

PLEASURE ISLAND: *D-Zertz*

DISNEY-MGM STUDIOS THEME PARK: *Min & Bill's Dockside Diner*.

DISNEY VILLAGE MARKETPLACE: *Donald's Dairy Dip*.

FRENCH-FRIED ICE CREAM

DISNEY INN: The *Disney Inn* restaurant. Ice cream served with a crispy crust offers a unique flavor.

LEMON SHERBET PUNCH

MAGIC KINGDOM: *Liberty Tree Tavern*.

INTERNATIONAL TREATS

EPCOT CENTER: Specialties at *L'Originale Alfredo di Roma Ristorante* include Italian concoctions like spumoni and tortoni. For a Mexican treat, visit *San Angel Inn* for helada con cajeta (vanilla ice cream with caramel topping).

DISNEY INN: The **Back Porch**, adjoining the *Disney Inn* restaurant, serves an assortment of specialty drinks and cocktails, plus some appetizers.

CARIBBEAN BEACH: The tropical theme of the hotel carries through to the lounges here.
  Captain's Tavern: Tropical drinks, beer, wine, and cocktails are served at this 200-seat lounge at Old Port Royale. Prime ribs, chicken, and crab legs also are available from 5 P.M. to 10 P.M.
  Banana Cabana: Drinks and a variety of snacks are available at this poolside bar.

DISNEY VACATION CLUB: The **Gurgling Suitcase** on the Turtle Krawl boardwalk serves an assortment of Key West specialties along with traditional cocktails, beer, wine, and soft drinks.

SWAN: A couple of lounges offer pleasant surroundings in which to sip a drink.
  Kimono's: Attractively decorated in a Japanese design, the bartender can mix up a variety of drinks, and sushi is served in the evenings.
  Lobby Court Lounge: The winding corridors of the hotel lobby have comfortable couches and chairs, punctuated by pianos where able musicians perform.

DOLPHIN: The entertaining hotel theme is carried through to its watering holes.
  Copa Banana: The wooden tabletops are designed as slices of fruit, and the Caribbean-style appetizers match the surroundings. Live music is featured in the evenings.
  Harry's Safari Bar: Join the peripatetic "Harry" for a drink and maybe a story or two.
  Carnivale Bar: Partake of the festival atmosphere at *Ristorante Carnivale*, even if all you want is a drink.
  Lobby Lounge: Appetizers and drinks are available in the very pleasant hotel lobby.

YACHT CLUB: A variety of nautical themes dominate the drinking spots here.
  Ale and Compass: Located in the lobby and offering a specialty drink menu including coffee and ale. The bar is open until 11 P.M.
  Crew's Cup Lounge: Styled after a New England waterfront pub, this lounge has a masculine feel to it. It's right next door to the *Yachtsman Steakhouse*, and is a choice spot for a drink before dinner.

BEACH CLUB: The two lounges here retain the beachfront feel of the rest of the hotel.
  Rip Tide Lounge: This lobby bar features California wines, wine coolers, and frosty drinks that are consistent with the hotel's beachside theme. It also is open until 11 P.M.
  Martha's Vineyard Lounge: A light and airy atmosphere prevails at this spot right next to *Ariel's*. Wines from an authentic Martha's Vineyard winery, as well as selections from California, Long Island, and European vineyards, are on the extensive list.

PORT ORLEANS: The hotel's New Orleans theme is reflected in the lounges.
  Scat Cat's Club: Traditional offerings from the bar plus light hors d'oeuvres and snacks.
  Mardi Grogs: Specialty drinks, popcorn, hot dogs, and hot pretzels are available at this poolside spot.

DIXIE LANDINGS: The two lounges each possess a certain degree of charm.
  Cotton Co-Op: Situated in a room designed as a cotton exchange, this lounge features specialty drinks and some light hors d'oeuvres.
  Muddy Rivers: The poolside bar serves snacks and drinks during pool hours.

WILDERNESS LODGE: The **Territory Saloon** located between *Artist Point* and the *Whispering Canyon Café* is a pleasant place to relax with a drink.

FORT WILDERNESS: Beer and sangría are served in Pioneer Hall. **Crockett's Tavern** serves cocktails, specialty drinks, appetizers, and full meals. For a change of pace, take a blue-flagged watercraft to the *Contemporary* resort. Be sure to check the operating hours before boarding so that you don't miss the last trip back. Or, if you have a car, make the short drive to the Disney Village Marketplace or Pleasure Island.

DISNEY-MGM STUDIOS THEME PARK: The settings of the lounges here are their main attraction.

Catwalk Bar: Above the *Soundstage* restaurant is the 90-seat full-service cocktail lounge designed to resemble a movie prop storage area. Appetizers, specialty drinks, beer, and wine are served.

Tune-In Lounge: A sitcom living room setting, with couches, chairs, and fold-up TV dinner tray tables is found at this lounge adjacent to the *50's Prime Time Café*. Waiters in V-neck sweaters play the roles of sitcom "Dads," and old television sets play scenes from beloved sitcoms. Appetizers, mixed drinks, beer, and wine are served.

DISNEY VILLAGE MARKETPLACE: Some of WDW's best lounges are here.

Baton Rouge Lounge: This spacious lounge on the main deck of the *Empress Lilly* is one of the liveliest spots in WDW, thanks to the musical comedy of John Charles. Specialty drinks are sold by the pitcher—things like Melancholy Baby (concocted of melon liqueur, rum, and orange, lemon, and lime juices), Old Man River (made with rum, vodka, triple sec, lemon and lime juices, and a splash of Coke), margaritas, and Singapore Slings. The Bayou chips—crunchy homemade potato chips sold by the basket—are delicious enough to make it easy to abandon dinner plans. Open from noon.

Empress Lounge: Almost as elegant as the *Empress Room*, whose guests this mahogany-paneled bar is meant to pamper before and after a meal. Aboard the *Empress Lilly*.

Cap'n Jack's Oyster Bar: Agleam with copper, right on the water, this bar serves delicious strawberry margaritas, made with strawberry tequila and real strawberries. The nibbles of steamed clams, oysters, and seafood marinara are good enough for a meal.

Village Lounge: This boîte, comfortable as a living room, is one of the World's best-kept secrets. Disney cartoons are shown in the evening to entertain kids while waiting for a table at the adjacent *Chef Mickey's Village Restaurant*.

PLEASURE ISLAND: All the clubs have bars that serve specialty drinks, beer, wine, non-alcoholic specialty drinks, and mixed drinks. the *Fireworks Factory* and the *Portobello Yacht Club* also have pleasant lounges.

EPCOT CENTER: All restaurants, including some of the counter-service establishments, offer alcoholic beverages with meals. Restaurants such as *The Land Grille Room* and the *San Angel Inn* have small lounges at which patrons may wait for tables.

Then there are a few places that specialize in spirituous liquid refreshments:

Rose & Crown Pub & Dining Room: The pub section of this watering hole that's part of the United Kingdom Pavilion is a veritable symphony of polished woods, brass, and etched glass. Beer is available along with a score of specialty drinks imported from the other side of the Atlantic.

Matsu No Ma Lounge: In addition to the exotic sake-based specialty drinks available here, this Japan Pavilion establishment offers a fine panoramic view over the whole of Epcot Center—including the World Showcase Lagoon with Spaceship Earth as a backdrop—one of the best vistas of the property available.

Biergarten: Just outside this restaurant in Germany there's a small shaded terrace where steins of beer and sausages are available.

MORE SPECIAL NIGHTTIME FUN

The Magic Kingdom, open late during several busy periods of the year, takes on additional dazzle after dark. In peak seasons, there's SpectroMagic, a procession so spectacular that it alone is worth the trip to WDW—even though it's necessary to visit it during a busy period in order to see it.

And Epcot Center is particularly lovely at night, when the lights sparkle on the Lagoon, Spaceship Earth is all aglow, and IllumiNations lights up the sky. At the Disney-MGM Studios Theme Park the Sorcery in the Sky fireworks show is a highlight. But there are always a dozen or so other special happenings and events going on after dark throughout WDW.

FIREWORKS: During summers and holidays when the Magic Kingdom and the Disney-MGM Studios Theme Park are open late, there are fireworks at 10 P.M. nightly. The shows last five to ten minutes, but pack as much dazzle as those shows many times their length.

ILLUMINATIONS: This nightly show is an absolutely spectacular display of music, laser lights, fireworks, and dancing water fountains that can be seen from any point on the Epcot Center promenade, usually at closing time. Check at Earth Station for the exact time.

SPECTROMAGIC: The Magic Kingdom's biggest extravaganza, this parade makes its way down Main Street twice each night during busy seasons. The advanced technology incorporates holograms, special lighting techniques, and a state-of-the-art sound system.

CAMPFIRE PROGRAM: This event at *Fort Wilderness*, held nightly near the Meadow Trading Post at the center of the campground, features a sing-along, Disney movies, and cartoons. Open only to Walt Disney World resort guests.

DISNEY MOVIES: A good choice when feet refuse to take even one more step. Full-length Walt Disney feature films are shown nightly at the *Contemporary* resort for WDW guests, in the theater near the Fiesta Fun Center—usually at 7 P.M. and 9 P.M. Movies are also shown at the *Fort Wilderness* resort every evening at the campfire (for resort guests only).

TENNIS: The courts at the *Contemporary* resort, the *Disney Inn*, *Fort Wilderness*, the *Yacht* and *Beach Clubs*, the *Disney Vacation Club*, the *Grand Floridian*, and the Lake Buena Vista Club are open until 10 P.M. year-round. (See *Sports*.)

ELECTRICAL WATER PAGEANT: Best seen from the nearest beach, this sparkling show is composed of a 1,000-foot-long string of illuminated floating creatures. Guest Services or City Hall can tell you when and where the Electrical Water Pageant can be seen—usually at 9 P.M. from the *Polynesian*, 9:20 P.M. from the *Grand Floridian*, 9:45 P.M. from *Fort Wilderness*, 10:05 P.M. from the *Contemporary* resort.

Index